Thinking for Decisions
Deductive Quantitative Methods

Thinking for Decisions
Deductive Quantitative Methods

C. West Churchman

University of California, Berkeley

Leonard Auerbach

University of California, Berkeley

Simcha Sadan

New York University

SCIENCE RESEARCH ASSOCIATES, INC.
Chicago, Palo Alto, Toronto
Henley-on-Thames, Sydney, Paris, Stuttgart

A Subsidiary of IBM

Library of Congress Cataloging in Publication Data

Churchman, Charles West, 1913–
Thinking for decisions.
Includes index.
1. Decision-making—Mathematical models. I. Auerbach,
Leonard, joint author. II. Sadan, Simcha, joint
author. III. Title.
HD69.D4C49   658.4'033   74-34494
ISBN 0-574-18225-X

To Our Parents

Preface

The pedagogy of this text is based on two theories, one related to learning and the other to the nature of mathematics. The theory of learning says that the student of decision making who is exposed to fairly rigid and precise materials needs constantly to be reaching out toward reality. Our purpose has been to create a text which proceeds as a pendulum; when the technical materials swing toward rigor, we introduce an example in which the student can sense the limits of rigor as well as its uses. The real world is basically ambiguous; rigor is one method of coping with ambiguity.

The theory of the nature of mathematics is extremely reactionary. We do not subscribe to the fairly recent notion that mathematics is an abstract language based, say, on set theory. In many ways it is unfortunate that philosophers and mathematicians like Russell and Hilbert were able to tell such a convincing story about the meaning-free formalism of mathematics. In Greek, mathematics simply meant learning, and we have adapted this original meaning to define the term as "learning to decide." Mathematics is a way of preparing for decisions through thinking. Sets and classes provide one way to subdivide a problem for decision preparation; a set derives its meaning from decision making, and not vice versa.

Subject topics and possible tours through the book   The text covers the basic topics of deductive reasoning as applied to decision making; it was designed to be read from beginning to end. Sometimes, it may not be necessary (or possible) to cover the entire text. In such cases, the chapters can be organized into topical units as follows: chapters 1, 4, 12; chapters 1, 5, 6, 7, 8, 12; chapters 1, 9, 10, 12; chapters 1, 11, 12. (See the chart on the facing page.)

Chapter 1 is recommended reading for all ensuing chapters. Chapters 2 and 3 are presented as review and explanatory material, and can be read in part or whole as needed.

The underlying structure for the methods presented in the text is the management information system described in chapter 1. For this, as well as for other reasons, it is a very good idea for all users of the book to read the first chapter. Chapter 2 lays out the design for deduction in general and the format for deductive systems. Set theory is covered in an appendix to chapter 2; we recommend strongly that the reader who is rusty on sets, and who will be reading chapters 5–9, read appendix 2.1. Chapter 2 can be read without extended study; it's the structure and flavor of the chapter that's important. This is also true of chapter 3, which contains a review of ordering, numbers, functions, variables, and a discussion of measures of performance. The appendixes to this chapter contain a review of some rules of algebra for those who've been away from the subject for a while. A knowledge of these rules is essential for understanding the material presented in the chapters that follow.

For those who know algebra, chapter 4 is self-contained, and can be read without the previous chapters. It covers present and future values and discounting, using arithmetic and geometric series.

Chapter 5, followed by 6, 7 and 8, covers decision making under uncertainty. Chapter 5 presents a deductive system for probability, followed by permutations and combinations. Permutations and combinations can be skipped if the reader so chooses, without loss of continuity for chapters 6, 7, and 8. Chapter 6 presents random variables and their distributions, for which the explanation of functions in chapter 3 is recommended for review. The characteristics of random variables, as they are related to measures of performance for decisions, are presented in the chapter 7. The topic of chapter 8 is the value of information (perfect and imperfect) and its relation to Bayes' Theorem.

Chapter 9 can be read directly after chapter 1; chapter 9, together with chapter 10, covers the topic of linear models. In chapter 9 systems of linear equations are examined, and the validity and usefulness of such models are discussed. Chapter 10 explores linear programming and duality, and their implications for decision makers.

The appendix to chapter 9 is designed as a review of slopes of lines for those who wish to cover this topic, *and can be read before chapter 9.* Chapter 11 is an introduction to differential and integral

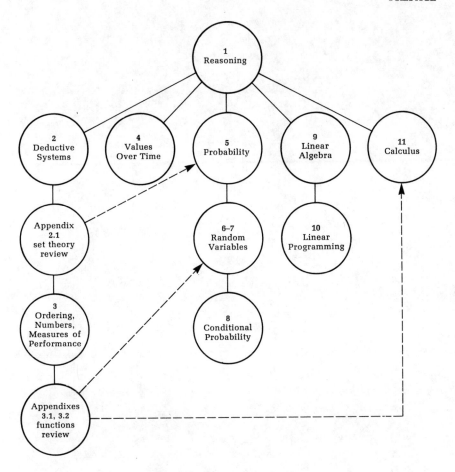

calculus. The appendix to Chapter 11 can be used to study multivariate calculus, the chain rule, and continuous probability distributions.

We would like to thank the many people who helped create this book. Some of them may find themselves in the Problems, but all should realize our deep gratitude.

Contents

Reasoning 1

1.1 Introduction

Quantitative methods are a very broad set of techniques that we use to prepare for decisions we must make in our lives. All of these techniques are based on two very important functions of the human mind, *reasoning* and *experience*. A great many of the techniques have become so common that you no longer have to learn about them in formal courses. For example, you decide to give a friend a birthday present. With a little reasoning about your financial situation and experience in buying birthday presents, you figure that you shouldn't spend more than $5. From experience you know your friend would dearly like to have a smooth-writing red fountain pen. As you look over the pens at the counter, you reject those that are significantly over $5; also, you reject those that are "too cheap," that is, significantly less than your "budget," because you don't want to show up at the party with a cheap present. Thus your common-sense quantitative technique narrows the choices so that you can easily make the final decision.

If you had to explain the reasoning and experience that went into your preparation for deciding on the present, you might put it this way: (1) experience says that the decision is narrowed down to the class of smooth red fountain pens; (2) reasoning and experience say my budget target is about $5; (3) reason says my decision rule is to select that pen with the smoothest writing, subject to the condition that the price is between $4 and $5. Of course, this is a pretty cumbersome way of saying "buy a red pen that writes smoothly and costs about $5," but we'll see that the more elaborate language can be extended to cover much more complicated situations, where there are hundreds of thousands of qualifications like *red, smoothness,* and $5.

Suppose, for example, that you had to help decide where to locate a service station for a gasoline company, or a hospital for a community. You'd still have a budget to worry about, of course, but now you'd have to concern yourself with many other things, like traffic, convenience of access, zoning laws, competition, age of inhabitants, and availability of doctors. But the considerations we've given for buying a fountain pen would still apply: (1) use experience to narrow down the options; (2) use experience and reasoning to specify a budget; (3) use reasoning and experience to develop a decision rule that tells you how to select the location with the best combination of access, traffic flow, competitive advantage, patient-doctor availability, and so forth, subject to the budget restraints. You'll see that the last instruction will involve some fairly elaborate reasoning to pinpoint what we mean by "best combination."

The important point you should grasp from these illustrations of deciding on fountain pens, service stations, or hospitals is that the techniques get their mileage by allowing you to *identify* the range of choices and to *refine* your method of choice. You can narrow your budget range, from $4 to $6, or $3 to $6, or $4.75 to $5.25, as you wish. You can specify smoothness as broadly or narrowly as you wish. Red can mean deep red, not pink, magenta, orange; or it can simply mean any color as long as it's reddish. In other words, your ability to identify the possibilities and make fine distinctions if you want to puts you in charge and gives you control of the situation. If you're running out of a burning building and see an exit sign, common sense says that's good enough; don't hunt around for an exit with a door that opens faster. But if you're hunting for a house or a job, you may want to consider many possibilities and introduce fine distinctions because you've got plenty of time to prepare for the decision.

The word *quantity* captures this point precisely. Of course, when you see *quantitative methods* you'll think of numbers and mathematical methods like algebra, geometry, and calculus. But throughout this text you should realize that above all you are trying to learn about decision making, and specifically about how to prepare for decisions — for your own life, for organizations, for society. Hence for you this is not primarily a course in mathematics, but we'll make use of mathematical techniques since they should provide you with an enormous addition to your power to control the preparations for decision. It *is* primarily a course in preparing for decision making using the tools of identification and refinement of choice, tools you may use at your own discretion. Hence "quantity" should mean not just numbers but other types of identification (such as verbal descriptions) as well as other types of refinement (for example, distinctions in color or taste) to which you may not normally assign numbers.

One of the most important aspects of refinement is the choice of the appropriate quantitative method (if any) to use. This choice depends on the *information* available to the decision maker. Using the quantitative method of addition makes little sense if your information is in terms of English pounds and French francs. The first method called for in this case is one that transforms the information into like units, say, dollars. Actually this dependence on information is even stronger since the relevance and usefulness of any method depends on the relevance and accuracy of the information available.

We will return shortly to the design of a systematic organization of information to help guide your study of the various quantitative techniques, but for the moment we should note one aspect of all management information that is very important if quantitative methods are to be useful: *stability*. If things change too rapidly or drastically, the information may not remain accurate or relevant, and the usual quantitative technique may no longer be appropriate. Not only do you believe that your friend wants a red pen, but you also believe he will still want one at the birthday party and that he won't find a red pen in every present he opens. You also believe that your budget will stay reasonably well fixed and that the smooth-writing pen will remain smooth. The fellow who decides to build a service station on a busy street had better know something about the plans of the traffic engineers, who may be about to build a freeway to reduce the traffic density; once the freeway is built, the service station customers may decline drastically.

Two important dimensions of the stability of information and the quantitative methods implied by the information are *time* and *location*. Location is important, because the criteria that work well in one locale for selecting a service station or hospital may not work well at all in another; if yours is a high-priced gasoline, the affluent may come in, but the poor will not. If the neighborhood of the hospital deteriorates rapidly, the type of patient and his ability to pay may also change rapidly. Note that if you can predict these changes accurately, then despite the changes the situation may still remain stable for you because you can plan by using the prediction and adjusting your decision accordingly.

You will see that the use of quantitative methods in decision making is very common. All of us use them all the time; also, governments, companies, schools, and doctors use them to decide what we should or can do. The Internal Revenue Service uses an information system and quantitative techniques to decide what income tax you should pay; the doctor uses them to see if you have a fever and should go to bed; your teacher may use them to decide if you should pass his course. Quantitative methods are as common in our lives as eating, sleeping, walking, making love. You may find it worthwhile for a time to keep a notebook in which you record now and then how they affect your life, from the ring of your alarm clock to your "it's time to go to bed." Your day is quantitative-methods dominated: 50% chance of showers, two pieces of bacon, one cup of coffee with a little sugar (if you are into organic diets, one-half bowl of Crunchy Granola, one cup of milk, and one whole-wheat cookie), the route you take to school or work, the time for this-or-that during the day, how long the report should be, when to eat, when to relax and how, and so on. Our society is quantitative-methods dominated: maximum speed limits, contents of this-or-that in foods, the price we pay to get foods and services, how highbrow or lowbrow we are (he has only read one play by Shakespeare!).

Associated with many common aspects of human living are what we call *technologies*; these vastly increase our capabilities. Most of us can transport ourselves from A to B by walking or swimming if the distance and dangers aren't too large; but the technologies of transportation vastly increase our capability of traveling at speeds up to 600 mph over all kinds of terrain. Similarly, most of us can keep ourselves in reasonably good health; but the technologies of medicine increase our capability of overcoming serious diseases and injuries that would otherwise kill us. This text is intended to teach you about the technologies of quantitative methods and their informational bases, technologies that may vastly increase your existing decision-making capabilities. In other words, you already use information for decisions and are well practiced in quantitative methods up to a certain level; this book should increase your level of proficiency significantly.

You should bear in mind that all technologies are both a blessing and a curse. Transportation technologies have increased speed and sometimes safety, but they have also increased air and noise pollution. Medical technologies have increased immunity to disease, but they have also increased drug abuse and second-order dangers. So, too, the information and quantitative-methods technologies, while increasing your ability to prepare for decision making, may result in unwarranted confidence in the methods themselves. Hence, when you think you understand a technique, always ask yourself: What are the dangers of using the technique? What could go seriously wrong? For example, you should be aware of the assumptions made when using any management information, as in the case of the prospective service station owner. You'll always find that such dangers exist, and you'll understand any quantitative method far better when you appreciate this point. "Appreciate" means to place a value on something, hopefully a realistic value. This is a course in appreciation of quantitative methods, and you should not end up thinking that these technologies can solve all life's problems or that they are largely irrelevant.

Throughout this course you should also be concerned with the *why* of the technique you are studying: Why will the technique increase the manager's power to make the right decision? If you understand the why, you will find that you can also understand the how-to-do-it far better. Of course, the two questions, the why and the how, will go together in your learning, since you'll have to learn some fundamental *how* techniques in order to understand the *why*. But merely being very clever in working out a technique won't improve your ability to use quantitative methods for decisions.

PROBLEMS 1.1

1. If you are enrolled in a school, can you describe how you made the decision to go there? To what extent did you use quantitative methods?

2. We live in an age of threatened shortages: of energy, food, paper, etc. To what extent have quantitative methods played a role in the creation of the shortages and in proposed solutions?

3. On a camping trip, you are using a recipe that calls for 2 quarts of water. You have no measuring device, but you do have a can which holds 5 quarts and another which holds 4 quarts. You also have plenty of water. Can you figure out how to get the required 2 quarts? Do you think that this example is very practical?

4. Your fireplace conveniently holds logs between 2 and 3 feet. You have a 13-foot tree trunk to cut up. How would you do it?

5. A fairly wealthy family figures it spends about $30,000 a year. Their expenditures for gasoline can be derived from the fact that they drive their two cars about 2000 miles a month at about 20 miles a gallon. When in 1974 the price of gas went from 40 cents a gallon to 60 cents, was this a very big calamity for them?

6. You own a gift shop and a salesman offers to sell you a lot of 400 plates for $1000. You're almost certain you can sell them for $5 apiece, provided you pay $300 for advertising. Should you accept the offer?

7. Precision of language ("quantity") often forces a sacrifice in flexibility of interpretation. Judge these ordinances in terms of precision and flexibility.
   a. No elevator operating in a commercial building shall be so crowded that the passenger may feel in danger of suffocation.

b. No elevator operating in a commercial building shall carry more than 15 passengers.

c. No elevator operating in a commercial building shall carry a load of more than 2000 pounds.

d. No child may be expelled from any public elementary school except when his conduct is deemed dangerous to others by the responsible authorities.

e. The speed limit on 25th St. is 25 mph.

f. The floor area of the mayor's office must not exceed 4000 square feet.

g. Only persons with sufficient education may be candidates for head librarian.

1.2   A Historical Example

Quantitative methods are not a new discovery that emerged with the advent of the computer. They may not be as old as all the hills, but certainly as old as some of them. It will be helpful to recount one quantitative method of using management information that dates back at least to 2000 B.C. in China because the reasoning and experience that were combined in this technique are very similar to that which we still apply today. The origins of the *I Ching** (the I is pronounced "ee"), *The Book of Changes*, probably go back to prehistoric times, and the book was certainly in use during the second millenium B.C. Its purpose was to provide decision makers with advice about their situation, and especially advice about how things will change (we would say today that the *I Ching* is a forecasting method). The method employed the technique of "throwing" stalks made from a yarrow plant.

By a fairly elaborate counting procedure, the final results of the throws end in one of four possibilities: an old or new "yang" or an old or new "yin." Whichever occurs, the result is written on a piece of paper. A yang is represented by an unbroken line, a yin by a broken line. "Old" is represented by a circle around the yang or yin line. This process of throwing and counting is repeated five more times, and each time the resulting line is placed above the one that came before it, as in figure 1.1. The six resulting lines are called a "hexagram," meaning a six-place figure. In the *I Ching* you look up the hexagram you obtained; the appropriate passage associated with your hexagram essentially describes the situation you are in, and gives some advice and commentary about what it is wise to do (the commentaries were written by many people over the ages, and include extensive passages

---

*The I Ching, Bolingen Series XIX, Princeton, Princeton University Press, 1971.

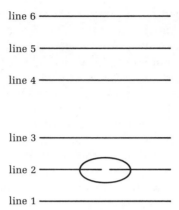

Figure 1.1   *I Ching* **Hexagram: "Fellowship with Men" (The circle around the second line indicates that it is an old yin, a changing line. Note that the lines start at the bottom.)**

by Confucius). Change is indicated by old lines; new lines indicate no change in the present situation.

The book is not a fortune-telling gimmick, since it is never specific, but rather is analogous to an expert who comments on the general situation — without telling you which choice to make. For example, you might be wondering whether to accept a job as a special assistant to a congressman in Washington; you "throw" the *I Ching* (nowadays, we are less patient and throw coins rather than yarrow sticks). You obtain all new yangs except for the second line which is an old (changing) yin. See figure 1.1. This hexagram is called "Fellowship with Men," and its judgment is "Fellowship with men in the open. Success. It furthers one to cross the great water. The perseverance of the superior man furthers." You might then interpret this to mean that Washington is the place to go; the "great water" is not the Potomac but the stormy waters of government. The commentary tells you about the need for a person like yourself with "clear, convincing, and inspiring aims and strength to carry them out." But watch out for the changing second line, which says that there is the strong possibility of factions based on personal interests which can lead to humiliation of yourself or others, as everyone who works hard in Washington comes to know.

Besides being a book of great wisdom, the *I Ching* provides us with a very important lesson about the use of quantitative methods and management information. The management information consists of the book, which interprets each of the 64 hexagrams. But why should throwing the yarrow sticks and counting lead us to the right hexagram, when "clearly" the whole operation is random? We'll see throughout this text that the meaning of random events is very important in decision making and that this meaning depends on what assumptions you are willing to make about how so-called random events take place in the whole world. For example, you might want to say that when you throw a coin the chances are exactly equal that the coin will come up heads or tails. But why? What do you assume about the world that justifies this belief? The Chinese sages would disagree with you. They believed that the whole world consists of two worlds, one of ideas, one of our everyday affairs. The events of the world of ideas "precede" the everyday events and influence their occurrence. Someone practiced in wisdom can succeed in getting the world of ideas to influence the yarrow sticks or coins so that they portray what is imminent in our everyday lives. To the Chinese sages "random" means a kind of mystical influence that occurs in the "real" world of ideas. None of this appears to be very scientific to our Western minds, which do not particularly appreciate such hidden explanations. But we'll see later, when we discuss the use of randomness for decision-making purposes, that even modern experts have to make strong assumptions about what is hidden in the natural world. So this need to make strong assumptions in using quantitative methods in preparing for decisions is the important lesson to be drawn from the ancient I Ching.

1.3   Reasoning as Deduction

We said that the method of the I Ching uses reason and experience; reason was used to develop and explain the theory of ideas which precede physical events, and to develop and explain the theory which ascribes a description of a situation for each hexagram. Experience was used to match the throws of the yarrow sticks with the appropriate description of the state you are in. Hence the methodology of the I Ching is an example of how reasoning and experience are combined to serve a decision maker. All quantitative methods are some combination of these two elements, reasoning and experience. Sometimes reasoning is the dominant element, sometimes experience; sometimes the two are intricately combined. When reasoning predominates, we call the quantitative methods used *deductive*: the information is primarily in the form of assumptions, and the quantitative method used essentially involves deducing results from these assumptions. If experience predominates, the quantitative method is called *inductive*: the quantitative technique tries to generalize from the data that experience provides, and the information is primarily empirical data. There is an intricate and richer combination of reasoning and experience called the *systems approach*.

This book concerns itself primarily with deductive methods. These methods consist of stating the assumptions of the problem precisely, along with defining the terms, and then deducing some consequences that will help solve the problem. Let's suppose you've accepted the *I Ching's* advice and have gone to Washington, where you live two blocks from your work. But one of the avenues connects the two places diagonally, like the hypotenuse of a right triangle. How should you decide to walk to work if you want to minimize the distance? Answer: Walk down the avenue. Why? Because the avenue is a straight line and it says in any elementary geometry text that the straight line is the shortest distance between two points; QED (which stands for *quod erat demonstrandum*, what was required to be demonstrated or deduced). Note that some experience was used to ascertain that the avenue was straight, but the important step was the use of the rational deductive method applied to a geometrical axiom (basic assumption).

By this time in your education you have had a chance to learn about a number of deductive systems, among which geometry and arithmetic have been most prominent. In chapter 2 we'll discuss the deductive process in general and the system of geometry in particular. We will also discuss techniques with such familiar names as calculus, linear algebra, probability, and decision theory. The emphasis in this book is on the way in which the preparation for decisions can be refined by these deductive methods.

PROBLEMS 1.3

The following are sets of assumptions; what can you deduce from each set?

1. All cats are animals; all animals eventually die.
2. Plan A will net this company one million dollars; Plan B will net two million dollars.
3. If X is a communist, he will keep a copy of Chairman Mao's sayings; he does in fact keep a copy of the book.
4. The world's population is increasing at a rate of 5% per year; the world's food supply is increasing at a rate of 1% per year.
5. Improbable events happen almost every day; what happens every day is probable.

1.4 Formal Organization of Management Information — A Management Information System

We have already referred repeatedly to the importance of information in management decisions and how the choice of quantitative methods is inextricably tied to the information made available to the decision maker. But the availability of relevant information may not be sufficient; for example, imagine trying to find out your grade in a university course if the records were available, but not organized. To systematically organize the information available is often imperative.

Nowadays we often refer to the organization of information and the resultant information structure used in preparing for decisions as a *management information system* (MIS). Although MIS is often tied to computer technology, it has a much more general meaning, which we will use throughout this text. It includes the procedures for gathering, organizing, and processing the information which is relevant to the decision maker, as well as providing information necessary for assessing what is a "correct" decision—that is, what goals are to be attained.

In this text we will use a particular management information system as a structure for preparing for decisions. We will introduce this MIS in the context of a problem which will emphasize one very important aspect of the MIS—namely, the degree of certainty you have about how things are going to turn out. For example, if you deposit your money in a very reliable savings account, you may safely assume that later on, when you come to withdraw your money, you will receive the principal plus interest. On the other hand, if you invest your money in a marketable security, such as stocks, you are uncertain as to your reward at some future date, since the price of the security may go up, stay the same, or drop. Let's see how this works in a practical example.

An Investment Problem

It is that exciting time at the end of the year when you expect a large bonus for your excellent work as the vice-president in charge of sales. Your hopes come true; the board of directors decides to show its appreciation by rewarding you with $10,000. After looking over your financial situation you wonder which of the following two options to invest the $10,000 in for one year: (1) deposit the cash in a savings account which yields a 6% interest at the end of one year, but stipulates that the money cannot be withdrawn during the year; (2) deposit the $10,000 in a passbook savings account which yields 5% annual interest and allows money to be withdrawn at any time.

If "making the most" from your investment were the only relevant consideration the problem would be simple; 6% is better than 5%. But there may be other considerations. For instance, suppose you and your coperson have decided to move into a new house as soon as you find one to your liking, if you have enough for the down payment. The town you live in is small, and after searching the limited possibilities you find one house that is ideal. The trouble is that the owner doesn't know whether he'll be transferred to another location and won't know until about July 1. He (and you) think that the chances are almost 50-50 that he will be transferred. If he sells to you, the down payment will be $10,000. Now which is the best investment option: the 6% "untouch-able" savings account or the 5% "pay on demand"?

Analysis: The introduction of the possibility that the dream house may become available no longer makes the second option ridiculous. If the owners move, you can withdraw your money with accumulated interest and buy the house, whereas if you choose the first option just to earn the higher interest, you must give up the house if it becomes available. Let us see how you might want to organize your information. The first thing you might want to do is list the possible *decisions,* which will be the first component of our MIS. In this case, there is a real choice between two decisions:

d_1 = deposit the $10,000 in a 6% interest savings account payable at the end of 12 months. Both principal and interest cannot be with-drawn before the year ends.

d_2 = deposit the $10,000 in a 5% interest passbook savings account where principal and interest are payable upon demand. (Interest is proportional to the length of time the cash is in the account.)

Together, we will call these two decisions D. An important character-istic of D is that you, the decision maker, have complete control over which of the decisions will be put into effect—that is, what decision, or option, you choose.

But your control over decisions does not always imply that you have control over the outcome resulting from your decision. If the house is a factor in your decision, you should realize that whether you'll end up with the house depends not only on your decision but also on whether the present owner will be transferred to a new location. The latter event is beyond your control.

Any number of such uncontrollable events may occur. One of these events is your receiving the $10,000 bonus, and another is that both savings accounts will live up to their terms and the bank won't fail. You are very sure of the occurrence of both of these events, but you are not at all sure about the availability of the house and must therefore consider the alternative uncontrollable possibility that the house does not become available. So you may be certain or uncertain about those events which are beyond your control.

In order to prepare for your decision (though in this case it is a bit tedious) you might want to spell out each of the possible relevant stories of your year. This will be the second component of our MIS, a list of decision-relevant stories of what might happen *outside your control,* which we call *states of the world* and denote by S. To save time and space we ignore those states of the world you are certain will *not* occur. For example, we do not include states which specify that you don't receive your bonus. What remains are two states of the world:

s_1 = you receive a \$10,000 bonus, both savings accounts remain intact, and house is available on July 1.

s_2 = you receive a \$10,000 bonus, both savings accounts remain intact, and house is not available on July 1.

Notice that your receiving the \$10,000 bonus and both savings accounts remaining intact do not vary from state to state, since you are certain they will occur. We will see that for this reason they need not be included in your MIS for this problem. Thus, the two states of the world in this investment problem can be described as:

s_1 = house is available on July 1.

s_2 = house is not available on July 1.

Having organized your information into decisions D and states of the world S, you can then specify the third component of our MIS: the possible *outcomes O* to you. *An outcome is a result of a decision that you make and a state of the world that prevails.* For example, if you decide to invest in the 12-months 6% option d_1, and the house becomes available s_1, the outcome to you could be described as "lost opportunity to buy the house, you receive 6% interest on \$10,000." Notice that for the given decision and state of the world, the outcome to you is unique.

In some decision situations there is only one state of the world that can occur: you are sure about everything that can happen relative to your decision. In this case we can associate a unique outcome with each decision. For example, before we introduced the house into the problem, the S component of the MIS would be: s_1 = you receive the \$10,000 bonus and the savings accounts remain intact. Thus d_1 would result in the outcome "6% interest on \$10,000," no matter what, and d_2 would result in "5% interest on \$10,000." We call the case where there is only one sure state of the world *certainty*.

In other cases there is more than one relevant state of the world that can occur for a given decision. Each decision can result in as many outcomes as there are states of the world. This case we call *uncertainty*. In either case we can compactly display the MIS we have developed so far by means of an outcome table, as in tables 1.1 and 1.2. In such an outcome table we list all the outcomes. Each outcome is associated with the appropriate state of the world and decision. You can see that you need not include the certain bonus in the states of the world in table 1.2, since the effect of the bonus on the outcome of your decision does not vary from state to state.

TABLE 1.1   Outcome Table, Certainty Case

DECISION	STATE OF THE WORLD
	$s_1 = \$10,000$ bonus, savings account intact
$d_1 = $ 12-month, 6% account	$o_1 = $ 6% interest on $10,000 for 12 months
$d_2 = $ 5% passbook account	$o_2 = $ 5% interest on $10,000 for 12 months

TABLE 1.2   Outcome Table, Uncertainty Case

DECISION	STATE OF THE WORLD	
	$s_1 = $ house available	$s_2 = $ house unavailable
$d_1 = $ 12-month, 6% account	$o_1 = $ lost house opportunity, 6% interest on $10,000 for 12 months	$o_2 = $ 6% interest on $10,000 for 12 months.
$d_2 = $ 5% passbook account	$o_3 = $ you get the house, 5% interest on $10,000 to July 1	$o_4 = $ 5% interest on $10,000 for 12 months

This systematic organization of the information of the problem is not necessarily complete, since in order to choose the "best" decision, we would like to state the above outcomes in terms that are more useful for comparison. That is, we are looking for the decision that yields "the most" on some scale, and we would like to specify the outcome in terms of this scale. We will defer discussion of how one might go about finding such a scale until later chapters. But, if we can in fact find such a scale, we can then attach a *payoff* to each outcome. This list of payoffs is the fourth component of our MIS. Payoffs are denoted by W (from the economic concept of "worth").

We can again use a table, this time to list the possible payoffs to you, as we have done in table 1.3 for the certainty case. Since we cannot readily find a scale which combines dollars and lost opportunities in the uncertainty case, that payoff table might look like table 1.4.

TABLE 1.3   Payoff Table; Certainty

DECISION	STATE OF THE WORLD
	s_1 = $10,000 bonus, savings account intact
d_1	w_1 = $600
d_2	w_2 = $500

TABLE 1.4   Payoff Table; Uncertainty

DECISION	STATE OF THE WORLD	
	s_1	s_2
d_1	w_1 = no house, $600	w_2 = no house, $600
d_2	w_3 = house, $250	w_4 = no house, $500

The MIS we will use throughout this book consists of D, S, O, and sometimes W, together with the criteria for choosing between decisions. In this example we did not specify a criterion combining lost-house opportunities and dollars. We will return to this MIS in the next chapter with a more precise discussion of its construction and other examples of its usefulness. In sections 1.6 and 1.7 we'll return to the choice criterion question. But for now, you should be able to see the importance of distinguishing between decisions, states of the world, outcomes, and payoffs. They will be familiar terms that can prove useful throughout your decision-making lives.

Before leaving the MIS, we should point out that many decisions are made by using our feelings rather than reason; if you decide to save the life of a drowning friend at considerable risk to yourself, you may do so out of love and not some calculation of dollar value, for example. This is why we have used W (for economic worth) rather than V as a symbol for payoffs; "value" is a very general term which includes feelings of aesthetics, power, and love, none of which has yet been quantified and presumably never will be.

PROBLEMS 1.4

1. Suppose you have the choice of two jobs. One pays $10,000 a year with a probability of 60% that you will lose the job within the year and lose an income of $4000 before finding another job. The second job pays $8000 a year with a 20% chance of losing the job within the year and losing $3000 income before finding another position. Construct the payoff table to help answer the question of which job you should take, considering your annual income only.

2. As manager of Sue's Shoes, you know from experience that on rainy days, about 15 customers per hour enter your store and on dry days about 25 per hour. Approximately three customers in five that are served make a purchase, and the average purchasing customer spends $10. Your barometer, which you trust, tells you that there is a 50% chance of rain today. If you call your part-time salesman for the day, it will cost you $24 for the eight hours, and all your customers will be served quickly. If not, and it rains, one customer in fifteen will leave because of slow service, and if it's dry, three in twenty-five will leave for that reason. If the extra sales-man accounts for $110 in expected hourly sales, he is worth the $24 you pay him. Construct a payoff table to prepare for the decision of whether or not to hire the extra salesman today, provided he works for eight hours in a day.

3. Explain how a checkbook is a mini information system. What are S, D, O? Is there a W?

4. You wish to design a simple management information system for running a parking lot at the baseball stadium. You receive crowd estimates which are lowest, highest, and "best guess," and you must decide how many employees to hire and how many lots to open. Show what an outcome table would look like, specifying typical states of the world and decisions. What criteria might you use to determine which decision to make? Suggest more than one!

5. Construct a D-S-O-W management information system for the following problem. You have two job offers when you leave school. Company A offers you $15,000 per year, with a 50-50 chance of a bonus of $2000. But you don't like its location. Company B offers $14,000, with no bonus but good location. Otherwise the two offers are quite similar (same kind of job, same type of personnel, same fringe benefits, etc.).

1.5   Classification of Assumptions

As we proceed to use this MIS in the text we will be refining assumptions so that we can deal with decision situations far more complicated than, though quite similar to, the investment problem discussed above. For the time being you should recognize some distinctions between the assumptions that are made.

First, there are several straight-out assumptions about reality: it is a "fact" that you have so much to invest, and it is a "fact" that you have two options. Such assumptions are *categorical* because there are no ifs, ands, or buts. They are also *descriptive* in that they tell us what exists. But the assumptions about O are different, because the MIS does not say that a specific o is a "fact." Rather, it says that if such-and-such a d is chosen, then that d together with an s implies such-and-such an o. Hence these assumptions are *hypothetical* because they are in the form *if A, then B.* The hypothetical assumptions are also descriptive, because they describe what would happen if a certain choice were made. Similarly, the transition from O to W is also based on hypothetical assumptions: if an o happens, then a value w is attained. Finally, we have some categorical assumptions which tell the decision maker how to use W in order to make a choice among the d's. The assumptions amount to saying something like "choose the d whose w is largest" or "choose the d whose o and w are least costly." These categorical assumptions are *prescriptive* because they prescribe a course of action.

Does this increase in your vocabulary help you? It should, because you should be aware of the kinds of assumptions you're putting into your use of quantitative methods and information. It makes quite a difference whether the assumptions are categorical or hypothetical. For example, some doomsday writers say that in another decade millions of people will die of starvation, while others say that millions will die *unless* we do so-and-so. The former assert categorically, the latter hypothetically. If the former are right, then it doesn't matter what we do (which d we choose), while if the latter are right, then we should make the choice that avoids mass starvation (assuming the categorical prescription "do not let humans starve").

Note also that the content of the entire MIS may be hypothetical. For example, you may not actually have $10,000, but you can dream, can't you? "If I had $10,000, what would I do with it?" is a perfectly respectable management question.

PROBLEMS 1.5

Identify each of the following assumptions in terms of categorical, hypothetical, descriptive, and prescriptive.

1.   All governments are essentially corrupt.

2. Corruption in government should be wiped out wherever it is observed.

3. Too many cooks spoil the broth.

4. Spoiled broth should not be drunk.

5. All private firms should try to maximize return on investment.

6. If a private firm operates legally, it should try to maximize return on investment.

7. "Eggheads of the world, unite! You have nothing to lose but your yolks." (Adlai Stevenson)

8. If proper steps are not taken, pollution will kill us all.

1.6 Making the Most (or Least)

There is one categorical-prescriptive assumption which will be used and discussed throughout this text. It is based on the idea that at least on some very important occasions in our decision-making lives we can properly evaluate our actions in quantitative terms. One obvious example you probably use all the time is to buy as cheaply as possible, all other things being equal. Thus, if you like Brand X tomato soup and there are two equally convenient stores selling it, one at 30 cents, the other at 33 cents, you "ought" to buy soup at the first. In the investment example given above, you might have used the dollar value of each outcome to "quantify" the payoffs; in that case the W's are completely quantified.

The categorical prescription based on a quantified W says, briefly, that you ought to minimize your losses and maximize your gains: in other words, *make as much as you can out of a situation*. If your sense of humanity makes this assumption sound rather crass and selfish, we should point out that the "you" in the prescription may be a family, or a community, or a nation, or mankind. Still, you may feel that there are "limits" on the use of the prescription; we have already mentioned some of these (aesthetics, power, love). For the time being, however, our task is to see how this prescription can be used in situations that are more complicated than buying similar cans of soup, or deciding on an investment in purely dollar terms.

For example, one brand of soup costs 30 cents but is not quite as tasty as the 33-cent brand. Then what does the prescription say? It is interesting to notice that it may say someting to you about how much you value the improved taste if you buy the 30-cent brand; the improvement in taste "isn't worth three cents" might be one reasonable way to decribe your preferences.

Similarly, in the investment problem you may put a value on having the house if it will be available; your prescription may tell you something about whether or not the additional 1% (from 5% to 6%) is worth the possible loss of your dream house. In some investment problems you may also put a value (cost) on investing in a morally dubious enterprise. The quantitative question is how much it is worth to you to avoid the chance of immorality. We should hasten to add that you also have a sound moral right to regard such questions as outrageous.

But moral issues aside, on technical grounds alone we can easily think of situations where it is astonishingly difficult to apply the prescription to "make the most," even when the facts seem reasonably clear. For example, suppose you are the manager of a car repair shop. You have two mechanics—one experienced and the other a relative novice—and 25 jobs on hand. You have a good idea how fast each mechanic can do a given job. How do you assign the work? You should notice right away that this problem needs to be formulated more precisely: what is it that you as the owner-manager should be trying to maximize? You obviously cannot restrict your consideration to the 25 jobs alone and will have to consider customer dissatisfaction over delays as well as the arrival of new jobs.

But even if you restricted your attention to the 25 jobs, the problem looks complicated. For example, suppose there was only one mechanic and that some jobs are easier to perform after other jobs because there is less need to move equipment or cars around. In what sequence should the jobs be done to minimize the total time? You can get some idea of the complexity of this "simple" problem if you consider the total number of ways in which 25 distinct jobs could be ordered. Any one of the jobs could come first, followed by any one of the remaining 24. So there are 25×24 ways in which you could have the first two jobs done, and any one of the 23 remaining jobs could be third; so there are $25 \times 24 \times 23$ ways of choosing the first three jobs. So it goes; there are $25 \times 24 \times 23 \times 22$ ways of choosing the first four jobs, and $25 \times 24 \times 23 \times 22 \times \ldots \times 4 \times 3 \times 2 \times 1$ ways of choosing the order of all 25 jobs. That this is a fairly large number is obvious enough; any mechanic who decided to be thorough and consider every possible sequence would probably spend the rest of his days computing the right sequence for any one day. Obviously, some clever shortcuts are required to analyze this very "simple" job-shop example. Since this type of problem is very common in decision making, we introduce a special notation for it. Instead of writing out $25 \times 24 \times \ldots \times 3 \times 2 \times 1$, we write 25!, read "25 factorial," and the result is called the number of possible *permutations* of the 25 jobs. Thus $1! = 1$, $2! = 2 \times 1 = 2$, $3! = 3 \times 2 \times 1 = 6$, and so on.

Few, if any, managers of auto repair shops try to solve their problems precisely, but if they are wise they will use some "quantitative methods," such as adopting the prescription to keep the highest paid mechanic as busy as possible on the difficult jobs (even if this means some idle time for the novice) or sequencing like jobs together. In later chapters we will explore in some depth allocation problems of the type discussed above.

PROBLEMS 1.6

1. You run a grocery store. A salesman offers to sell you 4000 cans of corn at a 10% discount on the price of 20 cents per can to be paid on receipt of the order. You have plenty of storage room and are not concerned about spoilage. You figure you can sell the 4000 cans in 12 months, but it will mean tying up capital in inventory—that is, an "opportunity cost" of capital which could be used for other purposes. You estimate that this cost is $90. On the other hand, you can decide to order the cans of corn every week, without a discount, but with some minor inconvenience in paper work and movement of goods which you estimate to be about 50 cents a week; the cost of capital for this decision is virtually zero. Which decision "makes the most"?

2. The engineering division of an automobile company has developed a safety device which it estimates will cut down the number of fatal accidents by 20%—from 500 to 400 drivers of their cars. The decision to add the safety device will drive up the price of each car by $100, with an estimated loss in sales of 30,000 cars per year from a total of 1,000,000 cars. The company nets $400 on each car sold regardless of whether it has a safety device. If they decide to add the safety device, what is the minimum dollar value they assume for the price of a life? Is this an appropriate question to ask?

1.7 Expected Value as a Choice Criterion

In this chapter we want to explore further the idea of uncertainty that arose in the investment problem in order to be more precise about the suitable choices to make. In the investment problem we could have simply ended by saying that it would be riduculous to risk losing the opportunity to buy the house for a few dollars in interest. But what if the situation is *not* all that obvious? As before, we begin with an example.

Problem: A Lottery Ticket ━━━━━━━━━━━━━

An impoverished friend of yours has bestowed upon you a lottery ticket for your birthday in hopes that you might appreciate his wishes for your future good fortune. There is a single prize for the one and only winner—$75.00 cash—but there are 100 ticket holders eligible to win.

Being a curious soul, you are interested in how much money you can "expect" to receive when the lottery drawing takes place next Tuesday.

Analysis: Now it is obvious that one of two things can happen. Either you will find that you are $75.00 richer on Tuesday, or you will be one of the 99 would-be winners who face Wednesday without the terrible decision of how to spend $75.00. In other words, either you win $75.00 or you win nothing. How, then, can you evaluate how much money you "expect" to receive? Do you "expect" to receive $75.00?

The first thing you might ask yourself in attempting to answer this question is, "What are my chances (What is the *probability*) of winning?" This is the same thing as asking, "What are the chances that my ticket will be drawn?" Well, if your friend is drawing the ticket and he can search for your particular number, your chances of winning are 100% (probability *one*). Thus you "expect" to receive $75.00.

But now suppose the drawing is "at random" in the sense that we assume the categorical description that each ticket has an equal probability of being drawn. Now you have a 1% chance of winning, or your probability of winning is 1/100. Your chances of losing are, of course, 99%, and the probability of losing is 99/100. On a percentage basis we could say that you "expect" to receive

$$\$75.00 \times \frac{1}{100} + \$0.00 \times \frac{99}{100} = \$0.75$$

on Tuesday.

How did we calculate this "expected value" of your ticket? There are four components in the calculation. Two of them are probabilities: 99/100 of losing, 1/100 of winning. Two of them are payoffs: $75, which is associated with a "winning" outcome, and $0, which is the monetary result of a "losing" outcome. The payoffs are "weighted" by the probabilities, yielding the expected value. This weighting is one way to define the term "expected value," and thus to help prepare for decisions under uncertainty.

Let us see how this newly learned quantitative method based on expected value actually works by adding a choice to the above example.

Problem: The Lottery Ticket Revisited ─────────────

What if your friend tells you that he will give you either a dollar for your birthday or the lottery ticket. Which would you take?

Analysis: You are now confronted with a decision problem, and you might want to use the MIS presented in section 1.4 to organize the information. The choice is between having one dollar in the hand,

TABLE 1.5   Outcome Table for the Lottery Problem

DECISION	STATE OF THE WORLD	
	s_1 = your ticket is drawn	s_2 = your ticket is not drawn
d_1 = take the dollar	o_1 = you receive a dollar	o_2 = you receive a dollar
d_2 = take the ticket	o_3 = you win the lottery	o_4 = you lose the lottery

TABLE 1.6   Payoff Table for the Lottery Problem

DECISION	STATE OF THE WORLD	
	s_1	s_2
d_1	$w_1 = \$1.00$	$w_2 = \$1.00$
d_2	$w_3 = \$75.00$	$w_4 = \$0.00$

d_1, or \$75.00 in the bush, d_2. Also, two relevant states of the world can occur, namely, that the ticket offered by your friend is drawn, s_1, or the ticket is not drawn, s_2. These decisions and states of the world determine the possible outcomes to you, as shown in the outcome table 1.5, and the payoffs associated with the above outcomes are described in table 1.6. In addition, you know the probability of getting the \$75.00 into your hand—namely, 1/100. How would you compare the two op-portunities, d_1 and d_2?

One way is to use the quantitative method of expected value to compare the expected value of decision d_2 to the expected value of d_1. You compute the expected value of d_1 in the same way that you compute the expected value of any decision. Weigh the payoffs by their probabilities, by multiplying the probability of an outcome associated with the decision times the payoff associated with that outcome, for example, 99/100 × \$1.00. Then add up these terms and get the expected value of that decision. There will be as many terms as there are states of the world. In this case the expected value of d_1 is:

$$\frac{99}{100} \times \$1.00 + \frac{1}{100} \times \$1.00 = \frac{100}{100} \times \$1.00 = \$1.00$$

You already know that the expected value of d_2, the ticket, is \$.75. However, note the prescriptive assumptions made in this analysis:

that you should compare decisions based upon expected value in the same way that you compare decisions involving sure dollars, and that expected value should be defined in such a way that a sure dollar is equal to an expected dollar for decision-making purposes. As always you must be careful when using quantitative methods in decision making to be fully aware of the assumptions involved. We will see in chapter 6 what happens if we drop these assumptions.

If you accept the assumptions, however, then the categorical prescription that you ought to make as much as you can tells you to take the dollar and let your friend wait out the results of the lottery. But, of course, the opposite decision is your best choice if he offers you 50¢ outright as the alternative to the ticket. Now ask yourself the following question: Accepting the assumption that expected value is equivalent to sure money, and the categorical prescription that you ought to make as much as you can, at what level of cash will you be "indifferent" between the lottery ticket and the monetary gift?

Let's review what you have just learned in a somewhat more complicated situation.

Problem: Which Route to Take to Work

After a late Wednesday night get-together with friends you have overslept your alarm clock, and it is 8:30 Thursday morning before you are ready to leave for work. You have three choices available to you. (1) Take the bus for 50 cents and arrive 30 minutes late to work. (2) Drive your car (gas and parking cost $1.50) and hope that the traffic is light, in which case you make it on time. If the traffic is normal, you will be 6 minutes late; if it is heavy, you will be 15 minutes late. (3) Take the subway at a cost of 30 cents; if you catch the next train, you arrive on time, but if you miss it, you will be 25 minutes late on the second train. You are docked pay at the rate of 10 cents a minute for tardiness since your hourly wage is $6. Fortunately, you know the probabilities for the last two choices. The probabilities of light, normal, and heavy traffic are 1/6, 2/6, and 3/6, respectively. The chance of missing the next train is 50%. What should you do?

Analysis: Again, let us see how the expected-value quantitative method applies. In this case assume that you are looking for the alternative with the smallest dollar loss (equivalent to "making the most you can"), and hence other considerations are not relevant in computing the payoffs. As in the previous problem, also assume that expected dollars are equivalent to sure dollars.

You can then decide by comparing the expected loss for each alternative decision. This calculation is made possible by the information provided in the statement of the problem.

1. You know the probabilities of the different arrival times for the different choices.

2. You know all the payoffs (in this case, costs) for the alternative outcomes (arrival times).

You can now compute expected and sure losses, compare your decisions, and make the "best" decision under all the assumptions.

d_1: *Take the Bus*

A sure loss of $.50 + $3.00 = $3.50 occurs no matter what the state of the world. We could also say that the chances of this alternative costing $3.50 are 100% (probability *one*) since

a. the probability of paying 50¢ is one (100% chance); and

b. the probability of arriving 30 minutes late is one (100% chance). You can therefore say that the expected loss if you ride the bus is $1 \times $3.50 = 3.50.

d_2: *Drive to Work*

Sure loss: $1.50.

Once you have decided to drive your car to work, there are three possibilities:

1. light traffic—you arrive on time and are not docked any pay;

2. normal traffic—you arrive 6 minutes late and get docked $.60;

3. heavy traffic—you arrive 15 minutes late and get docked $1.50.

The expected loss associated with driving, not including the sure loss of $1.50, is obtained by weighting the costs of these three events by their probabilities: $1/6 \times $0. + 2/6 \times $.60 + 3/6 \times $1.50 = $.95$. To get the total expected loss of decision 2, add to $.95 the sure loss of $1.50, yielding $2.45 as the total expected loss associated with driving your car to work.

d_3: *Ride the Subway*

If you ride the subway, there are two possibilities:

1. you catch the next train and arrive on time (probability 1/2) and are not docked pay;

2. you miss the next train and arrive 25 minutes late (probability 1/2) and get docked $2.50.

Expected loss (not including fare) = $1/2 \times $0.00 + 1/2 \times $2.50 = 1.25. Total expected loss (including fare) $= $1.25 + $.30 = 1.55.

So, you enjoy a ride on the subway, or you apply the systems approach and open up the whole problem by calling a friend and asking for a ride. (See page 8.)

PROBLEMS 1.7

1. Suppose you flip a fair coin (50% chance of heads or tails). If heads occurs, you win $3. If tails occurs, you win $1. What is the expected value of the flip?

2. A fair coin is tossed and if heads show you receive $1 but if tails occur you pay $1. What is the expected value of the toss?

3. You are offered the following bet: A six-sided die is tossed. The probability of each side is 1/6. If 1 or 2 occur you win $12; if 3 occurs, you win $3; otherwise you pay $2. What is the expected value of the bet? Is it worth it for you?

4. Suppose the lottery ticket you got from your friend earned you $75. You have the opportunity to spend all this money to buy another ticket in a ten-thousand-dollar-winner-takes-all lottery in which 200 tickets are sold. Should you try your luck again?

5. What job should you choose in problem 1, section 1.4? What assumptions have you made in this analysis?

6. Should you hire the extra salesman in problem 2, section 1.4?

7. Being late for the 9 o'clock meeting, you feel very lucky to find a parking place nearby. You try to put coins into the meter but it is out of order. After the meeting you approach the car and find a ticket on the windshield which could cost you $5 if you choose not to contest it in court. You discuss your problem with some "well informed" friends who estimate that your chances of acquittal in court are 70%, but if the judge decides to find you in violation of the parking regulation it will result in a $10 or $25 penalty with probability .25 and .05, respectively. Should you contest the ticket?

8. As you pass by a stand at a county fair, the owner shows you a deck of 52 cards, offers to let you shuffle them as you please, and bets $1 against your $5 that he can pick out the ace of spades when the cards are spread out face downwards. Should you accept the bet?

1.8   Modeling

It will be convenient in what follows to introduce one more technical term, *model*. *A model is a representation of reality, or what is taken to be reality.* Thus, when you write down the information about D, S, O, and W, and determine how to infer O from D and S, and W from O, you are constructing a model if you assume that all this information describes some aspect of the real world. Hence another way to explain the purpose of this book is to say that we are interested in extending and refining your capability to model reality in order to make decisions.

But you should realize that saying a model is a representation of reality hides the difficulties of practical decision making. The practical (and philosophical) question is: What is reality? Do I really know what it is? For example, is the set *D* really composed of all the decisions you could make? One of the creative acts in decision making is to come up with a real, available decision no one else has even dreamed of. Or, does *S* contain all the states of the world? Maybe your competitor is about to spring a new, better, and cheaper product on you and all your carefully laid market plans. Or, maybe God (the Supreme State of the World) helps those who help themselves. Will only the outcomes *O* occur, or are you in for some surprises when you buy that wonderful lot of land in the Michigan woods most of which happens to lie under a swamp? And finally, how much do you really value the outcomes: just their dollar worth, or their moral worth, or aesthetic worth, or just plain "people worth"?

But over and above these reality considerations is an overriding reality problem which asks, "Is this really an important problem for me to consider, and is this the right way to formulate it?" We have limited resources to consider problems, and presumably we should use them economically. A very elegant model for solving an unimportant problem is just that and nothing more: elegant.

Even in the exercises in this book, you should strive to think of other decisions that might be made, other states of the world that might ruin the decision, other outcomes and values, and above all, the importance of the problem. Then you'll begin to grasp the essence of modeling.

PROBLEM 1.8

Can you think of situations where it would be inappropriate to calculate expected value in making a risky decision?

1.9 Summary

Hopefully, you have begun to catch the spirit of the use of management information and quantitative methods in decision making. These points are worth repeating:

a. Quantitative methods is a technology which can increase your capabilities in preparing for decisions.

b. Using reasoning and/or experience, you can develop quantitative methods to identify the range of choices and to refine your methods of choosing between alternative decisions.

c. In this text we will be concerned primarily with deductive quantitative methods which rely predominantly upon reasoning.

d. Quantitative methods are only as useful and reliable as the accuracy and stability of the available information.

e. Quantitative methods, like all methods for preparing for decision, require strong assumptions, and, in general, these assumptions ought to be made explicit.

f. Quantitative methods may be tricky and deceptive because they are often so simple and "logical"; so use both reasoning and experience in applying them.

g. For the time being, in applying quantitative methods we will use the categorical prescription to "make the most you can," sometimes by maximizing expected value.

h. In applying quantitative methods to decisions it is often convenient to use a management information system that structures the information into four parts: D (the available choices), S (the relevant states of the world), O (the outcomes), and W (the values of the outcomes), where the w's help us decide which d to choose.

i. Maintain a constructive, critical attitude toward the use of models in decision making.

Deductive Systems 2

2.1   The Need for Deductive Systems of Thought

For a moment, let us place you back in time several thousand years, to the time of the Pharaohs in Egypt. You have just been appointed chief engineer of Rameses II's pyramid. Your predecessor lost his head for failing properly to judge spacial requirements for Rameses II's tomb area. Of course, you cannot turn down this "great honor," and you might (since you've read chapter 1) turn to the I Ching for some advice. But, unfortunately, China is very far away from Egypt, and there aren't many planes around since it's 2000 B.C. In any case, you've got a very specific problem at hand, and you may feel that the advice of the I Ching is a bit too general. What you would rather have is access to all the spacial information and experience of previous pyramid builders. It occurs to you that it might be nice if all their findings could be summarized in some compact form that would be of use to you. Unfortunately for you, however, Euclid isn't around just yet, but you can certainly sense that it might make your problems a lot easier (and safer) if his summary of knowledge about geometry were there to depend on.

The point of all this is that when faced with any decision problem (like that of the pyramid builder), it can be quite helpful to have a compact, unambiguous description of the current knowledge relevant to your decision. In the above case it was geometry; in the Lottery problem of chapter 1 you needed some knowledge of probability; later in this text, you may need calculus or some knowledge of linear mathematics for decision problems. The knowledge in these areas can be summarized by proceeding from basic ideas, definitions, and assumptions to consequences that follow directly from the assumptions. The consequences can then be used to help solve problems like that of the pyramid builder. This method of organizing knowledge and arriving at consequences was first introduced over 2000 years ago and is called the *deductive process*.

2.2   The Deductive Process

Probably the greatest contributor to the study of the deductive process was that marvelous organizer of human thought, Aristotle (384–322 B.C.), who, in his *Organon*, sets forth the basic method so clearly. The deductive process consists of basic ideas and definitions to remove ambiguity, assumptions, the rules of deduction, and theorems or consequences. A body of knowledge organized in this way is called a *deductive system*.

2.2.1   Removing Ambiguity by Definition   The first task in deduction is to be clear about your terms—that is, to express exactly what you mean. How can you create clear, unambiguous definitions? There is no one best way, but often we find that we can define our words by other words that are simpler, clearer, and less ambiguous, which we call basic ideas. For example, if we say that traffic into the St. Louis area is a fraction of the traffic into Chicago, the word "fraction" may be ambiguous. But if you know what a whole number is, and what it means to divide one whole number by another, then we can define the term "fraction" as any number which can be represented by one whole number divided by another larger whole number: 1/2, 2/3, 3/4, 5/8, and so on. If you didn't understand division, we would go on to define it in simpler language. For this method of defining to work, we must finally arrive at the simplest, clearest, and least ambiguous terms which therefore need no defining. For example, in geometry "point," "line," "straight line," and "plane" are often taken as the most unambiguous basic ideas, although there has been a long debate throughout the history of thought as to whether these are in fact the simplest ideas of space. For a decision maker what is or what is not simple and clear depends largely on how well a word or passage communicates the intended meaning of the speaker. In an organization that is working smoothly with a long experience of cooperation, a basic simple and clear language may emerge, where some ideas like "authority" or "responsibility" no longer need to be defined since they are well understood and relatively unambiguous. Of course, an organization may

assume that everyone understands its language in the same way and nevertheless be thoroughly deceived.

PROBLEMS 2.2.1

1. Suppose you understand what the number 1 means, and you understand what the successor of a whole number means. How would you define the number 2? Can you now define any positive whole number?

2. Which of the following ideas seem clear to you?

   a. net profit per year   b. authority
   c. right vs. wrong policies   d. one-half of a specified area
   e. gross sales   f. quality of life
   g. the environment   h. ecology

2.2.2   Assumptions (Postulates and Axioms)   The deductive process, besides requiring clear and simple terms, also requires *assumptions*, which logicians and mathematicians sometimes call *postulates* or *axioms*. Here again the history of thought has generated many different ideas about the role that assumptions should play in thinking through solutions to our human problems, and by now it's pretty difficult to create any very novel viewpoint. Some have argued that there must be basic axioms, or else where do we begin? Others have argued that every assumption we humans make is uncertain. Still others have said that the assumptions are conventions—much like the rules of a game: if you do not assume that bishops in chess move along the diagonals, you're not playing chess, that's all.

Assumptions play an essential role in management, because no organization can avoid chaos if its policies are continually in doubt. Of course, individuals in the organization may question any policy assumption, but a large part of the time the organization must act as though its basic assumptions were correct. In this regard, it is important that individuals in the organization understand the implications of general policies; that is, they should be capable of deducing the consequences. Hence, understanding the process of deduction in greater depth should enable you to understand better the application of managerial policies.

PROBLEMS 2.2.2

1. What assumptions did you make when you decided to apply to your school?

2. What assumptions does a school make in using grade point average, or a standard test score, as a criterion for admissions?

3. What assumptions does a manufacturer of clothes usually make?

4. What assumptions are hidden in the statement that "all men are created equal"?

2.2.3 Rules of Deduction Thus far the deductive process has been described in terms of clear and simple terms (basic ideas), definitions, and basic assumptions. To understand how implications are made from the assumptions, we also require the gasoline to run the motor. In this case we require rules that tell us how to go from assumptions to *consequences*, which are also called *theorems*. Your head is full of such rules which you use every day. For example, the sign in the hardware store says that 3-inch nails are 25 cents a pound, and you need 3 pounds, and have 53 cents in your pocket. Consequence? Not enough money. How did you get the theorem from the assumptions? You had a rule for deducing the total amount required from the assumption that the nails are 25 cents a pound, and another rule that told you that 75 is greater than 53, and so on, to your conclusion.

You'll note that this deduction relies very strongly on arithmetic, which is itself a deductive system. Logic is the most general deductive system in the sense that it is always used when we deduce consequences from assumptions. For example, logic tells you that once you have proven a theorem, you can use the theorem to prove other theorems; that is, you can use the theorem just as we use the original assumptions. The top management of a company may set an overall policy on pricing (for example, to meet the competitors' least price); each division will then adopt this policy for its own region; a retail store in a region can then use the regional policy, just as though it were the total company policy, without having to trace back to the original top management decision.

This process of reasoning is very common, and hence in deductive systems it is given a name, the *transitivity of inference*, which says that if you can infer proposition q from assumption p, and then infer proposition r from q, then you can act as though you had inferred r from the original assumption p; the deductive rule is:

a. if from p, infer q,

b. and from q, infer r;

c. then from p, infer r.

For example,

a. from "the interest rate goes up," infer "my costs increase,"

b. and from "my costs increase," infer "my prices must increase,"

c. then from "the interest rate goes up," infer "my prices must increase."

But, note that you may not be willing to accept the policy implications of (c). The final decision that must be made remains ambiguous because there may be other ways to cope with increasing costs (that is, (b) may not hold).

The word *transitive* will occur very frequently in quantitative methods, as it does implicitly in many decisions; "transitive" describes a property of a relationship. Transitive relationships such as "infer from" or "is greater than" or "is worth more" are relationships that enable us to go from a starting point and leap over the intermediate steps. Thus we often make the assumption (a) if x is worth more than y, (b) and y is worth more than z, (c) then x is worth more than z.

Not all relationships are transitive, of course. For example, you might try the scheme on the relation "is next to" by putting these words in place of "is worth more than" in (a), (b), and (c) in the preceding paragraph. Does (c) follow from (a) and (b) in this case?

Another very useful and common deductive rule consists of testing a possible consequence by assuming its negation and seeing what follows. For example, in the USSR there are very strict rules which forbid under-the-counter deals by factory managers. You wonder whether these rules really do imply that you'll get into trouble if you make such a deal. So you assume the opposite, namely that you can get away with a few deals despite the strict rules. You are caught and disciplined, and at some appropriate moment you can infer that the rules really do imply what they say. This is one form of the deductive rule which might be called a "reduction to disaster." A safer form is a reduction to absurdity: here we assume the opposite of the theorem to be proved, and derive a contradiction. For example, a retail store manager might wonder whether the company's policy of automatically meeting competitors' prices holds in the event of a prolonged price war. So he assumes the opposite of this assumption, and sees what would follow if he met every move of a competitor in a price war by lowering his price to the lowest offered. He would soon see that there were many small companies trying to beat the big ones by lowering their prices. He would also see that, in this situation, it would be disastrous to follow after every little mouse, when the real war was between the larger lions like his own company. Since it's ridiculous to follow a disastrous policy, he's deduced an absurdity from the assumption that the company's policy applies to all competitors in such price wars. Hence, the company's policies don't hold in such cases.

The scheme of this method of deduction is (a) if p is assumed, then q follows; (b) but q is false (absurd, ridiculous, deadly); hence (c) p is false.

PROBLEMS 2.2.3

Comment on the following deductions.

1. Scientists have established that there is a very high probability that intelligent life exists elsewhere in the universe. These intelligent beings may very well have answers to some of our most pressing problems (for example, cancer). *Therefore* we should try to communicate with them.

2. In Cleveland's first campaign, his opponents publicized the story that he was the father of an illegitimate child; *therefore* he should not be elected president because he was immoral.

3. Your marketing department forecasts to your satisfaction that Product A will have ten thousand sales at a profit of $5 each, while in the same period Product B will have five thousand sales at a profit of $12 each. *Therefore*, assuming you can make only one product, you should produce B.

4. If the communists wanted to infiltrate our political system they'd try to put fluoride—or something worse—into our water system. But people *are* trying to put fluoride into water systems. *Therefore* they're commies in disguise.

5. Many countries lack coal, oil, or water as sources of energy. But they desperately need energy. *Therefore* they should have nuclear plants.

2.2.4 Theorems To summarize, the deductive process consists of identifying basic ideas in terms of which other ideas are defined, plus assumptions, plus rules for deducing the consequences of the assumptions, and the consequences (theorems). Of course, the fruit of the entire effort is the theorems. If we can agree on the meaning of the basic ideas, and the assumptions and rules, then we must agree on all the consequences.

This is a very beautiful conception of decision making which has fascinated men over and over again throughout history. For instance, it so fascinated Benedict Spinoza (1632–77 A.D.) that he based a whole "systems approach" to decision making on it. In his *Ethics* he develops what he takes to be the basic postulates of the nature of reality, and from these deduces the proper rules of conduct for men. If Spinoza's dream had come true, all our petty and serious quarrels between people and nations would be over: we would have the basis for the perfect MIS for everyone and could deduce the right answers to all our problems from the basic certainties. Unfortunately or fortunately, depending on how you look at it, no one has been able to find the desired certainties, so that the deductive method has to be used in more specialized cases.

2.3   Geometry: An Example of a Deductive System

One of these specialized cases to which we have already referred is that of problems concerning space. Spacial problems are problems involving lengths, areas, volumes, locations, and so on, and the deductive system used to help solve them is called geometry.

In ancient times, the Babylonians and Egyptians "knew" many bits and pieces about space, as the Greeks did later and in greater depth. We don't know exactly when it occurred to someone to organize all this information, but the most famous attempt is that of Euclid, whose *Elements* were written about 300 B.C. The result of his efforts is an amazingly compact deductive system. Euclid's *Elements* was designed to organize and present the mass of knowledge about spacial problems in a way that would prove useful for decision makers (such as pyramid builders).

The structure of Euclid's description is based on the four components—*basic ideas, definitions,* and *postulates*—to which *logic* is applied in order to obtain theorems. He begins with

BASIC IDEAS   point, line, plane, and so on.

It's assumed that you have a good idea what these ideas mean.

Euclid's definitions were a mixture of fairly precise language and a rather ingenious set of images. Thus a straight line is defined as a line whose points "lie evenly on itself." This peculiar language was apparently used to evoke the image of turning the straight line so that it aims directly at your eye, in which case you would see only a point, whereas in the case of a crooked line you would see more than one point. A *segment* is the straight line between any two points, and the length of a segment is the *distance* between two points. A *circle* is the set of points equidistant from a given point. You can see how the language builds up in a systematic way: first line (a basic idea), then straight line, then segment and distance, then circle. This is not how most dictionaries work, but it is characteristic of the dictionaries of deductive systems. Thus, we have

DEFINITIONS   straight line, distance, circle, triangle, parallel lines, and so on.

Next, Euclid turns to assumptions, and chooses as his first assumptions some very simple "construction" postulates.

POSTULATE 1   Between any two points in a plane it is always possible to draw a straight line.

POSTULATE 2   A segment (piece of a straight line) can always be extended indefinitely in either direction.

POSTULATE 3   Given any point as center and any segment, a circle can always be drawn with the segment as radius.

You should also notice how these "ideal" postulates work. Suppose you are a city planner drawing a plan for new streets and parks. You write down some specifications: (a) connect the end of 17th Street with Mariposa by means of a straight street (postulate 1); (b) continue 18th Street one more block in a straight street (postulate 2); (c) make a circular street of diameter 100 yards with the center at the intersection of 19th Street and Green Avenue (postulate 3). These instructions are partially ambiguous as written in English: how wide a street, with what safety standards, sidewalks, paving, and so on? The precise geometrical postulates guarantee that *in principle* the instructions can be carried out: there are no purely geometrical obstacles. Thus postulate 1 does *not* say that between any two points a straight street can be constructed; but it does say that geometrically such a construction is feasible.

Euclid's first three postulates are often called the "ruler and compass" constructions, since the ruler allows us to perform the first two constructions and the compass the third.

Euclid's fourth assumption looks very odd at first sight, for it simply says:

POSTULATE 4   All right angles are equal.

Since you know (or should know) that a right angle is 90 degrees, this assumption merely seems to say that $90° = 90°$, and what's new? But the need to make this postulate reveals an important hidden lesson about how decision makers should use numbers. Let's trace back the idea of "right angle" in Euclid's definitional series; the origin is "intersecting straight lines," which are straight lines that have a point in common. The angles on the same side of two intersecting lines are called "adjacent." If these two adjacent angles are equal, then they are called "right angles" (note no mention of "degrees" yet). Euclid uses a "correspondence" test for equality: if the angles are placed on top of each other and they correspond in every regard (this is really another basic idea), then the angles are equal. Now by definition the two adjacent right angles are equal, but the question is whether two other adjacent and equal angles formed by another pair of intersecting lines will always produce the same "size" angle. Your intuition probably tells you they will: after all, carpenters have been using squares for centuries and their buildings hold up reasonably well. This is because the plane is "smooth"; if it were wrinkled, then equal adjacent angles would vary in size. Indeed, Euclid's fourth postulate is simply one fairly refined way of saying that the plane is smooth.

What is the lesson for decision making? Why, that simply assigning numbers to objects or events isn't enough for stable decision making to occur. It is only because right angles do not change over space that we can introduce the convenience of "degrees," "minutes," and "seconds," which are so essential in navigation, for example. If a degree in Hawaii is worth two degrees in Seattle, there would be real decision-making difficulties on the part of captains of ships. Or if you ask me what a 20-foot by 100-foot ocean view lot is worth in Bolinas, California, and I say 50 dollars, you may be astonished or angry, since the current asking price is about 1500 dollars. I meant that you could buy such a lot for 50 dollars in 1955; since then lots have become more valuable and dollars less valuable. It would *not* be safe to assume that "all Bolinas ocean view lots are equal in value," even though this is approximately true at any moment of time. However, if we can adjust for the increase in real estate values and decrease in the value of the dollar, we can arrive at a stable decision-making system; you could then take my answer "50 dollars" and adjust it to present values. Thus, hidden in Euclid's dry *Elements* is an important "systems" lesson on how to use numbers in decision making: You must search for the stability conditions in making measurements.

Euclid's fifth postulate became famous and almost infamous; possibly more attention was paid to it over the 2000 years after the *Elements* appeared than to any other mathematical problem. It'll make matters a bit more interesting if we explain it in a story which has no basis in historical fact. So there is Euclid working hard one night on his *Elements*. He's been proving theorems about parallel lines, which are lines in the same plane that never intersect. Around about 11:00 P.M., he proves that if two lines intersect a third so that the interior angles are all equal to right angles, the two lines are parallel. See figure 2.1. Now mathematicians live in intellectual patterns and like to keep things neat. When they prove that one proposition (all the angles are right) implies another (the lines are parallel), they wonder about the converse: does the second imply the first? Or, what is exactly the same thing logically, what happens if (in the figure) $B + D$ is *less* than two right angles? Certainly then ℓ_1 and ℓ_2 are converging on each other on the right side, but will they always meet? Prove it! At 3:00 A.M., Euclid is still trying to prove it; Mrs. Euclid has shouted at him four times to come to bed; he's tired, frustrated, so:

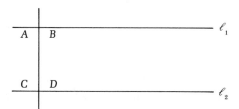

Figure 2.1   If $A = B = C = D = $ **Right Angle, Then** ℓ_1 **and** ℓ_2 **Are Parallel**

POSTULATE 5   If two lines intersect a third so that the interior angles on the same side are less than two right angles, the two lines are *not* parallel and intersect on this side.

Now it may not have been very sporting of Euclid to assume what he couldn't prove, and he certainly didn't provide a very good example for his students, who might be tempted to take any old exercise and postulate it instead of proving it. But there is another lesson for decision making in Euclid's story: If you really believe that certain hidden aspects of a situation must be happening, then you're well advised to trace back to one or more basic assumptions which will justify your belief. An interesting example of this principle occurs in card games, and perhaps in competition in general. If the *only* way you can win is to assume that one of your opponents holds a certain card, then assume that he does, and you will find that you can make inferences from this assumption that will determine your next play.

Euclid's fifth assumption became a problem for later mathematics because many people thought it could be proved, either from simpler assumptions or from the ones he previously made. We know now that this attempt of over 2000 years was futile: the postulate cannot be derived from anything simpler or from the other postulates.

These five assumptions are all geometrical; that is, they describe some of the basic properties of pure space. Euclid also introduces some of the rules of deduction, which he called "common notions." Many of these are arithmetical in character; for example, "things equal to the same thing are equal to each other."

We now come to the most important aspect of deductive systems: the ability to deduce consequences from the fairly simple and precise assumptions. From Euclid's assumptions we can deduce whether a given structure is geometrically feasible and what its geometrical properties will be (for example, size of angles).

Problem: Building a Pavilion ━━━━━━━━━━━━━━━━━━━━━━━━━━━

You have the honor and misfortune of running your county's annual fair. Someone comes up with the bright idea of a pavilion whose floor is to be an equilateral triangle (all sides equal). Is it geometrically feasible to lay out such a floor?

Analysis: The required construction is actually the first theorem of Euclid's *Elements*. His reasoning goes as follows:

THEOREM 1   On any straight line segment, an equilateral triangle can always be drawn (where "equilateral" means that all the sides are equal).

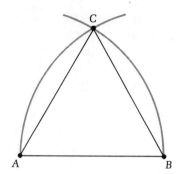

Figure 2.2 Constructing an Equilateral Triangle

PROOF Let AB be the line segment which represents one side of the proposed triangle (see figure 2.2).

With AB as radius and A as center, construct a circle (postulate 3 justifies this step).

With BA as radius and B as center, construct a circle (postulate 3).

Let C be the intersection of these two circles.

Draw AC and BC (postulate 1 justifies this).

$AB = AC$ (by definition of a circle).

$BC = BA$ (by definition of a circle).

$AB = BA$ (by meaning of equality of geometrical figures).

Therefore

$AC = BC$ (things equal to the same thing are equal to each other).

QED ("quod erat demonstrandum" — what was to be demonstrated).

Thus, from Euclid's elementary assumptions, we can prove that the required construction is geometrically feasible.

Later writers, especially in the last century, have pointed out that Euclid's deductive method is partially ambiguous and has loopholes; for example, he sneaked one in the proof just given: How does he know that the two circles will always intersect? But his method can be refined if one wants to (most teachers of geometry don't try because it would exhaust the patience of both teacher and student).

The *Elements* still stands as a great monument to man's thinking. It is really astonishing how many rich results follow from the postulates. For example, there is the well-known rule which says that in any right triangle the square of the hypotenuse is equal to the sum of the squares of the other two sides $(c^2 = a^2 + b^2)$. Certainly nothing in the postulates or definitions seems to hint at this remarkable result.

But more important from the point of view of management information systems is how very compactly and explicitly Euclid organized the geometrical information and knowledge available during his time. If you understand the basic ideas, you can then understand all the more complicated ideas by simply tracing back their meanings given in the definitions to the basic ideas. If you want to solve a complicated problem, you can trace back the correct solution to the basic postulates and axioms by proving that the solution is a theorem. And the most fantastic selling point from a managerial point of view is that your confidence in the solution—no matter how complicated—depends entirely on whether you are confident about the postulates and your deduction. If you are reasonably sure about these—and reasonably sure you understand the basic ideas—then you can be reasonably sure about the solution.

It would be nice to say that Aristotle's design method for deduction works for all managerial problems, but it does not. It works very well for practical geometry, arithmetic, mechanics, and some branches of engineering. It also works well for classification problems, and a deductive system for classification called *set theory* or *Boolean algebra* is presented in appendix 2.1. A deductive system for probability is presented in chapter 5. Aristotle's design is also widely used by economists who deduce economic solutions from "reasonable" assumptions, but even in economics there is considerable debate about how reliable these economic assumptions really are.

You may be interested in a postscript to Euclid's story to bring it up to modern times. Around 1700 a monk named Saccheri decided to "clear Euclid of every blemish"; that is, to "prove" the fifth postulate. To do so, he decided to use one of the logical schemes we discussed earlier, namely, to show that if he denied Euclid's assumption, an absurdity would follow. So he assumed (in effect) that the fifth postulate was false and began deriving the consequences. They were very strange, but not altogether ridiculous. For example, straight lines converge for awhile, then diverge; or they converge always but never meet; c^2 is greater than $a^2 + b^2$; a triangle has a maximum area; the sum of the degrees of a triangle is less than two right angles (180 degrees); and so on. What Saccheri didn't realize was that he was inventing non-Euclidian geometry, apparently for the first time. He thought he could deduce an absurdity, namely, that some straight lines can meet at infinity and have a common segment "thereafter"(?), which is more or less meaningless. Over a century later, non-Euclidean geometry was declared legal by the mathematical community, and later still opened up very significant theoretical possibilities for physics. So it was found that what was thought to be certain about the state of the world was actually uncertain. A deductive system based upon the negation of Euclid's fifth assumption is also plausible, and decisions can be made using non-Euclidean geometry as an alternative. This postscript shows, in effect, that even the most obvious assumptions may fail under deep scrutiny. Nevertheless, in the real world, Euclid's geometry is still the one to use if you're an earthly engineer or carpenter or real-estate man.

PROBLEMS 2.3

1. In normal accounting procedures, the financial statement always shows that assets = liabilities. What is the status of this "axiom" of accounting procedures—that is, why is it "true"?

2. In measuring length, you probably use a ruler, yardstick, or tape. But how do you know that these are accurate? How do you know that a message on a box on the grocery shelf which reads "contents not less than one pound" is correct?

3. Why should the fiscal year start July 1?

4. In economic theory it is usually assumed that if a consumer prefers commodity A to B, and prefers B to C, then he must prefer A to C. Why? What would you say about a consumer who was given the pairs A-B, B-C, and A-C, and chose A, B, C?

5. It seems obvious that the cause of an event must precede it in time. Is it? Why?

2.4   Deductive Systems and a "Systems Approach" Lesson

Euclid's geometry was intentionally developed in a fairly precise language in which the assumptions were relatively simple to understand and easy to accept as correct. But consider the following situation drawn from real life.

EXAMPLE   A city council, alarmed at the arrogant display of Nazi uniforms on the streets, passes the following resolution: That it shall be a felony punishable by a fine of $500 or three months in jail, or both, for any person to appear in public in the military uniform of a foreign power.

The council, however, forgets that a month ago it passed the following resolution: That the Veterans of America be permitted to exhibit a sham battle of the Alamo on the fairgrounds on July 4 of this year.

What can be deduced from these two resolutions? Maybe, that in the sham battle the "Mexicans" must wear suits, jeans, or nothing? A clever lawyer might argue that "appear in public" means ordinary appearance on the streets or other public places, but does not mean appearance in an authorized performance. The point is that it is very difficult, if not impossible, to understand clearly the implications of such resolutions which are written in a language which is ambiguous, and intentionally so.

But our intent in this book is to describe deductive decision making in language which is as unambiguous as possible. If the council passes an ordinance about drunk driving which says that "drunk" means more than k% alcohol in the blood stream, and there are accurate tests for inferring alcoholic content, then the language becomes unambiguous.

Unambiguous languages have the advantage of being precise, but the disadvantage of being relatively inflexible. For example, in the law the languages are flexible, but not precise; the languages of quantitative methods are precise, but not flexible. But you should recognize that practically every serious managerial problem in its initial formulation is expressed in an ambiguous language. If we feel that the MIS we have introduced is appropriate, then we do our best to translate the ambiguously formulated problem into a precise language which is relatively unambiguous. Within this precise language we infer a precise conclusion about the payoffs associated with each decision by means of assumptions about the states of the world and outcomes. But, once we have deduced the d with the highest associated w, we have to return to the ambiguous language of decision making. "Should you really implement the indicated decision?" is essentially an ambiguous question, since it brings in many considerations we had to leave out in formulating a precise D, S, O, and W. Figure 2.3 is a simplistic scheme which relates the three languages just mentioned. (Of course, in reality we may be in and out of the precise language frequently during our problem analysis.) You will have already noticed how the scheme is followed in the problems of this book. The English version of the problem is first stated, and the ambiguity is

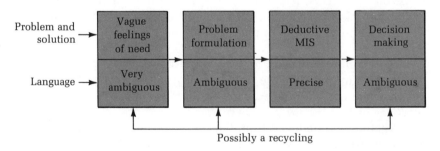

Possibly a recycling

Figure 2.3

apparent. (For example, in the Route to Work problem of chapter 1, what is meant by "subway"? There may be several choices.) Throughout this book we will occasionally return to ambiguity at the end of a problem, to remind you of the underlying ambiguous language of problem formulation and decision making. In this connection, even if you don't read appendix 2.1, you may want to read appendix 2.2, which raises questions about a management information system consisting of D, S, O, and W. (See also problem 7, 1.1)

2.5 Summary

Hopefully, you now have an understanding of the deductive process, some of its history, and how deductive systems like geometry and set theory have been and will continue to be useful to decision makers. These points are worth repeating:

a. The deductive method, as set forth by Aristotle, consists of identifying basic ideas and using them to form definitions and state basic assumptions or axioms. The basic assumptions or axioms and the definitions, together with the rules of logic, are then used to deduce theorems or consequences. The consequences themselves can then be used in turn as if they were basic assumptions.

b. If you accept the basic assumptions and the rules of logic, you accept the conclusions; so if you are a decision maker and accept the information as accurate and the quantitative method used as appropriate, you can have confidence in the conclusions reached.

c. The deductive system for set theory in the appendix provides you with a language which can be helpful in discussing your decision problems and will prove useful in describing and developing the quantitative methods of future chapters.

d. Even though the deductive process helps to formulate decision problems in an unambiguous manner, the real world of decision making remains ambiguous.

Appendix 2.1   A Deductive System for Classification: Boolean Algebra – Set Theory

We often classify objects and events by asking what, when, where, and how, all of which are important questions for decisions. The hinge on the door is loose, and you need to fix it. *What* do you need? A regular screwdriver. *When?* Now (not next Saturday). *Where* is the screwdriver, honey? Where you left it, dear. *How* do you use a screwdriver? If you don't know by this time, don't bother. Classification is a very refined way of preparing for decision making, because we can combine our specifications in various ways. Thus a job specification may call for a person who is under 30 years old, either male or female, trained as a typist, not ever convicted of a felony, and so on. Note that this description hangs together by means of such connectives as *and, either-or, not*. Our deductive task is to understand how these connectives work.

A deductive system for classification was first developed in the West by Aristotle, who set forth the general mode of argument in terms of four ways of stating the relationship between two classes: (1) one of them may belong entirely to the other ("all A is B": "all cats are animals"); (2) they may at least overlap ("some A is B": "some days are rainy"); (3) they may be completely separate and have no intersection ("no A is B": "no squares are circles"); (4) they may at least be different in some regard ("some A is not B": "some companies do not survive"). Aristotle then described how these forms, when combined in certain ways, provide a logical method of discourse. Thus *if* all A is B *and* all B is C, *then* all A is C, no matter what classes A, B, and C stand for. Or, somewhat more difficult, if some A is B and no B is C, then some A is not C (namely, the part of A that is in B). (These examples are called *syllogisms*.)

But, you should notice that problems of classification normally begin in an ambiguous language. Suppose the UN wants to appoint a commission to consider Indian problems. It might pose the ambiguous policy that "all members of the commission are Indians." A staff member suggests that "all Indians live in India or Pakistan." But the simple inference to "all members of the commission live in India or Pakistan" may be unacceptable, especially if one promising candidate is temporarily living in New York, or if "Indian," as far as the commission is concerned, also includes American Indians. Thus there is always a risk in passing from the ambiguous language of classification to a precise logic of classes.

Aristotle did not provide us with a complete logic of classes; this task was accomplished by several logicians of the nineteenth century, and principally by George Boole (1815–64), so that the logic of classes is often called "Boolean algebra." The word "algebra" is derived from an Arabic word meaning "putting together of broken parts," and specifically mending broken limbs. Mathematicians took over the idea and, in their usual style, abstracted its meaning into the combining ("putting together") of symbols according to rules. Hence "algebra" in mathematics is a much more general subject than the algebra of numbers you learned — and may have forgotten.

Boolean algebra, as a deductive system, is far simpler than the algebra of numbers. It sometimes helps your understanding if you think of classes in terms of circles in an area of a plane (called "Venn diagrams," after a logician of the nineteenth century). Figure 2.4 is an

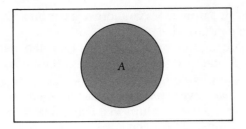

Figure 2.4   Example of a Venn Diagram for a Class A

example of a Venn diagram for a class A. The area enclosed by the circle represents the class A. The circle is placed in the plane, represented by the rectangle in the figure. This rectangle can be thought of as the *universal class*, the class that contains all other classes.

But you should beware of the utter simplicity of figure 2.4, which hides all the confusions and uncertainties about classification. Anyone in the health field who has ever tried to classify "healthy people" versus "unhealthy people" will quickly understand how vague are the boundary and inside of the class so glibly represented by the circle A, as well as the "universe" of all (relevant) people. As in the case of geometry, the logic of classes strips away most of the nasty considerations in order to speak precisely. Hence, whenever we illustrate a class by using the English language, you should be aware that the class is essentially ambiguous in the real-life struggle to classify.

We start with the first basic idea of the deductive system of classes, *elements*. Elements are the basic objects that make up a class. They may be physical objects such as "buildings over 25 stories in the state of California," or hypothetical objects, such as "the results of three flips of a coin." We will use small letters a, b, c, etc., to denote elements.

From this basic idea we proceed to the second basic idea, that of a *class*, also called a *set*. (Boolean algebra is also referred to as "set theory.") You can think of a class or set as a collection of elements. We will symbolize sets by capital letters A, B, C, and so on. For example, we write A = "the set of all owners of Fords in the U.S." Instead of using quotation marks, we can enclose the elements of a set in braces { }. For example, we write B = {all women under 25}, which is read "the set of all women under 25." Within the braces we may be able to list all of the elements of a set. For example, if your firm produces three products, then the set P, consisting of the names of products you produce, can be written P = {nuts, bolts, screws}.

Our third basic idea is that of *membership*. An element which is part of the collection which forms a set is said to be a "member of" or "belong to" that set. For example, "Income Statement for the First Quarter" is a member of the set S = {financial statements produced by your accounting department}. As another example, m belongs to {all letters in the Roman alphabet}.

If we are referring to a set A, we call a typical element of the set a and we write $a \epsilon A$ and read "a is a member of the set A," or "a belongs to the set A," or simply "a is an element of A."

At this point we have three basic ideas: *element*, *set*, and *membership*. Making use of these, we turn to a list of definitions and describe some special relationships between sets.

> DEFINITION 1   The set A is a *subset* of B if every element which is a member of A is also a member of B. We write this as $A \subset B$, and read "A is contained in B," or "A is a subset of B."

Figure 2.5 shows the set A as a subset of the set B. Note that both sets A and B are contained in U, the universal set.

EXAMPLE   A = {all women under 25} is a subset of B = {all women}; that is, $A \subset B$.

EXAMPLE   D = {a,b} is a subset of C = {a,b,c,d}; that is, $D \subset C$.

By carefully reading the definition of subset, we see that every set is considered to be a subset of itself.

EXAMPLE   The set C = {a,b,c,d} is a subset of itself, $C \subset C$, since every element of C is an element of C.

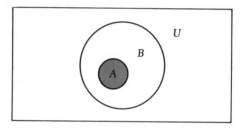

Figure 2.5   Venn Diagram for $A \subset B$

> DEFINITION 2   Two sets A and B are *equal* if they have exactly the same elements; that is, if each is a subset of the other. We can also say that two sets A and B are equal if A is contained in B ($A \subset B$) and B is contained in A ($B \subset A$), as in figure 2.6.

Occasionally when you are involved in a heated discussion, you may find that you and your adversary don't share the same frame of reference. "I don't believe that prices will go up more than 7%," may

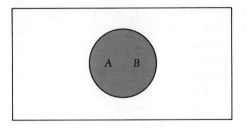

Figure 2.6 $A = B$

be a result of observing the behavior of the price index in the U.S. in the last decade. However, your adversary may be correct in disagreeing with you if he relies on world-wide price data for the same period. Using the notion of the universal set, we are able to clear up this type of confusion in communication.

DEFINITION 3   The *universal set*, denoted by U, is the set which contains all sets (and all elements). It is sometimes called the "universe of discourse."

If we took this idea literally, the universal set would include absolutely everything, but then it would be practically useless. Instead, in most conversations when we speak of "everything," we have a mutual understanding that "everything" refers to some specific "universe of discourse" which defines the topic. "I've tried every conceivable remedy and none of them works," would be absurd if "every" referred to anything, anywhere in the world; obviously, it refers to a more specific class of known potential remedies. In the broader systems approach, we can see how important these remarks are, because we need to think in terms of the "whole system and its environment" without necessarily thinking of everything in the whole wide world. Returning again to the MIS of section 1.4, we can see that S (the states of the world) and D (the decisions) make up the universe of relevant considerations at the outset, while O (the outcomes) and W (the payoffs) make up the universe of relevant considerations at the end.

Since U contains all the relevant elements, any set A which contains some of the elements is contained in U (by definition 1). Pictorially this is portrayed in figure 2.4. In the Lottery problem of chapter 1, if U is the set of all lottery tickets, then the set $A = \{99$ tickets which were not drawn$\}$ is contained in U.

Another point of frequent confusion is the idea of the empty set.

DEFINITION 4   The *empty set* (also called the *null set*) is the set which contains *no* elements. If is often denoted by the Greek letter phi, ϕ (pronounced "fee").

The empty set is associated with the ideas of "none" or "impossibility." But these notions, too, are relative. "No one speaks to a lady like that," might appear absurd if in fact you had just so spoken. But the sentence means "no one who is a gentleman speaks thus," with the implicit understanding that the universe (all that really "counts") is the class of all gentlemen and, therefore, the class of gentlemen who "speak to a lady like that" is empty.

The universal and empty sets are closely related in another way: they are said to "complement" each other. In general,

DEFINITION 5   The *complement of a set A*, symbolized by $\sim A$ and read "*not A*," is the set of all elements in U which are not in A. From a suitable set of assumptions it can be shown that the complement of the complement of A ($\sim\sim A$) is A itself, as seen in figure 2.7.

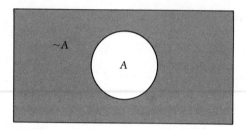

Figure 2.7 $\sim A$

EXAMPLE   The universal set is the complement of the null set, $\sim\phi = U$, since the set of all elements which are not in the empty set is the set of all elements U. By the same token, $\sim U = \phi$, since the set of all elements which are not in the universal set is empty.

EXAMPLE   A firm regards all families who live within a 100-mile radius as its potential customers. Thus, looking only at the customer aspect of its marketing problem, the universal set U consists of all these families. If R = the set of all families with incomes of \$10,000 or more, then $\sim R$ = the set of all families within the 100-mile radius who earn less than \$10,000. Note that both sets R and $\sim R$ are contained in U.

We often refer to "complement" as a *set operator* since it "operates on" a set and defines another set. Another operator which is useful for classification and clarification is *intersection*.

DEFINITION 6   The *intersection C* of two sets A and B, symbolized by $C = A \cap B$, is the set of all elements which belong to A *and* also belong to B. This is shown by the shaded area in figure 2.8.

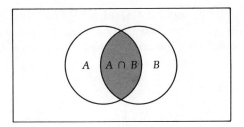

Figure 2.8 $A \cap B$

EXAMPLE If A is the set of all customers whose income is less than $10,000 and B is the set of all customers who have the highest credit rating, then $C = A \cap B$ is the set of all customers who have the highest credit rating *and* make less than $10,000 per year.

EXAMPLE If $G = \{a, b, c, d\}$ and $H = \{c, d, e, f\}$, then $H \cap G = \{c, d\}$.

In many cases in our decision-making lives we choose a decision which excludes all other alternatives. Such was the case in the Route to Work problem of chapter 1, where you could not take the bus and the subway at the same time; the choice of one alternative action excludes all other courses of action. When you fill out a questionnaire (for example, a product evaluation form), you are often given several categories as possible answers and you are asked to place some object or experience (elements) into one, *and only one*, of these categories; a product cannot be rated both "sweet" and "very sweet." This idea of exclusive classes can be defined in set theory as follows:

DEFINITION 7   If two sets have no elements (for example, products) in common, they are called *mutually exclusive*; that is, if $A \cap B = \phi$, then A and B are *mutually exclusive*.

EXAMPLE If $E =$ the set of courses which you rate as excellent and $F =$ the set of courses that you rate as fair, then $E \cap F = \phi$; that is, they are mutually exclusive sets, since a course cannot be rated as excellent *and* fair at the same time. This is depicted in figure 2.9.

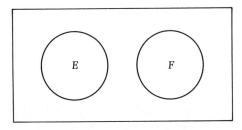

Figure 2.9   Mutually Exclusive Sets

EXAMPLE In the MIS of section 1.4, the set D of all decisions and the set S of states of the world are mutually exclusive, since D contains the elements that are within your control and S consists of all the elements that are beyond your control.

A third important operator is *union*.

DEFINITION 8   The *union* of two sets A and B, denoted $A \cup B$ and read "either A or B," is defined as the set of all elements which are either in A or in B (or possibly in both).

"Either-or" in English is ambiguous; sometimes it means "A or B, but not both" (as in "you can have either the blue plate special or a steak"), sometimes, as in the set theory operator *union*, "either A or B and maybe both" (as in "you are permitted to fish or swim off this beach"). The shaded area in figure 2.10 represents the union of the sets A and B. In the figure, some of the elements are only in A, some are only in B, and some are in both A and B.

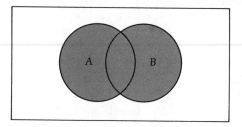

Figure 2.10 $A \cup B$

EXAMPLE The Commuter Airline operates two daily flights. The crew working flight 79 consists of Jeff, Ted, Eddie, Susan, and Kay, while on flight 89 Ted, Eddie, Susan, and Ray serve as the crew. Let A be the set of flight 79 crew and B the set of flight 89 crew members. Then the set C of crew of Commuter Airline employees is the union of A and B; that is,

$$C = A \cup B = \{\text{Ted, Eddie, Susan, Ray, Jeff, Kay}\}$$

Ted, Eddie, and Susan were counted only once. Note that the intersection of A and B

$$D = A \cap B = \{\text{Ted, Eddie, Susan}\}$$

EXAMPLE Let $G = \{a, b, c, d\}$ and $H = \{c, d, e, f\}$. Then $H \cup G = \{a, b, c, d, e, f\}$. The elements c and d which belong to both sets are listed in $H \cup G$ only once. Note that

$$H \cap G = \{c,d\}$$

EXAMPLE Let the set E be the set of courses which you rate excellent and F be the set of courses you rate fair. Then $H = E \cup F$ is the set of all courses that you rate either excellent or fair, shown as the shaded area in figure 2.11. Note that in this case E and F are mutually exclusive since they have no elements in common.

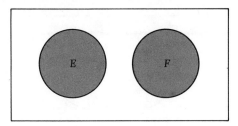

Figure 2.11 $E \cup F$

Very often we want an information system to include information about all relevant classes of items, for example, all product lines, where each product line is itself a set of elements. The complete list of product lines is an example of a list of sets that exhaust the universe.

DEFINITION 9   When we have a group of two or more sets (each set might consist of only one element) which cover all the possible elements in U, the sets are said to be *collectively exhaustive*. More formally, when the union of two or more sets is equal to U, the sets are said to be collectively exhaustive, since together they exhaust all the relevant elements.

EXAMPLE Let L be the set of all people born in or before 1946 and let M be the set of all people born after 1946. Hence, $M = \sim L$. As shown in figure 2.12, M and L are collectively exhaustive, since they exhaust the universal set of all people born. In this case, they are also mutually exclusive. We will make use of both these notions later when we develop our deductive system of probability.

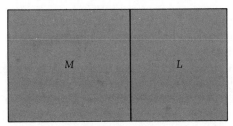

Figure 2.12 $M \cup L$

Our last definition in the deductive system for classes is called the "difference" of two sets.

DEFINITION 10   The *difference* of two sets A and B, denoted by $A - B$, is the set of all elements of A which are not elements of B, shown as the shaded area in figure 2.13.

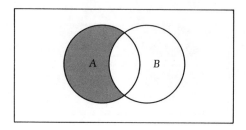

Figure 2.13 $A - B$

EXAMPLE   Let $G = \{a, b, c, d\}$ and $H = \{c, d, e, f\}$. Then $H - G = \{e, f\}$ and $G - H = \{a, b\}$.

If two sets A and B are mutually exclusive, then $A - B = A$ and $B - A = B$, since neither contains elements of the other. We can also define $A - B$ as the intersection of A and $\sim B$: $A - B = A \cap \sim B$.

Thus far we have introduced the basic ideas and important definitions of set theory. The next step in the deductive process is to present the basic assumptions and the rules of deduction. There are many ways of doing this, and all of them turn out to be quite simple, since the algebra of sets is itself quite simple. For example, all the important properties of sets can be derived from the following rather obvious assumptions.

1. $A \cap B = B \cap A$
2. $A \cap (B \cap C) = (A \cap B) \cap C$
3.   If $A \cap \sim B = \phi$, then $A \cap B = A$
4. $A \cap \sim A = B \cap \sim B = \phi$

The reasonableness of the first three assumptions can easily be examined by using Venn diagrams, although this examination is not a proof in the deductive sense. The last assumption says that the empty set is the same no matter how it is expressed: Square circles is the same set as dodo birds, if in fact there are no dodo birds.

From these assumptions, together with the definitions and some rules of deduction, we can generate a long list of relationships (theorems) between sets. Some of these theorems, for which you may wish to draw Venn diagrams, follow.

If A, B, and C are any sets and U and ϕ are the universal and empty sets, respectively, then

1. $A - \phi = A$
2. $A - A = \phi$
3. $A \cup \phi = A$
4. $A \cap \phi = \phi$
5. $A \cap U = A$
6. $A \cup U = U$
7. $A \cup B = B \cup A$ (analogous to assumption 1)
8. $A \cup (B \cup C) = (A \cup B) \cup C$ (analogous to assumption 2)
9. If $A \cup {\sim}B = U$, then $A \cup B = A$ (analogous to assumption 3)
10. $A \cup {\sim}A = B \cup {\sim}B = U$ (analogous to assumption 4)

In assumption (2) and theorem (8) above we have extended our deductive system for classes to more than two sets. All of the definitions and operators can be extended in this way.

Will this exposure to class logic help you make better decisions? If a friend gives you directions to his house ("Take either Market or Chestnut and turn on either 15th or 17th Street . . ."), will you now be able to follow more exactly? Probably not. Indeed, despite the many hours college students have spent on logic courses, it is doubtful if the reasoning powers of the great majority of them were changed one whit by the experience of studying the logic of classes. The main advantage of Boolean algebra is that it becomes a very convenient basic language for other precise deduction systems, or precisely defined situations.

So, as you progress with the text, you will find some uses of set theory (Boolean algebra). We will use it as a language that enables us to make general concepts more precise, as in the probability chapters 5–8, as well as a method by which we will be able to describe accurately and classify various aspects of problems which we will consider. For example, as we showed in chapter 1, when faced with a decision problem, you may find it helpful to structure the problem and organize its parts in a way that simplifies the analysis. Sometimes this may be hard to appreciate while studying a text, since the problems introduced are often well-structured and closely associated with the content of the section under consideration. But in reality such convenience is rare, and often, when preparing for decision, you have only some bits and pieces at your disposal. In these cases, the organization of the bits and pieces becomes an important but difficult part of the preparation for decision. One way to help ease this difficulty is to step back and try to use the MIS, first introduced in section 1.4. The development of this framework, which is particularly useful when uncertainty plays a role, is now presented again, this time with the assistance of set theory.

A Set Theory Organization of D, S, O, **and** W We can now return to the MIS of chapter 1 and clarify it in set theory language. To do this, we'll use the Route to Work problem discussed in section 1.7. To recall, the MIS consists of four relevant sets: (1) the set D of alternative decisions you can make, of which, for example, "take the bus" is a member; (2) the set S of relevant things that may happen that you cannot control but which matter, of which "heavy traffic" is a member; (3) the set O of results or outcomes that are important to you, of which "arriving 6 minutes late for work" is a member; and (4) the set W of values or payoffs to you associated with the outcomes, of which "$3.50" is a member. These four sets make up the information that is relevant to the decision maker, and therefore the universal class of information for the entire problem consists of

$$U = D \cup S \cup O \cup W$$

Note that this universe is "everything" only in the relative sense of "everything that is needed to prepare for the decision."

The first relevant set, the alternative decisions, consists of things which are under your control. In the Route to Work problem this set is $D = \{$drive to work, take the bus, take the subway$\}$.

The particular decision you make at a moment of time, we said, describes one aspect of the natural world at that moment. But in order to determine what will happen later on, you also need to describe occurrences that you do *not* control, like the behavior of traffic, or buses, or the state of technology. These properties, together with your decision, provide the basis for deducing the outcome. Hence, we require a set which describes these properties. Since it describes what happens "outside" of you and your decision, we have called it the set S of the states of the world.

It should be emphasized that the MIS of chapter 1 is based on a very strong categorical descriptive assumption about the world of decision making. This assumption says that the world behaves in a completely deterministic way. Laplace (1749–1827) put it this way: If the relevant properties of the world are known at any moment of time, then they can be determined for any other moment by the Laws of Nature. For example, if we know the positions, masses, and velocities of the planets and sun at noon on January 1, 1973, we can predict these properties for any other moment. Of course, we often don't know the exact properties of the relevant world, and have to estimate them or guess them. These estimates or guesses can sometimes be expressed in terms of probabilities, as we have seen in chapter 1. But note that this does not contradict the deterministic assumption; the uncertainty is grounded in the ignorance of the MIS designer (or the manager), and not in the natural world. In the more general systems approach we may want to question this strong deterministic assumption, but as in the problems of the last chapter we assume it in order to see how it helps in the design of the MIS.

In our case the deterministic assumption says that if we combine any element of D (for example, drive to work) with any element of S (for example, light traffic), then we can predict with certainty a unique element of O, the outcome set, in this case, arriving at work on time. Remember that the elements of D and S are complete descriptions. Thus, a knowledge of d and of s at one moment of time is sufficient to predict an o at a later moment of time. For example, if you take the bus, the outcome subset O_1, corresponding to outcomes resulting from decision d_1, contains only one element: $O_1 = \{$you are 30 minutes late$\}$. This is the outcome that always occurs when "take the bus" is combined with each element of S. For decision alternative d_2, however, three mutually exclusive and collectively exhaustive outcomes can occur. The subset of possible outcomes associated with d_2 is O_2 $= \{$arrive on time, arrive 6 minutes late, arrive 15 minutes late$\}$. When the decision results in an outcome set with a single member, as in alternative one, we said in section 1.4 that *certainty* prevails; for example, the MIS designer (or the manager) knows with certainty what will happen if he chooses d_1. However, when the outcome set contains several members, that is, several possible results could occur, then the decision is made "under uncertainty" since the designer is not certain what the outcome of the decision will be. Note as we said earlier that certainty and uncertainty describe the state of knowledge or ignorance of the decision maker.

We can now construct the outcome table based on the sets D, S, and O, which tells us what element of O will occur, as each element of D is combined with an element of S. This is shown in appendix table 2.1 for alternatives one and two in the Route to Work problem.

APPENDIX TABLE 2.1   Outcome Table

DECISION	STATE OF THE WORLD		
	$s_1 = light$ $traffic$	$s_2 = normal$ $traffic$	$s_3 = heavy$ $traffic$
$d_1 = take\ the\ bus$	you are 30 minutes late	you are 30 minutes late	you are 30 minutes late
$d_2 = drive\ to\ work$	you arrive on time	you arrive 6 minutes late	you arrive 15 minutes late

Associated with each outcome in the set of possible outcomes is a payoff which is the *unique* amount which you as the decision maker receive if a particular outcome obtains. The payoff, w_1, in the case of decision one, d_1, is "$3.50 loss," since there is only one outcome if you take the bus. However, there are three possible payoffs, w_2, w_3, and w_4, associated with alternative d_2 since there are three possible outcomes. If you chose d_2 (drive to work, and if s_1 (normal traffic) obtains, your outcome is "arrive on time" and your payoff, w_2, is "$1.50 loss." If d_2 is your choice and s_2 obtains, your payoff, w_3, is "$2.10 loss," while if s_3 obtains, $w_4 =$ "$3.00 loss" is your payoff. This set W of payoffs, $W = \{w_1, w_2, w_3, w_4\}$, and their association with states of the world and your possible decisions are summarized in a payoff table for d_1 and d_2 which is depicted in appendix table 2.2.

APPENDIX TABLE 2.2   Payoff Table

DECISION	STATE OF THE WORLD		
	$s_1 = light$ traffic	$s_2 = normal$ traffic	$s_3 = heavy$ traffic
$d_1 = take\ the\ bus$	$3.50 loss	$3.50 loss	$3.50 loss
$d_2 = drive\ to\ work$	$1.50 loss	$2.10 loss	$3.00 loss

We have already seen in chapter 1 how this payoff table can be used in an explicit way to derive the "best" decision, provided your aim is to make the most you can (or lose the least). Your knowing set theory might not have helped your understanding of that discussion, but it would have made our job of explaining it a lot easier! So you should appreciate from this review of the MIS of chapter 1 that the language of classes developed by Boole can help us better to communicate both old and new ideas. The usefulness of the language of sets in describing the MIS can be seen in the following problem which is similar to the problems at the end of chapter 1.

Problem: San Francisco Steel Works ━━━━━━━━━━

As manager of the Millbrae plant of San Francisco Steel Works you have been approached by a representative of Doputch Drug Company. He has offered to immunize your employees against the possibility of contracting a new strain of the American flu at a cost of $5 per employee. The flu has reached epidemic proportions on the East Coast. According to the Department of Public Health, there is a 10% chance that this flu will reach epidemic proportions on the West Coast, 10% chance that it will reach semi-epidemic proportions, and an 80% chance that it will strike only one person in 1000. You estimate that if an epidemic occurs, half of your employees will contract the flu, and if a semi-epidemic occurs, then 25% will be stricken. You have 2000 employees, and since the flu lasts three days, you estimate that each employee stricken will miss three days of work (considering that weekends don't count). The average employee-day lost costs you $30. Should you have your employees vaccinated?

Analysis: Our procedure is to design an MIS, along the same lines as we did previously, by completely specifying the sets D, S, O, and W.

The set D of decisions is $D = \{d_1, d_2\} = \{$immunize employees, do not immunize employees$\}$. The set S of states of the world is $S = \{s_1, s_2, s_3\} = \{$epidemic, semi-epidemic, no epidemic$\}$ The set O of outcomes can be represented as in appendix table 2.3.

APPENDIX TABLE 2.3   Outcome Table for S.F. Steel Co.

DECISION	STATE OF THE WORLD		
	$s_1 =$ epidemic	$s_2 =$ semi-epidemic	$s_3 =$ no epidemic
$d_1 =$ immunize employees	no employees get sick	no employees get sick	no employees get sick
$d_2 =$ do not immunize	50% of employees get sick	25% of employees get sick	2 employees $\left(\dfrac{1}{1000} \times 2000 = 2\right)$ get sick

You can now construct the payoff table for this problem, since there is one payoff attached to each outcome. To do so, simply compute the cost of each outcome to you. As an example of this calculation, look at the combination d_2 and s_2. If 25% of your employees get sick, then $2000 \times 25/100 = 500$ employees are stricken. This will cost you three days $\times$ \$30/day $=$ \$90 on the average if an employee gets the flu. Therefore, it will cost you

$$\$90/\text{employee} \times 500 \text{ employees} = \$45,000$$

if a semi-epidemic occurs and you do not accept the offer of Doputch Drugs. The payoffs are expressed in terms of costs and are shown in appendix table 2.4.

APPENDIX TABLE 2.4   Payoff Table for S.F. Steel Co.

DECISION	STATE OF THE WORLD		
	$s_1 = $ epidemic	$s_2 = $ semi-epidemic	$s_3 = $ no epidemic
$d_1 = $ immunize	$10,000 (vaccination cost)	$10,000 (vaccination cost)	$10,000 (vaccination cost)
$d_2 = $ do not immunize	$\dfrac{50}{100}$ $\times$ 2000 $\times$ $90 = $90,000	$\dfrac{25}{100}$ $\times$ 2000 $\times$ $90 = $45,000	$\dfrac{1}{1000}$ $\times$ 2000 $\times$ $90 = $180

You can now proceed to compare the payoffs for the two decisions on the basis of the chances (probabilities) that the three states of the world obtain. Clearly it costs you $10,000 if you immunize, no matter what state of the world obtains. If you assume expected dollars are equal to sure dollars, you can now multiply probabilities of states of the world by payoffs to get the expected payoff of decision 2, which is

$$\tfrac{1}{10} \times 90{,}000 + \tfrac{1}{10} \times 45{,}000 + \tfrac{8}{10} \times 180 = 9{,}000 + 4{,}500 + 144 = 13{,}644$$

Since the payoffs are in terms of costs, you might choose the decision which leads to the lowest expected cost, in this case d_1.

Of course, if you adopt the philosophical perspective that managers should decide on the basis of moral feelings, then the entire analysis may seem morally reprehensible since, in effect, it treats employees like one might treat machines, solely as means to the corporate goal, and not as ends in themselves.

Although this is primarily a text on deductive reasoning, we shall try to keep you from falling into the trap of believing that explicit and precise models of reasoning must inevitably lead to the truth.

PROBLEMS APPENDIX 2.1

1. Each of three salesmen — Adams (a), Duke (d), and Smith (s) — is to be assigned to either the northern region or the southern region.
   a. Describe the set U of salesmen in notational form.
   b. List all the subsets of U that correspond to possible sales forces in the northern region if only the southern region can be left without a salesman. (The northern region must always be assigned at least one salesman.)

c. List all the subsets of U that correspond to possible sales forces in the northern region if only the northern region can be left without a salesman. (The southern region must always be assigned at least one salesman.)

d. List all the subsets of U that correspond to possible sales forces in the northern region if either region can be left without a salesman assigned to it.

2. Define:

Cars = {Chevy, Buick, Pontiac, Oldsmobile, Ford, Lincoln, Mercury, Chrysler, Plymouth, Rambler}

G = GM cars = {Chevy, Buick, Pontiac, Oldsmobile}

F = Ford cars = {Ford, Lincoln, Mercury}

C = Chrysler cars = {Chrysler, Plymouth}

A = American Motors cars = {Rambler}

B = Big Three = {GM cars, Ford cars, Chrysler cars}

M = car manufacturers = {GM cars, Ford cars, Chrysler cars, American Motors cars}

a. Does $G \cup F$ exhaust Cars?

b. Are G and F mutually exclusive?

c. Does $G \cup F \cup C \cup A$ exhaust Cars?

d. Are G, F, C, and A mutually exclusive?

e. Can the set B be used in place of the original set Cars? Why?

f. Can the set M be used in place of the original set Cars? Why?

g. In a single lottery whose set of tickets is the pictures of Cars, we know that F has occurred. What can be said about the occurrence of B?

h. In the same lottery as in (g), we know that A has occurred. What do we know about the occurrence of F? Of G?

3. The purchasing department of your firm labels crates of incoming goods as either u (unsatisfactory) or s (satisfactory) after inspection. During a given day three crates of goods arrive.

a. Define the set S of all possible states of the world, each consisting of the results of the inspection of the three crates (consider order in inspection).

b. Suppose that two different decisions could be followed as a consequence of different outcomes:

d_1 = Return of all three crates if more than one is unsatisfactory, return of all unsatisfactory crates otherwise

d_2 = Return of all unsatisfactory crates

The firm may potentially return 0, 1, 2, or 3 crates. Which subsets of S correspond to each of the actions for each decision?

c. If there is a cost associated with returning crates, which decision will prove more expensive? Why?

4. Consider the following Venn diagram and note carefully the definitions of the sets D, E, F, and G given in the figure below, where A, B, and C correspond to the three circles, H is everything outside the three circles, and $D = A \cap B$; $E = B \cap C$; $F = A \cap C$; $G = D \cap E \cap F$. On the diagram indicate:

a. $(A \cap B) \cup C$
b. $(A \cup B) \cap C$
c. $\sim(A \cup B)$
d. $\sim(A \cup B) \cap C$
e. $(A \cap B \cap C)$
f. $F \cup G$
g. $\sim A \cap (\cup D)$
h. $\sim E \cap A$

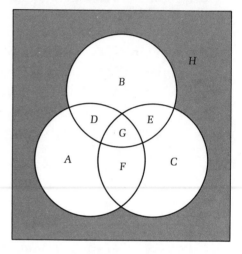

5. Consider a salesman's behavior during a certain day as an uncertain process the outcome of which is the number of customers contacted by the salesman. Assume a salesman could never contact more than 15 customers in a day.

a. Describe the set of outcomes O for this process.

b. Define a set T of the results of the salesman's behavior on three successive days.

c. The event E, "exactly two customers were contacted during the three days," is a subset of the set defined in (b). Define this event by listing all the components giving rise to its occurrence.

d. The event F, "at most one customer was contacted on any one day," is a subset of the set defined in (b). Define this event by listing all its components.

For parts (e) through (g) find the subset of T whose occurrence would make all three clauses in each of the sentences true. List every element in the subset.

e. $E \cup F$ has occurred; E has occurred; F has not occurred.

f. $E \cup F$ has occurred; E has not occurred; F has occurred.

g. $E \cup F$ has occurred; E has occurred; F has occurred.

6. Revisit problems 1–5, section 1.4, and problems 3–7, section 1.7, and identify in each the sets D, S, O, and W with their respective membership.

7. Mr. Classic plans to go to the afternoon performance of *Aida* in downtown San Francisco. He has already bought a ticket for $6. He is considering driving and computes gas costs as $1 and has to pay $.50 bridge toll. He can park in the city lot for $2 for the first hour, $1.50 for the next hour and $.60 for every one-half hour thereafter. Or he can park in a two-hour zone. A violation of two-hour parking is always caught in San Francisco and the fine is $5. To be assured of parking, he plans to arrive in San Francisco one-half hour before curtain time, which is at 1:30 PM, and wait in the lobby. The performance is exactly one hour long but there is only a 50% chance that it will start on time with a 25% probability that it will be one-half hour late and 25% probability that it will be one hour late. Mr. Classic is also a popcorn freak and consumes it at the rate of $.50 worth per half hour waiting. Of course, he can always catch a cab for $8.50 each way and thereby avoid going early.
   a. Set up an MIS system, taking care to define D, S, O, and W.
   b. If Mr. Classic used this MIS and made a decision based on expected monetary payoff, what can be said about his attitudes toward waiting?

8. The monthly report to the controller has arrived in your mail this morning. In reviewing it you notice that the painting department has accumulated an unusual number of unpainted units — 10,000 units to be exact — whereas the average end-of-the-month figure is 1000. You suspect that this large deviation may signal problems with the equipment, since the painting operation is fully automated. On the other hand, it is possible that the difficulties observed are due to some unsystematic, uncontrolled cause such as electrical current disruption. You ask your assistant to obtain information regarding the chances that a five-year-old piece of painting equipment, like the one your company uses, gets out of control and causes a large backlog. After several hours he comes to you with the required data; the company that produces the equipment estimates the probability to be .15. Further, the estimated cost of repairing the equipment is $10,000. You know that a repair job must be preceded by an investigation as to whether or not the difficulties have been caused by the equipment. Such an investigation is estimated to cost $4000. You also know that if such an investigation is not decided upon and the cause of the difficulties is with the equipment, your company stands to lose $60,000 in the coming month, until a new report may bring about an investigation. Should you order an investigation?

9. You are considering running a farm for one year on the West Coast. There are two farms available for lease at the following costs.

Farm	Lease cost per year
Santa Cruz	$5000
Monterey	$7500

You can either grow wheat or use the land to raise chickens. Because of soil differences, if you were to choose wheat growing, your annual costs of operation (all costs excluding lease) would be $9000 at Santa Cruz and $8500 at Monterey. Chicken farming costs $7000 (excluding lease) annually regardless of location. In wheat farming, weather conditions are crucial to the quality of the crop. The table below gives the estimated worth of your wheat crop, depending on location and weather, and also the estimated probabilities for the weather conditions for the next year.

		Wheat revenue	
Weather	Prob.	Santa Cruz	Monterey
Poor	30%	$10,000	$ 6000
Average	50%	18,000	15,000
Excellent	20%	25,000	35,000

Chicken farming is not sensitive to weather, and in one year you expect to generate a revenue of $18,000 if you are in the chicken business. State law requires that the same person cannot engage in both wheat and chicken production.

a. What is the set of all your possible decisions?
b. What is the set of all possible states of the world relevant to your decision?
c. Set up a payoff matrix giving the payoff for all combinations of decisions and states.
d. If you make your decisions on the basis of expected value, what is the expected value of each decision? Which should you choose?

Appendix 2.2 The MIS in Perspective

One might be inclined to generalize on this very simple example of an MIS by saying that *all* managerial decision making should use such a design. After all, it seems reasonable to say that in preparing for a decision we require just the four sets D, S, O, and W, and hence that the task of an MIS is completely specified: It should tell the manager what his alternatives are, D, what else is relevant in his world, S, and consequently what O to expect given any d and s, and what payoff occurs for each O.

A little exercise of systems thinking, however, will serve to dampen any overenthusiasm. There are two quite realistic criticisms of this approach to an MIS design. One is technical and the other philosophical. Technically, we have already seen that this design could easily become unmanageable or highly costly—when D, for example, has as many as 25! (25 × 24 × 23 × . . . × 2 × 1) elements, as in the car repair shop example of section 1.6. To build a complete outcome table for such a D would be an inexcusable waste of resources. Hence, the MIS needs some heuristic device to reduce the size of D, and such a device is not simple to construct. Similarly, the size of S may be enormous, because it, like D, may be based on millions of ways of combining elements. In effect this means that O will be very large as well. Finally, the manager may not want a complete payoff table, if it's going to cost him this year's profits to get one. He may be satisfied with a partial analysis, which leads to a "good enough" payoff. Nevertheless, we might want to say that this "ideal" MIS based on so much information is extremely useful, or even necessary, in designing a practical MIS, because it provides a standard in terms of which one can judge the value of the practical design, which is an approximation to the ideal.

The philosophical objection to using the MIS for all decisions attacks the whole idea of deriving "correct" decisions from an MIS based on D, S, O, and W and the assumptions we made. A mild form of this objection, which does not refute the usefulness of the MIS, is to argue that Nature is not deterministic, but rather an enemy of the decision maker. In this case, the outcome table is much more like a description of a game between two players. Nature is playing to win— that is, to minimize the decision-maker's payoff. Nature selects its "moves" from S, and you select your "moves" from D. If this is your view of reality, then you should make your decisions (that is, your plays in the game with Nature) so as to minimize the maximum loss that Nature can inflict—the so-called minimax principle. You would no longer be interested in expected value as a relevant choice criterion, and you can sense that, if you hold this pessimistic view of Nature, you will make quite different decisions from the ones you would make if you assume that Nature is deterministic. There are, of course, other choice criteria to be discussed in later chapters.

A much more radical philosophy denies that S and D exist as explicit sets and holds that real management decision making depends on intuition, feeling, and good judgment, none of which can be expressed in set-theory language. Such a philosophical viewpoint would argue that this "ideal" MIS, far from being ideal, is not even an approximation to the way in which managers should decide.

You may now expect that we will tell you once and for all which is the correct philosophy to adopt, especially if your past education is based on the notion that life consists of "problems" and "solutions." In its broader meaning, life is not the struggle to find closed solutions, but rather a continuous learning process in which your perspective keeps changing as experience, patience, hope, and other resources aid you in making it richer. If you are to become a successful decision-maker, you will have to continue to learn throughout your life, and this means changing your philosophical perspective a number of times while still being decisive and not frustrated.

Ordering, Numbers, and Measures of Performance 3

3.1 Introduction

A creature from outer space might well be amazed at the way in which our societies depend on orderings in making decisions. We hire people, flunk students, spend millions on defense, build countless statues, all because we believe in the importance of *first* and *last*, *more* and *less*. For example,

1. We should hire this man as a salesman because he had the *highest* sales record of any one of his region.
2. We should fail this student because he had the *lowest* grade on every test.
3. We should spend 20 billion more dollars on defense, because "they" have *more* boob-de-doop bombs than we do.
4. We should build a statue of George Washington in the town square because he was the *first* President of the USA.

The categorical prescription "you ought to make as much as you can" tells you to find the largest (smallest negative if you minimize losses) element in a set of possible payoffs. So in preparing for decisions in which you assume this prescription, you will want to order your decisions to pick out the one with the best payoff as you did in chapter 1. To understand better the idea of order we will present a deductive system for ordering in the familiar context of deciding which job to take.

3.2   A Deductive System for Ordering

Suppose you are about to make a decision to select one among a set of job offers. Hopefully, your set of job offers is *not* empty, and if it contains only one member, and you need a job, then there is no problem. Hence a problem exists only if the set of job offers has two or more members, which we'll assume. For the time being, we also assume that the set has a finite (limited) number of discrete members. In other words, in the symbolism of sets, $D = \{job_1, job_2, \ldots, job_n\}$, or, to abbreviate the notation, $D = \{x, y, z, \ldots\}$. Which job should you take?

The basic idea here is that you can compare any two job offers in terms of better or worse; suppose, just to abbreviate, we write xBy to stand for job x is better than job y. Of course, the big question is how you decide whether this relationship holds, but for the moment we are simply interested in what we must assume and deduce *if* it does hold.

Using the relation of xBy, we can define "is worse than," simply by saying that if xBy, then yWx (y is worse than x). Finally, we can define the "indifference" relation xIy (x is no better nor worse than y) by equating it to: *not xBy and not yBx.*

In order to use xBy to help you prepare for your decision, you may make these assumptions:

a. For any two members x and y of the set of decisions D, either xBy, or yBx, or xIy. [We sometimes say that B is "closed" with respect to the decision set.]

This assumption might appear obvious, for all it says is that either one job offer is better than another or you are indifferent between them. But, in fact, the assumption, so critical in many of our society's problems, is often attacked on the grounds that many objects and all people cannot be compared on a better-worse basis. Which is better, to sacrifice the lives of young men or save our country from dishonor? The answer for many cannot be indifference, nor one or the other; the choices, they say, are not comparable. But we do make such choices, and since for the time being we are trying to be rational, we must assume that despite our reluctance to make the comparison, it must be made. In any event, you should recognize that this first assumption is far from being obvious.

b. For any three choices x, y, z in the decision set D, if xBy and yBz, then xBz. [We say that the relation B is *transitive*, as you may recall from chapter 2, meaning that you can pass over or "transit" the intermediate y.]

Here again the assumption seems obvious; after all, if you believe x is a better offer than y, and you also believe y is a better offer than z, then you must believe x is better than z, mustn't you? Not necessarily, or perhaps not at all, unless you assume "is better than" to be like "is greater than" in arithmetic or geometry. But this is the crux of the matter: are our values like numbers and geometrical figures, or do they have a totally different character? No doubt a great deal of social policy making and legislation is based on the assumption that human values are like numbers. After all, we use budgets as a basis of decision making in many instances, and budgets are numbers. No doubt, also, many humanists believe that this assumption is wrong. So we ask you *both* to accept the assumption for the time being *and* to recognize that it is *not* obvious.

c. If xBy, then both xIy and xWy are false.

d. If xWy, then both xIy and xBy are false.

There is perhaps less reason to question these assumptions than the others, but we leave it up to your ingenuity to find grounds for doubt.

If you accept assumptions (a), (b), (c), and (d), then we can establish the existence of at least one decision that is not worse than any other:

THEOREM

e. There exists at least one choice, call it x_{max}, such that $x_{max}Wy$ is never true for all y's of the decision set.

Thus x_{max} is never "bettered" by any other choice. One way to deduce the theorem is simply to write down all the pairs of the decision set; we know from assumption (a) that for each pair we have either xBy, xIy, or xWy, and from (c) and its implications that only one of these three applies in each case. We also know that we can't have a circular trio like xWy, yWz, and zWx, because if xWy and yWz, then xWz by assumption (b) and hence zWy can't be right because of assumption (d). Hence, we can build up a hierarchy of choices, starting with those that are the worst and rising to the best. Of course, you may be indifferent between all job offers, in which case you really don't have a problem. Ideally, the top set has but one member, an assumption that often does not hold, but which we shall make to complete the picture.

f. There exists a unique x_{max} such that $x_{max}By$ for all other y in the decision set. Finally, if this ideal situation holds, then

g. One *ought* to choose x_{max}.

In the language of quantitative methods we often restate (g) to say that x_{max} is optimal, since "optimal" means the very best.

If (a)–(g) holds for a set of decisions $D = \{d_1, d_2, \ldots, d_n\}$, then we say that there is a "measure of performance" or "priority system" for D provided that the preference orderings are reasonably stable over some relevant time period. In this case, the measure of performance of a decision is its rank order relative to the relationship "is better than."

As we have pointed out, the ordering assumptions, and hence measures of performance, often seem to dominate our social lives, since we seem constantly to be evaluating ourselves, our government programs, teachers and their texts, corporations, and people. John Oxenham wrote:

> To every man there openeth
> A way, and ways, and a way,
> And the high soul climbs the high way,
> And the low soul gropes the low;
> And in between on the misty flats,
> The rest drift to and fro,

a poem that so well depicts the plight of the mediocre. Mediocrity refers to that vast class of people or events which fail to attain the glory of the highest or the fascination of the lowest. Yet almost everybody is mediocre. For the present, however, we are operating under the categorical prescription to make the most you can, and hence are interested not in the mediocre, but in identifying the decision with the highest measure of performance, which we call the "best" or "optimal" decision.

PROBLEMS 3.2

1. Try ordering the Presidents of the U.S.A. whom you remember in terms of their contributions to the growth of the country. What criteria do you use?

2. In each of the following, identify x_{max} if possible; if not possible, explain.
   a. aBb; bWc; cBd; aWc
   b. aIb; bWc; cBd; dBb; aIc
   c. aBb; bBc; cBa
   d. aId; bBc; cWd; bWd

3. The following is a schematic presentation of the "ontological proof" of the existence of God which was frequently used by rationalist philosophers of the past.
   a. God, by definition, is that entity which is highest in rank order on all positive properties (knowledge, power, etc.).
   b. An entity which is highest on all positive properties and exists is better than an entity which is highest on all positive properties and does not exist.
   c. Therefore God exists.
   Criticize this use of the postulates of ordering.

3.3 Numbers, Functions, and Variables

You should recognize that a measure of performance based on this deductive system for ordering alone may be very weak and uninformative. Suppose that D is the set of job applicants and their respective salary requests and that you, as a manager, wish to hire one of the applicants. One of the applicants may stand out from all the rest, or the applicants may differ just a little in their qualifications. A simple ordering of these qualifications might not help you decide how critical the salary differences might be. Suppose, for example, that the outstanding candidate requests $3000 more per year than any of the rest. Should you pay the difference? There is not sufficient information in the simple ordering to provide you with a basis for deciding this issue.

Hence in addition to the idea of ordering we may need the notion of *how much better x is than y*. This need takes us into the domain of *numbers*. Just as the properties of space, classes (sets), and ordering can be expressed in a compact deductive information system, so also the properties of numbers, which we call *arithmetic*, can be expressed deductively. The Italian mathematician Peano (1858–1932) first set forth the axioms for integers and we'll borrow from his work. Our main intent is to introduce you to the variety of numbers that can be used in decision making.

3.3.1 Integers and Functions Peano begins with positive whole numbers (integers) 1, 2, 3, . . . together with that most marvelous discovery of the ancient Hindus, the number 0. (You're probably so used to zero, it no longer occurs to you how creative it was to discover a "number for nothing"!) What are whole numbers? A little reflection will tell you that they are an ordered set with respect to "is greater than," because they satisfy the assumptions of order given above except for (f) and (g). But this fact hardly captures the richness of their meaning. Peano's genius lay in recognizing that the important idea behind the integers is that every integer has a uniquely determined successor. To generate the successor, we introduce the idea of "adding 1." Thus, $2 + 1 = 3$ is the successor of 2, $3 + 1 = 4$ is the successor of 3, and so on. Of course, the idea of a unique successor is not very remarkable, since in many ordered sets we can define unique successors —for example, the Presidents of the U.S. But, given a President, there is no explicit way of generating his successor, except to wait for history to unfold. But in arithmetic there *is* an explicit way of passing from one number to its successor, namely, by the rule of adding 1 to the number.

In general, what is important for you to recognize is that in arithmetic *there are explicit ways of passing from one number to another number*, a number's successor being one example. We call these explicit ways *functions*, which are the heart and soul of numerical quantitative methods. Thus "successor of" is a function, which we write as x + 1, and which tells you explicitly how to go from x to another number x + 1. We often denote a function like x + 1 as follows:

$$f(x) = x + 1$$

We read $f(x)$ as "f of x" and this notation says that if you start with any number x, the function takes the number and passes to its successor, x + 1. For example, if x is 6, $f(x) = 6 + 1 = 7$. Mathematicians generalize this idea of "passing" and think of functions as taking a member x from one *set* and passing to a member of another set. In the successor function, if the original set contains x, the new set contains x + 1. It's all very much like getting your driver's license, where you first go to one window, then to another where you hand in a form from the first window and get another form and are told to take a test at Window 3, except that in mathematics functions are meant to be very explicit and clear.

Another aspect of the idea of functions is the use of letters (like x) to express the rules for going from one set to another. Whenever you want to explain how to go from one number to another, you can express the idea in terms of letters that stand for any number you may want to select out of a specified set of numbers. We call these *variables* to reflect the idea that your choice can vary over the whole set of choices. For example, if $f(x) = 3x + 7$ is the cost of producing x units of some product, then the variable x can be any positive integer or zero.

As often happens with quantitative ideas, you've already seen and used functions even if you didn't know them by that name. For example, in our MIS of chapters 1 and 2 we said that a possible decision coupled with a state of the world implies an outcome. In the language of functions we would write

$$o = f(s, d)$$

and you can see that the idea here is to pass from a member of the set S together with a member of the set D to a member of the set O. In our Route to Work problem this means

f(normal traffic, drive to work) = you arrive 6 minutes late

Similarly, for each element of the set O we pass to a member of the set of payoffs W, $w = f(o)$. For example,

f(you arrive 6 minutes late) = $1.50 + 6 \times .10 = \$2.10$ loss

is a description in the language of functions of the payoff you are passed to if you arrive 6 minutes late.

Thus the idea of functions is not restricted to only one variable as you have just seen. You can express rules for passing from several variables to a single number in an explicit way which we call "functions of several variables." For example, if x is the level of production, y is the quantity sold, and z is the inventory at the beginning of a period, then

$$f(x, y, z) = z + x - y$$

is the explicit rule of *going from* the production, sales, and inventory on hand at the start of the period *to* the inventory f at the end of the period. Here x, y, and z can take on any positive number or zero since none of them make sense if they are negative.

In appendix 3.1 we recall for you some of the important functions of the arithmetic of integers, and some relations (rules) between these functions that you've seen before but may have forgotten. One very useful rule says that we can add to or multiply both sides of an equation by the same thing, and the results are equal.

RULE A   If $x = y$
then $x + a = y + a$
and $ax = ay$

3.3.2   Fractions and Negative Numbers   Note that all of the functions given in appendix 3.1 operate over the positive integers (and 0), in the sense that if you assign values to any of the variables, you land in a specific integer; thus $3^4 = 3 \cdot 3 \cdot 3 \cdot 3 = 81$ leads you from the function x^4, by assigning 3 to the variable x, to the specific number 81. But the reverse doesn't always work; if I tell you the number you'll land in, and ask what number you started with, you may not be able to tell me. For example, I tell you that the function is 3x and you land in 10; what number did you start with? You've surely seen this problem before in a form like $3x = 10$. The problem was to solve for x, and you may have called it "solving equations with one unknown." Now you can understand it as the reverse of the function: Given that you land in some number with such-and-such a function, where did you start?

But there's a problem with $3x = 10$, because there is no *integer* which makes it work. If you start with 3, 3x lands you in 9; and if you start with 4, 3x lands you in 12. You may remember that the required starting number is 10/3 or $3\frac{1}{3}$. If you do, you'll also realize that you found the answer by dividing both sides by 3. If you divide 3x by 3 you get x, and if you divide 10 by 3 you get 10/3. Hence if $3x = 10$, then $x = 10/3$. But what justified your doing this, and why do we think that 10/3 makes sense? The answer is that besides the integers there are some other numbers, sometimes called "fractions," sometimes called "rational numbers." These new numbers are introduced by a rule which says that, given any multiplication of positive integers, ax, and the number where you land, b, you can always find where you started. That is, solving $ax = b$ for x always has a solution, no matter what the specific positive integers a and b, and the solution is $x = b/a$. But watch out for zero! This is the blemish of pure arithmetic; if a is 0, then the rule doesn't work; if $0 \cdot x = 17$, what is x? You may have the urge to call x by a mysterious name, like "infinity," but the proper reply is that you can't find the reverse of 0.

We can go through the same procedure with addition. If $x + 7 = 3$, what is x? That is, if you start with the function $x + 7$ and land in 3, where did you come from? To make sense out of this question, we introduce minus numbers or negative numbers (as in the sentence "the temperature is 10 below zero outside"). With minus numbers added to the list, we have a rule which tells us that given any sum of positive integers $x + a$ and the number where you land b, there is one unique number where you started, and it is $b - a$. If a is larger than b, then $b - a$ is a minus number. For example, x in $x + 7 = 3$ is $x = 3 - 7 = -4$. This rule works even if a is zero. We can now reintroduce you to some other functions and rules, which use division and subtraction. These appear in appendix 3.2. Two important rules to recall are that you can subtract or divide both sides of an equation by the same number (except 0 for division) and the result is an equation.

RULE B   I   If $x + a = b$, then (subtracting a from both sides) $x = b - a$

II   If $ax = b$, then (dividing both sides by a, where a is not zero) $x = b/a$

These two rules often help solve equations by "taking one number – or variable – to the other side." For example, if for each unit sold, your company makes $5, total overhead is $5000, and you wish to compute the number of units to be sold in order to cover the overhead and make a $1000 profit, you can represent your problem by the equation $5x - 5000 = 1000$, where $x =$ number of units to be sold. You can solve for x by using rule B as follows:

by part I of the rule $5x = 5000 + 1000 = 6000$

by part II of the rule $x = \dfrac{6000}{5} = 1200$

Hence you need to sell 1200 units in order to make a $1000 profit.

3.3.3 Inequalities   Finally, we can generalize on these rules by considering *inequalities*. The symbol < means "is less than"; (for example, $3 < 5$ denotes that 3 is less than 5), ≤ means "is less than or equal to" (for example, $x \leq 3$ means that x can take on any number which is not greater than 3), $>$ means "is greater than," and $\geq$ stands for "is greater than or equal to." The rule of adding or subtracting any number from both sides of an inequality is very similar to the one we presented for equalities:

RULE C   If $x < y$, then $x + a < y + a$
If $x > y$, then $x + a > y + a$

That is, the relationship between the two sides doesn't change if we add the same number to both sides. For example, since $4 < 7$, adding 3 to both sides of the inequality we have $4 + 3 < 7 + 3$; or, since $9 > 7$, $9 + 3 > 7 + 3$.

But we must be more careful when we consider multiplication. Here we must distinguish three cases:

RULE D   I If a is positive, then for $x < y$ we get $ax < ay$, and for $x > y$ we get $ax > ay$.
For example, if $a = 3$, $4 < 7$ and $3 \cdot 4 < 3 \cdot 7$ since $12 < 21$; $11 > 7$ and $3 \cdot 11 > 3 \cdot 7$ since $33 > 21$.
II If a is zero, ax and ay are always zero regardless of the relationship of x to y.
III If a is negative, then for $x < y$ we get $ax > ay$, and for $x > y$ we get $ax < ay$.
For example, if $a = -3$, $4 < 7$ and $-3 \cdot 4 > -3 \cdot 7$ since $-12 > -21$; $11 > 7$ and $-3 \cdot 11 < -3 \cdot 7$ since $-33 < -21$.

In other words, multiplication of an inequality by a negative number changes the direction of the inequality.

With integers, rationals, minus numbers, equalities, and inequalities as part of your equipment, you can "solve" lots of familiar, daily problems, like buying a quart (1/4 gallon) of milk, figuring out whether it's cheaper to buy a gallon, balancing budgets, calculating distances, deciding which diet best controls weight, and so on. Even so, we haven't enough numbers to do all the jobs we want. In appendix 3.3 you can read about irrational and imaginary numbers including the most "imaginary" of all numbers, the infinite.

PROBLEMS 3.3

Additional material for solving the following problems appears in the appendixes that follow this chapter.

1.   If $f(x) = 5x + 8$, what is $f(3)$? $f(18)$?
2.   If $f(x) = 20$, what is $f(10)$? $f(20)$? $f(30)$?

3. If $f(x) = 2x^2 + 3x + 2$, what is $f(4)$? $f(0)$? $f(-2)$?

4. If $f(y) = \dfrac{1}{(y-a)} + (b-y)^2 - \dfrac{y^2 + c}{y}$,

     a. find $f(1)$ when $a = 4$, $b = 0$, $c = 1$.
     b. find $f(2)$ when $a = 4$, $b = 0$, $c = 1$.

5. If $f(x, y) = 5x + 6y + 15$, what is $f(4, 3)$? $f(0, 1)$? $f(0, 0)$?

6. If $g(x, y) = 2x^2 + 3xy - y^2$, what is $g(0, 0)$? $g(2, 1)$? $g(-3, 2)$? $g(-3, -2)$?

7. If $f(x) = 2x^2$, $g(x) = 3x + 7$, and $h(x) = f(x) - g(x)$, what is $h(3)$? $h(0)$? $h(-4)$?

8. If $f(x) = 2x^2$, $g(x) = 3x + 7$, and $h(x) = g(f(x))$, what is $h(5)$? $h(-8)$?

9. If $g(x) = 4x + 5$, $h(x) = \dfrac{x^2 - 2}{x}$, and $f(x) = h(x)/g(x)$, what is $f(3)$? $f(-6)$? $f(4)$?

10. If $f(x) = 3x^2$, and $g(x) = 2x + 3$, determine (a) $f(x)g(x)$, (b) $f(x)/g(x)$, (c) $f(x) + g(x)$, (d) $f(x)g(y)$, (e) $f(x)/g(y)$, (f) $f(y) + g(x)$.

11. Solve the following equations for x:
     a. $4x = 9$ b. $4x + 7 = 10$
     c. $2x - 4(x + 5) = 5 - 3(2x + 1)$ d. $x^2 = 16$
     e. $x^2 + 2x + 1 = 0$ f. $x^2 + 4x = -4$
     g. $x^2 - 4 = 0$ h. $x^2 + 4x - 7 = 2$

     Hint: Recall that if you have an equation of the type: $ax^2 + bx + c = 0$, then

$$x = \frac{-b \pm \sqrt{b^2 - 4ac}}{2a}$$

12. If $4x < 7$, is $x < 7/4$?

13. If $3x^2 + 2x < 3$, is $x < 0$?

14. If $2x - 7 < 4$, is $-2 \; x < 11$?

15. Simplify: (a) $x^2 + x^3$,   (b) $x^2 x^3$,   (c) x^2/x^3,   (d) $\dfrac{\sqrt{x}}{x^{\frac{1}{2}}}$

3.4   Measures of Performance

Suppose now we see how the set of numbers we've introduced may help improve preparation for decisions.

You've already seen how a simple ordering may not help you reach a decision; for example, when the best job applicant also requests the highest salary, and there is a partial conflict of the objectives of hiring the best person and of minimizing costs. Or, if you are the job seeker, an alternative choice may lead you to the most important objective of, say, job security in a choice among job offers, but may be far less satisfactory than other choices with respect to the other objectives (salary, location, people, etc.) Of course, if you could translate all your objectives into money, you might then count up the blessings and costs of any choice, using the number system we've just discussed. But you may also try a more general approach. Suppose you accept the idea that attaining each objective is like receiving a certain amount of value, which could be pleasure, welfare, or whatever. (Some of you may balk at this supposition, and it certainly doesn't always work, but at least listen for a bit.)

Here are some steps by means of which you might quantify the value of each job offer.

1. List your objectives—in this case the relevant aspects of a job— and place them in a rank order representing your preference. For example, for a very cautious type, they might come out to be:

    A_1: job security (meaning, let us say, the probability of being fired within five years is very small)
    A_2: salary (more than adequate for your needs)
    A_3: location (near the ocean or mountains, nice climate)
    A_4: people (interesting and compatible people to work with or live near)

    There are probably a number of other objectives relevant to a job, but these will suffice for our purposes.

2. Of course, if only one job offer satisfies all the relevant objectives, you've no further problem. But suppose this is not the case. You may, however, be able to assign numbers to the objectives which convey how much value each one has for you. One way to do this is to assign 100 to the top objective, and numbers from 1 to 99 for the others. For example,

$$V(A_1) = 100, \ V(A_2) = 80, \ V(A_3) = 50, \ V(A_4) = 40$$

    where V is a function which assigns a value number to an objective.

3. Now you make a very strong assumption, namely that these "values" can be added; that is, that they behave just as numbers normally do. This means that the value of A_1 and A_2 (security and salary) is $100 + 80 = 180$, and $V(A_2$ and $A_3) = 80 + 50 = 130$, and so on. This is by no means an obvious assumption, because, for example, security and a good salary combined may make a value far exceeding the sum of their respective values. Hence, you have to judge whether the assumption applies to you. Note that the connective "and" needs explaining, since the way in which objectives combine may be very critical (oysters *and* chocolate sauce are all right in one meal if the oysters come first, and the chocolate sauce is served over a dessert, but not all right if served together).

4. If you accept the *additivity* assumption of step 3, then you can test your answers in step 2 by asking yourself whether you really do value A_2 *and* A_3 (salary and location together) more than A_1 (security), because your numbers indicate you do: $V(A_2$ *and* $A_3) = 130$ which is greater than 100. If this is *not* the case and security is more important than salary and location, you then adjust the values of A_2 and A_3 downwards. The same test can be applied to other combinations of the objectives.

5. Finally, you take your list of job offers (decisions), and determine which objectives a given job will or will not attain. The resulting scores will help you prepare for the decision if you can safely rely on the assumptions and judgments.

We have now arrived at a numerical *measure of performance* for this problem where the numbers assigned to each decision obey the rules of addition, multiplication, subtraction, and division. To do so, we have made some very strong assumptions; for example, about the additivity of values. We have already used another numerical measure of performance in chapters 1 and 2 — namely, *expected value*. Expected value also assigns a value to each decision, but it does so in two steps. First, a value w, for example, dollars, is assigned to each possible outcome o of each decision. Then for each decision the assigned payoffs are weighted by the probabilities that they occur. For example, in the Route to Work problem of chapter 1, for the decision $d_1 =$ drive your car, the probabilities are:

$$p_1 = \tfrac{1}{6}, \ p_2 = \tfrac{2}{6}, \ p_3 = \tfrac{3}{6}$$

and the payoffs (expressed as minus numbers to indicate losses) are

$$w_1 = -\$1.50, \ w_2 = -\$2.10, \ w_3 = -\$3.00$$

and the expected value of d_1 is

$$EV(d_1) = \tfrac{1}{6} \times (-1.50) + \tfrac{2}{6} \times (-2.10) + \tfrac{3}{6} \times (-3.00) = -\$2.45$$

With this in mind, we can now further clarify the idea of a measure of performance.

A measure of performance is a rule for passing from a specific decision to a number that measures the value of the decision.

We said earlier that a function was a rule for passing from one number to another. A function may also be a rule for passing from an element of a set (for example, accepting the job offer) to a number (the value to you of the job). So, a measure of performance is also a function that enables you to go from each decision to the value of the decision. We call these *objective functions*, since they reflect the objectives that will occur or will not occur if a given decision is made.

3.5   Some Difficulties in Measuring Performance

3.5.1   Comparability   To return to the Route to Work problem of chapter 1, suppose we add a realistic twist to the problem you face after waking up late for work. You are not completely secure in your job, and if you arrive late too often, you will lose it. Then how would you order your choices? What measure could you use to combine the possibility of job loss with the cost of a subway ride?

You now face the same difficulty as in the problem of choosing the right job offer. It is one of finding a unit of measurement by which to compare your alternatives according to the prescriptive criteria "you ought to make as much as you can" (lose as little as possible). This general comparability problem is often not an easy one to solve, as in this case. The question of cost versus benefit in a proposed project, such as the building of a hospital or construction of an additional defense plant, often leads to the same dilemma of finding a suitable unit of measurement. For example, how do we compare the loss of life or limb of a construction worker with the benefit of the hospital or plant? In order to answer the question of making a comparison, you might suggest that more information is needed to choose the unit of measurement for comparison. More information would also be desirable in order to compare the loss of a job with subway fare.

Since in this text we are mainly concerned with preparing for decisions for which *all* the information is embedded in the assumptions or in the statement of the problem, measurement is relatively easy. If you can reasonably and confidently assume how numbers can be assigned, then the comparability problem may be more or less automatically solved. But in a larger systems context, we'll need observation and judgment to support our assumptions. For the moment, we need to emphasize that all the problems solved by deductive methods presume the existence and knowledge of the unit of measurement, as well as a categorical prescription which orders the alternatives according to that measure.

As we have said, beyond comparability lies an even stronger assumption for transforming the values of outcomes into numbers which obey the rules of arithmetic; we assume not only that we can compare the values of outcomes, but also that we can add, subtract, multiply, and divide these values. Of course, if we are satisfied with dollar evaluations, there is no problem. But it is always pertinent to ask whether such monetary representations of human values are appropriate.

3.5.2 Separability The problem of measurement and hence ordering is not always solved even after a unit of measurement has been established. Consider the following decision problem.

Problem: Two Products, Inc. ────────────────

As president of Two Products, Inc. you have decided to make available an extra $100,000 in advertising money for each of your products, if the manager in charge of each product line feels it would be worthwhile; that is, if the revenue from additional sales of the product caused by the additional advertising is greater than the sum of the cost of production and sales plus the $100,000 in additional advertising costs. The manager of department A, who is responsible for tape recorders, already spends $500,000 on advertising, as does the manager of department B (turntables). Thus each has the choice of continuing to spend $500,000 on advertising for his product, or to use the additional $100,000 available to each.

It seems reasonable to you to assume that the unit of measure for Two Products' performance is *net* profit dollars. If so, no problem of comparability exists. You have asked each of the product managers to maximize net profits in his own department. Is this a good idea?

Analysis: It turns out that such a policy may *not* be optimal from the firm's point of view. This can occur if the advertising of one product affects the sale of the other product.

Suppose, for a moment, that you are the manager of department A. You think that manager B will spend $500,000 (as before) on advertising turntables, and so you look at your projected net profit figures based upon his spending $500,000. Manager B bases his decision on your spending $500,000 on advertising tape recorders. But since both products bear the name Two Products, Inc., additional advertising by manager B on turntables may help your sales, and thus the net profits on tape recorders, and vice versa.

Using some data obtained from past experience the marketing division is able to provide you with table 3.1, information which you assume to be reliable. If you look at this table, which shows net profits for your department (A) in the double box, you will see that it is wise for you to use the additional $100,000 in advertising (thus spending $600,000) if you assume that manager B will be spending $500,000 as before. Similarly, manager B's net profits (table 3.2) are maximized if he spends $600,000, if he assumes that you will spend $500,000. Thus you might both choose to use the extra $100,000 available. But is it the best decision to have the individual department managers maximize their net profit separately?

TABLE 3.1 Net Profits for Department A in Thousands of Dollars*

Department B / Department A		Advertising budget	
		500	600
Advertising budget	500	100	125
	600	130	125

*Net profits for department A appear in the double box. The four alternative net profits figures are associated with the four combinations of advertising expenditures of the two departments. For example, if department A manager chooses to spend $500,000 on advertising and department B manager decides on $600,000 advertising budget, then the net profit for department A is $125,000.

TABLE 3.2 Net Profits for Department B in Thousands of Dollars

Department B / Department A		Advertising budget	
		500	600
Advertising budget	500	110	130
	600	120	125

Looking at table 3.3, the total net profits *of the firm* based upon the above myopic decisions are $250,000. But notice that due to the interaction of product advertising, net profits are maximized if manager A spends $500,000, as before, and manager B spends $600,000, yielding $255,000 net profit for the firm as a whole.

TABLE 3.3   Net Profits for Two Products, Inc., in Thousands
of Dollars

Department A \ Department B		Advertising budget	
		500	600
Advertising budget	500	210	255
	600	250	250

The type of problem that arose in the above example is one of *separability* of the objective function. You cannot always *suboptimize* (maximize net profits on each product) without consideration of the actions of the other decision makers, and expect the organization's value to be maximized. This can be done, in general, only when the optimal solution of subproblems (in this case, that of the manager of each department) does *not* depend on the optimal solution of another subproblem (the action of the other manager). Often this separability is deemed desirable for decision making in large organizations since one man (or department) has limited capabilities for information collecting and decision making. If the objective is separable, then local (decentralized) decision makers can solve their subproblems (suboptimize), and this will still lead to an optimal solution for the entire organization. However, from a larger systems point of view, there is always the question whether *apparent* separability is *real* separability. Many of us have come to suspect that if the systems we live in are viewed in a larger perspective, separability *never* occurs.

3.6   The Maximum, Minimum, and Satisfaction—Our Prescriptive Operators

To summarize our discussions of measurement of performance so far, we have seen what such measurements enable us to do and when we can feel reasonably assured that they are serving us well and not fallaciously. What they do is to enable us to pass from a set of alternative decisions D, specified either in a common language or arithmetically, to the corresponding numerical values of the decisions by way of the outcomes. The rules for passing from the elements of D to their numerical values in W are reliable if comparability and additivity are appropriate, and if we have correctly considered the separability problem.

There is one further function to consider with respect to the measure of performance. This is the function which enables us to select the maximum valued element of D (or minimum if the values are represented as costs or losses). In the examples so far, we can do the job of this function simply by scanning the values. Thus, in the advertising budget example we considered four alternative actions that you as president may take, listed in table 3.4. The unit of measure has been determined to be dollars, and the measure of performance (which "solves" the comparability and separability problem) is total net profits. In this example, once you place the categorical prescription on the decision maker's behavior to make as much as he can, it is easy to "operate" on the figures in order to choose the optimal decision, since you can see at a glance that d_2 is best. In general, however, it may not be so easy to determine the desirable d—that is, to "operate" on the values in this simple a manner.

TABLE 3.4   Advertising Budget

Decision	Department A	Department B	Total Net Profit
d_1	$500,000	$500,000	$210,000
d_2	$500,000	$600,000	$255,000
d_3	$600,000	$500,000	$250,000
d_4	$600,000	$600,000	$250,000

Note that the operator maximum, however devised, operates on the set D, and in the above instance it cranks out the number 255,000. In other words, the operator maximum is a function which starts with the members of D and lands in the maximum. But if your objective is simply to reach a certain "satisfaction level," say, $200,000, then the operator would select a decision which meets at least this level without necessarily searching all the decisions. We would still say that the operator "maximizes," since you are indifferent with respect to decisions that produce results higher than $200,000.

The example given above is very simple since the naked eye can easily scan a set of four elements and the respective payoffs. But if there are 100 or 250, or an infinity of elements, it would be far too costly in time and dollars to scan in this manner. Thus, one of the central values of quantitative methods will be to provide you with

techniques for scanning large sets of alternatives in a precise but relatively cheap and short manner. We will discuss some of these methods
in detail in chapters 8–11. In 3.7 we will examine one such method.

PROBLEMS 3.6

1. Comment on the following frequently used measures of performance:
   a. for a university, the number of student credit hours minus the
      cost.
   b. for a government program (health, education, safety, etc.), the
      total of increases in income for persons served by the program
      minus the cost.
   c. for a public park, an estimate of what citizens are willing to pay,
      multiplied by the number of users, minus the cost.
2. Can you think of decision-making situations in which a measure
   of performance is totally inappropriate?
3. Do grades in courses measure student performance?
4. What measure of performance should be used in buying a car?
5. What measures of performance are often used in advertising the
   following: aspirin, laundry soap, toothpaste?

3.7   Marginal Analysis

One technique for abbreviating the search for the maximum (or
minimum) is called "marginal analysis," which is based on a quite
simple and frequently used idea: decide one unit at a time on the best
available alternative for the next unit. This way you don't have to keep
track of the history of what you've been doing nor do you need to look
too far into the future. This technique, however, is not always a good
one and can be used only under some conditions as you shall see. To
introduce you to marginal analysis we will take a look at a (deliberately)
simple problem.

Problem: Good-Natured Foods ⸺⸺⸺⸺⸺⸺⸺⸺⸺⸺

As the owner of Good-Natured Foods you sell fresh strawberries
for which there is a demand at your store of 100 pounds per day. Your
supplier, however, only delivers every third morning, and you have to
buy your strawberries for the next three days at that time. He sells 100-
pound crates of strawberries for $41.50 each, and your selling price is
$.50/lb. From experience, you feel it is safe to assume categorically that

each of the first two nights a crate of strawberries is stored, 10% of the unspoiled quantity left will be spoiled by morning. You also know that all strawberries kept for more than three days spoil and cannot be sold. How many crates should you order each time from the distributor?

Analysis: We assume that you are interested in maximizing profits. However, this statement of your objective is imprecise since we have not specified the *time period* over which you wish to maximize your profits. The specification of length of time (which we call *horizon*) is a very important element to remember when time plays a role in decision making. In this problem the choice of a horizon is straightforward. Since strawberries kept for more than three days yield no revenue (they are spoiled) and since the distributor visits you every three days, each three-day period is a *separable* problem. Thus you can limit your efforts to solving a three-day horizon problem and keep using the solution over and over every three days or as long as the conditions remain unchanged. Note how this reduces your computational problem to a manageable size.

The statement of the problem indicates that the resource—strawberries—is relatively unlimited. (In the terminology of quantitative methods this means that you are not *constrained* by the availability of the resource.) Thus you can order one, two, three, four, five, or more crates of strawberries. But since you know that unsold strawberries that are kept for more than three days are spoiled and you also know that the maximum quantity you can sell in a three-day period is 300 pounds, you find it worthless to consider an order of more than four crates (400 pounds, because you might want to order an excess to take care of spoilage during the first two days). Based on these remarks, the relevant management information for your problem is summarized in tables 3.5 and 3.6. Table 3.5 provides data on the inventory and sales of strawberries in pound terms, and table 3.6 gives the necessary money figures from which you can derive the solution.

The first column of table 3.5 represents your order in terms of crates. Each crate contains 100 pounds of fresh strawberries. The second column has, for a given order, the quantity of strawberries available for sale in the morning of the day you receive the new order. The third and the fourth columns show the quantities available for sale in the second and third mornings, respectively, and the last column is the total quantity sold in a three-day period for the given order.

The numbers in this table are derived as follows: Say you order two crates; you then start with 200 pounds the first day. After the first day, you sell 100 pounds and have 100 pounds left, 10% of which spoil overnight (10% × 100 lbs. = 10 lbs.). So you have $100 - 10 = 90$ pounds to start the second day with. Your demand is 100 pounds again so you sell all 90 for a total of $100 + 90 = 190$ pounds.

TABLE 3.5   Inventory and Sales of Strawberries

No. of Crates Ordered	Pounds of Unspoiled Strawberries Left to Sell			
	First day	Second day	Third day	Total no. of pounds sold in 3 days
0	0	0	0	0
1	100	0	0	100
2	200	90	0	190
3	300	180	72	272
4	400	270	153	300

TABLE 3.6   Marginal Profits Computations

No. of Crates Ordered	Total No. of Pounds Sold	Total Revenue	Marginal Revenue	Total Cost	Marginal Cost	Total (Net) Profit	Marginal Profit
0	0	0	0	0	0	0	0
1	100	$ 50	$50	$ 41.50	$41.50	$ 8.50	$ 8.50
2	190	$ 95	$45	$ 83.00	$41.50	$ 12.00	$ 3.50
3	272	$136	$41	$124.50	$41.50	$ 11.50	$ -.50
4	300	$150	$14	$166.00	$41.50	$-16.00	$-27.50

To obtain the figures in table 3.6 we used the results of table 3.5 and the monetary information given in the statement of the problem. The first column of this table again represents your order alternatives. The second column is the last column of table 3.5; that is, the pounds of strawberries sold. The third column of table 3.6 is total revenue, derived by multiplying the total number of pounds sold (column 2) by $.50/lb. The fourth column represents the *addition to* or *increment* in *total* revenue achieved by ordering an additional crate. Notice this is just the *difference in total revenues* between ordering a given number of crates (x crates), and ordering one additional crate (x + 1 crates). Similarly, columns 5 and 6 represent *total cost* of ordering 0, 1, 2, 3, or 4 crates and the *marginal cost* of ordering the one additional crate. Column 7 is total (net) profit, that is, total revenue minus total cost, and column 8, *marginal profit*, is the additional *profit* obtained from ordering an additional crate. Notice that column 8 can be derived, for a given order, from the differences in total profit, or by subtracting the appropriate marginal cost from marginal revenue.

Clearly, all of the alternatives with positive total profit (1, 2, 3 crates) are worthwhile if you are interested just in making profits. But recall that your objective is *maximizing* profits. To find the decision (number of crates) which yields the most profits you can scan with the operator maximum the list of profits: max {$0, $8.50, $12, $11.50, $−16} = $12, so you order two crates.

But you can also arrive at the same result by successively asking "Is ordering another crate worthwhile?" The marginal profits column gives you the answer—it's worthwhile only if the marginal profits from the additional crate are greater than zero. When marginal profits become negative (as when you order the third crate), total net profits, which you want to maximize, go down even though the total profit may remain positive. You can see that the total profits must go down since marginal costs exceed marginal benefits for this crate.

To summarize, you can solve the problem by examining the total (net) profits and picking the largest, or by using marginal analysis to examine marginal profits. In fact, the marginal profits are derived by taking the differences in the totals. The idea is that when the marginal benefits from an activity (sale of strawberries) exceed the marginal cost of the resource (strawberries), then you continue to allocate (buy) additional units of the resource until the reverse is true. By doing so, you satisfy the categorical prescription to make as much as you can.

Using marginal analysis in the above problem may not seem to have been particularly helpful in saving computation time or making the problem more manageable. However, it did serve to introduce you to the idea of marginal analysis, which will prove to be computationally beneficial in the problem to follow. In the case above you chose the alternative that was the *most* worthwhile in the sense of yielding the *most* profit. You found you could accomplish this by examining each additional allocation of strawberries to see if it *by itself* was worthwhile—that is, yielded net marginal benefit. In the problem to follow, since you will have limited resources, marginal analysis will dictate that you examine each additional allocation to see if that additional allocation is the most worthwhile. Using this method, you will arrive at the alternative which provides the most total benefit, satisfying the profit-maximizing prescription.

Problem: Good-Natured Foods II ——————————————

It is several years later. You have applied marginal analysis so well that now you own a chain of Good-Natured Foods Stores. You no longer purchase strawberries from outside distributors since now you grow your own. Every day you harvest six crates (100 pounds each) which you distribute to your four stores. You know that there are differences between the stores, such as location, customer demand, and efficiency in operations, that cause differences in profits. You also know that because of packaging costs, it is not worthwhile to split any crate between stores. Based on these considerations, you arrive at the profits presented in table 3.7. The first column represents possible allocations of crates to stores. The second column provides the profits of store 1 for each allocation of crates to store 1. For example, if store 1 receives no crates, its profits from strawberries sales is zero; if it receives one crate, the profit is $400; if it receives two or more crates, total profit is $700. Columns 3, 4, and 5 give the profit information for stores 2, 3, and 4, respectively.

TABLE 3.7   Profits for Good-Natured Foods II in Hundreds of Dollars

No. of Crates	Store			
	1	2	3	4
0	0	0	0	0
1	4	2	6	5
2	7	4	9.5	6
3	7	6	10	7
4	7	8	10	8
5	7	10	10	9
6	7	12	10	10

How should you allocate the daily harvest of six crates so as to maximize your profits?

Analysis: You now have the problem of allocating a limited resource — you are constrained to six crates per day — to activities which compete for the resource (sales in each of the four stores). When you encounter such a problem the question to be answered is not just "is this additional allocation worthwhile?" but "is it the most worthwhile?" As you can see from table 3.8 (which provides you with the marginal profits associated with alternative allocations of crates to stores), 17 crates could be allocated with positive marginal profits (that is, are worthwhile), but only six crates are available. Therefore you must refine your method of marginal analysis so that you can use it to solve your current problem. You could, of course, examine each alternative allocation and compare the total profits for each. But this would be quite a cumbersome task, as you can see if you try it. However, by placing the positive marginal profits in a decreasing order (table 3.9), you can arrive at the solution to your problem.

TABLE 3.8   Marginal Profits

No. of Crates Allocated	Store			
	1	2	3	4
1	4	2	6	5
2	3	2	3.5	1
3	0	2	.5	1
4	0	2	0	1
5	0	2	0	1
6	0	2	0	1

TABLE 3.9   Ranking of Marginal Profits

Marginal Value	6	5	4	3.5	3	2	2	2	2	2	2	1	1	1	1	1	.5
Store	3	4	1	3	1	2	2	2	2	2	2	4	4	4	4	4	3

Marginal analysis dictates that you allocate the crates one at a time: The first crate should be sent to the alternative which is the *most* worthwhile (yields the most marginal profit) — that is, to store 3; the second crate should be sent to store 4 where the marginal profit is $500; the third should be shipped to store 1 ($400 marginal profit); the fourth to store 3; the fifth to store 1, and the last to store 2. In summary, the allocation that yields the most profits to you is given in table 3.10.

TABLE 3.10   The Optimal Allocation

Store No.	No. of Crates Sent
1	2
2	1
3	2
4	1

As always, though, you must be careful in using new quantitative methods. What if, in the above case, you lost money on the first crate at, say, store 4 due to high delivery costs, but on additional crates made very high profits, like $2000, at store 4 since it costs the same to deliver one crate as to deliver 10? Well, marginal analysis wouldn't let you get that first crate into the store to get the high profits on the second or third crates! So be aware that this "discrete" marginal analysis only works if the total amount you make at any one store doesn't increase at a *higher rate* the more crates you order.

PROBLEMS 3.7

1. You have an advertising budget of six million dollars to be allocated among three departments. The net profits for each department for each level of spending on advertising are as follows.

Advertising Allocated (in millions of dollars)	Profits (in millions of dollars)		
	Department A	Department B	Department C
0	5	4	7
1	8	8	9
2	11	11	11
3	14	13	13
4	16	14.5	15
5	17.5	15.5	17
6	18	16.5	19

   For example, if four million advertising dollars are allocated to Department B, the profits will be 14.5 million dollars.

   You cannot allocate a fraction of a million dollars because all advertising packages are designed in multiples of million dollars. What is the optimal allocation of your advertising budget?

2. The board of directors has decided to allocate half a million dollars for reducing the pollution emitted by your four plants. Each pollution reducing device costs $100,000, but its effectiveness is different from one plant to another. The following table shows the reduction of pollution in units of pollution for each number of

devices. For example, if three devices are installed in plant 4, the total reduction of pollution is 2700 units.

No. of Devices	Reduction of Pollution			
	Plant 1	Plant 2	Plant 3	Plant 4
1	1000	1400	2000	1800
2	1900	2200	3900	2400
3	2800	3000	4700	2700
4	3400	3600	5300	2800
5	3600	4100	5500	2850

How much of the half a million dollars should be allocated to each plant if the desire of the board is to reduce pollution as much as possible?

3. You are about to put in an order for six new conveyors. You consider three suppliers from whom you have received the following price data:

No. of Conveyors Ordered	Total Costs (in thousands of dollars)		
	Supplier 1	Supplier 2	Supplier 3
1	2	2.2	1.8
2	4.5	4.8	3.8
3	7.0	7.5	6.2
4	9.5	11.0	8.6
5	12.0	15.3	11.9
6	14.8	19.9	16.0

How many conveyors should you order from each supplier, assuming you'd like to pay as little as possible?

4. Your knitting firm considers investing $700,000 to increase its capacity in three areas: warping, knitting, and finishing. The increased capacity will yield incremental profits as given by the following table:

Investment (in units of $100,00)	Incremental Profits (in thousands of dollars)		
	Warping	Knitting	Finishing
1	220	290	300
2	380	400	500
3	450	510	680
4	500	620	840
5	540	730	980
6	580	840	1100
7	620	950	1100

For example, if $500,000 are invested in increasing the warping capacity, the incremental profits will be $540,000. You cannot invest a fraction of $100,000 since all investment plans in these three areas are in multiples of $100,000. How should you allocate the $700,000 among the three areas?

5. In these days of full employment you feel fortunate since five of the local high school graduates have come to you seeking work. You can assign them to any one of four departments. You estimate the increased production due to additional labor as follows:

Additional Labor	Increased Production			
	Department I	Department II	Department III	Department IV
1	1000	900	1200	1400
2	800	800	700	700
3	600	700	300	350
4	400	600	100	175
5	200	500	0	80

The sales price and the per unit cost of production for the four departments are:

Department	Unit Price	Unit Cost of Production
I	$12	$6
II	$10	$3
III	$9	$3
IV	$7	$2

How should you assign the five additional people if your objective is to maximize additional profits?

3.8   Conclusion

In this chapter we have examined ways of evaluating decisions by quantitative methods, starting with simple orderings and going on to quantitative assessments. The whole idea has been to provide a *measure of performance* which can be used to select the best decision.

In concluding the discussion, it is important to notice that the categorical prescription to *make the most you can* has turned out to have somewhat different meanings on the surface. Sometimes we are so built into a problem area by our assumptions that we have a reasonably small number of possible decisions to examine, and without a significant computational cost, we can deduce the optimal one—that is, the one that results in the greatest payoff. In other cases—as in the auto shop example of section 1.6—it is far too costly to examine all the alternatives, and we may be satisfied with one that is *good enough*. In principle, we could still speak of *making the most* and of an *optimal* in this larger case, if we could measure the cost of computation, because then we would maximize the gross worth minus the (usual) cost minus the cost of searching and computing. Unfortunately, there are some horrendous problems of analysis and measurement to overcome if one tries to proceed in this manner. Instead, we often proceed with a feel for the situation, which some writers call a *satisfaction level* or *aspiration level*: We strive, not for the pure optimal, but for what we feel or judge to be good enough. This happens in the case of studying for an examination, where clearly you can't scan all alternative tactics of studying, but rather rely on a feeling for how much is required to attain the grade you will be satisfied with or aspire to. Thus the *measure of performance* need not always be as precise as it has been in the problems of this chapter.

3.9   Summary

Hopefully, you have now begun to understand the importance of explicitly specifying your measure of performance when preparing for a decision. You also should begin to appreciate the difficulties in specifying and using such a measure. It would be useful to review the following points.

a. In order to satisfy the prescription "make as much as you can," it is helpful to order decisions using a relationship like "is better than" or "is greater than."

b. Sometimes such an ordering is not enough, and you can refine the ordering with the use of numbers.

c. Whole numbers have the property that a successor exists for every integer; succession is an example of a *function*, which is one of the most important concepts in quantitative methods for decision.

d. A function passes from one set to another; a specific function called a "measure of performance" passes from the set of decisions to the set of values associated with that decision.

e. Examples of measures of performance are dollars, value, and expected dollars or expected value.

f. There are many difficulties in specifying useful measures of performance; two of them are comparability and separability.

g. Associated with measures of performance, or objective functions, are prescriptive operators like maximum, minimum, or aspiration level.

h. Quantitative methods exist which can help you reduce problems that occur in measuring performance; you can sometimes ease the computational load by specifying the time horizon of a problem and by using marginal analysis when it is appropriate.

Appendix 3.1   Important Functions and Rules

Functions

1. ax (i.e., add x to itself a times)
2. $ax + b$, called a "linear function," because, as we shall see, it can be represented as a straight line; $3x + 7$ is an example
3. x^n (i.e., multiply x by itself n times), sometimes called the nth power of x
4. $ax^2 + bx + c$, called a "quadratic function," which is nonlinear; it can be represented graphically by a curved line
5. $ax^n + bx^{n-1} + cx^{n-2} + \ldots + kx + l$, called a "polynomial function" (of degree n)

Rules

The rules for any numbers, variables, or functions x, y, z, a, b are:

1. $x + y = y + x$ (Addition is commutative.)
2. $x + (y + z) = (x + y) + z$ (Addition is associative.)
3. $xy = yx$ (Multiplication is commutative.)
4. $x(yz) = (xy)z$ (Multiplication is associative.)
5. $x(y + z) = xy + xz$ (Multiplication is distributive with respect to addition; this rule enables us to "factor" expressions, so that $y(x + 1) + y^2(x + 1) = (x + 1)(y + y^2) = (x + 1)y(y + 1)$, for example.)
6. $x^a \cdot x^b = x^{a+b}$ (Note that a and b can be any numbers, but x must be the same number.)

Appendix 3.2   Additional Functions and Rules

The functions, where a represents a constant number, are:

1. $x - a$, and
2. x/a.

The relationships (rules), where a, b, x, y, and z are constants, variables, or functions are:

1. $a(x - y) = ax - ay$ (Multiplication is distributive with respect to subtraction.) Note that subtraction is neither commutative nor associative: in general, $a - b$ does not equal $b - a$, nor does $(a - b) - c$ equal $a - (b - c)$.

2. $x - x = 0$

3. $-(-x) = x$

4. $-(-(-x)) = -x$, and so on

5. $-(a + b) = -a - b$

6. $-(a - b) = -a + b$

7. $x(-y) = -xy$

8. $(-x)(-y) = xy$

9. $\dfrac{x}{y} \cdot \dfrac{y}{z} = \dfrac{x}{z}$ (We always assume that the denominator, the "bottom" number, is not 0.)

10. $\dfrac{x}{\left(\dfrac{y}{z}\right)} = \dfrac{xz}{y}$

11. $(1/z)(x - y) = \dfrac{x - y}{z}$ (Note that division is neither commutative nor associative.)

12. $x^{-1} = \dfrac{1}{x}$

13. $x^{-2} = \dfrac{1}{x^2}$, and so on

Appendix 3.3   Irrational Numbers, Imaginary Numbers, and the Infinite

It is important to mention briefly some other numbers because they will appear later on. If we tell you that where you land is 2, and the function is x^2, what is the number you started with? It's surely not 1 or 2, but somewhere in between. Euclid showed that the number, which we write as $\sqrt{2}$ ("square root of 2"), is not a fraction either. We call it an *irrational* number. So there are other numbers (lots of them!) besides positive and minus rationals and 0. Some of these, like the number $\pi = 3.1416 \ldots$, have immense practical importance, because they enable you to estimate the circumference of a circle (a wheel, for example) if you know the diameter. Others, like the number $e = 2.718 \ldots$, which we'll introduce later, enable you to make computations more simply.

There is a really odd set of numbers which arises when you land, say, in -1 and the function is x^2. This may seem absurd, because when you multiply a number by itself, the answer is always positive: $1 \times 1 = 1$ and $-1 \times -1 = 1$. So how could you ever land in -1 when the function is x^2? The answer is another set of numbers, called *imaginary*, because for a long time people did not believe in their existence. These numbers are generated from $\sqrt{-1}$, which is symbolized by the letter i; thus $a \cdot i$ is an imaginary number for any a drawn from a list of "real" numbers.

Finally, we must mention that most "imaginary" of all numbers, the *infinite*. The concept of the infinite, like the concept of zero, has always puzzled philosophers and mathematicians. The Greeks of the fifth century B.C. understood the paradoxical nature of the infinity of points that lie on a straight line. You can appreciate their puzzlement if you think of a line that is one foot long. Between any two points on this line there must always be a third which is distinct from both of them. If the points, for example, are fractions of a foot, like 3/4 and 7/9, then the average of the two fractions, which is $(3/4 + 7/9)/2 = 55/72$, lies between the two. And another fraction, 109/144, lies between 3/4 and 55/72, and so on. So the number of points on a line one foot, or one inch, or one thousandth of an inch long must be very large, and he who sets out to count them could never finish the task. But we move about over these distances with ease! If you walk one foot, you must have an infinity of tasks to perform to get through every point, and yet you do "get through" all these tasks. But "logic" says you can't! Luckily for practical you, you can relegate discussion of this paradox to leisure time; based on some clever theory developed a century ago, it appears that you'll be perfectly safe in assuming that you can deal logically with sets that have infinite membership. For example, sometimes the set D of alternative choices is infinite, as when you have to decide on the size of a ball bearing, the weight of an automobile, the area of a building, hours to study for an exam, and so on. But, as you'll see later, you don't have to construct an outcome and payoff table for such a D, because there are techniques presented in chapters 9–11 which will guide you to the optimal choice in a relatively few steps.

Values Over Time 4

4.1 Stable Measures of Performance

Thus far, we have mainly been studying the preparation for decision making in one specific situation. In the Route to Work problem, for example, we were interested in how you should solve the problem for one particular day. In this chapter we want to consider some of the reasoning that goes into decision making where the outcomes are spread out over a number of periods of time.

At the outset it is important to recognize that the value w of an outcome o may change dramatically over time, as happens when you offer a boy of six the choice between a love affair and a box of candy, and compare the results with a similar offer to a boy of eighteen. We say that a value determination, that is, the measure of performance, is "stable" if you can predict changes in value over time; hence, there is nothing unstable about changes in the value of sex and candy between six and eighteen, since you can reasonably well predict how these values will change. In this chapter we shall assume that the decision maker is sufficiently aware of how the values change in time; that is, we shall concern ourselves with stable measurements of performance.

4.2 Notation for Time Periods

Suppose you have been given the set of profit figures of your firm for the past five years. The set might look like $P = \{\$100,000, \$98,750, \$210,000, \$231,000, \$196,000\}$. Since you would like to do some projections of future profits based upon this data, you would like to distinguish among the years that the set of profits are associated with; in other words, you would like to sequentially order the data on past profit. Since you want to order the profit figures, it is convenient to attach a symbol with a subscript to each element of the set, thus identifying each element as well as the order desired. So, if you call an arbitrary element of the set of profits p, you can call the first year's profit p_1 (which is read "p sub-one"), the second p_2, and last year's profit p_5 (p sub-five). If $p_1 = \$100,000$, you know then that the profit of five years ago was $\$100,000$, and you can refer to it as p_1, which will tell you it is the first number in the set of profit figures. This is a concise, unambiguous way of referring to a particular year's profit.

In general, we can use subscripts to represent periods of time. If there are n time periods, then we assign the numbers $1, 2, 3, \ldots , n$ to these periods. Suppose we are using the letter a to represent costs. The ith element in the sequence is written symbolically a_i (read "a sub-i"). The next element after the ith element is referred to as the "i plus first" element and is written a_{i+1} (read "a sub-i-plus-one"), and the element before the ith element is written a_{i-1} (read "a sub-i-minus-one").

For example, in the sequence of cost numbers 20, 21, 22, 23, 24 called a_1, a_2, a_3, a_4, a_5, if $i = 3$, then

$$a_i = 22 \qquad a_{i+1} = 23 \qquad a_{i-1} = 21 \qquad a_{i+2} = 24$$

We will sometimes use the subscript "zero," such as in a_0, as the first term of a sequence.

You may sometimes want to add up a sequence of n numbers, $a_1, a_2, a_3, \ldots , a_n$. We can represent the sum of the sequence by the mathematical symbol

$$\sum_{i=1}^{n} a_i$$

This symbol is read "the sum from i equals one to n of a-sub-i." This means you start with $i = 1$, or a_1, and increasing i by one each time to 2, a_2, 3, a_3, and so on, adding up all the a_i's until $i = n$, a_n. The symbol Σ is the Greek capital letter sigma, and you can remember that the "s" in "sigma" is like the "s" in "sum." A few computational examples will illustrate this notation.

EXAMPLES   If $a_1 = 21$, $a_2 = 23$, $a_3 = 27$, $a_4 = 3$, and $a_5 = 22$, then

$$\sum_{i=1}^{2} a_i = a_1 + a_2 = 21 + 23 = 44$$

$$\sum_{i=1}^{5} a_i = a_1 + a_2 + a_3 + a_4 + a_5 = 21 + 23 + 27 + 3 + 22 = 96$$

$$\sum_{i=2}^{4} a_i = a_2 + a_3 + a_4 = 23 + 27 + 3 = 53$$

We use i as the subscript because you will see this letter used most often for subscripting in other books and communications. The letters $j, k, l,$ and m are also often used as subscripts.

We can also use the summation symbol to represent the sum of a sequence of numbers not necessarily represented by subscripted variables; for example,

$$\sum_{i=1}^{3} i(i+1) = 1 \times 2 + 2 \times 3 + 3 \times 4 = 20$$

PROBLEMS 4.2

1. If $a_1 = 3$, $a_2 = 33$, $a_3 = 45$, $a_4 = 52$, $a_5 = 67$, $a_6 = 82$, what are the values of the following?

    a. $\sum_{i=1}^{2} a_i$

    b. $\sum_{i=1}^{4} a_i$

    c. $\sum_{i=3}^{6} a_i$

    d. $\sum_{i=2}^{5} a_i$

2. If $a_1 = 1$, $a_2 = 2$, $a_3 = 3, \ldots, a_{10} = 10$, what are the values of the following?

    a. $\sum_{i=1}^{3} a_i$

    b. $\sum_{i=1}^{5} a_i$

    e. $\sum_{i=3}^{7} i$

    c. $\sum_{i=6}^{10} a_i$

    d. $\sum_{i=3}^{7} a_i$

3. If $a_1 = 2$, $a_2 = 4$, $a_3 = 6$, $a_4 = 8$, $a_5 = 10$, $a_6 = 12$, what are the values of the following?

    a. $\sum_{i=1}^{2} a_i$

    b. $\sum_{i=1}^{4} a_i$

    c. $\sum_{i=4}^{6} a_i$

    d. $\sum_{i=4}^{6} 2^i$

4. Solve the following.

    a. $\sum_{i=1}^{7} 3i$

    b. $\sum_{m=1}^{5} m^2$

    c. $\sum_{j=6}^{10} 2j$

    d. $\sum_{k=1}^{100} 5$

    e. $\sum_{i=1}^{5} (i+3) + \left(\sum_{j=1}^{3} 3j\right) \Big/ \left(\sum_{k=1}^{6} k^2\right)$

5. Consider the following table (each entry is doubly indexed according to its row and column, and denoted by a_{ij}; read "a sub ij").

Row i	Column j			
	1	2	3	4
1	3	8	11	14
2	6	9	15	11
3	2	3	7	0

What are the values of the following?

a. $\displaystyle\sum_{i=1}^{3} \sum_{j=1}^{4} a_{ij}$

b. $\displaystyle\sum_{i=1}^{2} \sum_{j=1}^{3} a_{ij}$

c. $\displaystyle\sum_{j=1}^{4} a_{ij}$, where $i = 2$

d. $\displaystyle\sum_{i=1}^{2} a_{ij}$, where $j = 4$

4.3 Arithmetic Series

Let us see how this notation helps us display time-period problems in a neat and precise manner.

Problem: School Enrollment _____

The board of education has asked you, the superintendent, to prepare a five-year master plan for enrollment. You know that this year's enrollment is 1000 students and that each year enrollment can safely be assumed to increase by 200 students. (1) What do you predict the enrollment will be in each of the next four years? (2) What do you predict will be the *total* number of students over the five years including this one (the sum of the five years' enrollment)?

Analysis: To answer the first question, start with 1000 as the enrollment this year. Call this year's enrollment a_0. You can then compute the successive enrollments in two ways. One way is to add 200 to the previous year's enrollment:

Predicted enrollments

this year's enrollment = 1000 students = a_0

year 1 enrollment = year 0 enrollment + 200 = 1200 students = a_1

year 2 enrollment = year 1 enrollment + 200 = 1400 students = a_2

year 3 enrollment = year 2 enrollment + 200 = 1600 students = a_3

year 4 enrollment = year 3 enrollment + 200 = 1800 students = a_4

Now let d be the constant increment (difference) in enrollment between two successive years. Then the method used above for computing a_i when you know d and you know the value of a_{i-1} (the previous year's predicted enrollment) is

$$a_i = a_{i-1} + d$$

For example, in computing enrollment for year 4, after having computed enrollment for year 3, you can write

$$a_4 = a_3 + d \quad \text{or} \quad a_4 = 1600 + 200 = 1800$$

There is a second systematic way to solve the superintendent's first question which allows you to answer questions like "What is the predicted enrollment four years from now?" without having to compute intermediate figures:

Expected enrollments

this year's enrollment $= \qquad\qquad$ 1000 students $= a_0$

year 1 enrollment $= 1000 + (1) \times 200 = 1200$ students $= a_1$

year 2 enrollment $= 1000 + (2) \times 200 = 1400$ students $= a_2$

year 3 enrollment $= 1000 + (3) \times 200 = 1600$ students $= a_3$

year 4 enrollment $= 1000 + (4) \times 200 = 1800$ students $= a_4$

In general, by the above method, the predicted enrollment in year i would be

$$a_i = a_0 + i \cdot d \tag{1}$$

where: a_0 is the number of students enrolled this year;

$\quad\quad\;\;\;$ d is the constant difference in enrollment each successive year;

$\quad\quad\;\;\;$ a_i is the expected number of students enrolled in year i from now, as before.

This quantitative formula can be used when you are interested in finding the value of some variable (school enrollment in this case), where the variable grows or declines by a *constant* amount each time period. A sequence of numbers that change by a constant amount each time period is called an *arithmetic series*. Formally,

$\quad\quad$ if $a_i = a_{i-1} + d$ (d can be negative), then the sequence

$\quad\quad\quad$ $a_0, a_1, a_2, \ldots$ is an *arithmetic series*

As another example, if you know that your expected income this year a_0 is \$5000 (the variable a is expected yearly income, the initial value a_0 is \$5000) and you expect a raise each succeeding year of \$500 per year (the increment d is +\$500), then 16 years after this one, your expected yearly income is

$$a_{16} = 5000 + 16 \times 500 = \$13,000$$

To answer the superintendent's second question, that of total enrollment in the next five years, you can again proceed in two ways. One obvious way is to add up the a_i's (computed by either method in answer to question (1)):

$$S_4 = \sum_{i=0}^{4} a_i = 1000 + 1200 + 1400 + 1600 + 1800 = 7000$$

where S_4 is the sum of enrollments up through four years from now. However, there is a convenient quantitative method for computing the sum of an arithmetic series in general, and in particular for computing the sum of the five years' enrollments. Using the same notation as before, and calling the final time period n (in this case $n = 4$), the formula for the sum of an arithmetic series is

$$\sum_{i=0}^{n} a_i = \frac{(a_o + a_n)(n + 1)}{2} \qquad (2)$$

where: a_0 = the initial variable value;

   n = the subscript of the final element in the series to be summed (the number on top of the summation sign);

   a_n = variable value in year $n = a_0 + n \cdot d$;

   d = the increment.

So you can compute the sum of the five terms using the formula

$$\sum_{i=0}^{4} a_i = (1000 + 1800)\,\frac{5}{2} = 7000$$

Using formula (2) in the special case where $d = 1$ and $a_0 = 0$, it follows that the sum of the digits from 0 up to n is given by

$$(0 + n)\,\frac{n + 1}{2} = \frac{n(n + 1)}{2}$$

Thus the sum from 0 up to and including 6 is $6 \cdot 7/2 = 21$, as you can readily confirm.

Sometimes in using quantitative methods we like to have on hand several different versions of the same formula. This is done because at different times we have different versions of the relevant information readily available. For example, to use formula (2), you need a_0, a_n, and d. However, you may not have a_n at your disposal—perhaps all you know is a_0, n, and d. You can then use formula (1) and substitute it for a_n in formula (2) to get (3).

From (1):
$$a_n = a_0 + n \cdot d$$

and plugging in for a_n in (2):
$$\sum_{i=0}^{n} a_i = \frac{[a_0 + (a_0 + nd)](n + 1)}{2}$$

which yields:
$$\sum_{i=0}^{n} a_i = \frac{[2a_0 + nd](n + 1)}{2} \qquad (3)$$

In (3) all you need to know is n, a_0, and d. Of course, you might argue that this is just playing mathematical games; we don't deny this, but point out that we do this kind of game-playing not only because it can be great fun, but also because a formula for the same sum may be more readily identified as useful in an alternative form, such as (3). In the future, we will state or show how the same formula may appear in different, useful forms, sometimes by using the equality relationship, such as

$$\sum_{i=0}^{n} a_i = \frac{(a_0 + a_n)(n + 1)}{2} = \frac{[2a_0 + nd](n + 1)}{2}$$

In the School Enrollment problem, you might also have preferred to start the sequence of a_i's by calling the current year a_1. In that case, the subscripts all change, the final year is a_5, and the formulas are

$$a_i = a_1 + (i - 1)d \qquad (1')$$

and

$$\sum_{i=1}^{n} a_i = \frac{(a_1 + a_n)n}{2} \qquad (2')$$

where: a_1 = the variable value for the initial period 1;
         a_n = the variable value for the final nth period;
         d = the increment.

So if you had wanted to know the sum of the next five years' enrollments, then next year's enrollment $a_1 = 1200$, $a_5 = a_1 + (5 - 1)200 = 1200 + 800 = 2000$, and

$$\sum_{i=1}^{5} a_i = (1200 + 2000)\frac{5}{2} = 8000$$

To convince yourself of the power of these quantitative methods for summing up arithmetic series, solve the school problem for total expected enrollment over the next 17 years if 200 is the yearly increment, by summing up the numbers. Then use formula (2′)!

Predicted total enrollment $= (1200 + (1200 + 16(200)))17/2$ $= 47{,}600$. Compare your computational time.

PROBLEMS 4.3

Solve the following, assuming the a_i's are terms in an arithmetic series.

1. If $a_0 = 5500$, $d = 230$, what are the values of the following? (a) a_5, S_5; (b) a_8, S_8; (c) a_{15}, S_{15}.

2. If $a_0 = 3000$, what are the values of the following?
    a. S_4, if $a_4 = 11{,}000$ b. S_7, if $a_7 = 24{,}000$
    c. a_9, if $d = 2000$ d. a_{23}, if $d = 1500$
    e. d, if $a_8 = 35{,}000$ f. d, if $a_4 = 9{,}000$
    g. S_{10}, if $d = 1750$ h. S_{30}, if $d = 2800$

3. You purchased a car on January 1, 1972, for which you paid $4200. You plan to keep it until December 31, 1976, and to sell it then for $200. You use the car solely for business so the IRS allows you to deduct depreciation on the car as a business expense. You choose to deduct an equal amount for each year you plan to have the car.
    a. Set up the problem (model) as an arithmetic series. Identify a_0, n, a_n, d.
    b. What is the annual depreciation expense?

4. As the manager of a ski resort you are requested by the owners to provide them with information about future earnings. The resort opened on January 1, 1968, and attracted 5000 skiers during the first year of operations. Since then it has been growing constantly at an annual increment of 1500 skiers a year. You know that each skier contributes $80 to the resort's revenues. You also estimate that each skier will use up $60 worth of variable resources. Your fixed costs are $3000 per year (regardless of the number of skiers). Predict the profit (loss) for each of the next five years. For 10 years from now. What is the sum of the next 10 years' profits?

5. A survey has shown that to satisfy the hospitalization needs of the community 280 new hospital beds must be added each year. Currently there are 1200 beds available.
    a. How many beds will be needed at the end of ten years from now?
    b. On the average 26 people per bed are hospitalized each year. How many people will be hospitalized in the next 5 years?
    c. What assumption have you made in this analysis?

∗ 4.3.1   A Geometric Proof of Formula (2) We said in chapter 2 that when reasoning deductively the real fruits of our labor are the theorems

---

∗Starred sections can be omitted without loss of continuity. (In other words, if you don't dig it, don't do it.)

(consequences) which follow from the definitions and assumptions that we start with. Often it may not be very instructive to prove results formally—for example, formulas (1) and (2) above. However, some of us are curious, or skeptical, while some feel better when we can "see" algebraically or geometrically the reasoning behind such deductive results. A geometric proof of formula (2) goes as follows.

The enrollment figures for the five years can be depicted graphically as in figure 4.1.

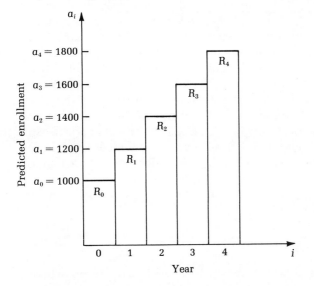

Figure 4.1

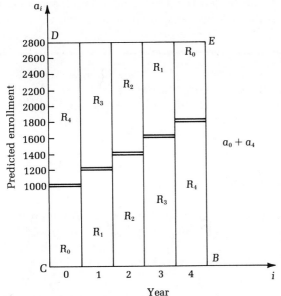

Figure 4.2

The total predicted enrollment over the five years can be represented by the sum of the areas of rectangles R_0, R_1, R_2, R_3, and R_4. The area of each rectangle is computed by multiplying the base (the length of which is 1) by the height (length a_i). For example, the area of rectangle R_0 in the figure is $1 \times a_0 = 1 \times 1000 = 1000$. In figure 4.2 we have placed above rectangle R_0 the rectangle representing year 4 (whose base is 1 and height is 1800). Note that you can obtain the a_i needed (if you know a_0 and d) by using formula (1): $a_i = a_0 + i \cdot d$. Rectangle R_3 is above rectangle R_1, rectangle R_2 is added to itself, rectangle R_1 is above rectangle R_3, and rectangle R_0 is added to rectangle R_4. A super-rectangle now appears, whose corners are denoted by B, C, D, E. The area of this rectangle (you should recall from basic geometry) is the product of the base $\overline{BC}$ and the height $\overline{BE}$. The length of the base is the total number of original rectangles (which is equal to the number of terms in the series, in this case 5, which is $n + 1$ if the series starts with a_0), and the height $\overline{BE}$ can be seen as the sum of the first and the last terms of the series, $a_0 + a_4$. Since the area of rectangle B, C, D, E is *twice* as large as the sum of the original arithmetic series (each term is included twice in rectangle B, C, D, E), we must divide it by 2 in order to get the sum of the arithmetic series; that is, $S_4 = (a_0 + a_4)(n + 1)/2 = (1000 + 1800) \times 5/2$.

Of course, this geometric proof for the superintendent's problem can be generalized for any a_0, d, and n.

4.4   Geometric Series

We have been examining the case of arithmetic series where a series increases by *adding* an increment. Often, however, a series increases by *multiplying* an increment. Let's see how this works.

Problem: Ike Kennedy ──────────────────────────

As a public relations man for congressional candidate Ike Kennedy, you have decided to use the marketing "theory of diffusion" to bring his message to the people. This theory describes the communications of information about products (a candidate can be viewed as a "product" to be "sold" to a wide variety of potential consumers (voters) through a network of information carriers). The "message" is first communicated to so-called opinion leaders in the community, who "diffuse" the information by relaying it to subleaders, who then relay it to sub-subleaders, and so on.

You have selected a group of 1000 opinion leaders to whom you have sent the information, and you believe that each of them will receive the information today and tell two people tomorrow, who will in turn tell two new people the next day, up through the election day which is five days from now. You would like two questions answered: (1) How many new people will get Ike Kennedy's message each day? and (2) How many people will get his message by election day?

Analysis: To answer the first question, as before, there are two ways available. The first method is simple multiplication.

$$a_0 = \qquad\qquad\qquad\qquad\qquad 1000 \text{ people}$$
$$a_1 = a_0 \times 2 = (1000) \quad \times 2 = \quad 2000 \text{ people}$$
$$a_2 = a_1 \times 2 = (2000) \quad \times 2 = \quad 4000 \text{ people}$$
$$a_3 = a_2 \times 2 = (4000) \quad \times 2 = \quad 8000 \text{ people}$$
$$a_4 = a_3 \times 2 = (8000) \quad \times 2 = 16{,}000 \text{ people}$$
$$a_5 = a_4 \times 2 = (16{,}000) \times 2 = 32{,}000 \text{ people}$$

where a_i is the number of new people getting Ike Kennedy's message on the ith day from today. The formula here is

$$a_i = a_{i-1}q$$

where q is the "rate of diffusion" ($q = 2$ in this case).

The second way of computing the number of new people getting the message has the same advantage as our second arithmetic method. When asked for the number of new people i days from now, you need not compute each day's amount as above. The general formula is

$$a_i = a_0 q^i \tag{4}$$

where $a_0 =$ the initial number of people informed and q is the diffusion rate. For example,

$$a_5 = (1000) \times (2)^5 = 32{,}000$$

When the value of some variable (such as new people getting Ike Kennedy's message) increases (or decreases) each time period *by some factor q*, the sequence of variable values is called a *geometric series*, and the variable value at any time i can be calculated by formula (4). This is the same as saying:

A *geometric series* is a sequence of numbers where the *ratio* of two successive numbers in the sequence is a constant q.

The second question facing you as PR man can also be answered in two ways. First, by summing directly the six terms:

$$S_5 = \sum_{i=0}^{5} a_i = 1000 + 2000 + 4000 + 8000 + 16{,}000 + 32{,}000 = 63{,}000$$

where S_5 is the sum of all the people getting the message. The second way is again by use of a general formula, this time for the sum of a *geometric* series:

$$S_n = \sum_{i=0}^{n} a_i = \frac{a_n q - a_0}{q - 1} \tag{5}$$

if you know a_0, a_n, and q; or

$$S_n = \sum_{i=0}^{n} a_i = \frac{a_0(q^{n+1} - 1)}{q - 1} \tag{6}$$

if you know a_0, q, and n.

In the current problem

$$S_5 = \frac{1000(2^{(5+1)} - 1)}{2 - 1} = \frac{1000(63)}{1} = 63,000$$

which is the total number of people receiving Ike Kennedy's message by election day.

═══

As in the case of arithmetic series you may wish to start with a_1. The formulas then become

$$a_i = a_1 q^{i-1} \tag{4'}$$

and

$$S_n = \sum_{i=1}^{n} a_i = \frac{a_n q - a_1}{q - 1} \tag{5'}$$

Let us put the new quantitative methods of the last two sections in a decision-making context.

Problem: Choice of Pension Plan ───────────────

You want to buy into a pension plan for yourself, and an insurance agent has offered you a choice between two alternative plans, both of which yield the same retirement pensions after 30 years. However, the difference in the plans is that payments are made as follows:

Plan I   Down payment $2000
          Yearly payments $50 additional per year for the next 30 years

Plan II   Down payment $10
          Yearly payments   1.3 times the previous year's payment for 30 years (e.g., $13 next year)

Your objective is to minimize the total amount of money put into the fund. Which plan should you choose? What will the last payments be under each plan?

Analysis: To help prepare for this decision, first notice that plan I involves an arithmetic series of payments, $2000, $2050, $2100, $2150, . . . , and that plan II's payments are a geometric series, $10, $13, $16.90, $21.97, ... There are 31 total payments under both plans, so if the first period is denoted period 0, then $n = 30$.

Under plan I your total dollar payments will be

$$S_{30} = \sum_{i=0}^{30} a_i = \frac{(2a_0 + 30d)(30 + 1)}{2} = \frac{(2 \times 2000 + 30 \times 50)31}{2}$$
$$= \$85,250$$

and your last payment is

$$a_{30} = (a_0 + 30d) = 2000 + 30 \times 50 = \$3500$$

Under plan II your total dollar payments will be

$$S'_{30} = \sum_{i=0}^{30} a_i = \frac{a_0(q^{(30+1)} - 1)}{q - 1} = \frac{10(1.3^{31} - 1)}{1.3 - 1} = \$113,499.81$$

and your final payment will be

$$a'_{30} = a_0 q^{30} = \$26,199.56$$

So your decision, based upon your objective of least total dollar payments, will be to choose plan I, since

$$S_{30} < S'_{30}$$

You should note here that our earlier discussion of values changing over time is relevant. In this example we've made a large assumption about your attitude towards money over time; your objective of least dollar payment implies that paying a dollar today is worth exactly the same to you as paying a dollar 15, 20, or 25 years from now. That is, we've neglected to incorporate in your objective the cost of not having money available during a certain period of time because it is allocated elsewhere. For example, if you put $2000 down now in plan I, you forego the opportunity of earning 5% interest in the bank for the next 30 years. This notion is quite important in areas of public and private finance such as project investment, portfolio selection, and credit management. We will turn in a moment to the quantitative analysis of the cost of lost opportunities (called *opportunity cost*) after introducing the ideas of the present and future value of money. Geometric series will play an important role in this analysis.

PROBLEMS 4.4

1. Which of the following are geometric series? Identify a_0 and q.
   a. 1, 2, 4, 8, 16, 32
   b. 1, 4, 8, 16, 32
   c. 4, 6, 9, 13.5
   d. 3, 9, 27, 81, 243

2. If $a_0 = 3$, what are the following values?
   a. a_4, if $q = 10$
   b. S_6, if $a_2 = 27$
   c. S_3, if $a_2 = 396.75$
   d. a_{20}, if $q = \frac{1}{2}$
   e. S_{10}, if $q = 10$

3. In the Pension Plan problem of this section, suppose in plan II the yearly payments are 1.2 times the previous year's payment, and the down payment is $500. Which is the better plan now?

4. Greasy Slick, halfback for the Hawaiian Haoles of the newly formed Trans-American football league, recently tore his Achilles tendon and will be out for the rest of the season. As a hard-drinking, hard-smoking 30-year-old halfback, Greasy doesn't plan to retire until he has played six more seasons (after this one). His salary today is $100,000, but because of his problems, Slick feels that he is worth the same amount next year; once the general manager finds out what terrible shape he is in, however, Greasy figures that his salary will decrease by 20% per year thereafter.

   Greasy is starting a food franchising operation ("Greasy's III") and would like to know what his salary will be four, five, and six years from now as well as his total income from football over the next five years. What should you tell him?

5. The owner of the Hawaiian Haoles, Charley O. Lokl, has figured out that his attendance figures should start going up by 30% every year for the next five. This year the Haoles drew 900,000 fans. His profit on Primo Concessions was $63,000, based on a total volume of $1,260,000 in concession revenues. He began to make profits on the concessions after the $1 million mark. If concession sales will increase in proportion to attendance, and profits in proportion to concession volume over $1 million, what can he count on as total (sum of) profits over the next five years?

4.5 Opportunity Cost of Money: Future Value and Present Value

4.5.1 Future Value of Money

Problem: Where to Bank ━━━━━━━━━━━━━━━━━━━━━━━━━━━━━

You have just received a $4000 inheritance, and your friendly banker, Mr. Van Puten, suggests that you deposit it in a five-year savings account at 5% interest, compounded annually. "Compounded annually" means that at the end of one year, the 5% interest is declared (in the first year this amounts to .05 × $4000 = $200) and added to your balance so that you have $4200 in your account. In the second year you earn 5% interest on the new balance of $4200, which amounts to .05 × $4200 = $210. (If the terms were 5% *simple* interest, you would earn only $200 per year interest for each of the five years.)

A rival banker, Mr. Long, urges you to borrow an extra $1000 from him for which you must *pay* 8% interest (compounded annually), and hence be in a position with your $4000 to buy a $5000 federally insured bond from him which yields 7% annually compounded interest. You are interested in the alternative which yields the most money at the end of five years. Which offer should you choose, the straight 5% or the borrow-bond combination?

Analysis: To prepare for this decision, it is useful to introduce the term *future value of money*. At the 5% interest rate, the "one-period" future value of $4000 is 1.05 × 4000 = $4200, where the length of the "period" is one year. The two-year future value is 1.05 × $4200=$4410. In general, if P is the original principal available and r is the interest rate per period, then the *n-period future value of the principal*, F_n, is

$$F_n = P(1 + r)^n$$

For example, $F_5 = \$4000 \, (1+.05)^5 = \$5,105.13$ is the 5-year future value of $4000 at 5%. This formula for F_n is the same as that for evaluating the nth element in a geometric series:

$$a_n = a_0 q^n$$

where $a_0 =$ the principal, $a_n =$ the n-period future value of the principal, and $q = (1 + r)$.

By evaluating the future value of your $4000 in five years, you have answered the question of how much money you will have at the end of five years if you bank with Mr. Van Puten: $F_5 = \$4000 \, (1.05)^5 = \$5,105.13$. If you bank with his rival, your $5000 deposit will earn you

$$5000 \times (1.07)^5 = \$7012.76$$

the five-year future value of $5000 at 7%. (This $5000 follows a geometric series over time: $5000, 5000 × 1.07 = $5350, 5350 × 1.07 = $5724.50, ... That is, $F_i = F_{i-1}q$, where $q = 1.07$.) But you will not have $7012.76 at your disposal at the end of the five years. You are going to pay back the $1000 loan, with interest. The amount you'll have to pay is

$$1000 \times (1.08)^5 = \$1469.32$$

which is the five-year future value of $1000 at 8% interest rate.
   At the end of five years you will have

$$\$7,012.76 - \$1,469.32 = \$5,543.44$$

which is more than the $5105.13 that you'll get from Van Puten. So you accept the loan and do business with Mr. Long, unless you have an aversion to borrowing.

Numbers like $(1 + r)^n$ will occur often in this chapter, and we have included appendix 4.2 for your convenience to save time in computation. (Appendix tables 4.1 and 4.2 can be found on pages 123–24.)

4.5.2   Present Value of Money and Calculation of Interest Rates

Problem: Revisiting the Bank ───────────────

   Mr. Van Puten has now told you that if you give him your $4000 today, he will repay you $4250 in one year. Other banks are offering a 6% annual interest for a one-year deposit of $4000. Again you are interested in maximizing your cash position at the end of the year. Is Van Puten's offer better than the other banks' offer?

Analysis: There are three ways to solve this problem. The first is to use the method of analysis of the previous subsection. The future value next year of $4000 at 6% is: $F_1 = 4000 (1.06)^1 = \$4240$. Van Puten's offer is better.
   A second way to look at this problem is to find the interest rate that Mr. Van Puten's $4250 offer represents. Your objective can be rephrased as maximizing the interest rate on your money. To calculate this, we introduce the interest rate r, which is "unknown," and solve for it in an equation. If the interest rate is r, then $F_1 = \$4250 = \$4000(1 + r)^1$. To solve for r, first divide both sides of the equation by $4000, yielding

$$\frac{4250}{4000} = 1 + r$$

or

$$1.0625 = 1 + r$$

Subtracting 1 from both sides gives .0625 = r. Clearly, an interest rate of .0625 is better than .06, so you have verified that banking with Mr. Van Puten is a wise choice.

The third way to compare the choices is to evaluate the *present value* of Mr. Van Puten's offer, given your alternative of investing at 6%. The $4250 will *not* be placed in your hands today, but one year from today. But what is $4250 one year *from now* worth to you in terms of today's dollars? The present value of the $4250, which you receive one year from today, is calculated by using what is called a *discount rate*. A discount rate is the rate at which you could earn interest or other returns by investing your money in some alternative opportunity such as a bank account. In general, the present value (denoted by PV) of F dollars available to you n periods from today is

$$PV = \frac{F}{(1 + r)^n}$$

where r is the discount rate. The reasoning behind this formula is that you should "discount" the F dollars because you'll receive the money in the future. The "rate of discounting" is r.

In this case the discount rate is r = .06, and the present value of the $4250 offered to you one year from now is

$$PV = \frac{\$4250}{1.06} = \$4009.43$$

This must be compared with the present value of what the other banks offer. If you put the $4000 in another bank at 6% interest, you'll receive

$$\$4000 \times 1.06 = \$4240$$

next year. Discounting back to the present, at the discount rate of 6%:

$$PV = \frac{\$4240}{1.06} = \$4000$$

which is not surprising, since you used the bank's interest rate as your rate for discounting.

Obviously, a present value of $4009.43 is better than $4000, so you have another argument for accepting Van Puten's offer.

We have presented this analysis in three ways because all three are in current use, and you will need to be able to compare offers that employ different schemes. For example, to finance the purchase of an automobile, you may have three options: (1) the dealer may offer to loan you $1000 for monthly payments by you of $60 for two years; (2) a bank may offer to loan you $1000 for two years, at 8% interest payable at the end of each year, the principal to be paid back in one lump sum at the end of two years; or (3) you can take the $1000 out of your savings account which earns 5% interest. You should be able to decide by using either total payment by you, or interest rate paid over two years, or present value as the criterion for decision.

The three methods all come from the same basic equation in which two of the three variables are specified in the information, and you have to solve for the third. This basic equation is

$$F_n = PV(1 + r)^n$$

where n is the number of years. We first evaluated F_1 using the r from alternative banks. Second, we solved for the r in Van Puten's deal, using his F_1 and your P. Third, we solved for PV, which we called the present value, using Van Puten's F_1 and the other banks' r.

Problem: Van Puten III _____

The elated Van Puten now makes an alternative offer of $4510 at the end of two years. This makes you curious as to why he did not offer $4500, since he offered you only $4250 at the end of one year. The reason for this is the *compounding* of interest since you earn interest not only on the original $4000 in the second year, but also on the $250 interest earned in the first year. You want to see how generous Van Puten's *new* offer really is.

Analysis: One way to examine whether Van Puten's newest offer is more generous than the one you just accepted is to compare the interest rates, sometimes called *rates of return*. Since you deposit $4000 now and you get $4510 after two years, the following relationship holds:

$$4510 = [4000(1 + r)](1 + r) = 4000(1 + r)^2$$

where r is the rate of return. To solve for r, divide both sides of the equation by 4000 and take the square root of both sides:

$$\sqrt{\frac{4510}{4000}} = \sqrt{(1 + r)^2}$$

or

$$1.062 = 1 + r$$

Therefore, $r = 1.062 - 1 = .062$. In general, if you know the amount P you are about to invest, and the proceeds F to be received n years from now, you can find the rate of return r by the formula.

$$r = \sqrt[n]{\frac{F}{PV}} - 1$$

As an alternative to evaluation of the rate of return of Van Puten's offer, you could have calculated the present value of his offer based upon the 6% discount rate—the interest offered by other banks:

$$(1.06)^2 PV = 4510$$

Solving for PV yields:

$$PV = \frac{4510}{(1.06)^2} = \$4013.88$$

In general, the present value of F dollars n years from today, where r is the discount rate, is

$$PV = \frac{F}{(1 + r)^n}$$

4.5.3   The Time Value of Money   We have discussed examples in this chapter in which either

1.   there has been a stream (flow) of cash payments over time *without* consideration of the time factor in evaluating such payments (the Pension problem), or

2.   the time-value of a *single* cash payment was considered (the Bank problems).

Evaluation of the flow of cash payments over time is an essential element in financial decision making. In our lives the flow of income in the future is of great interest for such decisions as choosing between jobs, what stocks to buy, insurance purchases, and choice among loan alternatives. All such decisions involve evaluation of both the total amount of the payments (as in the pension example) and the *scheduling* of such payments (which considers the time value of money).

The problems which follow will involve decisions in which a cash *flow* over time is under consideration, *and* the time value of money is included in the categorical prescription "you ought to make as much as you can." The measure of performance (which quantifies how much you make) is assumed to be dollars today. Therefore dollars to be received or paid out in the future (as part of a flow of cash) are *discounted* to their *present values* for purposes of comparability. Once all the cash in the stream is in terms of today's dollars, the stream whose total (sum) is largest is preferred, provided you have no other basis for valuing future versus present payments.

Problem: Leeson Label Company

As financial analyst for Leeson Label Company, you are asked to decide whether purchase of an additional label press is worthwhile. The purchase price of the press is $13,500, and the increased capacity it will provide the company is expected to result in increased sales of $4000 per year, while production and sales costs will be $2000 per year for the additional labels produced. Thus the *net* cash receipts provided by purchase and use of the machine will be $2000 per year. It is further projected that the machine will be obsolete at the end of 10 years, and at that time, you will be able to sell the press for $4000 (this is called the "salvage value" of the machine). It is assumed that the company can borrow any reasonable amount from the bank at 6% and has no other more profitable use of money; hence, you use 6% as the discount rate, sometimes called the *cost of capital*, by which you discount future cash flows. Should Leeson Company buy the label press?

Analysis: In order to prepare for this decision, several assumptions are made. First (as throughout this chapter), the amount of the payments and receipts is assumed to be known with certainty. Second, the entire net cash receipts for a given time period are assumed to be received at the *end* of the period. Thus, the $2000 each year is discounted as if the entire amount had the same present value. Third, the discount rate of 6% is assumed to remain the same over the 10 years under consideration.

Having made these assumptions, recall that the present value of the $13,500 to be paid is exactly that: $13,500. The present value of the (net) cash flow generated by the machine is

$$\frac{2000}{(1+.06)} + \frac{2000}{(1+.06)^2} + \cdots + \frac{2000}{(1+.06)^{10}} + \frac{4000}{(1+.06)^{10}}$$

$$= 2000 \sum_{i=1}^{10} 1/(1+.06)^i + \frac{4000}{(1+.06)^{10}} \tag{7}$$

The summation term of (7) is the sum of a geometric series, while the second term of (7) represents the present value of salvaging the machine.

You should by now be able to calculate the sum of the terms under the summation sign, by using formula (5') for the sum of a geometric series, where $q = \dfrac{1}{1+.06}$, and $a_1 = \left(\dfrac{1}{1+.06}\right)$:

$$\overset{a_n}{} \qquad \overset{q}{} \qquad \overset{a_1}{}$$

$$\sum_{i=1}^{10}\left(\frac{1}{1.06}\right)^i = \frac{\left[\dfrac{1}{1+.06}\left(\dfrac{1}{1+.06}\right)^9\right]\dfrac{1}{1+.06} - \dfrac{1}{1+.06}}{\dfrac{1}{1+.06} - 1}$$

$$= \frac{\left(\dfrac{1}{1.06}\right)^{10}\dfrac{1}{1.06} - \dfrac{1}{1.06}}{\dfrac{1}{1.06} - \dfrac{1.06}{1.06}}$$

$$= \frac{\left(\dfrac{1}{1.06}\right)^{11} - \dfrac{1}{1.06}}{-\dfrac{.06}{1.06}} \qquad\qquad (8)$$

The numerator of (8) can be factored to yield

$$\frac{1}{1.06}\left[\left(\frac{1}{1.06}\right)^{10} - 1\right]$$

so multiplying the numerator and denominator of (8) by 1.06 yields

$$\frac{\left(\dfrac{1}{1.06}\right)^{10} - 1}{-.06}$$

Finally, multiplying numerator and denominator by −1 yields

$$\sum_{i=1}^{10}\left(\frac{1}{1.06}\right)^i = \frac{1 - \left(\dfrac{1}{1.06}\right)^{10}}{.06}$$

Fortunately, you need not do this complicated (but straightforward) algebra for every problem, since, in general:

$$\sum_{i=1}^{n}\left(\frac{1}{1+r}\right)^i = \frac{1 - \left(\dfrac{1}{1+r}\right)^n}{r} \qquad\qquad (9)$$

Numbers like $\dfrac{1}{(1+.06)^{10}}$ will appear frequently in such problems, so a table containing $\dfrac{1}{(1+r)^n}$, for various values of n (the number of periods) and r (the discount rate), is included in appendix 4.1. Looking at this table for $r = .06$ and $n = 10$, you'll find that $\left(\dfrac{1}{1.06}\right)^{10} = .558$. Using (9) you get

$$\sum_{i=1}^{10} \frac{1}{1.06} = \frac{1 - \left(\frac{1}{1.06}\right)^{10}}{.06} = \frac{(1 - .558)}{.06} = 7.366$$

and therefore (7) equals

$$\$2000 \times 7.366 + \$4000 \times .558 = \$14,732 + \$2232 = \$16,964$$

So the *net present value* (present value of the cash flow minus present value of the investment) of the machine is

$$\$16,964 - \$13,500 = \$3464$$

You clearly recommend purchase of the machine. This problem could also have been solved using the geometric series $\frac{2000}{1.06}, \frac{2000}{(1.06)^2}, \cdots$ with $a_1 = \frac{2000}{1.06}$, $q = \frac{1}{1.06}$, and $n = 10$.

===

You have just seen a very convenient management information system (MIS), based essentially on a set D of alternative decisions made up of $D = \{$buy, not buy$\}$, or, in a more general case, $D = \{$buy, rent, not buy$\}$. Each member of D leads directly to one unique w or "payoff," by means of an interest rate (or discount rate) plus a salvage value, plus an "income stream" that the purchase or rental may generate; S is known with certainty. This use of the MIS often proves very useful, because individuals, companies, schools, government agencies, and other organizations frequently have to consider this type of decision. But, in a larger systems perspective, this method clearly does not provide final answers, not only because there are usually great uncertainties about the assumptions, but also because D itself is only a subset of a larger set of alternatives. It is not true that Leeson Labels can borrow any amount it wants to at 6% interest; the banks wouldn't permit it to, and its stockholders would become alarmed at the debt-equity ratio. Hence, the company's problem of "buy-not buy" is embedded in a larger decision set of other opportunities* for borrowing; the return of $3464 may be significantly less than other returns it could acquire.

Nevertheless, this simplified MIS may be very useful for decision makers, especially if we generalize on its design a bit. For example, in the general case of evaluation of the present value of a cash flow, the payments or receipts may be different in different periods.

---

*The cost of foregoing investment in alternative options is sometimes called the *opportunity cost* of a decision.

Problem: Psychedelic Candle Factory ━━━━━━━━━━━━

As the owner of a psychedelic candle-making factory, you currently purchase preshaped wax candle bases, with wicks, from a wholesale producer. The wholesale price is $50 per thousand. A machine which produces the wax bases with wicks has been offered to you at a price of $2000, and you can pay $1000 now and $1000 a year from now. You are a growing firm, and expect to sell 12,000 candles next year, 15,000 the year after, and increase sales by 2000 each year after that. The machine can produce 30,000 candle bases with wicks per year, and your cost of production will be $20 per thousand if you buy the machine. You expect the machine to last five years, at which time it will be worthless (salvage value, zero). Your discount rate is 8%, since you can earn that much by reinvestment in other areas of your firm. Should you make your own bases (buy the machine) or continue to purchase them from the wholesaler?

Analysis: The savings provided by the machine are depicted in appendix table 4.1.

Note that we again assume that the discount rate (return on investment) is stable at 8%, and that the savings are realized at the end of the period. The present value of the investment in the machine is

$$\$1000 + \frac{1000}{1 + .08} = \$1925.93$$

The present value of the savings from the machine is

$$PV = \frac{\$360}{1.08} + \frac{\$450}{(1.08)^2} + \frac{\$510}{(1.08)^3} + \frac{\$570}{(1.08)^4} + \frac{\$630}{(1.08)^5}$$

From appendix table 4.1, with $r = .08$,

$$PV = \$360 \times .926 + \$450 \times .857 + \$510 \times .794 + \$570 \times .735$$
$$+ \$630 \times .681$$
$$= \$1971.93$$

The net present value of the investment in the machine is

$$\$1971.93 - 1925.93 = \$46.00 > 0$$

Therefore, you should purchase the machine, assuming that no other investment opportunities are available.

Note that you might have solved the problem by combining payments and receipts and calculating the net present value directly:

$$\text{Net Present Value} = -\$1000 + \frac{(-\$1000 + \$360)}{1.08} + \frac{\$450}{(1.08)^2} + \frac{\$510}{(1.08)^3}$$
$$+ \frac{\$570}{(1.08)^4} + \frac{\$630}{(1.08)^5}$$

yielding the same result, a net present value of $46.00 for the investment.

The general formula for the present value of a cash flow for n years, where F_i is the cash flow to be received or paid out i years from now, and r is the discount rate, is

$$\sum_{i=1}^{n} \frac{F_i}{(1 + r)^i} \tag{10}$$

With this formula you can now evaluate the Pension Plan problem (section 4.4) under the more realistic assumption of a personal time value for money. Certainly you would rather have a dollar today than wait 30 years to get it, since you can always bury it until then. By the same token you would rather pay a dollar next year than today. Once you have decided on the time value of the money to you, in terms of a discount rate, you can then compare the pension plans with this refinement in your objective. The analysis in section 4.4 assumes a discount rate of zero. To save computational time we could use a simple computer program first to generate the two series of payments and then to evaluate the plans in terms of present value for the different interest rates (using (10)). If you did this you would find that plan I is the best option until your discount rate becomes 3% (actually a little less than that is the point at which the present value of the payments is equal), and for all rates above it, you ought to choose plan II. At the high rate of 15%, plan II's payments have a very low net present value, since the geometric series of payments are very small at first, and very large in the distant future. In general, *the higher the discount rate gets, the less important payments made in the future become, and the farther away in time the payments are, the less important they are.* Of course, if you have a strong personal preference for pay-now rather than pay-later, this rule may not hold.

Once you get the basic idea of using future projections to help you prepare for present decisions, you can readily extend the methods to other examples. The following section is one illustration of this extended design, in which the two ideas of an arithmetic series and a geometric series are combined.

PROBLEMS 4.5

1. What is the future value of
    a. $5000 at 5% interest rate 10 years hence?

    b. $7500 at 8% interest rate 5 years hence?

    c. $8000 at 3% interest rate 15 years hence?

2. You plan to deposit $2500 at the beginning of each of the next 3 years in a special savings account which yields 7.5% compound interest. How much money will you be able to withdraw from the account five years hence?

3. Troublemaker Len asks for another raise in salary amounting to $5000 annually. Knowing the kinds of difficulties he can cause and the frequent demands he makes for raises, you offer to deposit the additional annual $5000 in a special account which yields 6.5% interest, compounded annually. T. M. Len will not be able to touch these moneys for three years. How much richer will he be after this waiting period?

4. What is the present value of
    a. $5000 received 2 years hence, at 6% discount rate?
    b. $7800 received 4 years hence, at 5% discount rate?
    c. $18,000 received 6 years hence, at 8% discount rate?

5. What is the present value of
    a. $3000 received annually for the next 5 years, at 3% discount rate?
    b. $4000 received annually for the next 10 years, at 6% discount rate?
    c. $2000 received a year hence, $5000 received 2 years hence, and $8000 received 3 years hence, at 5% discount rate?

6. The next five years' maintenance costs for one of Leeson's press machines are estimated to be $1000, $1200, $1200, $1200, and $1200, respectively. After this period the press must be sold for scrap, for the anticipated price of $200. Leeson is considering purchasing a new press which will produce the same as the present press, but its annual maintenance cost will be $100, $200, $300, $300, $300 for the five years, respectively, and its value at the end of five years will be $600. The investment needed for a new press is $3000. Should Leeson spend the $3000, if he can sell the old machine for $1000 now?

7. a. Billy Blue has been lamenting his signing of a $63,000 contract with the Fresno Freaks. Billy figures that as long as he stays with the team, the most his salary can be cut is 10% of his previous year's salary. His base salary was $50,000 for this year, and $13,000 was an agreed-upon bonus. Billy, being a country boy from the bayous and the winner of the Cy Young award, has an 8% discount rate. If he stays with the team for the next 10 years and then quits, what is the present value of his contract if he gets the maximum cut every year? (Assume this year's amount is not discounted, and next year's is by one year.)

b. If Billy begins blazing again, he expects an additional $15,000 per year each year for 5 years over the previous year's base salary, at which time he gives his manager the shaft. What is the present value of his association with the Freaks under these conditions?

4.6 Finite-Difference Equations—Combination of Arithmetic and Geometric Series

Problem: Expansion, Inc. ─────────────────────────

You are the market strategist for Expansion, Incorporated, and the production department has asked you for an estimate of the number of units to be produced each year for the next five years. You know that your projection for sales growth in regions where your product is available is 5% compounded per year and current sales are 15,000 units per year. Also, you plan to enter one new region each year, and in these new regions, first year sales will be 1000 units, after which sales follow the same growth pattern, increasing by a factor of 1.05 per year. What is your estimate?

Analysis: Let a_i denote the sales in year i with $a_0 = \$15,000$, the current sales. Next year's sales will then be:

$$a_1 = 15,000 \times 1.05 + 1000$$
$$a_2 = a_1 \times 1.05 + 1000$$
$$\vdots$$
$$a_5 = a_4 \times 1.05 + 1000$$

and, in general,

$$a_i = a_{i-1}q + d$$

where $q = 1.05$, $d = 1000$. So, your estimates are:

$$a_1 = \$16,750$$
$$a_2 = \$16,750 \times 1.05 + 1000 = \$18,587.50$$
$$a_3 = \$18,587.50 \times 1.05 + 1000 = \$20,516.88$$
$$a_4 = \$20,516.88 \times 1.05 + 1000 = \$22,542.72$$
$$a_5 = \$22,542.72 \times 1.05 + 1000 = \$24,669.85$$

In the above problem there are two growth factors involved: the constant difference between two time periods, d, and the constant ratio, q. Mathematicians call an equation representing a relationship of this type a *finite-difference equation* and you can, too, if you want to impress somebody. If $q = 1$ in the general finite-difference equation

$$a_i = a_{i-1}q + d$$

then the sequence of a_i's is an arithmetic series. If $d = 0$, then the a_i's form a geometric series.

It turns out that if you want to predict sales 20 years from now in the Expansion, Incorporated, problem you need not evaluate all the intermediate terms. As will be proven in the next section:

$$a_i = a_0 q^i + d\left[\frac{q^i - 1}{q - 1}\right] \tag{11}$$

so you can predict the sales of Expansion, Incorporated, 20 years from now to be

$$a_{20} = 15{,}000 \times (1.05)^{20} + 1000\left[\frac{(1.05)^{20} - 1}{1.05 - 1}\right] = \$72{,}865.42$$

This generalized formula (11) enables us to prepare for a number of decisions which involve growth and/or decline: growth-decline of cities, epidemics, markets, water resources, and so on.

We'll illustrate the idea of difference equations by means of a problem, the design of an annuity plan, by showing the versatility of the equation represented by (11). You will see that, as in any equation, you not only can solve for the left-hand side when it is the value you are searching for, but you can solve for *any* single unknown variable when the rest of the variables in the equation are known.

Problem: Annuity Plan ————————————————

Suppose that you have \$5000 in the bank now, and place \$1000 in the bank each year for the next 20 years. The bank pays 5% interest, and you want to know the amount of money that will be in your account at the end of that time. Assume that interest is declared on the last day of the year, and the first deposit is made on December 31, and so are the succeeding deposits.

Analysis: Letting a_i represent the balance (after deposit) of your account at the end of year i,

$$a_0 = \$5000 \text{ (no interest earned for one day)}$$
$$a_1 = (\$5000)1.05 + \$1000$$
$$a_2 = a_1 \times 1.05 + \$1000$$
$$\vdots$$
$$a_{20} = a_{19} \times 1.05 + \$1000$$

Then a_{20} represents the amount you will have in the bank after declaring interest on the balance in your account 19 years hence and depositing the last $1000. From equation (11), where $i = 20$, $q = 1.05$, $a_0 = 5000, and $d = 1000:

$$a_{20} = \$5000(1.05)^{20} + \$1000 \frac{(1.05)^{20} - 1}{1.05 - 1}$$

From appendix table 4.2, with $r = .05$, $n = 20$, you can see that $(1.05)^{20} = 2.6533$ and you can directly solve for $a_{20} = \$46,332.50$, the balance in your account 20 years from now.

Suppose you have, say, $5000 in the bank and you want to have $46,332.50 (or any other amount) in the bank 20 years from now. If you had not solved the above problem, and wanted to know how much to put in the bank each year in *equal* deposits to achieve that figure, you could have used equation (11) also. In this case you know a_{20}, but want to solve for d. Recalling (11):

$$a_i = a_0 q^i + d\left[\frac{q^i - 1}{q - 1}\right]$$

You can solve for d in two steps: Isolating the d term on one side,

$$a_i - a_0 q^i = d\left[\frac{q^i - 1}{q - 1}\right]$$

and then multiplying both sides by $\left(\frac{q - 1}{q^i - 1}\right)$ to get d,

$$d = \frac{[a_i - a_0 q^i][q - 1]}{[q^i - 1]} \tag{12}$$

Solving the problem using (12) with $46,332.50 as a_{20} and appendix 4.2 for $(1.05)^{20}$:

$$d = \frac{[\$46,332.50 - \$5000(1.05)^{20}][1.05 - 1]}{(1.05)^{20} - 1}$$

yields $d = \$1000$, as expected. Note that, if you know the equal payments d you were willing to make, and the final balance a_i you desired, and want to solve for the initial balance a_0, you can also derive the general equation for a_0.

This concludes our discussion of how to prepare for decision making over time by means of arithmetic and geometric series, and their generalization to difference equations. We note at this point that the quantitative methods based on these ideas are mainly applicable when there are a specific number of discrete steps (months, years, etc.) and you know ahead of time what will happen at each step if you make some decision (for example, buy or not buy) at the beginning. If the changes are continuous, and you cannot feasibly approximate what happens by discrete steps, then more general techniques are required. Some of these are discussed in chapters 9–12.

* **4.6.1 Proof of Equation (11)** A finite difference relationship is represented by

$$a_i = a_{i-1}q + d \tag{13}$$

Also,

$$a_{i-1} = a_{i-2}q + d = (a_{i-3}q + d)q + d = a_{i-3}q^2 + d(q + 1) \tag{14}$$

So, from (13) and (14)

$$a_i = (a_{i-1})q + d = a_{i-3}q^3 + d(q^2 + q + 1) \tag{15}$$

In general, working your way backward, if you are given a_0 to start with

$$a_i = a_0 q^i + d \sum_{j=0}^{i-1} q^j \tag{16}$$

Recall that $q^0 = 1$, since any number taken to the power zero is 1. You should recognize that $\sum_{j=0}^{i-1} q^j$ is a geometric series with $a_0 = 1$, $n = i - 1$ and $q = q$, so we can restate (16) as

$$a_i = a_0 q^i + d\left[\frac{q^i - 1}{q - 1}\right]$$

PROBLEMS 4.6

1. Presently the population of Eilat is 100,000. The net migration into the city is 5000 people per year. The local annual birthrate exceeds the death rate by 10%. What will be the population of Eilat (a) next year; (b) after five years; (c) after 20 years?

2. Suppose you place $10,000 in the bank now and add $500 to the account each year for the next 10 years. The bank pays $4\frac{1}{2}\%$ compound interest on the balance. What will you have 10 years from now?

3. Your boss offers you the following option: (i) $50,000 bonus now and a salary of $50,000 for the next ten years; or (ii) a $100,000 bonus now and a salary of $30,000 for the next ten years.
    a. Which would you prefer?

b. What discount rate, if any, did you use to decide?

c. How high would the bonus (or salary) have to be in the worse offer to make you "indifferent"?

d. What assumptions have you made in your analysis?

4. You have $100,000 to put in the bank. You don't want to put it all in now, but you want to have $100,000 after 6 years. So you put $50,000 in now, and want to know how much of the remaining $50,000 you can spend if the bank pays 8% interest and you make equal deposits for the next 10 years.

a. What must those deposits be?

b. How much does that leave to spend?

5. Suppose you knew d and a_i in equation (11). Deduce a general formula for a_o.

4.7 Summary

In this chapter we have examined methods of preparing for decisions, where the outcomes and payoffs may be spread out over a number of periods of time. Throughout, the state of the world has been assumed to be known with certainty: if you made a deal for 6% compound interest, we assumed that you'd get the money for sure at the end. A few points are worth repeating.

a. *Subscripting* is a very useful notation for representing a series of payoffs over time.

b. An *arithmetic series* is a series of numbers which have a common difference between successive numbers; there exist useful *formulas* for calculating the ith term of such a series as well as the sum of the terms in a series.

c. Such formulas also exist for *geometric series*; in a geometric series there is a constant ratio between successive terms.

d. These formulas are very useful in calculating *present values* and *future values*, which are one way of comparing alternative opportunities.

e. In the present-value calculations, the method is to *discount* future payoffs by using a *discount rate*, which can be determined by considering lost opportunities such as an alternative investment.

f. Other outcome and payoff streams can be represented by *finite-difference equations*, which are combinations of arithmetic and geometric series; annuities, for example, can be evaluated using finite difference equations.

g. Some helpful tables, listing present and future values of one dollar, appear in the appendixes.

Appendix Table 4.1 Present Value of $1 at Annual Rate r% for n Years, $\dfrac{1}{(1+r)^n}$

n	1%	2%	3%	4%	5%	6%	7%	8%	9%	10%	11%	12%	13%	14%	15%
1	0.9901	0.9804	0.9709	0.9615	0.9524	0.9434	0.9346	0.9259	0.9174	0.9091	0.9009	0.8929	0.8850	0.8772	0.8696
2	0.9803	0.9612	0.9426	0.9246	0.9070	0.9000	0.8734	0.8573	0.8417	0.8264	0.8116	0.7972	0.7831	0.7695	0.7561
3	0.9706	0.9423	0.9151	0.8890	0.8638	0.8396	0.8163	0.7938	0.7722	0.7513	0.7312	0.7118	0.6931	0.6750	0.6575
4	0.9610	0.9238	0.8885	0.8548	0.8227	0.7921	0.7629	0.7350	0.7084	0.6830	0.6587	0.6355	0.6133	0.5921	0.5718
5	0.9515	0.9057	0.8626	0.8219	0.7835	0.7473	0.7130	0.6806	0.6499	0.6209	0.5935	0.5674	0.5428	0.5194	0.4972
6	0.9420	0.8880	0.8375	0.7903	0.7462	0.7050	0.6663	0.6302	0.5963	0.5645	0.5346	0.5066	0.4803	0.4556	0.4323
7	0.9327	0.8706	0.8131	0.7599	0.7107	0.6651	0.6227	0.5835	0.5470	0.5132	0.4817	0.4523	0.4251	0.3996	0.3759
8	0.9235	0.8535	0.7894	0.7307	0.6768	0.6274	0.5820	0.5403	0.5019	0.4665	0.4339	0.4039	0.3762	0.3506	0.3269
9	0.9143	0.8368	0.7664	0.7026	0.6446	0.5919	0.5439	0.5002	0.4604	0.4241	0.3909	0.3606	0.3329	0.3075	0.2843
10	0.9053	0.8203	0.7441	0.6756	0.6139	0.5584	0.5083	0.4632	0.4224	0.3855	0.3522	0.3220	0.2946	0.2697	0.2472
11	0.8963	0.8043	0.7224	0.6496	0.5847	0.5268	0.4751	0.4289	0.3875	0.3505	0.3173	0.2875	0.2607	0.2366	0.2149
12	0.8874	0.7885	0.7014	0.6246	0.5568	0.4970	0.4440	0.3971	0.3555	0.3186	0.2858	0.2567	0.2307	0.2076	0.1869
13	0.8787	0.7730	0.6810	0.6006	0.5303	0.4688	0.4150	0.3677	0.3262	0.2897	0.2575	0.2292	0.2042	0.1821	0.1625
14	0.8700	0.7579	0.6611	0.5775	0.5051	0.4423	0.3878	0.3405	0.2992	0.2633	0.2320	0.2046	0.1807	0.1597	0.1413
15	0.8613	0.7430	0.6419	0.5553	0.4810	0.4173	0.3624	0.3152	0.2745	0.2394	0.2090	0.1827	0.1599	0.1401	0.1229
16	0.8528	0.7284	0.6232	0.5339	0.4581	0.3936	0.3387	0.2919	0.2519	0.2176	0.1883	0.1631	0.1415	0.1229	0.1069
17	0.8444	0.7142	0.6050	0.5134	0.4363	0.3714	0.3166	0.2703	0.2311	0.1978	0.1696	0.1456	0.1252	0.1078	0.0929
18	0.8360	0.7002	0.5874	0.4936	0.4155	0.3503	0.2959	0.2502	0.2120	0.1799	0.1528	0.1300	0.1108	0.0946	0.0808
19	0.8277	0.6864	0.5703	0.4746	0.3957	0.3305	0.2765	0.2317	0.1945	0.1635	0.1377	0.1161	0.0981	0.0829	0.0703
20	0.8195	0.6730	0.5537	0.4564	0.3769	0.3118	0.2584	0.2145	0.1784	0.1486	0.1240	0.1037	0.0868	0.0728	0.0611
21	0.8114	0.6598	0.5375	0.4388	0.3589	0.2942	0.2415	0.1987	0.1637	0.1351	0.1117	0.0926	0.0768	0.0638	0.0531
22	0.8034	0.6468	0.5219	0.4220	0.3418	0.2775	0.2257	0.1839	0.1502	0.1228	0.1007	0.0826	0.0680	0.0560	0.0462
23	0.7954	0.6342	0.5067	0.4057	0.3256	0.2618	0.2109	0.1703	0.1378	0.1117	0.0907	0.0738	0.0601	0.0491	0.0402
24	0.7876	0.6217	0.4919	0.3901	0.3101	0.2470	0.1971	0.1577	0.1264	0.1015	0.0817	0.0659	0.0532	0.0431	0.0349
25	0.7798	0.6095	0.4776	0.3751	0.2953	0.2330	0.1842	0.1460	0.1160	0.0923	0.0736	0.0588	0.0471	0.0378	0.0304
26	0.7720	0.5976	0.4637	0.3607	0.2812	0.2198	0.1722	0.1352	0.1064	0.0839	0.0663	0.0525	0.0417	0.0331	0.0264
27	0.7644	0.5859	0.4502	0.3468	0.2678	0.2074	0.1609	0.1252	0.0976	0.0763	0.0597	0.0469	0.0369	0.0291	0.0230
28	0.7568	0.5744	0.4371	0.3335	0.2551	0.1956	0.1504	0.1159	0.0895	0.0693	0.0538	0.0419	0.0326	0.0255	0.0200
29	0.7493	0.5631	0.4243	0.3207	0.2429	0.1846	0.1406	0.1073	0.0822	0.0630	0.0485	0.0374	0.0289	0.0224	0.0174
30	0.7419	0.5521	0.4120	0.3083	0.2314	0.1741	0.1314	0.0994	0.0754	0.0573	0.0437	0.0334	0.0256	0.0196	0.0151
35	0.7059	0.5000	0.3554	0.2534	0.1813	0.1301	0.0937	0.0676	0.0490	0.0356	0.0259	0.0189	0.0139	0.0102	0.0075
40	0.6717	0.4529	0.3066	0.2083	0.1420	0.0972	0.0668	0.0460	0.0318	0.0221	0.0154	0.0107	0.0075	0.0053	0.0037
45	0.6391	0.4102	0.2644	0.1712	0.1113	0.0727	0.0476	0.0313	0.0207	0.0137	0.0091	0.0061	0.0041	0.0027	0.0019
50	0.6080	0.3715	0.2281	0.1407	0.0872	0.0543	0.0339	0.0213	0.0134	0.0085	0.0054	0.0035	0.0022	0.0014	0.0009

Appendix Table 4.2 Future Value of $1 at Annual Rate r% for n Years, $(1 + r)^n$

n	1%	2%	3%	4%	5%	6%	7%	8%	9%	10%	12%	14%	15%	16%	18%	20%
1	1.010	1.020	1.030	1.040	1.050	1.060	1.070	1.080	1.090	1.100	1.120	1.140	1.150	1.160	1.180	1.200
2	1.020	1.040	1.061	1.082	1.102	1.124	1.145	1.166	1.188	1.210	1.254	1.300	1.322	1.346	1.392	1.440
3	1.030	1.061	1.093	1.125	1.158	1.191	1.225	1.260	1.295	1.331	1.405	1.482	1.521	1.561	1.643	1.728
4	1.041	1.082	1.126	1.170	1.216	1.262	1.311	1.360	1.412	1.464	1.574	1.689	1.749	1.811	1.939	2.074
5	1.051	1.104	1.159	1.217	1.276	1.338	1.403	1.469	1.539	1.611	1.762	1.925	2.011	2.100	2.288	2.488
6	1.062	1.126	1.194	1.265	1.340	1.419	1.501	1.587	1.677	1.772	1.974	2.195	2.313	2.436	2.700	2.986
7	1.072	1.149	1.230	1.316	1.407	1.504	1.606	1.714	1.828	1.949	2.211	2.502	2.660	2.826	3.185	3.583
8	1.083	1.172	1.267	1.369	1.477	1.594	1.718	1.851	1.993	2.144	2.476	2.853	3.059	3.278	3.759	4.300
9	1.094	1.195	1.305	1.423	1.551	1.689	1.838	1.999	2.172	2.358	2.773	3.252	3.518	3.803	4.435	5.160
10	1.105	1.219	1.344	1.480	1.629	1.791	1.967	2.159	2.367	2.594	3.106	3.707	4.046	4.411	5.234	6.192
11	1.116	1.243	1.384	1.539	1.710	1.898	2.105	2.332	2.580	2.853	3.479	4.226	4.652	5.117	6.176	7.430
12	1.127	1.268	1.426	1.601	1.796	2.012	2.252	2.518	2.813	3.138	3.896	4.818	5.350	5.936	7.288	8.916
13	1.138	1.294	1.469	1.665	1.886	2.133	2.410	2.720	3.066	3.452	4.363	5.492	6.153	6.886	8.599	10.699
14	1.149	1.319	1.513	1.732	1.980	2.261	2.579	2.937	3.342	3.797	4.887	6.261	7.076	7.988	10.147	12.839
15	1.161	1.346	1.558	1.801	2.079	2.397	2.759	3.172	3.642	4.177	5.474	7.138	8.137	9.266	11.974	15.407
16	1.173	1.373	1.605	1.873	2.183	2.540	2.952	3.426	3.970	4.595	6.130	8.137	9.358	10.748	14.129	18.488
17	1.184	1.400	1.653	1.948	2.292	2.693	3.159	3.700	4.328	5.054	6.866	9.276	10.761	12.468	16.672	22.186
18	1.196	1.428	1.702	2.026	2.407	2.854	3.380	3.996	4.717	5.560	7.690	10.575	12.375	14.463	19.673	26.623
19	1.208	1.457	1.754	2.107	2.527	3.026	3.617	4.316	5.142	6.116	8.613	12.056	14.232	16.777	23.214	31.948
20	1.220	1.486	1.806	2.191	2.653	3.207	3.870	4.661	5.604	6.728	9.646	13.743	16.367	19.461	27.393	38.338

A Deductive System for Probability and Some Applications

5

5.1 Introduction

In section 1.4, and again in the appendixes to chapter 2, we discussed the design of an MIS (management information system) made up of four sets: D (your possible decisions), S (states of the world), O (outcomes), and W (payoffs). The usefulness of this MIS depended very strongly on what assumptions you could legitimately make, especially regarding how members of O are caused by the members of D and S. In the last chapter we examined the case where O is stretched out over periods of time, but where each occurrence is entirely predictable, given your decision to invest, buy, not buy, and so on.

In this chapter we will be examining problems in which *uncertainty* plays a role. To help prepare for this long journey, keep in mind that we are operating under one very strong assumption: namely, that either

a. you are given information about how the states of the world S are generated, from which you can deduce the chances that any state of the world s will occur; or

b. you know outright the chances that each state of the world s will occur.

In other words, you can always find or are given the probability of each s. To see when this assumption holds, and when it doesn't, compare two situations, one where you are playing a game of poker or bridge with friends, and the other where you are wandering about a county fair. In the friendly game of bridge, it may become critical for you to guess which of two players has the king of spades (which of two states of the world occurs); you have no other information about this other than the assumption you are quite willing to make that the cards were dealt fairly. From this assumption you can deduce that the chance that a specific player holds the king of spades is 1/2. On this basis you may decide how to play your cards, since for each choice you can deduce the probability (chances) of success or failure. But now imagine that you are wandering about a county fair, and there is a table on which this character throws eight pennies, and they all come up heads! He says to you, "Hey, kiddo, want to bet a buck I can't do the same thing again?" If you think deductively, you might deduce that he'd offered you an easy chance to "make the most of it." If the toss is fair, the probability of getting eight heads is very small; as we'll soon see, it's 1 over 2 raised to the 8th power, or 1/256. Your chances of winning are therefore 255/256, or virtual certainty. But if you have any sense, you will think again about taking the bet, because you'll figure perhaps the coins were all biased to turn up heads. In other words, you'll think about a state of the world (all heads) and try to guess what process might have generated it; you'll pass from the states of the world back to guesses about their probability.

When, as in the friendly game, you know or can find the probability of any s, the quantitative methods are designed to go from knowledge or assumptions about D and S to conclusions about O, and hence are primarily deductive; when you go from experience or observation about O back to estimates about S, the process is primarily inductive. When we question whether a given D, S, O, and W are sufficient for an adequate definition of the problem, we ask questions at a higher or broader level—that is, we ask systemic questions.

Now, even though the deductive applications of the D, S, O, W MIS are limited, the design of such an MIS will be very useful in understanding the inductive process as well. If you know the pathways from D and S to O, then you'll have a map to help you in the reverse direction when you come to decisions involving induction. Hence your best preparation for the details of this chapter is to appreciate the broader implications of the deductive quantitative methods, even when the examples seem quite limited or contrived.

Also, you should realize that each detail by itself is not nearly as important as the basic logic that permits us to justify the technique in back of the detailed example. This basic logic always deals with the structure of the sets S and O and your relation to them. We will generate a much more detailed description of the states of the world and outcomes than we did in chapter 1 or 2; but in each case we will assume, as we did then, that a given state of the world coupled with a given decision will cause a unique outcome. This is what scientists sometimes call a "closed system," to indicate that no additional information is needed to account for what is going on. However, your relation to the states of the world is that you most often don't know which has occurred. But you have, as we stated, some very important information about S; namely, the probabilities of the occurrence of its members.

The idea of using probabilities in describing the world seems first to have been explored by Carneades, who flourished in Greece in the fourth century B.C. Carneades argued that nothing about the world is known with certainty, but nevertheless we often make "appropriate" judgments. The words "appropriate" and "probability" have the same roots in our language, and the deductive probabilistic MIS is basically an information system made up of appropriate judgements.

Our first task, in developing a deductive system of probabilities, is to refine the description of S (and hence of O), as we do in the next section.

PROBLEMS 5.1

1. How does the weather service determine the probability of rain?

2. How did you determine the probabilities of "winning" and "not winning" in the Lottery problem of chapter 1?

3. Is there a difference in the methods used in problems 1 and 2?

4. What is the probability of a head in a toss of one fair coin? What are the probabilities of "all heads" in a toss of two fair coins? three fair coins? four fair coins?

5. One morning you arrive at your auto shop and find three of your best customers waiting for service. They are in a hurry and insist on being served early. You have no information about the order of their appearance so you decide to give each one of them an equal chance to be serviced first, second, or third. How can you accomplish it? *Hint:* Recall the auto shop example in section 1.6.

6. In a game of craps the number 7 can be obtained by various combinations of certain sides of two six-sided dice. What is the chance of 7 showing, if every side of each dice has an equal probability? Will your answer change if you know that one die has the number 5 on two sides and no number 3?

5.2 Some Primitive Notions for Probability

It will help you to understand the method of describing the set of states of the world if you keep in mind the "friendly game," where you can safely assume that everything is happening fairly and no one is cheating. For the moment, we'll restrict our attention to coins, dice, or cards. Suppose the game is the simple one of tossing three coins and betting on the result. We need to consider two closely connected aspects of the situation: What can happen to each individual coin and what can happen to all three together. We call the first an *atomic event* and the second an *elementary event*. This distinction, as you shall see, is solely a matter of convenience in computing probabilities.

We assume all along that the coins can be identified as first, second, and third. For each coin there are two possible *atomic* events, heads (H) and tails (T). If the game is fair, you can assume that the probability of either atomic event is 1/2. A little patience will reveal that there are eight *elementary* events: HHH, HHT, HTH, THH, HTT, THT, TTH, and TTT. Here again, if the game is fair, you can assume that the probability of each of these elementary events is 1/8. At least this much should seem reasonable to you, and in the next section we'll establish the reasonableness by means of a deductive system. For the moment, however, we can safely rely on your common sense to see again how probabilities work in our MIS.

Problem: A Friendly Bet ————————————————

Your friend offers you the following choice: He will flip three coins and you are free to choose in advance from the three bets below, with the payoffs as listed. What is your "best bet"?

Bet (decision)	If you win, you get	If you lose, you must pay
1. exactly 2 heads	$2	$1
2. at least 2 heads	$2	$2
3. all heads	$5	$1

Analysis: Of course, you can refuse to play. Hence, D is 1, 2, 3, and 4, where 4 = no bet. You can define S as having *eight* states of the world, one for each elementary event. In that case, the outcome and payoff tables have 32 combinations of decisions and states of the world; to illustrate, the payoff table is depicted in table 5.1.

Recall that you read the payoff table as follows: if you choose d_1 (that is, you bet "exactly two heads") and s_1 turns out to be the state of the world (that is, HHH appears), then your payoff is $\$-1$. If you choose d_3 and s_1 obtains, you win $5.

Each of the states of the world has probability 1/8 since the coin is fair, and you can use the table to find the decision with the highest expected payoff. You should recall from chapter 1 how to calculate expected payoff: by multiplying, for each decision, the payoffs by their

TABLE 5.1   A Payoff Table for Your Betting Decision in Dollars

DECISION	STATE OF THE WORLD							
	HHH s_1	HHT s_2	HTH s_3	HTT s_4	THH s_5	THT s_6	TTH s_7	TTT s_8
d_1	$\$-1$	$\$2$	$\$2$	$\$-1$	$\$2$	$\$-1$	$\$-1$	$\$-1$
d_2	$\$2$	$\$2$	$\$2$	$\$-2$	$\$2$	$\$-2$	$\$-2$	$\$-2$
d_3	$\$5$	$\$-1$	$\$-1$	$\$-1$	$\$-1$	$\$-1$	$\$-1$	$\$-1$
d_4	$\$0$	$\$0$	$\$0$	$\$0$	$\$0$	$\$0$	$\$0$	$\$0$

respective probabilities, and then summing up these products to yield the expected payoff for that decision. For d_1 the expected payoff is $.125, for d_2 it is $0, for d_3 it is $-.25, and for d_4 it is, of course, $0. Therefore, you would choose the first bet *if* your sole aim is to maximize expected payoff.

━━━━━━━━━━

Notice, however, that you could have effectively combined the elementary events in a fashion more sensible for each decision. When we do so, we call such a combination a *compound event*. For example, "at least two heads" is made up of the combination of elementary events HHH, HHT, HTH, and THH. The probability of this compound event is calculated as the sum of the four elementary events; thus, the probability of the compound event "at least two heads" is 1/2. So for d_2 the probability of winning is 1/2, as is the probability of losing. Accordingly, you could have calculated the expected payoff using only these compound events:

$$\tfrac{1}{2} \times (\$2) + \tfrac{1}{2} \times (\$-2) = \$0$$

You can often avoid the complexity of displaying all the elementary events by thinking in terms of the relevant compound events. *You can do this whenever several different elementary events give rise to the same outcome for a given decision.* There are some fairly simple rules, to which we will soon turn, that allow you to calculate the probabilities of these compound events without resort to listing and counting all the elementary events.

You can see the usefulness of these rules if you consider a coin betting problem involving 10 coins. The method of displaying all the elementary events as states of the world quickly becomes cumbersome since there are $2^{10} = 1024$ such states of the world.

As another example, consider a pair of dice. Would you make an even bet (for example, get $1 if you win, pay $1 if you lose) on throwing a seven or an eleven? In this case, we say that each side of a single die is an *atomic* event: [⚀], [⚁], [⚂], [⚃], [⚄], [⚅] ; six possible atomic events can occur in *one* toss of one die. For two dice, the set of *elementary* events is [⚀][⚀], [⚀][⚁], [⚀][⚂] . . . , [⚅][⚅] 36 in number. It's feasible but tedious to list all these; if you do, you'll find that there are six ways of getting a seven:

[⚅][⚀], [⚄][⚁], [⚃][⚂], [⚀][⚅], [⚁][⚄], [⚂][⚃]

and similarly, exactly *two* ways of getting an eleven. In other words, there are *eight* ways of winning and hence $36 - 8 = 28$ ways of losing. Since winning and losing are the two relevant outcomes, you can think in terms of only two compound events, "seven or eleven in a single throw of a pair of dice" and "neither seven nor eleven," instead of 36 elementary events. Obviously, it would be useful to be able to calculate the probabilities of these compound events independently of listing all the elementary events. Quantitative methods that aid us in such calculations are the subject matter of this chapter.

But first we need to make clear some of the things we have been doing in the examples given above. Otherwise, you may very well fall into some bad traps. We've been adding, subtracting, and multiplying as though we knew exactly when these operations are appropriate. But consider this friendly offer. I have five cards which I lay face down on the table; they are the ace, king, queen, jack, and 10 of spades. I give you five chances to pick up the ace, each time shuffling the five cards fairly and laying them out again. If you pick up the ace in any of the five tries, you win $1. If you fail to pick up the ace in the five tries, you must pay me $5. Is this a good bet? If you're not careful, you may say to yourself "the probability of picking the ace on the first try is 1/5, and hence in five tries it should be $1/5 + 1/5 + 1/5 + 1/5 + 1/5 = 1$. So how can I lose?" This would be very faulty reasoning, as you'd find out if you accepted the bet. Of course, you can lose, namely, by *failing* to pick up the ace five times in a row; this is unlikely, to be sure, but not impossible. In fact, as you'll see, it happens with a probability of about 1/3. Hence your expected payoff is $\$1(2/3) - \$5(1/3) = \$-1$, not a very appetizing payoff.

Therefore we must specify exactly when you can add or multiply probabilities, if the quantitative methods presented in this chapter are to be of aid to you in preparing for decisions. This means we must explain the deductive system of probabilities that forms the basis for using these methods.

PROBLEMS 5.2

1. Two fair coins are flipped.

    a. What are the atomic events here? How many are there?
    b. What are the elementary events? How many are there?
    c. What is the probability of each of the following events:
        i at least one tail   ii at least one head
        iii at most one head   iv exactly two tails
        v all heads   vi no heads

2. What would be your answers to parts (a), (b), (c) of problem 1 if four fair coins are flipped?

3. What would be your "best bet" in the Friendly Bet problem in this section if four coins were flipped?

4. A lottery ticket is held and each ticket is identified by a unique five-digit number. Each digit is a whole number between zero and four, inclusive.
    a. How many *different* lottery tickets can be printed?
    b. In this lottery what are the atomic events? How many are there?
    c. What is an elementary event? How many are there?
    d. What is the probability that the winning ticket (there is only one prize) starts with the number 4?
    e. What is the probability that the winning ticket starts with the number 40?

5. Your entrance ticket to the county fair entitles you to participate once in a dice game. There are two games for you to choose from. One involves two fair dice and you win $1 if either a 2 or 12 appears. In the other, three dice are thrown and if 3 or 11 appear, you win $10. Which game do you prefer? (Try the prescription of "making the most expected gain you can.")

6. Your friend offers you the following choice: He will flip a fair coin and a fair die and add up the outcomes (heads is considered 0 and tails 1). If 7 occurs you receive $6; if 4 is the total that shows up, you get $3. Otherwise you must pay him $2. Should you take the bet?

5.3   A Deductive System for Probability

5.3.1   Basic Ideas and Definitions   The examples just discussed indicate the two *basic ideas* of a deductive system for probability: atomic events (like H in a toss of a coin) and elementary events which describe the states of the world (as in HTH in the toss of three coins). We can note that S is in a sense a *universe of discourse* (appendix 2.1), since it represents all possible states of the world that are relevant to the decision we are about to make. We note, too, that the elementary events are generated by allowing the atomic events to take on all possibilities. If two coins are tossed, there are two possibilities for each coin, H and T, and hence four possible elementary events, $e_1 = HH$, $e_2 = HT$, $e_3 = TH$, and $e_4 = TT$.

Our chief interest is in calculating the probabilities of *compound events*, which, as we said, are constructed by combining elementary events. In the example of two coins, we can generate the following compound events (as well as others):

not e_1 (at least one T appears)*

e_1 or e_4 (both coins will be alike)

e_3 and e_4 (the impossible or null event)

5.3.2 Assumptions We can begin our *assumptions* about probability with the fairly obvious notion that probability measures range from absolute impossibility up to certainty. We let the corresponding measure of probability range from 0 (zero), which means that the event is impossible, to 1, which means that it is certain. If we let $P(E)$ stand for the probability of an event E (elementary or compound), then our first assumptions read:

ASSUMPTION 1   If an event E cannot occur, then the probability of E, $P(E)$, is zero.

For example, the probability of three heads in two tosses of a coin is zero. The probability of $E = (e_3$ and e_4 *both* occur) above was zero.

ASSUMPTION 2   If the event E must occur, then $P(E) = 1$.

For example, if there are four elementary events, then $P(e_1$ or e_2 or e_3 or $e_4) = 1$.

Now we can turn to events whose probabilities lie between zero and one. As a first step, suppose two events, elementary or compound, are mutually exclusive, meaning that they could not possibly occur together (for example, HH and HT).† What is the probability that one or the other will occur? We see that for HH and HT in a toss of two fair coins, the answer is 1/2, since HH and HT are exactly one-half of the possible elementary events. We are, in a sense, "adding" the two exclusive events together, and this is the basis of the following assumption.

ASSUMPTION 3   If A and B are mutually exclusive events (elementary or compound), then $P(A$ or $B) = P(A) + P(B)$.

We can readily see that the same assumption applies to three, four, or any number of exclusive events: The probability that any one of them will occur is simply the sum of the probabilities of each one.

---

*For those of you who studied appendix 2.1, we construct compound events from elementary events by using the Boolean operators $\sim$, $\cap$, $\cup$; for example, $\sim e_1$, "not e_1," is "at least one T appears."

†See appendix 2.1 for a discussion of mutually exclusive sets.

In order to use assumption 3, we need to put some numbers besides 0 and 1 into the system. This can be done by means of the implicit
assumption we made in the examples at the beginning of this chapter—
namely, that the elementary events all have the same probability. This
assumption is not necessary for a deductive system of probability, but
it is a reasonable one to make in games that are "fair," for example.
Hence, we won't introduce it as a formal assumption of the system but
will assume it for convenience for the time being. It now follows from
this convenient assumption that if there are n elementary events, each
of which has an equal chance of occurring, then the probability that
any one of them will occur is $1/n$.

Assumption 3, together with the equiprobable assumption, already
gets us some mileage. Suppose you want to bet that heads will appear
at least once in tossing two fair coins. Should the bet be even, or what?
The question can readily be answered, since "at least one head" means
"either HH or HT or TH." But HH, HT, and TH are mutually exclusive
events, each having a probability of 1/4 since for two coins there are
four elementary events. Hence the answer (by assumption 3) is 1/4
+ 1/4 + 1/4 = 3/4.

You could have obtained this same answer by introducing a consequence (theorem) of the assumptions made thus far:

THEOREM 1 $P(\text{not } A) = 1 - P(A)$ for any event A, elementary or
compound.

Thus $P(\text{at least one head in two tosses}) = P(\text{not TT}) = 1 - P(\text{TT})$
$= 1 - 1/4 = 3/4$.

We can now go back to the treacherous card game (getting the ace
at least once in five tries, using five cards). How should your chances
of winning be calculated? Well, adding the probabilities of getting an
ace on any given try (1/5) is *not* sanctioned by assumption 3, because
whatever happens on the first attempt clearly does not exclude any
result on the second attempt; the fact that you got a king on the first
try doesn't tell you anything about what you can or can't get on the
second try, since the cards are shuffled each time.

In order to handle this kind of problem, you need to calculate probabilities of two or more events which take place *independently* of each
other, as in reshuffling the cards and making a new attempt. Or, as
another example, my success or failure at cards tonight would seem to
have very little to do with your success or failure with a slot machine
in Las Vegas. This is pretty tricky ground, of course, because all events
that could conceivably take place may be linked in mysterious and
deeply hidden ways. Some experts, for example, think that there are
persons who have "extrasensory perception," so that they can perceive
how cards are being dealt in a completely separate room; the skeptics

argue that the two events, the card deal and the subject's guesses, are independent, and have no linkages unless someone is cheating.

The idea of *dependence* and *independence* is one of the basic ideas of our decision-making lives. We have been using the idea frequently in this text, as we explored the consequences of certain assumptions we were willing to make. And we will keep coming back to the idea frequently as we proceed. Right now we can notice a rather obvious application to the present topic, by observing that our uncertainties often change *given* that certain events have occurred. For example, if I draw a card from a 52-card deck and truthfully tell you that it's a black card, I've done something to your uncertainty about the card. Without the information, the card could be any one of 52 cards; with the information it is any one of 26 cards, since half the cards are red and half black. But suppose I'm about to toss a coin, and tell you truthfully that the last time I tossed that coin it came up heads. It's reasonable to assume that this is irrelevant with respect to what will happen on the coming toss; that is, what I tell you doesn't change your uncertainty. In the card-drawing case we say that the events "the card is black" and "the card is the king of spades" are dependent, while in the coin-tossing case we say that the events "heads on the first toss" and "tails on the second toss" are independent.

Now let us see how you can use the idea of dependence and independence of events. What is the probability of throwing two sixes with a pair of dice? It is reasonable to assume that what happens on one die is independent of what happens on the other die. The probability of a 6 on the first die is 1/6. Even if the first die does turn up a 6, the second can still be a 1, 2, 3, 4, 5, or 6 with equal chances, since the events are independent. So the 1/6 chance of a 6 for the first die has to be distributed over the six possibilities of the second. This reasoning suggests that we multiply the two probabilities together, $1/6 \times 1/6 = 1/36$, to calculate the probability that *both* the independent events occur.

ASSUMPTION 4   If two events (elementary or compound) are *independent*, then the probability that they *both* occur is the multiplication of their respective probabilities.

Thus, if $P(E_1)$ is the probability that event E_1 will occur, and $P(E_2)$ is the probability that a second event E_2 will occur, then $P(E_1) \times P(E_2)$ is the probability that they will both occur *if* the two events are independent.

Suppose now you go back to the offer to bet on getting the ace at least once in five tries with five cards. Since the deck is shuffled each time, it is reasonable to assume that what occurs on each try is independent of what occurs on other tries. But how do you use this idea to help decide on what should be bet? Well, what are the events that you're interested in? Getting an ace at least once, in which case you win, *and* never getting an ace in five trials, in which case you lose. There are lots of ways in which the first of these could happen, but there is only one way the second could occur, namely, "not-ace" five times in a row. How likely is "not-ace" five times in a row? The probability of "not-ace" on the first try is 4/5, since the probability of "ace" is 1/5 (see theorem 1 above). But the events are independent. Hence the probability of "not-ace" twice in a row is $4/5 \times 4/5 = 16/25$. By the same reasoning the probability of "not-ace" five times in a row is $4/5 \times 4/5 \times 4/5 \times 4/5 \times 4/5$; if we use "power notation" it is $(4/5)^5$, which is approximately 1/3. In other words, the probability that you will lose the bet is (about) 1/3, and hence the probability that you will win it is 2/3.

We can immediately derive a practical application of this lesson in probability.

Problem: Forbe's Electric Light Company ▬▬▬▬▬▬▬▬▬

Suppose you manufacture electric light bulbs and wish to determine whether a lot of 10,000 light bulbs has a significant number of defects. You could, of course, examine every one, but this might be far too costly. Instead, you decide to sample 100 bulbs and test these. You find no defects in the sample. Now you'd be very unhappy if the total lot of 10,000 had as many as 1% defects. *Could* the lot have 1% defects and yet none occur in a sample of 100?

Analysis: This is exactly like the ace-drawing example. Could you altogether miss a defect in 100 tries? If the sample is drawn "fairly," the probability of a defect being found on any try is 1/100, assuming that the lot is 1% defective. Therefore, the probability of *not* finding a defect is 99/100. Since what happens on one tested bulb is presumably independent of what happens on any other, the events are independent. Hence the answer to the question "What is the probability of missing a defect 100 times in a row?" is obtained by multiplying 99/100 by itself 100 times: $(99/100)^{100}$. This could be pretty tedious, but you may recall how to use logarithms to help you;* the result is .364. You therefore may not feel very comfortable with a sample of 100, because even if no defects occur, there is still a real chance that the lot is 1% defective.

▬▬▬▬▬▬▬▬▬▬▬▬▬▬▬▬▬▬▬▬▬▬▬▬▬▬▬▬▬▬▬▬▬▬▬▬▬▬▬

Since we are dealing here with a fairly simple formulation of probabilities, we have presented the rule of multiplication in terms of independent events. But in the more complicated real world of decision

---

*Using logarithms: $\log 99 = 1.9956$; $\log 100 = 2$; $100(1.9956 - 2) = -.44$; antilog $(-.44) \approx .364$.

making, most of the relevant events you face are dependent, and later on in chapter 8 we'll discuss some techniques for calculating probabilities of dependent events (often called *conditional probabilities*). It's worth noting here two closely related ways in which dependent events arise. One way occurs when knowledge of one event cuts down on the possibilities of the second. This happened when we told you the card drawn from the bridge deck was black; the information cut the possibilities of the specific value of the card in half. The second way occurs when one event is a cause or partial cause of the second. We know that cancer often causes death; hence if someone has cancer, the probability of his dying is greater than it is if he is in good health.

To summarize what you have learned from this deductive system: For the time being we assume that the probabilities of n elementary events are each equal to $1/n$; you can *add* probabilities of mutually exclusive events; you can *multiply* probabilities of independent events. Simple as these assumptions are, they enable you to calculate rather complicated-looking probabilities; for example, the probability of making a point in a game of dice, of filling a bobtail straight in poker, of finessing successfully in bridge. If you don't gamble, or play cards for fun, still the system may help you guess the probability of rain three days in a row in your region in a given month, or of you and your spouse dying on the same day (note that because you live together the events are not independent), and, most important for our practical decision-making purposes, the probabilities of shipping defective consumer items or of your purchasing such items.

Nevertheless, because the system is fairly simple, its use will have to be restricted to situations where you believe you can make safe categorical assumptions about the probabilities of atomic or elementary events. But, for practical management purposes, the system provides rich ways of exploring hypothetical assumptions, as we did above in the case of inspection of light bulbs: what *if* the probability of such-and-such an event is p; am I then likely to make such-and-such a mistake?

PROBLEMS 5.3

1. Can all past events be considered to be known with certainty to a decision maker?

2. "It's possible but improbable" is a widely used phrase. What is the difference between "possible" and "probable" in terms of the assumptions of probability?

3. Explain the underlying assumptions you made in obtaining the probabilities in problems (a) 4, section 5.1, (b) 5, section 5.1, (c) 1, section 5.2, (d) 5, section 5.2.

4. As the owner of a beer concession at the neighborhood ball park you must make a decision every Sunday on how many vendors to hire for the day's sales. One relevant factor in the preparation for the weekly decision is the weather. So, prior to every Sunday, you try to obtain probability information about the possible weather states. You distinguish between wet and dry weather. You subdivide the category "wet" into snow, freezing rain, and rain, and the "dry" condition into sunny and cloudy.

   a. You have received the new weather report for the coming Sunday indicating the probability of snow to be .01, that of freezing rain to be .05, and rain .2. Also, you know the probability of cloudy sky to be .3. What is the probability of next Sunday being sunny?

   b. You know that in addition to the weather, the winning position of the home team is an important, though independent, factor in determining your profits. There are three winning categories that prove worth paying attention to: The home team leads in the first half, the home team trails in the first half, and a tie position exists in the first half. For the coming Sunday's game you assess the probabilities of these three possibilities to be .4, .1, and .5, respectively. List all the states of the world which affect your Sunday profits. Note that each state is a combination of weather conditions and the winning position.

5.4 Calculating Probabilities: Quantitative Methods for Counting

We begin the development of computational rules for calculating probabilities by noting that if we make the assumption that the elementary events are equiprobable, then the knowledge of the total number n of elementary events in S is the key to our calculations. Under the equiprobable assumption, the probability of each elementary event is $1/n$. So we shall turn our attention now to obtaining n, and hence $1/n$.

5.4.1 Independent Atomic Events Going back to our flipped coin or thrown die, assume that each toss is independent of any previous toss. You can readily see that for a flip of two coins there are four elementary events ($n = 4$), for three coins $n = 8$, and if you try it for four coins, you'll find that $n = 16$. Your hunch should be that as the number of coins, k, increases, n also increases as the powers of 2, since 2 is the number of atomic events associated with each coin. Thus $n = 2$ if there is one coin ($k = 1$), $n = 2^2$ if $k = 2$, $n = 2^3 = 8$ if $k = 3$, and so on. So we have a way of calculating n for any number of coins.

Now consider a die of six faces. Here the number of atomic events is 6 ($n = 6, k = 1$). If two dice are thrown ($k = 2$), the number of elementary events is $36 = 6^2$, as you have seen. If three dice are thrown ($k = 3$), $n = 6^3 = 216$, and so on. The underlying rule can be stated as follows.

RULE 1   a. Suppose an elementary event is made up of k atomic events, each of which can happen in m different ways (for example, $m = 2$ for a coin, $m = 6$ for a die), then the number n of elementary events in S is:

$$n = m^k$$

b. It follows that if the atomic events in part (a) are equiprobable, then the probability of each elementary event is:

$$1/n = 1/m^k$$

Thus if you spin a dial with 10 places marked on it from 1 to 10, how many different results could you get in two tries? Here $m = 10$, $k = 2$, $n = 100$ (not surprisingly!), and the probability of any number pair (for example, a 3 followed by a 6) is 1/100.

Now suppose we use this rule to analyze a betting problem.

Problem: Tossing a Fair Coin

A very reliable friend offers you the following bet: A fair coin will be tossed three times. If three tails in a row occur, you get $8, and if the compound event "at least two heads in a row" occurs, you get $4. If anything else happens you lose the $2 you pay to play the game. Should you take the bet?

Analysis: This problem is similar to the Friendly Bet problem of section 5.2, but now we can be more precise in our analysis. Assume, as we did in chapter 1, that you are indifferent between an expected dollar and a sure dollar, and that your objective is to make as many dollars as you can. Then your task is to compute the expected value of the bet, for which you need to know the probabilities of the three relevant events: (1) three tails in a row, (2) at least two heads in a row, and (3) neither of these (you lose). Each event is associated with a different payoff.

Rule 1 tells you that there are eight equiprobable elementary events; since $m = 2$ and $k = 3$: $2^3 = 8$. Therefore each elementary event has a probability of 1/8 by the equiprobability assumption. So to obtain the required probabilities you can count the number of elementary events in each of the relevant compound events. The relevant information is shown in figure 5.1. You can see that the event "three tails in a row" consists of only one elementary event (TTT) and therefore its probability is 1/8. The event "at least two heads in a row" is composed of three elementary events (HHH, HHT, THH), implying that its probability is $3 \times 1/8 = 3/8$. (Remember, by assumption 3 you can add the probabilities of mutually exclusive events.) Also the probability of event 3 is 4/8, since it is composed of 4 (mutually exclusive) elementary events. Or, you could arrive at the same result by noting that the probability of (1) TTT or (2) "2 heads in a row" is $1/8 + 3/8 = 4/8$, and hence the probability that (1) or (2) will *not* occur is $1 - 4/8 = 4/8$.

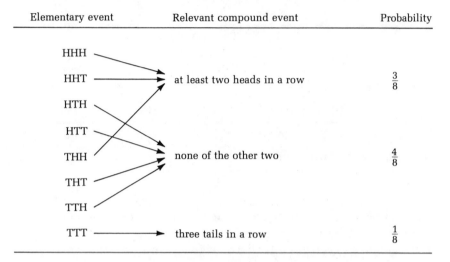

Elementary event	Relevant compound event	Probability

Figure 5.1   Probabilities of Relevant Compound Events

Using the probabilities of the *compound* events, you can now compute directly the expected value of the decision to bet:

$$(\$8 - \$2) \times \frac{1}{8} + (\$4 - \$2) \times \frac{3}{8} + (\$0 - \$2) \times \frac{4}{8} = \$.50$$

Comparing this to the $0 expected return if you don't bet, you accept the bet happily.

Let us see exactly what you did in terms of our old friend, the MIS of chapters 1 and 2. The elementary events are the states of the world, and since there are 8 equiprobable elementary events, the probability of any state of the world is 1/8. Given these probabilities, you calculated the probabilities of three compound events. Each of these compound events represented a distinct outcome. You then multiplied the probabilities of each compound event (outcome) by the associated *payoff* to get the expected value of the decision to bet. If you had calculated directly from the familiar MIS table instead, the payoff table would have looked like table 5.2, and the expected value of the decision to bet would have been calculated as:

$$\$2 \times \frac{1}{8} + \$2 \times \frac{1}{8} - \$2 \times \frac{1}{8} - \$2 \times \frac{1}{8} + \$2 \times \frac{1}{8} - \$2 \times \frac{1}{8} - \$2 \times \frac{1}{8} + \$6$$

$$\times \frac{1}{8} = \$.50$$

TABLE 5.2   Payoff Table

DECISION	STATE OF THE WORLD							
	$s_1 =$ HHH	$s_2 =$ HHT	$s_3 =$ HTH	$s_4 =$ HTT	$s_5 =$ THH	$s_6 =$ THT	$s_7 =$ TTH	$s_8 =$ TTT
$d_1 =$ bet	$2	$2	−$2	−$2	$2	−$2	−$2	$6
$d_2 =$ don't bet	0	0	0	0	0	0	0	0

You can use the same reasoning on a dice game, by deciding whether or not to accept the following offer from your reliable friend: He will toss three fair dice and if three sixes show up, he will pay you $200. Otherwise you pay $2. This one is easy since you know that $n = 6^3 = 216$ from rule 1, and that three sixes can occur in only one way. Hence the probability of winning is 1/216, and the expected payoff is $(200) \times (1/216)$, or less than one dollar. Don't play but be polite; after all, your friend may not know probability theory as well as you do! Now suppose we examine a somewhat more complicated situation.

Problem: A Die and a Coin ———————————————

Your reliable friend comes up with a new offer: He will toss a fair die *and* a fair coin and if 6 and H appear, he will pay you $14; otherwise you pay him $1. Should you accept the offer?

Analysis: As opposed to the previous bet, here you are concerned with two gambling devices, each associated with a different number of possible atomic events: the die has six sides (six atomic events) while the coin has two sides (two atomic events). Therefore, your common sense tells you that the number of possible pairs, each consisting of a die's side and a coin's side, is $6 \times 2 = 12$ elementary events. What are the probabilities of the two compound events of interest? Since both the die and the coin are fair (recall also that your friend is reliable), and the results of a toss of either do not affect the results of the other (the two tosses are independent), the probability of each elementary event is 1/12. The event associated with winning is elementary since there is only one way to get a 6 *and* a head. Therefore the probability that you will be $14 richer is 1/12. The losing event is clearly "not winning" and by assumption 4 its probability is $1 - 1/12 = 11/12$. How much do you expect to make this time?

$$\frac{1}{12} \times \$14 + \frac{11}{12} \times (-\$1) = \$.25$$

So, you gratefully accept the bet.

This last example involves a more general structure than rule 1, where the number of atomic events is always equal. In this structure the elementary events consist of atomic events which are selected from sets of different sizes: the die is associated with a set having six atomic events (size 6), and the coin with a set of size 2. To obtain the number of these elementary events you can enumerate all of them, but generally it is simpler to apply rule 2.

RULE 2   a. Suppose an elementary event is made up of a sequence of k atomic events, in which the first atomic event can happen in m_1 different ways, the second atomic event in m_2 different ways, and the kth atomic event in m_k different ways. Then S contains

$$n = m_1 \times m_2 \times \cdots \times m_k$$

elementary events.

b. It follows that if the atomic events in each case are equiprobable, then the probability of each elementary event is

$$1/n = \frac{1}{m_1 \times m_2 \times \cdots \times m_k}$$

Using this rule you find, as before, that the number of elementary events in tossing a die and a coin is $m_1 \times m_2 = 6 \times 2 = 12$, and the probability of each such an event is 1/12. Let's use this new rule in another example.

Problem: Slot Machine

You have been selected to head the annual student body party. To add excitement to the party you have decided to rent a slot machine which works as follows: To play you put a nickel in the coin slot and pull a lever which starts three disks spinning inside the machine. The first disk has 8 figures on its surface, the second has 10, and the third has 13. On each disk one of the faces is a joker. If three jokers appear in the window in front of the machine, then you win the jackpot; otherwise you get nothing. The rental company assures you that each figure on the disk has an equal probability of appearing in the window, and that the rotors operating each disk run independently. You are free to set the amount of the jackpot. How much should the jackpot be if you want the machine to be absolutely fair? In other words, you want the gross expected payoff to the player to be 5 cents to match the 5 cents he put in, so that the net expected payoff is zero.

Analysis: You would like to determine the value of a "fair" jackpot. You know that if you play you must pay a nickel; in return you either receive the jackpot if three jokers appear, or you simply lose the nickel. What are the probabilities of these two outcomes?

In preparing for this decision you can look at the three discs as the generators of the atomic events: the first disk contains $m_1 = 8$ atomic events (figures), the second disk contains $m_2 = 10$ atomic events, and the third contains $m_3 = 13$ atomic events. By rule 2, the number of elementary events (combinations of figures in the window) is

$$n = m_1 \times m_2 \times m_3 = 8 \times 10 \times 13 = 1040$$

and since the three rotors operate independently, and the atomic events are equally likely, the probability of each elementary event is 1/1040. Knowing that there is only one joker in each of the three disks, you deduce that there is only one way to hit the jackpot; that is, three jokers appearing in the window is an elementary event whose probability is 1/1040.

Since any other combination of figures is a losing event you know that $P(\text{losing}) = P(\text{not 3 jokers}) = 1 - P(\text{3 jokers}) = 1039/1040$ by theorem 1.

For the game to be fair, you want to find the appropriate prize so that the expected payoff of the machine is 5 cents. In other words, you want to find a prize X such that:

$$\frac{1}{1040} \times X + \frac{1039}{1040} \times 0 = .05$$

Solving for the jackpot prize X, you compute that:

$$X = .05 \times 1040 = \$52$$

Quite a nice prize for a nickel! But note that on the average someone will win only one time in 1040, so that you can expect a lot of complaints.

PROBLEMS 5.4.1

1. What is the probability of 12 dots appearing in a toss of two fair six-sided dice?

2. What is the probability of three dots appearing in a toss of three fair six-sided dice?

3. Each roll of a "one-armed bandit" has 15 pictures. What is the probability of the same picture appearing on the three rolls in the window simultaneously?

4. Suppose the left roll of a "one-armed bandit" has 10 pictures, the middle roll 8 pictures, and the right roll 12 pictures. Each roll has only one picture of a jackpot. What is the probability of the three jackpot pictures appearing in one turn?

5. a. How many license numbers can California have if each number consists of three letters and three digits in that order?
   b. What is the probability of your friend receiving license plate USA 123?
   c. How many additional plates can be issued if each of the six positions can be either a letter or a number?
   d. What assumption have you made in the analysis of (b)?

6. In a game of craps you make 30 to 1 if in a throw of two fair six-sided dice the outcome totals 2. Should you rush to the craps table with the dollar you've just found to bet on the outcome of 2?

7. What are your chances to end up with $923,521 in four consecutive bets on the outcome of 2 in the game of craps in (6) if you start with $1?

8. On any given day the price of the stock you hold can advance, decline, or remain unchanged, with identical chances.
   a. What is the probability of 10 successive advances?
   b. What is the probability of at least two advances in three days?
   c. Your friend has just advised you to purchase some other stock which has advanced for 25 days consecutively. What are the chances of the stock repeating this route?
   d. What assumption have you made in this analysis?

9. Upon entering Steve's Casino you are given a ticket entitling you to a $5 bet on an outcome of 3 in the craps game, and a $1 bet on a number on the roulette wheel. The craps game pays $75 if you win. The roulette pays $100 if you win. There are 38 numbers on the roulette wheel, 36 of which can be gambled on, and 0 and 00, which cannot be gambled on, and hence if either is the outcome, the cash gambled is lost.
   a. How many outcomes of the two gambling devices are favorable to your enrichment?
   b. How many outcomes will contribute nothing to your wealth accumulation?
   c. How much richer do you expect to be after exercising the ticket's privileges?

5.4.2 Drawing Without Replacement (Dependent Atomic Events): Permutations

Thus far we have presented rules for cases in which elementary events consisted of independently chosen atomic events. But now consider the practical case of sampling to determine whether there are any defects in a lot of, say, 100 items (considered as 100 atomic events). You draw one item, test it, and determine that it is not defective. So you package it and send it out. Now there are 99 left. If there were one defect in the lot, and you sampled fairly, you had a 1/100 chance of finding it on the first try. Since you didn't find it, you now have a slightly increased chance of finding it on the second try, namely, 1/99.

The process you followed is called *drawing without replacement*. Another example in which such a process occurs is the draft lottery used during World Wars I and II and after. Before the lottery starts there are 366 possibilities (atomic events), each representing a date of the year. However, once the first date is drawn, 365 dates remain for the second draw, since the first date chosen is not replaced.

You can view this case as a particular application of rule 2. After each selection is made the size of the set of atomic events which are candidates for the next selection is reduced by one. We can refine rule 2 for this special case as follows:

> RULE 3   a. Suppose an elementary event is made up of a sequence of k atomic events, in which (as in drawing without replacement) the first atomic event can happen in k different ways, the second atomic event can occur in $k - 1$ different ways, and so on, so that the kth atomic event can occur in only one way. Then S contains
>
> $$n = k \times (k - 1) \times (k - 2) \times \cdots \times 2 \times 1 = k!$$
>
> elementary events. Recall from chapter 1 that $k!$ is read "k factorial."
>
> b. If the (remaining) atomic events at each draw are equiprobable, then the probability of each elementary event is:
>
> $$\frac{1}{n} = \frac{1}{k!}$$

Problem: Choice of Flicks ———————————————————

You and three of your friends have decided to spend the next four evenings in the movie theatre where a series of four oldies but goodies will be shown. Tickets are sold early each morning for that day's show, and since demand for the series is large you must get up early each morning to obtain the tickets for that day. The four of you can't agree on who should get up early on each day. You suggest to your friends that they decide on who buys on what day by lottery. They agree and ask you to prepare a bunch of slips of papers, listing the four names in different orders. Your friend Bill then chooses one slip, and the first on that slip will have to get up early tomorrow; the second on that slip will buy tickets the following day, and so on. How may slips of paper do you need to list all the possibilities?

Analysis: Your task in this problem is equivalent to determining how many different elementary events can occur. An elementary event in this case consists of choosing one of you to go first, one of the remaining three to go second, one of the remaining two to go third, and the remaining one fourth; that is, an elementary event is a series of draws without replacement from four people (the atomic events). So $k = 4$, and by rule 3, there are $4! = 24$ elementary events, so you'll need 24 slips of paper.

There is an alternative way that you could have viewed this problem. Each slip of paper represents one way of placing your names in a specific order. You are interested in the number of possible ways to order the four names. You may recall from section 1.6 (the auto shop example) that we called such an ordering a permutation. In that case no reference was made to atomic or elementary events. Here one such permutation is (John, Bill, Sam, you), while another is (Sam, Bill, John, you). In general, if a set contains k things and you place all k of them in order, such an ordering is called a permutation of size k from a set of size k. So the number of slips of paper is the number of possible permutations of size 4 from a set of size 4.

Sometimes you may face problems where an elementary event consists of the ordering of *some* (but not all) of the possible atomic events. For example, in some card games it is valuable to find the number of ways of drawing two cards from a single deck. If the order in which you draw a hand counts, then drawing the two of clubs first and *then* the ace of spades is a *different* "pair" of cards from the ace of spades first, and two of clubs second. Each of these "ordered pairs" is called a *permutation of size 2 from a set of size 52* (there are 52 cards in one deck), denoted by P_2^{52}. From rule 2(a) you know that if the first draw has 52 possible atomic events and the second has 51 atomic events (since the drawing is without replacement), then $P_2^{52} = 52 \times 51$. That is, there are 52 candidates for the first draw and 51 for the second and final draw. Therefore, the number of all possible pairs is the product of the two, 2652.

In general, if r atomic events are successively drawn without replacement from a set containing k atomic events $(r \le k)$, the r elements form an ordered arrangement called a *permutation of size r from a set of size k*. From rule 2 we deduce that the number of these permutations (denoted P_r^k) is:

$$P_r^k = k(k-1)(k-2) \cdots (k-r+1) = \frac{k!}{(k-r)!}$$

The reasoning goes as follows: The first position of such a permutation can be filled by one of the k atomic events, the second can be chosen from the $(k-1)$ remaining atomic events, the third from $(k-2)$, and so it goes, with $(k-r+1)$ elements being the candidate for the rth (last) position.

In the above example, the number of ways to draw two cards from 52 is:

$$P_2^{52} = 52 \times 51 = \frac{52!}{(52-2)!} = \frac{52 \times 51 \times 50 \times 49 \times \cdots \times 1}{50 \times 49 \times \cdots \times 1} = 52 \times 51$$

Now, try your own hand at this: How many different ways can you draw 5 cards from 52?

We can summarize the above by

RULE 4   a.   Suppose an elementary event consists of a sequence of r different* atomic events ($r = 2$ in the blackjack case) chosen from a set of k atomic events ($k = 52$ in the blackjack example); that is, each elementary event is a permutation of size r from a set of k atomic events. Then S, the set of all elementary events, contains

$$n = P_r^k = \frac{k!}{(k-r)!}$$

members; that is, P_r^k is the number of permutations of size r from a set of size k.

b.   If the (remaining) atomic events at each draw are equiprobable, the probability of each permutation is

$$\frac{1}{n} = \frac{1}{P_r^k} = \frac{(k-r)!}{k!}$$

It is interesting that when $k = r$, we are back to rule 3. How? Well, $P_k^k = k!/(k-k)! = k!/0!$. Now, we haven't talked about 0! before, but it turns out that our computation theory becomes most convenient if we let $0! = 1$ (there are other mathematical reasons as well). Hence, $P_k^k = k!/1 = k!$.

---

*"Different" in the sense of drawing the atomic events without replacement.

Problem: A Blackjack Deal ─────────────────────────────

While driving through the Nevada desert you become thirsty and decide to pull over at the next town. At the door of the town inn a lovely young hostperson hands you a ticket which entitles you to a special free game of blackjack. In this game you win $5 if you are dealt a "blackjack." A hand consists of two cards dealt from a 52-card deck. You win if one of the cards is an ace and the other is a card of value 10 (a 10, jack, queen, or king). How much do you expect to win if you sit down to play with a free ticket?

Analysis: Since a blackjack hand consists of two cards, you would first like to find out how many ordered pairs (elementary events) can be dealt from a single deck. Or, in our new quantitative terms, how many permutations of size 2 from a set of size 52 can be generated? Applying rule 4 you obtain

$$P_2^{52} = \frac{52!}{(52 - 2)!} = 52 \times 51 = 2652$$

Since the deck is well shuffled, the probability of each permutation is 1/2652. Next you would like to know how many such permutations are blackjack hands. Since it doesn't matter whether an ace is dealt first and a value 10 card is dealt second or vice versa, you must count the number of hands in both cases. Applying rule 2, notice that if an ace is dealt first, then $m_1 = 4$ (there are four aces in a single deck of cards), and $m_2 = 16$ (4 tens + 4 jacks + 4 queens + 4 kings). Therefore, the number of ways to obtain such a hand with the ace drawn first is $4 \times 16 = 64$. On the other hand, if an ace is preceded by a face card or a 10, then $m_1 = 16$ and $m_2 = 4$, yielding $16 \times 4 = 64$ ways of being dealt a hand of a value 10 card followed by an ace.

Now you are in a position to compute the probability of a black-jack hand from a well-shuffled deck. If you denote by O_1 the compound event "a blackjack hand," then

$$\text{Probability } O_1 = \frac{\text{no. of elementary events in } O_1}{\text{total no. of elementary events}} = \frac{64 + 64}{2652} = \frac{128}{2652}$$

which is about 1/20. (Notice that you *add* 64 + 64, since the events "blackjack with ace first" and "blackjack with ace second" are mutually exclusive.) So, if you play 100 hands in an evening, then the expected number of pure blackjack hands you may receive is about $100 \times 1/20$ or 5.

In this case you win $5 with probability 128/2652 and you walk out empty-handed with probability $1 - 128/2652 = 2524/2652$ (by assumption 4). Therefore you "expect" to win

$$\frac{128}{2652} \times \$5 + \frac{2524}{2652} \times 0, \text{ which is approximately } \$.24$$

But, remember that the "expected" may very well *not* occur, just as in a bet you often will not receive your "expected" payoff.

Thus the lovely young hostperson at the inn has handed you a free ticket that is "worth" about a quarter. But all is not generosity. The inn figures that the probability is high that you'll want to play some more of this game of blackjack at the regular price of 40¢ a game; and *they* "expect" to make $40 - 24 = 16$ cents on each additional game you play.

PROBLEMS 5.4.2

1. How many ways can you order 10 jobs in an auto shop?

2. How many ways can you order 60 products on the supermarket's shelves?

3. How many ways can you choose a subcommittee of three from the six members of the student council?

4. Each student council member serves a term of two months as chairperson of the council. The succession of the six members' service is determined at random. Explain how this procedure can be implemented. What is the probability of each possible succession order?

5. Having to write five equally important papers during the holidays and being worried about the short time, you have decided to choose the order in which you'll write the papers in a random fashion. How many orders do you have to consider? What is the probability of each such an order?

6. In a game of poker each player is dealt, at the outset, five cards from a well-shuffled deck of 52 cards. What is the probability of being dealt a hand consisting of the ace, king, queen, jack, and 10 of spades?

7. In a version of blackjack a winning hand is a pair that adds up to 11. What is the probability of such a hand, if the cards are drawn from a 52-card well-shuffled deck?

8. As the producer of a new TV game show, you must provide the prizes which will be given on the show. Each show is planned to consist of 20 turns. In each turn the contestant is asked to predict the order of five cards in a well-shuffled five-card deck. A correct prediction is worth $5000 to the contestant.

a. How much money do you need to have on hand before the beginning of each show in order to pay *all* the possible winners?

b. How much do you *expect* to pay for each turn?

c. How much do you *expect* to pay in each show?

9. Your friend, the owner of York's Casino, has asked you to help him determine the prizes for a new gambling game he plans to introduce. The game involves a deck of 52 cards. Three of them are dealt to the bettor, who wins the prize if the order of the cards dealt is ace, king, and queen of spades. Your friend expects 500 players to participate in this game every day, each playing three turns. He estimates that each player will pay $1 per turn. What should the prize per turn be if your friend is to *expect* to make $250 per day profit on the game?

5.4.3 Order Doesn't "Count"—Combinations Up to this point we have mainly been interested in elementary events, so that when you toss three coins, you think in terms of HHH, HHT, HTH, and so on. But, in some situations you may be interested in arrangements generated by drawing atomic events without replacement, and are *not* concerned with the order in which the atomic events are drawn. Such was the case in the blackjack game; either an ace followed by a value 10 card, or a value 10 card followed by an ace is a blackjack hand. Or, when asked for the probability of throwing exactly two heads with three tosses of a coin, you don't really care whether the result is HHT, HTH, or THH. Again, when you sample a lot of size 100 for defectives, it usually doesn't matter whether the defective was found in the first test or the hundredth. In such cases the set of several elementary events representing the different *arrangements* or *ordering* of the same atomic events is called a *combination*. Formally, *a combination is a set of elementary events, each elementary event consisting of the same atomic events in a different order. A combination of size r from a set of size k* is such a set of elementary events, where each elementary event consists of r different atomic events (as in choosing without replacement) chosen from a set of k atomic events. The different elementary events making up the combination have the various atomic events in different order.

Problem: Party Games ━━━━━━━━━━━━━━━━━━━━━━━━━━━━━━━

You and your "old person" are at a party with nine other couples, and you decide to play a game involving teams. In the first game there are teams of size 5, and all team members are of equal importance. In the second game each team has a captain, a lieutenant, a sergeant, a corporal, and a private. How many teams are in each game?

Analysis: In the first game the order of the members of the team is not of importance. Therefore, if you want to know the number of different teams, you count the number of *combinations* of size $r = 5$ chosen from $k = 20$ people. We'll see in a moment how to calculate this number. In the second game, if Jim is captain and Joy a lieutenant, then that team is different from the one in which Joy is captain and Jim lieutenant. That is, order counts, and the number of possible team arrangements is the number of *permutations* of size 5 from a set of size 20 (which you know to be $20!/(20 - 5)! = 20 \times 19 \times 18 \times 17 \times 16$).

The difference between combinations and permutations can also be illustrated using the notion of sets (appendix 2.1). For example, look at the set A which contains the atomic events a_1, a_2, a_3: $A = \{a_1, a_2, a_3\}$. Let us now list all the elementary events, which are *permutations of* size 2 from this set: $P_1 = (a_1, a_2)$, $P_2 = (a_2, a_1)$, $P_3 = (a_1, a_3)$, $P_4 = (a_3, a_1)$, $P_5 = (a_2, a_3)$, $P_6 = (a_3, a_2)$. Since a combination is an arrangement which is independent of the order of its elements, P_1 and P_2 count as the compound event which is a single combination, consisting of the atomic events a_1 and a_2. The same is true for the pairs P_3, P_4 and P_5, P_6. That is, the *combinations of* size 2 from the set A are:

$$C_1 = (a_1, a_2), \ C_2 = (a_1, a_3), \ C_3 = (a_2, a_3)$$

The notation most commonly used for the *number of combinations of size r from a set of size k* is C_r^k or $\binom{k}{r}$ which is read "k choose r."

RULE 5   a.   Suppose an elementary event consists of a sequence of r different atomic events chosen from a set of k atomic events as in rule 4. Then the number of such elementary events was shown to be $k!/(k - r)!$. If you are *not* interested in the order of the atomic events, all the different elementary events containing the same atomic events are considered a combination. The number of *different* combinations of size r chosen from a set of k atomic events is:

$$C_r^k = \binom{k}{r} = \frac{k!}{r!(k - r)!}$$

b.   It follows that if the (remaining) atomic events at each draw are equiprobable, then the probability of each combination is:

$$\frac{1}{C_r^k} = \frac{1}{\binom{k}{r}} = \frac{r!(k - r)!}{k!}$$

In the Party Game problem, the number of "different" teams in the first game is:

$$\frac{20!}{(20-5)!5!} = \frac{20 \times 19 \times 18 \times 17 \times 16}{5 \times 4 \times 3 \times 2 \times 1}$$

quite a bit less than the number of different team configurations in the second game. In general, notice that the rule applies only if $k \geq r$ (that is, you can't choose 50 different atomic events from 45).

Recall the convention that $0! = 1$. Hence C_k^k, the number of possible combinations using *all* members of the set, is

$$\frac{k!}{k!(k-k)!} = \frac{k!}{k!0!} = 1$$

which is not very surprising if you think about it.

Instead of just accepting rule 5, you might want to see the deductive reasoning that leads to its verification. This is very simple to give: Each of the groups of atomic events that constitute a single elementary event in a combination can be arranged in r! different ways (rule 3); that is, there are r! elementary events in each combination. But for combinations, all these different orders are irrelevant and count as a single combination, so that the number of combinations is equal to the total possible number of permutations (elementary events) divided by r!. That is, $C_r^k = P_r^k/r!$.

Problem: "86" Gas

Your neighbor, the owner of Joe's "86" gas station, has come to you for advice about a promotion plan he has been thinking about. With each fill-up he wants to give every customer a card on which there are 10 circles, each with a number from 1 to 10 printed inside the circle. There is a wax covering on each circle so that you can't see the numbers. The customer rubs off five of the circles and if the sum of the numbers revealed exceeds the number printed on the top of the card, the customer wins a dollar's worth of gas. Leeson's Expanded Label Company can produce such cards, and have designed their label machine and number distributions so that the numbers on the top of the card can be exceeded by exactly one combination of five circles on the front. So if the customer chooses the right five waxed circles (which he can't see beforehand, of course), he wins. Joe wants to know how many winners he can "expect" each week if he fills 1000 tanks a week. What should you tell him?

Analysis: Joe wants to know how many winning cards he can expect among the 1000 customers who have their tanks filled. To compute this he needs the probability that a customer will rub off the correct five circles on the card he receives. Once that probability is established, multiplying that probability by 1000 customers will give him the expected number of winners.

To compute the probability, assume that the customer chooses the circles to rub off at random, and hence the chances of a customer's rubbing off any combination of five circles are equiprobable. Since only one such combination is a winner (*combination* — since the order in which he rubs off the circles doesn't matter), all you need to do is compute the total number of such combinations that are possible. Rule 5 tells you that the number of ways of choosing five objects (circles) from a set of 10 (the number of combinations of size 5 from a set of size 5) is

$$C_5^{10} = \binom{10}{5} = \frac{10!}{5!(10-5)!} = \frac{10!}{5!5!} = \frac{10 \cdot 9 \cdot 8 \cdot 7 \cdot 6}{5 \cdot 4 \cdot 3 \cdot 2 \cdot 1} = 252$$

So there are 252 combinations, only one of which is a winner. Since each combination is equiprobable, the probability that any customer wins is 1/252. The expected number of winners per week is 1/252 × 1000, which is about 4. But as a friend of Joe's, you should point out to him that he is not to "expect" that the number of winners will be 4 each week, week after week. Would it be unusual for there to be zero winners? Or 10 winners? Note that Joe as a manager is really interested in this question of a likely range of winners, since if there are very few his customers may think his offer is a fake, and if there are very many then he's giving away too much gas. You would best serve him as a consultant if you could give him a likely *range* of winners in which he can have a great deal of confidence — that is, a "confidence interval." We will discuss this concept later in the book. You should keep such objectives in mind while preparing for decisions.

PROBLEMS 5.4.3

1. How many distinct three-card hands can you deal from a well-shuffled 52-card deck? What is the probability of each hand?

2. What is the probability of being dealt the ace, king, and queen of spades from a well-shuffled deck with 13 spades?

3. What is the probability of being dealt a heart royal flush (that is, ace, king, queen, jack, and 10, all of the heart suit) in a game of straight poker (five cards are dealt from a well-shuffled deck)?

4. In every lot of 100 units there are three defectives. They must be identified and repaired before the lot is shipped out. Recently, you have observed that your quality control person doesn't keep pace with the production of new lots. Her argument is that in the last five lots she has inspected, the defectives happened to be the last

three among the 100 units of the lot. What is the probability of such an event?

5. In order to attract gamblers to the blackjack table your friend the casino manager has proposed to increase the prize for a blackjack (a hand of 2 cards dealt from a well-shuffled deck of 52 in which one of the cards is an ace and the other is a king, queen, jack, or 10) from $5 to $10. To enter the game a player pays $1. What will be the effect of the proposed policy on the casino's daily expected profits, if the number of players increases from 1000 to 1500 per day?

6. How long do you expect it is going to take for you to become a millionaire if you are given a permit to open a gambling table to play the following game: You deal to the gambler four cards from a well-shuffled deck of 52 cards. You pay $50 if all four cards are aces; otherwise you receive $5. You expect 1000 bets every day.

7. Will your expectation in problem 6 change if you pay for a hand of four kings as well but charge $10 to play?

*** 5.4.4   More Complex Cases**   We can now combine several of our rules to help handle more complicated situations that may arise. You have seen the relationship between combinations and permutations and it turns out that some problems, like the blackjack example, can be solved using either method. In the examples that follow you will probably find one or the other of the methods used to be more suited to your own intuition, and since we don't know in advance which you prefer, we will solve the problem using both techniques. This should also give you the flavor of the relationship between permutations and combinations.

Problem: An Example from Cards ────────────────

Two cards are drawn from a well-shuffled deck. Would you be willing to put up $5 to get $25 if both cards are spades?

Combination Analysis: The number of possible distinct* hands consisting of two cards drawn from a deck of 52 cards is:

$$C_2^{52} = \frac{52!}{(52-2)!2!} = 1326$$

since the draw is without replacement and the order is not important (rule 5). The number of distinct ways that you can draw 2 spades from a deck which includes 13 spades is (rule 5)

---

*"Distinct" means that if we draw the same hand in different order, it is not considered a different hand.

$$C_2^{13} = \frac{13!}{(13-2)!2!} = 78$$

Since all hands are equiprobable, the probability of 2 spades is 78/1326 = 1/17. Your gross expected payoff is therefore $1/17 \times 25 + 16/17 \times 0$ = $1.47, which is clearly less than $5; so don't bet (assuming you want to "make the most you can").

Permutation Analysis: The total number of hands where order counts (drawing the same two cards in different order is considered a *different* hand) of size 2 drawn from a deck of 52 cards is

$$P_2^{52} = \frac{52!}{(52-2)!} = 52 \times 51 \text{ (rule 4)}$$

The number of these hands in which both cards are spades is $P_2^{13} = 13 \times 12$ (rule 4). Since all hands are equiprobable, the probability of two spades is

$$\frac{13 \times 12}{52 \times 51} = \frac{12}{204} = \frac{1}{17}$$

and the expected value is about $1.50 as before.

Problem: Another Card Example ━━━━━━━━━━━━━━━━━━━━━━━━

In one form of poker, five cards are dealt to each player from a well-shuffled deck of 52 cards. After being dealt a hand of five cards, each player may exchange up to three of his cards for other cards. One evening your reliable friend offers to bet you that he can deal himself a flush (all cards of one suit) without having to draw any extra cards. If he does, you pay him $10; if he doesn't, he pays you 50 cents. Is this a profitable bet?

Combination Analysis: The number of possible distinct poker hands is C_5^{52} (rule 5). The number of distinct ways of getting dealt a flush of a specific suit is C_5^{13}, because there are 13 cards of the suit in the deck. Since there are four suits, the number of ways of getting a flush of any of the four suits is $4 \times C_5^{13}$. This is an application of rule 2, where each elementary event consists of (1) a suit chosen from (spades, hearts, diamonds, clubs) and (2) a hand of five cards chosen from that suit. That is, $m_1 = 4$, $m_2 = C_5^{13}$.

Thus if you assume the deck is well-shuffled, the probability of being dealt a flush is

$$\frac{\text{no. of different flush hands}}{\text{no. of distinguishable poker hands}} = \frac{4 \times C_5^{13}}{C_5^{52}}$$

$$= \frac{4 \times \dfrac{13!}{(13-5)!5!}}{\dfrac{52!}{(52-5)!5!}}$$

$$= \frac{4 \times 13 \times 12 \times 11 \times 10 \times 9}{52 \times 51 \times 50 \times 49 \times 48}$$

$$= \frac{33}{16,660} = .002$$

Since the order does not matter, we could have described each elementary event as consisting of (1) a five-card hand of some specific suit chosen from a 13-card deck of that suit, and (2) a suit from the set of four suits. In other words, our choice of which to pick from first did not matter, because $4 \times C_5^{13} = C_5^{13} \times 4$.

Permutation Analysis: The number of ways (order counts here) that you can be dealt a five-card poker hand is $P_5^{52} = 52 \times 51 \times 50 \times 49 \times 48$ (rule 4). The number of ways that you can be dealt a flush, by rule 2, is $52 \times 12 \times 11 \times 10 \times 9$, which is explained as follows: The suit of the first card doesn't matter, but once it has been dealt you must draw the next four cards from the same suit. If the first card dealt is a spade, for example, there are then 12 spades left to be chosen from for the second card, 11 from the third, and so on. So, the first atomic event in the sequence is chosen from the set of all cards; that is, $m_1 = 52$; the second is chosen from the set of remaining cards in the same suit as the first card chosen; that is, $m_2 = 12$; and so on.

Thus, the number of ways to deal a flush (where order counts) is $52 \times 12 \times 11 \times 10 \times 9$. Since all hands are equiprobable, the probability of a flush is

$$\frac{\text{the no. of ways to be dealt a flush}}{\text{total no. of ways to be dealt 5 cards}} = \frac{52 \times 12 \times 11 \times 10 \times 9}{52 \times 51 \times 50 \times 49 \times 48}$$

$$= \frac{33}{16,660} = .002, \text{ as before.}$$

Hence your expected payoff for the bet is

$$-\$10 \times (\text{probability he draws a flush}) + \$.50$$
$$\times (\text{probability he doesn't}) =$$
$$-(10) \times (.002) + (.5) \times (.998) = -.02 + .499 = +.479$$

so you accept the bet, if the small risk of losing \$10 is worth it.

You can determine, also, what would have constituted a "fair" bet if you receive 50 cents whenever you win. To get a fair return, your *net* expected payoff should be zero. Let X be the amount you should pay if the expected value of the bet is zero for both of you. You want to solve for X in the following equation where the expected payoff is zero:

$$\text{Expected payoff} = -X(.002) + (\$.50) \times (.998) = 0$$

$$\text{or } .002X = .499$$

$$\text{and } X = \frac{.499}{.002} = \$249.50$$

Problem: Mark's Motel

As the manager of Mark's Motel, you would like to select a representative committee of employees to be present at a meeting with the owners. You have 31 room and service employees, 21 of whom are women, 10 of whom are men. You also have 14 desk personnel, half of whom are men. You have decided to be fair and choose the committee of three at random, but it turns out that there are no women on the committee. How likely is this? Six months later you find yourself selecting a new committee of three for the same purpose. This time you find that there is exactly one committee member who is a desk clerk. How likely is this?

Combination Analysis: The number of distinct three-person committee combinations is, by rule 5, C_3^{45}, where 45 is the total number of employees. The number of distinct committees with no women on them (where the order in which the members are chosen is irrelevant) is C_3^{17}, since 17 is the number of men. Since the choosing of committee members is at random, the probability of having no women on the committee is

$$\frac{\text{no. of distinct committees with no women}}{\text{no. of distinct committees}} = \frac{C_3^{17}}{C_3^{45}} = \frac{\dfrac{17!}{14!3!}}{\dfrac{45!}{42!3!}} = \frac{68}{1419}$$

Similarly, the probability that one desk clerk is chosen, using rule 5 and rule 2, is

$$\frac{C_2^{31} \times C_1^{14}}{C_3^{45}} = \frac{\dfrac{31!}{(31-2)!2!} \times \dfrac{14!}{(14-1)!1!}}{\dfrac{45!}{(45-3)!3!}} = \frac{217}{473}$$

Notice again that since the order did not matter, you could have chosen first from the desk employees, and then from the service personnel, yielding the equivalent answer

$$\frac{C_1^{14} \times C_2^{31}}{C_3^{45}} = \frac{217}{473}$$

Permutation Analysis: The number of different ways of choosing the three members of the committee, where the order in which they are chosen counts, is P_3^{45} by rule 4. The number of different ways of choosing a committee with no women is P_3^{17}. So the probability of having no women on the committee is

$$\frac{P_3^{17}}{P_3^{45}} = \frac{17 \times 16 \times 15}{45 \times 44 \times 43} = \frac{68}{1419}$$

Similarly, the number of ways of choosing exactly one desk employee is, by rule 2 and rule 5, $C_1^3 \times 31 \times 30 \times 14$. This may throw you at first, but can be explained as follows: the first atomic event, in rule 2, is chosen from the set of all ways in which you can place the one desk clerk in three positions; there are $C_1^3 = 3$ different ways in which you can place the one desk clerk in the three available positions, by rule 5. Once you have chosen a place in the committee of three for the desk clerks, you have 31 choices for the first room and service employee, 30 for the third atomic event — the second room and service employee, and 14 choices for the desk clerk. Rule 2 says that you multiply these, where $m_1 = C_1^3 = 3$, $m_2 = 31$, $m_3 = 30$, and $m_4 = 14$. Again, you could have chosen the order of the above atomic events differently for rule 2, but the same result would have occurred; thus the probability of one desk clerk being chosen is

$$\frac{C_1^3 \times 31 \times 30 \times 14}{45 \times 44 \times 43} = \frac{3 \times 31 \times 30 \times 14}{45 \times 44 \times 43} = \frac{217}{473}$$

In the above analysis, as well as throughout this section, you could have used the fact that

$$C_r^k = C_{k-r}^k$$

For example, placing the two room and service employees in the three positions is identical to placing the one desk clerk in the three positions; that is,

$$C_1^3 = C_2^3 = 3$$

In general,

$$C_r^k = \frac{k!}{r!(k-r)!}$$

and

$$C^k_{k-r} = \frac{k!}{(k-r)!(k-(k-r))!} = \frac{k!}{(k-r)!r!} = \frac{k!}{r!(k-r)!}$$

are always equal.

PROBLEMS 5.4.4

1. In a game of bridge each of the four players is dealt a 13-card hand from a well-shuffled 52-card deck. Suppose that you are playing bridge and that the hand you have just been dealt contains no aces. What is the probability that the hand held by your partner (the player opposite to you) contains exactly two aces?

2. Defective communication units have been mistakenly installed in four of a group of 10 jets. It is not known which jets have the defective units. What is the probability that in a random check of four of the jets no defective unit will be found?

3. Is it true that the probability of receiving a blackjack hand where the order of the cards you are dealt is ace followed by a value-10 card is larger than the probability of getting a value-10 card succeeded by an ace?

4. What is the probability of being dealt a pair in a game of five-card poker? (A poker hand containing two matching cards — same face — and three nonmatching cards is called a pair.)

5.4.5 Summary of Counting Rules The rules presented in section 5.4 form a hierarchical structure (figure 5.2) that gives you a taste of the deductive process to which we so often refer.

The most general rule, from which all the others can be derived, is rule 2. It covers cases in which elementary events are constructed by drawing from k sets of atomic events; the first set contains m_1 atomic events, the second contains m_2 atomic events, and so on. A special case of his process occurs when all k sets contain the same number of atomic events; that is, $m_1 = m_2 = \cdots = m_k$. The rule that applies in this case is rule 1, which can be deduced from rule 2. Rule 4 is again a refinement of rule 2 for the case in which the first position of the arrangement (elementary event) is filled by one of k atomic events ($m_1 = k$), the second position is filled by one of the $k-1$ atomic events left after the first draw is made, and so on to the rth position for which there are $k - r + 1$ candidates; that is, $m_1 = k$, $m_2 = k - 1, \ldots, m_r = k - r + 1$. A special case of this last process occurs when $r = k$ so that $m_1 = k$, $m_2 = k - 1, \ldots, m_{r-1} = 2$, $m_r = 1$. The refinement here is quite simple:

$$\frac{k!}{(k-r)!} = \frac{k!}{(k-k)!} = \frac{k!}{0!} = k! \text{ (rule 3)}$$

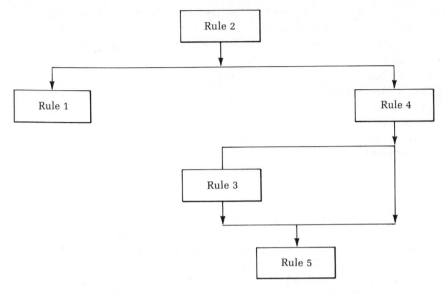

Figure 5.2   Deductive Hierarchy of Counting Rules

Finally, rules 3 and 4 are used to derive a combinations rule: P_r^k is given in rule 4, and from rule 3 $P_r^r = r!$ Since the order of the elements in any combination of size r does not matter:

$$C_r^k = \frac{P_r^k}{P_r^r} = \frac{\dfrac{k!}{(k-r)!}}{r!} = \frac{k!}{(k-r)!r!} \text{ (rule 5)}$$

5.5   Decision Making in a P-C World

What have you gained as a result of studying these various rules for calculating permutations and combinations? Your lesson for decision making is that the size of S, the set of states of the world, is often extremely large. Nonetheless, there are methods of handling these immensities in a rational and not too laborious manner. For example, if the order of the atomic events is of no importance you can go directly to the compound events which are represented by combinations. This chapter is primarily concerned with S, and as you saw, we purposely narrowed D, the set of decisions available, down to a few, and often just two choices (for example, to bet or not to bet). Nevertheless, since the computational rules are fresh in your mind, it will be useful to say a few things about D when it is large.

Whichever rule you used, it's obvious that in many real situations the number of ways you can arrange things to serve one purpose is very large. Suppose, for example, that you could design a meeting of 12 persons for an hour, where each person gets to speak only once for five minutes. You'd like to design the meeting so that you "optimize" the sequence of speakers. Rule 4 tells you that the number of designs is 12! or about 500 million. Of course, in real meetings the number is much higher, because the duration of a speech is not fixed, and people can (and some usually do!) speak more than once, or not at all. And yet people do seem to be able to conduct meetings without a great deal of stress, and sometimes everyone feels that the meeting was "well run." Clearly, no one scanned the large number of designs to select the one with the highest payoff. What decision rules are followed, if any, in running a meeting?

One common sense decision rule could be called the "rule of urgency": Do those things first which appear to be most urgent. Urgency is often the basis on which meetings are run. Some people believe that what they have to say is very urgent, and they, in cooperation with the chairman, get the floor first. Or, if you think the house is on fire, you have several options: call the fire department, get a hose, go warn others, run out of the house, or throw a blanket over the fire. Hence there are at least 5! or 120 sequences you can follow; you won't scan these, but rather you'll do what appears to you to be the most urgent first, for example, run out if it's obvious that the building is about to collapse. Note that the rule of urgency is at best only an approximation to the optimal, since it's based on your perception of what is most urgent.

A generalization of the urgency rule says to do the most important things first, or at least what appear to be the most important. This common sense rule is often violated in running meetings, when the chairman elects to "get a few administrative matters settled before turning to the important items on the agenda," only to find that the unimportant trivia occupy the whole time. Here again the decision rule may not even approximate the optimal, for one reason because it may violate another sensible decision rule—namely, to do those things in sequence that belong together in some sense. One of the most obvious applications of this last rule is the design of product development, from the initial idea through a prototype of production and market distribution. Here the items in the sequence follow each other by the logic of necessity: one step is required in order to perform the next step. In recent years, quantitative methods have been developed to help you design such sequences and forecast completion time, notably Critical Path Analysis (CPA) and Program Evaluation and Review Technique (PERT).

This much on the subject of large D's will suffice for the moment. Suppose we turn now to recall what we have been saying about large S's. If you had to consider the consequences of each element of D coupled with each element of S, and S is composed of 12! possibilities, you'd be in a similar computational impasse. But note how we have overcome the difficulty. We have all along assumed that "Mother Nature," in making her decisions, is operating "at random," by making the events independent and equiprobable so that we can calculate the probability of a limited number of outcomes. Then, for each d from a small-sized D, you can calculate a very large number of possibilities that could occur; but if you're only interested in the possibility of drawing all of one suit, then you can cut down tremendously on the inspection of the consequences. In the next chapter we will further examine this idea of reduction of the number of possibilities and study methods which will assist us in this task. We also reexamine our widely used decision criterion — expected value — look at its rationale and limitations, and discuss several alternatives as well as extensions of this criterion in chapter 7. We should, however, warn you that starting with the next chapter we often *assume* the probabilities of the various states of the world outright as a *given* part of the decision problem, whereas throughout most of this chapter, we *deduced* the relevant probabilities from the information given.

5.6   Summary

In this chapter we have begun to examine in detail decision problems in which you are *uncertain* about which of *several* (or many) states of the world will occur or has occurred. One way to *quantify* this uncertainty is through the use of *probabilities*. The following points are worth repeating:

a.   Since this is a book about *deductive* quantitative methods, we *assume* in all of the decision problems that either you know the probabilities of the states of the world outright, or you can generate the probabilities through use of the *deductive system* for *probability* developed in this chapter.

b.   The states of the world are associated with *elementary events*, which can sometimes be usefully combined together into *compound events*; this is especially useful when the outcomes associated with different states of the world are identical.

c.   You also need the deductive system for probability to specify when you can appropriately *add, subtract, or multiply probabilities* together; the notions of *mutually exclusive events* and *independent* events help us deduce the probabilities of states of the world and compound events or outcomes.

d.   You also can use this deductive system to develop *rules* and *quantitative methods* that vastly reduce the computational load involved in obtaining probabilities, and to define more precisely the assumptions you make about the states of the world (and hence the outcomes) and their chances of occurring.

6 Random Variables and Their Distributions

6.1 From Events and Their Probabilities to Random Variables and Their Distributions

In the previous chapter we discussed the difficulties that arise when you are confronted with a large number of states of the world (elementary events). We have suggested a method for overcoming these difficulties in the case where the number of distinct outcomes for a given decision is less than the number of states of the world. We said that in such cases you could list only those events (which we called compound, since they may consist of more than one elementary event) that give rise to distinct outcomes. For example, on a winter day you can describe the possible weather conditions (states of the world) in many different ways. But for a decision like whether to take an umbrella, you are interested in only two weather descriptions—that is, two compound events: "wet weather" and "dry weather," in preparing for your decision.

In some decision contexts, the list of relevant compound events can also be so large that the sheer size of the required information and computation makes the problem unmanageable. For example, flash back to those three rather worn coins we've been tossing. You are made an offer in which you receive as many dollars as the number of heads showing on the three coins but must pay $5 if no heads show. Recall that the number of states of the world (elementary events) is eight. However, you are not actually interested in the *eight* states of the world *separately*, since, for example, HTT is identical to THT as far as the dollar *outcome* to you is concerned. Instead you are interested in *four* distinct relevant events, each of which gives rise to a distinct outcome:

0 heads show

1 head shows

2 heads show

3 heads show

In this case, the listing of the relevant events is still manageable, but imagine a bet involving a hundred coins or a million coins!

In chapter 2, we explained that sometimes you can use a precise language expressed in symbols to define your ideas. For example, we have used S to denote the set of states of the world, and $s_1, s_2, \ldots, s_N$ to specify particular states which might occur. In chapter 3 we discussed the concept of function, which is simply a rule for passing from one set to another set. Probabilists discovered that you can combine these two ideas to develop a precise language for communicating the list of all relevant elementary or compound events pertinent to any decision under consideration. The idea is to associate a number with each decision-relevant event by creating a function which passes from the set of events to the set of numbers. The function is represented by a symbol, say, X. For example, in the above example of three coins, you can define the function: X = numbers of heads in three tosses of a coin. The values that X can take on are 0, 1, 2, 3, which stand for "no heads," "one head," "two heads," and "three heads," respectively. If you had flipped 100 coins and defined X in the same way, X could take on the values $X = 0, 1, 2, \ldots, 100$. X is called a *random variable* since X can have many values, each with the probabilities of the corresponding events. For the present, we denote a random variable by a capital letter. In the three coins example, the probability of $X = 0$ (no heads) is $(1/2)^3 = 1/8$, which is written as $P(X = 0) = 1/8$. The probability of one head is $P(X = 1) = 3/8$, and the probabilities of two and three heads are $P(X = 2) = 3/8$ and $P(X = 3) = 1/8$. Note that the four probabilities 1/8, 3/8, 3/8, and 1/8 add up to 1, which is not surprising since one of the four events must occur (they are collectively exhaustive — see (the appendix to chapter 2). We say that the complete set of probabilities, $P(X = 0)$, $P(X = 1)$, $P(X = 2)$, $P(X = 3)$, is the probability distribution of the random variable X. *A probability distribution describes completely the probability that a random variable like X takes on each of its various values.* The probability distribution of X = number of heads in three tosses, and its relationship to the elementary events, is portrayed in table 6.1.

TABLE 6.1   Distribution of a Random Variable and Its Relation to Events

Elementary event	Relevant compound event	Value x of random variable X	Probability distribution P(X = x)
TTT ⟶	zero heads	0	$\frac{1}{8}$
TTH			
THT ⟶	one head	1	$\frac{3}{8}$
THH			
HTT	two heads	2	$\frac{3}{8}$
HTH			
HHT	three heads	3	$\frac{1}{8}$
HHH			

In earlier chapters you have already encountered both the notion of a random variable and its probability distribution. Recall the Lottery problem of chapter 1 in which for the decision to buy the ticket, the payoffs of $75 and $0 are associated with the compound events "your ticket is drawn" and "your ticket is not drawn." The first event had probability 1/100 and the second event had probability 99/100. You can now describe this information in terms of the random variable W whose values are the possible payoffs associated with the buy decision. W is a random variable whose possible values are 0 and 75 and whose probability distribution is $P(W = 0) = 99/100$, $P(W = 75) = 1/100$.

Similarly, in the Route to Work problem of chapter 1, for the decision "drive to work" the three possible payoffs can be viewed as the values of the random variable W, which can take on three possible values: $1.50, $2.10, or $3.00. The distribution of this random variable W is given by

$$P(W = 1.50) = \frac{1}{6}, \ P(W = 2.10) = \frac{2}{6}, \ P(W = 3.00) = \frac{3}{6}$$

In the same problem you could also have defined another random variable, Y = number of minutes late you arrive to work. The possible values of Y would be 0, 6, 15, and the probability distribution of Y is given by

$$P(Y = 0) = \frac{1}{6}, \ P(Y = 6) = \frac{2}{6}, \ P(Y = 15) = \frac{3}{6}$$

The point of this last example is that you are free to define the random variable function in the way that makes most sense for your decision-making purposes.

PROBLEMS 6.1

1. Write down the distributions of the following random variables.
    a. $X =$ number of heads in four tosses of a fair coin
    b. $Y =$ number of boys in a family of size 3, if the probability of a girl is .53
    c. $Z =$ number of changes from heads to tails in three tosses of a fair coin

2. In each of the following problems specify the values that the random variable can assume and the distribution of the random variable:
    a. Two six-sided dice are tossed. They are both fair. What is the distribution of the sum of the two numbers which appear?
    b. Three fair dice are tossed. What is the distribution of the number of ones that can appear?
    c. A fair coin is flipped until a head appears. What is the distribution of the numbers of flips?
    d. Two fair six-sided dice are tossed. If the random variable of concern is the larger value appearing on either die, what is its distribution? (Assume that if the same value appears on both, the larger is the common value.)
    e. Six fair coins and a fair six-sided die are tossed. You receive as many dollars as the number of heads appearing, and pay as many dollars as the number which appears on the die. What is the distribution of your payoff?

Let's now look at some specific, widely used distributions of random variables.

6.1.1 Discrete Uniform Distribution—Equiprobable Events

In several of the examples already encountered, the elementary events that could occur were equally likely. Recall the Lottery problem where each ticket had an equal chance of being drawn as well as the various examples discussed in chapter 5. In each of these cases you can define a random variable where values of the random variable correspond to different equiprobable events. Such a random variable is said to have a *discrete uniform probability distribution*. Examples of uniform distributions are plentiful. The famous draft lottery used by the USA to assign numbers to potential draftees is supposed to have created a uniform distribution where the values that X can take on range from 1 to 366, each with probability 1/366. (Leap years' February 29 makes the business a bit sticky, but this can be overcome by various techniques.)

Problem: Ice Cream Concession ——————————————————

You are offered an ice cream concession at a three-day county fair for which you pay $100 per day. Based upon past experience, you know that nice-weather days attract large crowds, in which case you net $300 per day (gross return minus wages, ice cream, and the $100). Rainy or cold-weather days result in a $100 loss (net). Reliable weather data establishes for you that the probability of zero, one, two, or three nice days is about the same. Should you accept the concession?

Analysis: The random variable of interest to you is net profit. Let Y = net profit for the three days. Then Y can take on four different values: $-300, +100, +500$, or $+900$, as shown in table 6.2. For example, the second value ($Y = 100$) is computed as follows: The $100 corresponds to one nice day out of three. You make (net) $300 on that day and lose $100 on each of the other two days. The result is $300 - $200 = $100 profit over the three days.

Since there are four possibilities and each has an equal chance of occurring, the probability of each is 1/4. So, Y is a uniformly distributed random variable.

If your objective is to maximize expected payoffs, then, using your old friend, expected payoff, with the information displayed in table 6.2, accept the offer — unless you have a more profitable way of spending the three days.

TABLE 6.2   Ice Cream Concession

$Y = y$ (net profit)	$P(Y = y)$	$yP(Y = y)$
$3 \times (-100)$ $= -300$	.25	-75
$2 \times (-100) + 1 \times 300 = 100$	.25	$+25$
$1 \times (-100) + 2 \times 300 = 500$	.25	$+125$
$3 \times 300 = 900$	.25	$+225$
		$+300$ = total expected profit

Of course, whether or not you decide to take the ice cream concession now becomes an ambiguous "systems problem": are there better options? is your health up to it? and so on.

PROBLEMS 6.1.1

1. Is the random variable "the number of heads in two tosses of a coin" uniform?

2. Review the problems in the text of sections 5.4.1, 5.4.2, 5.4.3, and 5.4.4. In each of the problems identify a random variable which has a discrete uniform distribution. Specify the values each random variable can assume and the probability of each such value; that is, write down the distribution.

3. Give examples of uniformly distributed random variables. For each example write down the probability of each value of the random variable.

6.1.2   The Bernoulli Distribution   We now turn to one nonuniform distribution of a random variable which is compatible with the view, sometimes useful in decision making, that there are only *two* relevant events associated with a decision. These two events can be described in terms of "yes" or "no," "success" or "failure," "positive" or "negative," and the like. Sometimes the two events are the only ones that can occur; sometimes you *choose* to look at the situation as resulting in only one of two possible events: when you bet on a horse to place first in the races, the fact that your horse comes in second by a nose is irrelevant to the payoff you receive. Hence you choose to consider only the events: "your horse comes in first," "your horse doesn't come in first."

In the Lottery problem of chapter 1, your ticket will be drawn in next Tuesday's lottery (success), or it won't (failure); Proposition 9 on the June ballot will pass (yes) or not (no). Other examples are: you will be awarded a contract with the government (success), or you will not (failure); two heads in three tosses of a fair coin will appear (success), or they will not appear (failure). In this subsection, then, we will explore this two-sided world and its uncertainties.

Many people have thought and written about this two-sided world, but the mathematician James Bernoulli seems to have been one of the first to give it a clear, formal description. In his honor we say that a random variable associated with such a world is a *Bernoulli random variable*. For ease of communication, the Bernoulli random variable is often given the values 0 and 1. In a single flip of a fair coin, if you define

$$X = \text{the number of heads in a single flip}$$

then either $X = 0$ or $X = 1$, and $P(X = 0) = \dfrac{1}{2}$ and $P(X = 1) = \dfrac{1}{2}$

Or, in the Lottery problem

$$X = \begin{cases} 1 \text{ if your lottery ticket is drawn} \\ 0 \text{ otherwise} \end{cases}$$

and

$$P(X = 1) = \frac{1}{100}$$

$$P(X = 0) = \frac{99}{100}$$

In general, if the probability of success is called p, then the probability of failure, denoted by q, is $(1 - p)$, by theorem 1 of section 5.3. The probability distribution of a Bernoulli random variable X can be represented by:

Event	Value x of Bernoulli Random Variable X	Probability $P(X = x)$
Failure	0	$q = 1 - p$
Success	1	p

PROBLEMS 6.1.2

1. Write down the distribution of the Bernoulli random variable "one flip of a fair coin."

2. If you are looking for defective items in a production lot, show how each item can be represented by a Bernoulli random variable.

3. In each of the following cases specify the relevant Bernoulli random variable and the probabilities associated with it.
    a. An inspection of a unit produced by a machine whose specifications allow for one defective in 100 units manufactured
    b. A winning number in a 1000-ticket lottery
    c. A rainy day for which the weather service predicts 30% chance
    d. A sunny day for which the weather service predicts 30% chance

6.1.3   The Binomial Probability Distribution   Some cases in life are "single shot" affairs; if you were the oldest of three brothers in a fairy tale, you'd inevitably fail to solve the king's riddle and you'd lose your head and that would be that as far as you're concerned. But most of the time for most of us, life is a sequence of successes and failures of various kinds, and we're interested in our chances of getting a "satisfactory" combination of successes among the failures.

In the simplest case, a situation can be described by a sequence of what are called *independent identically distributed Bernoulli trials*, as when you flip a fair coin three times. *Independent trials* means in this case that you flip the coin three times and the outcome of any flip (trial) does not depend on whether you got heads or tails on any of the previous trials. *Identically distributed* means that the *probability p* of heads (success) is the same on each flip or Bernoulli trial. In the language of chapter 5, independent identically distributed trials correspond to successive draws from the same set of atomic events where the atomic events have the same probabilities of being drawn each time. By counting the number of successes in such a sequence, you get a new random variable called a *binomial random variable.* The binomial random variable "counts" the number of successes in a sequence of independent identically distributed Bernoulli trials (in each elementary event, it counts the number of atomic events which are "successes") and has that number of successes as its value. Thus, the random variable

X = number of heads (successes) in three tosses of a coin

is an example of a binomial random variable. The binomial random variable X can take on the values 0, 1, 2, and 3.

You have seen this several times before, but now are equipped to talk about *any* sequence of independent identically distributed Bernoulli trials. If you start with the assumption that the probability of a success on any single trial is p, and perform n independent Bernoulli trials, then the random variable

X = number of successes in n trials

is said to have a binomial distribution with "parameters" n and p. We call n and p parameters because they characterize the specific binomial distribution of the random variable under consideration. Clearly, four tosses of a coin with .4 probability of heads (n = 4, p = .4) is different from five tosses of the same coin (n = 5, p = .4) or four tosses of a fair coin (n = 4, p = .5).

The notation used to denote that a random variable X is binomial with parameter n and p is

$$X \sim B(n, p)$$

which tells us that X "is distributed binomially with parameters n and p."

The values that the binomial random variable X can take on are 0, 1, 2, . . . , n (the fewest number of successes is zero, and at most there are n successes in n trials).

It turns out that the probability of r successes (r is, of course, a number between 0 and n) in n trials is

$$P(X = r) = \binom{n}{r} p^r q^{n-r} \tag{1}$$

where, as before,

$$q = 1 - p$$

and, from section 5.4.3:

$$\binom{n}{r} = \frac{n!}{r!\,(n-r)!}$$

You can use this formula as a shortcut for visiting an old friend: the probability of exactly two heads in three tosses of a fair coin. The number of heads (successes), X, is binomially distributed with $n = 3$ and $p = q = 1/2$. Hence the probability of $r = 2$ heads is

$$P(X = 2) = \binom{3}{2} \left(\frac{1}{2}\right)^2 \left(\frac{1}{2}\right)^{3-2}$$

$$= \frac{3!}{2!(3-2)!} \left(\frac{1}{2}\right)^2 \left(\frac{1}{2}\right)$$

$$= \frac{3}{8}$$

which is identical to the result of section 5.4.3. At that time, the probabilities were derived by *counting* the different combinations of two heads after spelling out all the possible elementary events generated by tossing a coin three times. But now, with the new quantitative method of random variables, you have a tool with which to obtain the desired probabilities in seemingly unmanageable problems like 100 flips of a coin: you can generate the probabilities of any binomial random variable directly. For example, consider the probability of drawing no more than one defect in a sample of 10 units from a large lot of items, knowing that the true probability of a defect in the lot is .05. You know that each unit of the sample can either be defective (success) or not (failure) with probability $p = .05$ and $q = .95$, respectively. Therefore, the random variable

$$X = \text{number of defects in a sample of 10 units}$$

is binomial with parameters $n = 10$ and $p = .05$. In order for the sample not to contain more than one defect, it must have either no defects ($X = 0$) or exactly one defect ($X = 1$). Hence the desired probability consists of the sum of the probabilities of two mutually exclusive events

$$P(X = 0) + P(X = 1) = \binom{10}{0} (.05)^0 (.95)^{10} + \binom{10}{1} (.05)^1 (.95)^9 = .9138$$

You can see that even with the formula, performing the necessary computations can become tedious if the number of trials n is large. For this reason, tables which contain binomial probabilities for some common values of the parameters n and p are given in appendix 6.1. You can verify any of the numbers in the table by calculating the probabilities yourself from formula (1).

*   To convince those of you who are dubious that formula (1) for computing the probabilities of a binomial random variable is correct, we will deduce the formula from basic assumptions. As before, we (arbitrarily) give "success" the value 1 and "failure" the value 0 at each trial. Then a series on n trials can be represented by a string of 0's and 1's. Each such string corresponds to one elementary event, and an example would look like this: 0010110111001010 . . . . For example, if heads is success and a coin is flipped three times, the elementary event HTH would be represented by 101. Since a binomial random variable counts the number of successes, it is simply the number of ones in such a string. Now, since the trials are *independent*, the probability of *any* elementary event with r successes and hence $(n - r)$ failures in a particular order is just the *product* of the probabilities of the atomic events at each trial, by assumption 4, section 5.3.

For example, $r = 4$ successes and $(n - r) = 3$ failures in the particular order 1100101 occurs with probability

$$p \times p \times q \times q \times p \times q \times p$$

where the p's occur 4 times and the q's occur 3 times. The probability is thus $p^4 q^{7-4}$. In general, the probability of r successes and $n - r$ failures in a *particular* order is $p^r q^{n-r}$. Hence if you have a coin which is biased toward heads so that heads appears 60% of the time $(p = .6)$, if you flip the coin three times, the probability of HTH = 101 is

$$(.6)(.4)(.6) = (.6)^2(.4)^1 = p^2 q^{3-2}$$

Now the probability that the binomial random variable X takes on the value r is just the sum of the probabilities *of all the mutually exclusive elementary events with r successes*. Each of these elementary events has the r successes in different order: for example, for $n = 7$, $r = 3$, 1110000 and 1101000 are two such events. But there are $\binom{n}{r}$ distinguishable elementary events of r successes in a sequence of n trials (section 5.4.3), since that is the number of different ways that we can arrange r ones in the n slots available. So the probability that $X = r$ is the sum of the probabilities of $\binom{n}{r}$ mutually exclusive events, each of which has probability $p^r q^{n-r}$. So:

$$P(X = r) = \binom{n}{r} p^r q^{n-r}$$

Recall also from section 5.4 that $\binom{n}{r}$ is equal to $\binom{n}{n-r}$, so we could have placed the $(n - r)$ zeros in the n slots and gotten the same result.

Problem: Screwy Nut Corporation ────────────────────

As quality control manager for the Screwy Nut Corporation, you have determined that 2% of the screws you produce are defective. Screwy Nut has a prospective contract with a radio manufacturer who uses 10 screws for the installation of radios in their housings. The manufacturer has found that if three or more of the screws are defective, the housing will fall apart and he will lose customers. He has asked your company for the percentage of times this will occur if he contracts with you. How would you calculate the information he desires?

Analysis: Because the radio manufacturer is concerned with each individual radio for which 10 screws are used, the random variable of relevance to you is the number of defective screws in a lot of size 10. You wish to find the probability that the random variable

$$X = \text{number of defective screws}$$

is greater than or equal to 3, denoted by $P(X \geq 3)$.

That is, that the random variable X can take on any of the values 3, 4, 5, 6, 7, 8, 9, 10.

Since you know that 2% of the screws produced are defective and you assume that the lot of 10 screws for each radio is chosen randomly, the probability of a "success" on a single trial (since X counts bad screws, "success" here means a bad screw) is $p = .02$. So $X \sim B(10, .02)$, which is read "X is a binomially distributed random variable with parameters $n = 10$; $p = .02$."

By our probability assumption 3, $P(X \geq 3)$ is the sum of the probabilities of the eight mutually exclusive events represented by $X = 3$, $X = 4$, $X = 5$, $X = 6$, $X = 7$, $X = 8$, $X = 9$, and $X = 10$. You can compute the probability of each of these events by using the binomial distribution formula (appendix 6.1 does not contain values for $p = .02$), and you come up with the following:

$$P(X=3) = \binom{10}{3}(.02)^3(.98)^7 = \frac{10!}{(10-3)!\,(3!)}[.000008 \times .8682] = .0008$$

$$P(X=4) = \binom{10}{4}(.02)^4(.98)^6 = 210 \times 16 \times 10^{-8} \times .8859 \approx 0^*$$

$$P(X=5) = \binom{10}{5}(.02)^5(.98)^5 = 252 \times 32 \times 10^{-10} \times .9040 \approx 0$$

$$P(X=6) = \binom{10}{6}(.02)^6(.98)^4 = 210 \times 64 \times 10^{-12} \times .9224 \approx 0$$

───

* $\approx$ means "approximately equal to."

$$P(X=7)=\binom{10}{7}(.02)^7(.98)^3=120\times128\times10^{-14}\times.9412 \qquad \approx 0$$

$$P(X=8)=\binom{10}{8}(.02)^8(.98)^2=45\times256\times10^{-16}\times.9604 \qquad \approx 0$$

$$P(X=9)=\binom{10}{9}(.02)^9(.98)^1=10\times512\times10^{-18}\times.9800 \qquad \approx 0$$

$$P(X=10)=\binom{10}{10}(.02)^{10}(.98)^0=1\times1024\times10^{-20}\times1 \qquad \approx 0$$

The sum of these eight terms is $P(X \geq 3)$, which is the probability that the housing will fail: $\approx .0008$.

You can considerably reduce the amount of computation by using the fact that the probabilities of the two compound events, $X \geq 3$ and $X < 3$, must sum to 1. (By theorem 5.1, $P(X \geq 3) = 1 - P(X < 3)$.) You know that $P(X < 3) = P(X \leq 2) = P(X=0) + P(X=1) + P(X=2)$. Thus you can obtain the desired probability by computing only three probabilistic terms:

$$P(X=2)=\binom{10}{2}(.02)^2(.98)^8 = 45 \times .0004 \times .8508 = .0153$$

$$P(X=1)=\binom{10}{1}(.02)^1(.98)^9 = 10 \times .02 \times .8338 = .1668$$

$$P(X=0)=\binom{10}{0}(.02)^0(.98)^{10} = 1 \times 1 \times .8171 = .8171$$

The sum of these is .9992, which is the probability that the housing will be O.K. The probability it will fail is then $1 - .9992 = .0008$, as above.

There is still another way to compute the probability that the housing will fail. Instead of counting the number of defectives, you can define the random variable

$$Y = \text{number of good screws in a lot of size 10}$$

where a success corresponds now to a good screw, and the probability of a success is $p = .98$; that is, $Y \sim B(10,.98)$.

As you have seen, the event "housing will fail" is associated with $X \geq 3$; but "three or more defectives" is identical to "seven or fewer good screws," so the probability of the event of interest in terms of the random variable Y is $P(Y \leq 7)$. You can obtain $P(Y \leq 7)$ by adding up the probabilities of the mutually exclusive events, $Y = 0,1,2,3, \ldots ,7$. Again, to reduce computation you can use the fact that

$$P(Y \leq 7) = 1 - P(Y > 7) = 1 - [P(Y=8) + P(Y=9) + P(Y=10)]$$

where each of the terms in brackets is calculated by using the binomial formula. For example,

$$P(Y = 8) = \binom{10}{8}(.98)^8(.02)^{10-8} = \frac{10!}{8!(10-8)!}\ [(.851)(.0004)] = .0153$$

See if you get the same result, .0008, using Y instead of X.

PROBLEMS 6.1.3

1. What is n and what is p in the binomial random variable "three tosses of a fair coin"?

2. Verify the fact that the probability of one success in 10 trials is .3874 if the probability of success is .10 by using the binomial formula.

3. In the Screwy Nut Company problem suppose that 5% of the screws are defective. What is the probability that three or more screws are defective? What if the screws are defective 20% of the time? Use appendix 6.1 to calculate your results.

4. What is the probability of six or more successes in eight tosses of a fair coin? In 10 tosses? Use appendix 6.1.

5. Upon returning from Las Vegas your friend announces that he has accomplished the "impossible"; he has won ten consecutive times in betting on the color red in the game of roulette. (There are 16 red slots, 16 black slots, and two green slots on a roulette wheel. The chances of landing in any slot are equal). How "impossible" is this feat?

6. How much more "possible" is it to win *exactly* five out of 10 bets on red in a roulette game?

7. You are in charge of a manufacturing process which is intended to produce electrical fuses with approximately 1% defectives, and you have decided to conduct a check every hour by trying 10 fuses selected at random from each hour's production. If one or more of the 10 fuses fails, the process is halted and carefully examined. Is it probable that the process will be examined needlessly in a given instance?

8. Would the above probability change if the hourly sample is
   a. reduced to five fuses?
   b. increased to 20 fuses?
   c. What is your conclusion based on the results obtained in (a) and (b), taking into consideration the fact that testing involves manpower time, and that the fuses tested cannot be reused?

9. Your friend who is a distributor of bean seeds knows that 5% of a large batch will not germinate. He sells his seeds in packages of 200 and guarantees 90% germination or more. He wonders about

the chances he is taking that a given package will not satisfy the guarantee and asks you to help him calculate the desired probability. What should you tell him?

10. You think that 40% of the people in California are Republicans. After sampling 1000 Californians randomly, you find that 350 of those you sample are Republicans. How would you calculate the probability of your getting this few a number or fewer, assuming that 40% is an accurate number? How might you explain the 350 in the sample? (Assume, for now, that tables exist for large n).

6.1.4 The Multinomial Distribution Often, in our decision-making lives, the viewpoint of a two-sided world, which is the basis of the binomial random variable, is too narrow-minded. If an item is defective, it doesn't necessarily mean that it has to be dumped. Sometimes it may be quite reasonable to fix it and then put it up for sale. And in some industries, products called "seconds," "thirds," and so on are alternatives for a somewhat defective item.

When you go to the grocery store, you notice that eggs are sold in any one of several grades. The same is true for potatoes, oranges, and other raw agricultural products. So the idea of categorizing things and results into several classes is not strange and unfamiliar to decision making, and therefore expanding your ability to represent events and compute probabilities based on this extended world view may prove fruitful.

In the last subsection, each trial could result in only one of two atomic events; now we assume that a trial can result in any one of k possible atomic events. For example, if you are a hen keeper and the hen's eggs can be classified into any one of five possible grades, each grade corresponds to an atomic event that may occur at any laying.

The extension of the classification scheme from 2 to k (k can be any integer) categories also changes the representation of each elementary event. While in the binomial case, a string of 1's and 0's has done the job, now we have a string of numbers that can range between 1 and k. For example, 431453221511 is a representation of five possible grades of a dozen eggs "layed at random" by your hen. The first egg's grade is 4, the second has grade 3, and so on. If the probability of an egg being of grade 1 is p_1 and probability of it being of grade 2 is p_2 and so on up to probability of it being of grade 5 is p_5, then the probability of this particular combination of grades of the dozen eggs is

$$p_4 \times p_3 \times p_1 \times p_4 \times p_5 \times p_3 \times p_2 \times p_2 \times p_1 \times p_5 \times p_1 \times p_1$$
$$= (p_1)_4(p_2)^2(p_3)^2(p_4)^2(p_5)^2 \text{ where } p_1 + p_2 + p_3 + p_4 + p_5 = 1$$

since each egg must fall (without breakage!) into one of the five grade categories.

Your decision, however, may not be affected by the order of the atomic events in the sequence but rather by the distribution of the total into the k different classes; an egg buyer for a large supermarket is not interested in the grade of any particular egg in the lot but the knowledge of the grade distribution of eggs is very important for his purchasing decisions. For these purposes, there is another random variable, called multinomial, which (in contrast to the binomial) has k different components: $X_1, X_2, X_3, \ldots, X_k$. The relevant questions that you can ask about such a random variable in n trials (for example, for the eggs, n = 12) are these: What is the probability that $X_1 = 3$, $X_2 = 7$, and so on up to X_k? For example, what is the probability that among 12 eggs, four are of grade 1 ($X_1 = 4$), two are of grade 2 ($X_2 = 2$), two are of grade 3 ($X_3 = 2$), two are of grade 4 ($X_4 = 2$), and two are of grade 5 ($X_5 = 2$)? In probability notation, what is

$$P(X_1 = 4, X_2 = 2, X_3 = 2, X_4 = 2, X_5 = 2)?$$

There are many strings of grade numbers that have $X_1 = 4$, $X_2 = 2$, $X_3 = 2$, $X_4 = 2$, and $X_5 = 2$; one is 431453221511 and another is 341453-221511. It turns out there are 12!/4!2!2!2!2! ways that satisfy the spread of X_i's; if the numbers in the string (trials) are independent, each string has probability $p_1^4\, p_2^2\, p_3^2\, p_4^2\, p_5^2$ of occurring. Hence

$$P(X_1 = 4, X_2 = 2, X_3 = 2, X_4 = 2, X_5 = 2) = \frac{12!}{4!2!2!2!2!}\, p_1^4\, p_2^2\, p_3^2\, p_4^2\, p_5^2$$

In general if there are n independent trials, each of which can result in one of k atomic events with probabilities $p_1, p_2, \ldots, p_k$ with $p_1 + p_2 + \ldots + p_k = 1$, then we can compute the probability that the n trials will result in the distribution: m_1 belonging to class 1, m_2 belonging to class 2, and so on up to m_k belonging to class k, namely

$$P(X_1 = m_1, X_2 = m_2, \ldots, X_k = m_k)$$

$$= \frac{n!}{m_1!m_2! \ldots m_k!}\, p_1^{m_1} p_2^{m_2} \ldots p_k^{m_k} \tag{2}$$

Of course, $m_1 + m_2 + \ldots + m_k = n$ since each trial result is in one of the k classes. This is the general formula for the probability distribution of a multinomial random variable.

Problem: Kitty's Klothing Korner ━━━━━━━━━━━━━━━━━━━━━

As manager of Kitty's, you have received a shipment of "factory reject" blouses which you are selling at half the regular price. You know that there are four different types of mistakes in the blouses and have been told that the production process which makes the blouses has the probabilities of each type of error among the defective blouses as shown in table 6.3.

TABLE 6.3   Probability Distribution of Errors

Type of Error	Probability
$e_1 = $ imperfect darting	.4
$e_2 = $ uneven seam	.3
$e_3 = $ uneven collar	.2
$e_4 = $ uneven sleeve length	.1

There are no cases on record of two or more errors in the same blouse. In the last shipment of 20 blouses, 10 had uneven collars, 4 had uneven seams, 4 had uneven sleeve lengths, and only 2 had imperfect darting. Since it is easiest to sell blouses with uneven darting and hardest to sell those with uneven collars, you feel that perhaps the distribution of errors you have been given is wrong, and therefore perhaps the price should go down. So you ask yourself: What is the probability of getting 20 blouses like the ones you just got?

Analysis: For each defective blouse, there are four possibilities: e_1, e_2, e_3, e_4. The probability of each type of error is given in table 6.3, and, of course, they sum to one. You have four possibilities (instead of two, as in the binomial case), and the process can be described by a random variable which has four components X_1, X_2, X_3, and X_4 representing the number of blouses with imperfect dartings (e_1), uneven seams (e_2), uneven collars (e_3), and uneven sleeve lengths (e_4), respectively. The total number of blouses is $n = 20$, so $X_1 + X_2 + X_3 + X_4$ must add to 20.

To compute the probability of getting a lot of size 20 with $X_1 = 2$, $X_2 = 4$, $X_3 = 10$, $X_4 = 4$, you can use the multinomial distribution formula (2). You know that $p_1 = .4$, $p_2 = .3$, $p_3 = .2$, $p_4 = .1$. So

$$P(X_1 = 2, X_2 = 4, X_3 = 10, X_4 = 4) = \frac{20!}{2!4!10!4!} \times .4^2 \times .3^4 \times .2^{10} \times .1^4$$

which is practically zero, so you are even more suspicious about the ratios of the four types of errors given to you.

PROBLEMS 6.1.4

1. What is the probability of getting a lot of size 10 with the same proportions of the four mistakes as in Kitty's Klothing Korner, provided the probabilities of the mistakes are as given in the problem?

2. In Kitty's Klothing Korner, what is the probability of three blouses with imperfect darting, three with uneven seams, three with uneven color, and one with uneven sleeve lengths in a lot of 10?

3. The probability of a defective in Kessem Knitting Mills' sweaters manufacturing process is .08. Three-quarters of the defects can be sold as "seconds," but the rest must be scrapped. What is the probability of four "seconds" and no rejects in a lot of 50 sweaters if the process is according to specifications?

4. On any January day there is 25% probability that the temperature is above normal and 30% probability that it is normal. The first week of this year's January was "unusually warm" according to the weather bureau; there were four above normal days, two normal, and one below normal. What is the probability of such a week?

5. A priori, you know that any new credit customer your firm does business with has a probability of 1% default and a 5% chance to renegotiate the credit terms. The last report you received from your sales manager shows that of the 100 new credit customers four defaulted and six asked for renegotiation of terms. What is the probability of such a report, provided the distribution of new credit customers hasn't changed?

6.2 Cumulative Distributions of Random Variables

As you saw in the Screwy Nut Company problem, there are decision problems in which you may want to know the probability that a random variable takes on any one of a set of values *below some critical value*. In the problem you were interested in the event that the housing will fail, which occurred when the random variable "Y = number of good screws" took on any value less than or equal to seven. This probability was obtained by adding up the probabilities that the random variable Y takes on each of the possible values less than or equal to seven; that is,

$$P(\text{housing will fail}) = P(Y \le 7) = P(Y = 0) + P(Y = 1)$$
$$+ P(Y = 2) + \ldots + P(Y = 7) = \sum_{i=0}^{7} P(Y = i)$$

In Kitty's problem, you may be interested in the likelihood (probability) of two *or fewer* imperfectly darted blouses out of 20. In general, for any random variable X and any value x, you can compute the probability of X being less than or equal to x. $P(X \le x)$ is a function, since for each value x there corresponds a value between 0 and 1. The function is called the *cumulative distribution function of a random vari-*

able X, abbreviated c.d.f. The values of the cumulative distribution for any value x are obtained by adding up all the probabilities of the values for which the random variable is less than or equal to x. Symbolically,

$$P(X \leq x) = \sum_{i \leq x}^{x} P(X = i)$$

Problem: The Corner Grocery Store ———————————————————

As manager of the Corner Grocery Store, you know that the random variable, which you call X, representing the number of customers who are in your store at any moment of time, has the probability distribution given in table 6.4.

TABLE 6.4   Probability Distribution of X

x = No. of Customers in Store	P(X = x)
0	.07
1	.04
2	.06
3	.07
4	.16
5	.1
6	.11
7	.1
8	.1
9	.06
10	.05
11	.05
12	.03

You are expecting the fire inspector to show up any day now to inspect your store, and the law says that a grocery store which has more than seven people in it at any time must have special fire equipment installed. Not having this equipment, you would like to estimate the probability that you won't get caught with more than seven people in your store. What is the probability?

Analysis: What you are looking for here is the probability that seven customers or fewer are in the store at any given time, which is equivalent to the value of the c.d.f. of X at x = 7, P(X ≤ 7). From table 6.4, you can compute the c.d.f. of X up to and including a value x by adding up the probabilities of the values for which X ≤ x. The results are given in table 6.5.

TABLE 6.5   The c.d.f. of X

x = No. of Customers in Store	P(X ≤ x)
0	.07
1	.11
2	.17
3	.24
4	.40
5	.50
6	.61
7	.71
8	.81
9	.87
10	.92
11	.97
12	1.00

Another way of presenting the c.d.f. appears in figure 6.1.

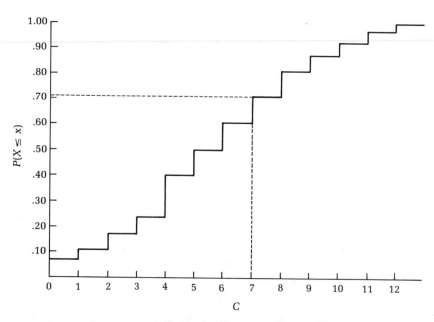

Figure 6.1   The c.d.f. of X

From table 6.5 and figure 6.1, $P(X \le 7) = .71$. Hence your chances are better than 50-50 that the inspector won't catch you.

Sometimes you may be interested in the probability that the random variable is *greater* than some number. Such was the case in the Screwy Nut Company where the event of interest—the housing will fail—was associated with the random variable

$$X = \text{number of bad screws}$$

being greater than 2. One way to obtain the probability of $(X > 2)$ is to use theorem 5.1:

$$P(X > 2) = 1 - P(X \leq 2)$$

In our new terminology $P(X \leq 2)$ is the value of the c.d.f. at $X = 2$, so if you know the cumulative distribution of the random variable X, it is easy to find $P(X > 2)$.

In general, for any value x

$$P(X > x) = 1 - P(X \leq x)$$

and

$$P(X \geq x) = 1 - P(X < x)$$

Thus if you wish to know the probability that more than seven customers will enter the store during the time of inspection, you can calculate it:

$$P(X > 7) = 1 - P(X \leq 7) = 1 - .71 = .29$$

Still another probability value of interest can be obtained if the c.d.f. is known. Suppose the fire inspector will force you to buy the fire equipment if the number of customers is greater than nine, but if it is seven, eight, or nine he returns in a few days for another inspection. You are now interested in

1. the probability that $(X > 9)$ which corresponds to the outcome "must purchase fire equipment," and

2. the probability that $(7 \leq X \leq 9)$, which is associated with the outcome "a citation and a further visit."

1. $P(X > 9) = 1 - P(X \leq 9) = 1 - .87 = .13$

2. $P(7 \leq X \leq 9) = P(X = 7) + P(X = 8) + P(X = 9)$
$$= .1 + .1 + .06 = .26$$

Using the c.d.f. values, $P(7 \leq X \leq 9) = P(X \leq 9) - P(X < 7)$
$$= P(X \leq 9) - P(X \leq 6)$$
$$= .87 - .61$$
$$= .26$$

In general, if you are interested in the probability that some random variable X takes on values not to exceed some number b and greater than or equal to some number a, then

$$P(a \leq X \leq b) = P(X \leq b) - P(X < a)$$

Also,

$$P(a < X \leq b) = P(X \leq b) - P(X < a)$$

and

$$P(a \leq X < b) = P(X < b) - P(X < a)$$

PROBLEMS 6.2

1. Using the distribution of customers given in table 6.4 in the text, calculate the following:
    a. $P\,(C \leq 5)$
    b. $P\,(C < 5)$
    c. Explain the difference between (a) and (b).
    d. $P\,(C \geq 3)$
    e. $P\,(C > 3)$
    f. Explain the difference between (d) and (e).
    g. $P\,(3 < C < 5)$
    h. $P\,(3 < C \leq 5)$
    i. $P\,(3 \leq C < 5)$
    j. $P\,(3 \leq C \leq 5)$

2. Use appendix 6.1 to find the cumulative distribution of a binomial random variable with $n = 9$, $p = .4$.

3. Write down the cumulative distribution of X = number of heads in four tosses of a fair coin. What is $P(1 \leq X \leq 4)$?

4. What is the probability that the winning number in a turn of roulette is between 10 and 20? There are 38 slots (37 consecutive numbers, from zero to 36, and one "double zero") on a roulette wheel; the probabilities of landing on any number are equal.

5. In the context of problem 7, section 6.1.3: What is the probability that the process will needlessly be examined in a given instance if the procedure you follow is to examine only if three or more of the fuses in the sample of 10 are defective?

6. As a prosperous manufacturer of bolts you are currently shopping for a new machine to increase your production capacity. You know that your customers are very strict about meeting their specifications; therefore you've ordered that all bolts whose diameters deviate from .25 by more than .05 must be scrapped. You also know

that a machine which is expected to produce more than 20% beyond the above tolerance specifications is unprofitable. You are reviewing written material concerning a particular machine. It explains that the machine will tolerate diameters between .18 and .4. The probability that you get the exact diameter that you set is .1; the probability of a deviation being +.01 is 5%, −.01 is also 5%, and the occurrence of any other deviation, measured in hundredths, is equally likely. Should you purchase this machine?

7. You are about to contract for the construction of a filling station. The regional gasoline supplier has informed you that the delivery of gasoline will be once every week. You assess the probability of the weekly volume of sales X (in thousands of gallons) to be

$$P(X = x) = \frac{1}{2^x}; \quad x = 1, 2, 3, \ldots$$

and you need to decide on minimum capacity of the tank to be constructed in order to meet the weekly demand with probability of 93.75%. What should be your specifications to the contractor?

6.3 Summary

When you left chapter 5, you were searching for a way concisely to represent the probabilities of decision-relevant outcomes. Random variables turn out to be a convenient way of doing so. The following points are worth repeating:

a. Some phenomena, such as the two-sided and several-sided world of decisions, can be adequately represented by random variables with specific distributions such as the multinomial and binomial.

b. The cumulative distribution of a random variable may be useful for reporting information about the probabilities needed for a decision.

Appendix 6.1

Individual Binomial Probabilities $p(x)$ (If $p > .50$, work in terms of the complementary event "failure" instead of "success.")

n	r	.05	.10	.15	.20	.25	.30	.35	.40	.45	.50
1	0	.9500	.9000	.8500	.8000	.7500	.7000	.6500	.6000	.5500	.5000
	1	.0500	.1000	.1500	.2000	.2500	.3000	.3500	.4000	.4500	.5000
2	0	.9025	.8100	.7225	.6400	.5625	.4900	.4225	.3600	.3025	.2500
	1	.0950	.1800	.2550	.3200	.3750	.4200	.4550	.4800	.4950	.5000
	2	.0025	.0100	.0225	.0400	.0625	.0900	.1225	.1600	.2025	.2500
3	0	.8574	.7290	.6141	.5120	.4219	.3430	.2746	.2160	.1664	.1250
	1	.1354	.2430	.3251	.3840	.4219	.4410	.4436	.4320	.4084	.3750
	2	.0071	.0270	.0574	.0960	.1406	.1890	.2389	.2880	.3341	.3750
	3	.0001	.0010	.0034	.0080	.0156	.0270	.0429	.0640	.0911	.1250
4	0	.8145	.6561	.5220	.4096	.3164	.2401	.1785	.1296	.0915	.0625
	1	.1715	.2916	.3685	.4096	.4219	.4116	.3845	.3456	.2995	.2500
	2	.0135	.0486	.0975	.1536	.2109	.2646	.3105	.3456	.3675	.3750
	3	.0005	.0036	.0115	.0256	.0469	.0756	.1115	.1536	.2005	.2500
	4	.0000	.0001	.0005	.0016	.0039	.0081	.0150	.0256	.0410	.0625
5	0	.7738	.5905	.4437	.3277	.2373	.1681	.1160	.0778	.0503	.0312
	1	.2036	.3280	.3915	.4096	.3955	.3602	.3124	.2592	.2059	.1562
	2	.0214	.0729	.1382	.2048	.2637	.3087	.3364	.3456	.3369	.3125
	3	.0011	.0081	.0244	.0512	.0879	.1323	.1811	.2304	.2757	.3125
	4	.0000	.0004	.0022	.0064	.0146	.0284	.0488	.0768	.1128	.1562
	5	.0000	.0000	.0001	.0003	.0010	.0024	.0053	.0102	.0185	.0312
6	0	.7351	.5314	.3771	.2621	.1780	.1176	.0754	.0467	.0277	.0156
	1	.2321	.3543	.3993	.3832	.3560	.3025	.2437	.1866	.1359	.0938
	2	.0305	.0984	.1762	.2458	.2966	.3241	.3280	.3110	.2780	.2344
	3	.0021	.0146	.0415	.0819	.1318	.1852	.2355	.2765	.3032	.3125
	4	.0001	.0012	.0055	.0154	.0330	.0595	.0951	.1382	.1861	.2344
	5	.0000	.0001	.0004	.0015	.0044	.0102	.0205	.0369	.0609	.0938
	6	.0000	.0000	.0000	.0001	.0002	.0007	.0018	.0041	.0083	.0156
7	0	.6983	.4783	.3206	.2097	.1335	.0824	.0490	.0280	.0152	.0078
	1	.2573	.3720	.3960	.3670	.3115	.2471	.1848	.1306	.0872	.0547
	2	.0406	.1240	.2097	.2753	.3115	.3177	.2985	.2613	.2140	.1641
	3	.0036	.0230	.0617	.1147	.1730	.2269	.2679	.2903	.2918	.2734
	4	.0002	.0026	.0109	.0287	.0577	.0972	.1442	.1935	.2388	.2734
	5	.0000	.0002	.0012	.0043	.0115	.0250	.0466	.0774	.1172	.1641
	6	.0000	.0000	.0001	.0004	.0013	.0036	.0084	.0172	.0320	.0547
	7	.0000	.0000	.0000	.0000	.0001	.0002	.0006	.0016	.0037	.0078

						p					
n	r	.05	.10	.15	.20	.25	.30	.35	.40	.45	.50
8	0	.6634	.4305	.2725	.1678	.1001	.0576	.0319	.0168	.0084	.0039
	1	.2793	.3826	.3847	.3355	.2670	.1977	.1373	.0896	.0548	.0312
	2	.0515	.1488	.2376	.2936	.3115	.2965	.2587	.2090	.1569	.1094
	3	.0054	.0331	.0839	.1468	.2076	.2541	.2786	.2787	.2568	.2188
	4	.0004	.0046	.0185	.0459	.0865	.1361	.1875	.2322	.2627	.2734
	5	.0000	.0004	.0026	.0092	.0231	.0467	.0808	.1239	.1719	.2188
	6	.0000	.0000	.0002	.0011	.0038	.0100	.0217	.0413	.0703	.1094
	7	.0000	.0000	.0000	.0001	.0004	.0012	.0033	.0079	.0164	.0312
	8	.0000	.0000	.0000	.0000	.0000	.0001	.0002	.0007	.0017	.0039
9	0	.6302	.3874	.2316	.1342	.0751	.0404	.0207	.0101	.0046	.0020
	1	.2985	.3874	.3679	.3020	.2253	.1556	.1004	.0605	.0339	.0176
	2	.0629	.1722	.2597	.3020	.3003	.2668	.2162	.1612	.1110	.0703
	3	.0077	.0446	.1069	.1762	.2336	.2668	.2716	.2508	.2119	.1641
	4	.0006	.0074	.0283	.0661	.1168	.1715	.2194	.2508	.2600	.2461
	5	.0000	.0008	.0050	.0165	.0389	.0735	.1181	.1672	.2128	.2461
	6	.0000	.0001	.0006	.0028	.0087	.0210	.0424	.0743	.1160	.1641
	7	.0000	.0000	.0000	.0003	.0012	.0039	.0098	.0212	.0407	.0703
	8	.0000	.0000	.0000	.0000	.0001	.0004	.0013	.0035	.0083	.0176
	9	.0000	.0000	.0000	.0000	.0000	.0000	.0001	.0003	.0008	.0020
10	0	.5987	.3487	.1969	.1074	.0563	.0282	.0135	.0060	.0025	.0010
	1	.3151	.3874	.3474	.2684	.1877	.1211	.0725	.0403	.0207	.0098
	2	.0746	.1937	.2759	.3020	.2816	.2335	.1757	.1209	.0763	.0439
	3	.0105	.0574	.1298	.2013	.2503	.2668	.2522	.2150	.1665	.1172
	4	.0010	.0112	.0401	.0881	.1460	.2001	.2377	.2508	.2384	.2051
	5	.0001	.0015	.0085	.0264	.0584	.1029	.1536	.2007	.2340	.2461
	6	.0000	.0001	.0012	.0055	.0162	.0368	.0689	.1115	.1596	.2051
	7	.0000	.0000	.0001	.0008	.0031	.0090	.0212	.0425	.0746	.1172
	8	.0000	.0000	.0000	.0001	.0004	.0014	.0043	.0106	.0229	.0439
	9	.0000	.0000	.0000	.0000	.0000	.0001	.0005	.0016	.0042	.0098
	10	.0000	.0000	.0000	.0000	.0000	.0000	.0000	.0001	.0003	.0010

From *Handbook of Probability and Statistics with Tables* by Burlington and May. Copyright © 1970 by McGraw-Hill, Inc., Second Edition. Used by permission of McGraw-Hill Book Company.

7 Random Variables and Measures of Performance

7.1 The Expected Value or Mean of a Random Variable

In most of the uncertainty examples up to this point, the expected value of the payoff has been the measure of performance upon which you have based your decisions. For each combination of a decision and state of the world, a payoff has been deduced, and for each decision the relevant payoffs for the various states of the world have been integrated into a single measure using expected value. Using the newly learned idea of random variables, the expected value associated with a decision can now be viewed as the expected value of a random variable representing payoff, as in the Ice Cream Concession. In general, the symbol $E[X]$ is used to represent the expected value of any random variable X; if X has the values $x_1, x_2, \ldots, x_n$, with probabilities $P(X = x_1)$, $P(X = x_2), \ldots, P(X = x_n)$, then

$$E[X] = x_1 P(X = x_1) + x_2 P(X = x_2) + \ldots + x_n P(X = x_n)$$

In summation notation, this is written

$$E[X] = \sum_{i=1}^{n} x_i P(X = x_i)$$

In the Lottery problem of chapter 1, the random variable X, whose values represent payoffs for the decision to accept the ticket, assumes two possible values, $x_1 = \$75$ and $x_2 = \$0$ with probabilities $P(X = x_1) = 1/100$ and $P(X = x_2) = 99/100$. Thus

$$E[X] = 75 \times \frac{1}{100} + 0 \times \frac{99}{100} = .75$$

as before.

You can also use the idea of expected value with respect to outcomes or states of the world. For example, the random variable $Y =$ number of minutes late you arrive to work if you take your car, whose values represent outcomes in the Route to Work problem of chapter 1, has possible values 0, 6, 15 with probabilities 1/6, 2/6, 3/6, respectively. In this case the expected value of Y

$$E(Y) = 0 \times \frac{1}{6} + 6 \times \frac{2}{6} + 15 \times \frac{3}{6} = 9\tfrac{1}{2} \text{ minutes}$$

is the number of minutes you "expect" to be late if you take your car. Of course it is unlikely that you will be *exactly* $9\tfrac{1}{2}$ minutes late; the expected value of a random variable is just an indicator of the "average" or "mean" value of the phenomenon that the random variable represents. Indeed, the expected value is sometimes called the average or mean value.

The usefulness of the expected value or mean as an indicator of the central value of a random variable is seen in the following example.

Problem: More War ━━━━━━━━━━━━━━━━━━━━━━━━━━━

As advisor to Fun 'n Games, Incorporated, who produce the game More War, you have good reason to believe that the method of making the game results in one defective game out of 30. The managers note that last year 290 defective games had to be discarded and are now wondering whether this is unusual. You know that the company produces 10,000 games a year. On the basis of this information, what should you tell them?

Analysis: The managers are concerned with the performance of the production department of More War. One way to evaluate performance is to compare the actual result (290 defective games) with some number which represents a standard or "expected" number of defective games. Let the random variable

$X =$ number of defective games produced in a year

The values X can take on are 0,1,2, . . . ,10,000, since any number of games (even none or all of them) could turn out defective. You may recognize X as the *sum* of *Bernoulli* random variables (section 6.1.2) which can take on either the value 0 or 1. These values are associated with the atomic events "nondefective" and "defective," respectively. You know from the statement of the problem that the probability of a "defective" is 1/30. From the discussion about the binomial distribution (section 6.1.3) you know that the sum of the 10,000 Bernoulli random variables, each with probability 1/30 of success, constitutes a binomial random variable with $n = 10,000$ and $p = 1/30$.

If you did not know any other quantitative methods, you might have to go through the laborious process of calculating

$$P(X = x) = \binom{10,000}{x} \left(\frac{1}{30}\right)^x \left(\frac{29}{30}\right)^{10,000-x}$$

for $x = 0,1,2, \ldots ,10,000$. Then the desired $E[X]$ would be the sum:

$$E[X] = \sum_{x=0}^{10,000} x \, P(X = x) = 333\frac{1}{3}$$

So you report that the 290 defective items last year is "below normal" for the year, since the normal is $333\frac{1}{3}$ games. (Note again that the expected "normal" never occurs, since usually you can't get $\frac{1}{3}$ of a defective game, but, nonetheless, $333\frac{1}{3}$ is the *expected* number of defectives by definition.)

There is a much easier way to calculate $E[X]$ in this case, which we will state as a theorem. The theorem can easily be proven using the deductive system of probability and the definition of expected value.

THEOREM 7.1   The expected value of the sum of random variables is equal to the sum of the expected values of the random variables. Thus, if X and Y are two random variables, and a new random variable, $Z = X + Y$, is defined, the rule says that

$$E[Z] = E[X + Y] = E[X] + E[Y]$$

For example, if

$X =$ the number of heads on one flip of a fair coin, and
$Y =$ the number of heads on one flip of another fair coin,

then if $Z = X + Y$,

$$E[Z] = E[X] + E[Y] = .5 + .5 = 1$$

In the More War problem, X is the sum of 10,000 Bernoulli random variables; all you need to do is calculate the expected value of each Bernoulli random variable and add them together. The Bernoulli random variables take on the value 1 if a defective occurs, 0 if not, with probabilities 1/30 and 29/30, respectively. Thus, if you call any one of the 10,000 Bernoulli random variables Y_i,

$$E[Y_i] = \frac{1}{30} \times 1 + \frac{29}{30} \times 0 = \frac{1}{30}$$

Since all the Y_i have the same expected values

$$E[X] = E\left[\sum_{i=1}^{10,000} Y_i\right] = \sum_{i=1}^{10,000} E[Y_i] = \sum_{i=1}^{10,000} \frac{1}{30} = 10,000 \times \frac{1}{30} = 333\frac{1}{3},$$

by theorem 7.1.

We can also use theorem 7.1 to deduce a very important result about *any* binomial random variable B:

$$E[B] = np$$

The deduction goes as follows: If Y is a random variable with *Bernoulli* probability distribution and p is the probability of "success," then $E[Y] = p$. This is shown easily:

$$E[Y] = 1 \cdot p + 0 \cdot q = p$$

Now suppose B is a random variable with a *binomial* distribution with probability p of success of each of n trials. Since a binomial random variable in the sum of n independent Bernoulli random variables Y_i, theorem 7.1 says that if $B = \sum_{i=1}^{n} Y_i$, then:

$$E[B] = \sum_{i=1}^{n} E[Y_i] = \sum_{i=1}^{n} p = np$$

PROBLEMS 7.1

1. What is the expected number of customers per hour in the Corner Grocery Store of section 6.2? (Use table 6.4.)

2. Suppose that, in the More War problem, Fun 'n Games produces 15,000 games per year. What is the expected number of defective games, if the probability of a defective is 1/30? 1/20?

3. As the assistant controller in your company you are requested to determine the standard price of a raw material for the cost accounting system. In your inquiry, you find that most dealers in this raw material predict the unit price in the coming year to be in the range of 60¢ to $1 with equal chances assessed to these two values as well as any 10¢ increment in-between. What should be your standard price recommendation? Why have you chosen this answer?

4. Fun 'n Games, Incorporated, produces 10,000 More War games and 20,000 Joe the Killer games. The probability of a defective game is 1/30 for the first game, and 1/20 for the second. How many games

do they "expect" will be faulty, total? Define a random variable representing faulty games. How does theorem 7.1 apply?

5. Every day during the last 10 years (3652 days), your friend has participated in a lottery. Three thousand tickets are sold daily at $1 each for a single prize of $3000. His total wins during his long participation are zero, and he is furious with the organizers. Should he have expected more favorable results?

6. Your friend has found a new gambling arena. It's a lottery with 200 tickets and a single prize of $110. Each ticket is sold for 50¢. But 150 of these 200 tickets can also be purchased together with a stub which independently may bring a prize of $50. The combination of a ticket and stub is sold for 60¢. What can your friend expect from these opportunities? Should he purchase either of the two types of available tickets?

7. During a stereo-warming party that you threw to celebrate the acquiring of your new system, your friend Dick, who is an insurance salesman, suggested that you ought to purchase a fire-theft policy for the system. During the party you didn't pay too much attention to his advice but during the night you started thinking about it, and you felt that protecting your hard-earned stereo was worth a thought. So the following morning you took the time to gather some data from your neighborhood police station, and from it you inferred that the chance of the theft of your new stereo system was 1.2% (per year). You also learned that the chance of your apartment catching fire was 0.5%. Feeling uncomfortable with these surprisingly high rates, you called up Dick to find out about the annual premium involved in purchasing an insurance policy. He gave you the following schedule:

> theft insurance only: $9.30
>
> fire insurance only: $3.10
>
> a special discount rate for theft and
> fire insurance combined: $11.25

All these rates are for a policy which pays $620, the amount you paid for your new stereo system. It is now the time for your decision. What should you do?

8. As the manager of the defectives' repair section you are asked to assist the department head with budgeting the costs of repairing defectives. You know that the cost of repairing a unit is $5, and that there are five machines in the production department with probability of turning out defective units of .01, .02, .005, .01, and .015, respectively. Each machine is expected to manufacture 10,000 units in the next year. What should your repair budget recommendation be?

7.2 The Need for Other Measures of Performance than Expected Payoff

Suppose in Old Uncle Jim's will you are offered a choice between

a. $400,000 in your hand, and

b. a bet in which you receive $1,010,000 if the result of a fair coin flip is heads, while if tails appears, you pay $10,000.

Many of you are probably not wealthy enough to take such an offer lightly, and would choose the sure $400,000 and never look back. But half a chance at a million-plus has an expected value of $500,000, which is more expected dollars than the $400,000 you accepted! So, expected payoff really doesn't capture your choice criteria in this case.

Now suppose your boss has asked you to forecast the total earnings your division will generate in the coming year. Clearly, the profit you'll generate depends on the decisions you'll make during the year, but your problem right now is to choose which target you'd like him to judge you by. Should you give him your "expected" earnings as your target? Perhaps some other number which minimizes the probability of deviation would be better. So it looks as if in some cases at least, expected payoff does not fully represent your real measure of performance.

In the coin flip offer and the target decision, factors like the spread or dispersion of the payoffs become important. There is a wide range in the second, or bet, alternative (from a loss of $10,000 to a gain of over a million dollars) and none in the first (you get 400 grand no matter what).

The inclusion of various factors like spread in a measure of performance is not unique to cases of uncertainty. When choosing a job (chapter 3), location, salary, and stability are all factors to be considered. But, for now, we are concerned with cases where uncertainty prevails. In some cases, you might be interested in some minimum target level — for example, return on investment. Perhaps you'd even be willing to give up possibilities of large gain due to the "risk" that you'll lose money, as in the million-dollar coin flip offer. What all this suggests is that a search is needed for some additional ways besides expected payoff to measure the performance of some decisions. In terms of the MIS, new ways of combining the various payoffs associated with the different outcomes for a given decision may be called for. As we will see in the sections to follow, the "best" relevant measures will depend upon the nature of the decision problem at hand.

PROBLEMS 7.2

The questions raised by the following problems are elaborated upon in future sections of this chapter.

1. Suppose we flip a fair coin; you pay $10 to play and bet that heads will appear. For you to accept this deal, how much would we have

to offer you as a reward for the appearance of heads? How much would we have to offer you as reward in this deal to prefer it to 50 sure dollars?

2. When you gamble in Las Vegas, are you maximizing expected value? Then why do you gamble (if you're a gambler)?

3. If you're a gambler at all, why do you buy insurance? Isn't your expected return from the purchase of insurance negative? (If your answer is no, please let us in on your insurance company, so we can buy some, too.)

4. You have $40 and need an additional $40 to fly home from Las Vegas. You can get the badly needed funds by risking the $40 in one of two ways: (1) a bet that has a 40% chance for you to end up with $80, and 60% chance to lose everything and (2) a gamble with 10% chance for $400, 10% for $60, and 80% for ending up empty-handed. What is your best choice, considering you are determined to go home?

7.3 Some Measures of the Spread of Random Variables

7.3.1 The Range   A measure of the spread of payoffs that immediately comes to mind is simply the difference between the two extreme values that a random variable can take on. *The difference between the two extreme values of a random variable is called the range of the random variable.* For example, the range of the random variable,

$$X = \text{profits},$$

when X can take on the values −$50,000, $10,000, $200,000, and $300,000 with probabilities .15, .25, .4, and .2, respectively, is

$$300,000 - (-50,000) = 350,000$$

If the decision alternative results in a sure thing like $400,000, the random variable "payoff" has only one possible value and the range is zero — no spread. The range in (b) in the million-dollar bet of section 7.2 is

$$1,010,000 - (-10,000) = 1,020,000$$

This measure seems appropriate if your purpose is to order the various alternatives according to differences between extremes; but now suppose Uncle Jim offers you a third alternative. It is also a bet, but now you get $5,000,000 if the coin flipped is heads and nothing if tails appear. Wouldn't you take this bet rather than (b) in 7.2, even though the range is larger? What about the third and first? What if the occurrence of a head (and hence $5,000,000) is 80%? 90%?

You can see that the choices you make in terms of the range are partly a matter of your life-style; no universal logic applies in determining how to use the range. But perhaps we can do better than the range.

7.3.2   Expected Deviation from the Mean   Another way to measure the spread of a random variable like payoff is to subtract the mean or expected payoff from each payoff value; the resulting numbers are the *deviations* of the payoffs from the mean payoff. For example, if the random variable W has distribution

$$P(W = 0) = .2$$
$$P(W = 1) = .4$$
$$P(W = 2) = .3$$
$$P(W = 3) = .1$$

then

$$E[W] = 1.3$$

and the deviations, D, are

$$
\begin{aligned}
D &= 0 - 1.3 = -1.3 & \text{if } W = 0 \\
D &= 1 - 1.3 = - .3 & \text{if } W = 1 \\
D &= 2 - 1.3 = + .7 & \text{if } W = 2 \\
D &= 3 - 1.3 = +1.7 & \text{if } W = 3
\end{aligned}
$$

These deviations themselves form a random variable, just as payoffs form a random variable. The deviation random variable D above takes on the values $-1.3, -.3, +.7, +1.7$. The probabilities are the same as the probabilities of the corresponding payoffs, so the distribution of D is

$$P(D = -1.3) = .2$$
$$P(D = - .3) = .4$$
$$P(D = + .7) = .3$$
$$P(D = +1.7) = .1$$

Weighting the deviation of each payoff from the mean payoff by its probability and summing the numbers gives a measure called the *expected deviation from the mean*. If the deviations are labeled D and the payoffs W, then

Expected Deviation from the Mean $= E[D]$

$$= \sum_{\text{all } d_i} d_i \times P(D = d_i)$$

$$= \sum_{\text{all } w_i} (w_i - E[W])P(W = w_i)$$

This measure is called the *expected* deviation, since $E[D]$ is the expected value of the random variable D. Unfortunately, this measure proves useless since the expected sum of deviations of any random variable X from its mean is *always* zero! Deductively,

$$\sum_{\text{all } x_i} (x_i - E[X])P(X = x_i) = \sum_{\text{all } x_i} (x_i P(X = x_i) - E[X]P(X = x_i)) \quad (2)$$

which can be split up into two summations,

$$= \sum_{\text{all } x_i} x_i P(X = x_i) - \sum_{\text{all } x_i} E[X]P(X = x_i)$$

Since $E[X]$ is a constant,

$$(2) = \sum_{\text{all } x_i} x_i P(X = x_i) - E[X] \sum_{\text{all } x_i} P(X = x_i)$$

But

$$\sum_{\text{all } x_i} P(X = x_i) = 1$$

no matter what X's distribution is, and

$$\sum_{\text{all } x_i} x_i P(X = x_i) = E[X]$$

by the definition of expected value of a random variable X. So

$$(2) = E[X] - E[X] \cdot 1 = 0$$

7.3.3 Expected Absolute Deviation from the Mean   The trouble you ran into in weighting the deviations from the mean can be avoided by using the *absolute values* of the deviations. The absolute value of a number n, represented by $|n|$, is the magnitude of n irrespective of sign, so that $|3| = |-3| = 3$. The *absolute deviation from the mean* is also a bona fide random variable, with its own probability distribution. However, the probabilities may not be exactly the same as the probabilities of the payoffs. For example, if

$$P(W = -3) = .2$$
$$P(W = -1) = .3$$
$$P(W = +1) = .3$$
$$P(W = +3) = .2$$

then

$$E[W] = 0$$

Now, if we denote by A the absolute deviation of W from its mean $E[W]$, then A can take on two values:

$$A = 1 \quad \text{if } W = -1 \text{ or } W = +1$$
$$A = 3 \quad \text{if } W = -3 \text{ or } W = +3$$

and the probability distribution of A is

$$P(A = 1) = .3 + .3 = .6$$
$$P(A = 3) = .2 + .2 = .4$$

Using these probabilities to weight the absolute deviations from the mean and adding up the resulting terms yields the expected absolute deviation from the mean. If W represents payoffs and A the absolute deviations, then

$$\text{Expected Absolute Deviation} = E[A]$$
$$= \sum_{\text{all } a_i} a_i \times P(A = a_i)$$
$$= \sum_{\text{all } w_i} |w_i - E[W]| \times P(W = w_i)$$

In the above example,

$$E[A] = 1 \times .6 + .3 \times .4 = 1.8$$

Returning to the million-dollar bet, you can immediately see that the expected absolute deviation of alternative (a) is zero since

$$|400,000 - 400,000| \times 1 = 0$$

That is, the expected absolute deviation of any sure thing from its mean is 0; a very reasonable result! In (b) the expected absolute deviation of the random variable payoff is

$$|-10,000 - 500,000| \times \frac{1}{2} + |1,010,000 - 500,000| \times \frac{1}{2}$$
$$= 510,000 \times \frac{1}{2} + 510,000 \times \frac{1}{2} = 510,000$$

Different versions of this measure of spread are used widely, particularly in budgetary decision-making and standard cost-accounting systems. In large and complex organizations, decision makers often face the problem of how to manage the subordinate units effectively. This includes taking into account two basic factors: (1) having sufficient control over the managed units, and (2) letting the subordinates have some autonomy over their own affairs. One method that addresses this problem is management via the budget or management via standards; the subordinate unit is given a standard or a budget for its activities, and its performance is measured in terms of absolute deviations from these standards or budget figures. Based upon past data and other information, probabilities can be assessed for each possible value of revenues and expenditures for the year. The mean of these possible values can be used as the standard, the expected absolute deviation as a measure of the "expected" deviation from the standard. However, the mean is not the only applicable standard in all cases. We will see an example of this in the next section.

PROBLEMS 7.3

1. What is the range of the possible values of the random variable:
   a. the number of dots that may appear after tossing three six-sided dice
   b. the number of heads in flipping five coins
   c. the number of switches from heads to tails or from tails to heads in flipping a coin eight times
   d. the total number of defectives in the More War problem (section 7.1)
   e. the number of customers per hour in the Corner Grocery Store problem (section 6.2)

2. Show that the expected deviation from the mean—or expected value—is zero in the following random variables:
   a. number of heads in four tosses of a fair coin
   b. total number of defectives in the More War problem
   c. the number of customers per hour in the Corner Grocery Store problem

3. In part (b) of problem 1 what is the expected absolute deviation from the mean?

7.4   The Median (as Minimizer of Absolute Deviations)

Problem: Kipon Trucking ━━━━━━━━━━━━━━━━━━━━━━━━

You have finally secured your first job; you've been hired as terminal manager with Kipon Trucking Corporation. Your terminal is given a budget every year, and your boss has asked you for an estimate of expenses for next year, upon which to base your terminal's budget. You know that your boss looks mainly at the absolute deviation of actual expenses from the budgeted amount (in either direction) to evaluate promotion possibilities at the end of the year.

Based upon past data, your confidence in your own ability to cut costs, and the possibility of a truckers' strike, you estimate that there is a 20% chance you'll spend $300,000 next year, a 25% chance of spending $350,000, 10% chance of $400,000, 40% chance of $450,000, and a 5% chance of a strike, meaning you'll have to spend $600,000. What budget figure should you suggest to your boss?

Analysis: Your goal, assuming you want a promotion or to quit with a good letter of recommendation, involves being as close as possible to your recommended budget at the end of the year, due to your boss's measure of performance. Of course, you can't recommend a budget that's too high; your boss isn't likely to accept it and you might have to spend money frivolously at the end of the year to meet it. On the other hand, if the budget's too low, you may not be able to come close to it even by taking drastic belt-tightening measures. So perhaps the best budget figure to recommend is one which *minimizes* the absolute deviations that you expect will result at the end of the year.

In quantitative terms, this says you may want to suggest a budget or standard M such that if your cost estimates for the year are c_1, c_2, c_3, . . . , c_n, and your assessed probabilities for their occurrence are $P(C=c_1)$, $P(C=c_2)$, $P(C=c_3)$, . . . , $P(C=c_n)$, then you want to find M which minimizes the sum,

$$\sum_{i=1}^{n} |c_i - M| \times P(C = c_i)$$

It turns out that the expected value or mean of your cost estimates, in general, does *not* minimize; that is, in general, M is *not* $E(C)$.

The number M that *does* minimize the expected absolute deviation from it is called the *median* of the probability distribution. The median, like the mean, indicates the "center" of a distribution. It is the value that divides the set of all possible values of the random variable into two regions, so that the probability is 50% or more that the random variable will take on any value less than or equal to the median, while the probability that the random variable takes on a value greater than or equal to the median is also 50% or more. For example, in the Corner Grocery Store problem of section 6.2, the median is 5 since

$$P(X \leq 5) = .5 \quad \text{and} \quad P(X \geq 5) = .5$$

In the current example the c_i's and their probabilities are:

$$c_1 = 300{,}000 \qquad P(C = c_1) = .20$$
$$c_2 = 350{,}000 \qquad P(C = c_2) = .25$$
$$c_3 = 400{,}000 \qquad P(C = c_3) = .10$$
$$c_4 = 450{,}000 \qquad P(C = c_4) = .40$$
$$c_5 = 600{,}000 \qquad P(C = c_5) = .05$$

and the median of the random variable, C, is 400,000 since

$$P(C \leq 400{,}000) = .55 \quad \text{and} \quad P(C \geq 400{,}000) = .55$$

which are both greater than 50%. To see that the expected absolute deviation from the median is less than the expected absolute deviation from the mean in this example, calculate

$$|300{,}000 - 400{,}000| \times .20 + |350{,}000 - 400{,}000| \times .25$$
$$+ |400{,}000 - 400{,}000| \times .10 + |450{,}000 - 400{,}000| \times .40$$
$$+ |600{,}000 - 400{,}00| \times .05 = \$62{,}500,$$

which is less than the $62,750 obtained by using the mean instead of the median:

$$E[C] = 397{,}500$$

and

$$|300{,}000 - 397{,}500| \times .20 + |350{,}000 - 397{,}500| \times .25$$
$$+ |400{,}000 - 397{,}500| \times .10 + |450{,}000 - 397{,}500| \times .40$$
$$+ |600{,}000 - 397{,}500| \times .05 = \$62{,}750$$

So, you recommend the median of your anticipated expenditures, $400,000, to your boss as the budget if expected absolute deviation is your measure of performance to be minimized.

To summarize, the median of a random variable, like the mean, is a useful measure which indicates the center of a distribution; it also turns out to be the standard which minimizes the "expected" absolute deviation. Such a standard is useful as your "target" if you wish to minimize the expected deviation of your performance from the standard. Of course, this depends upon your accurate assessment of the probabilities of earnings, as well as the strong assumption that very large deviations are not penalized much more heavily than small ones.

PROBLEMS 7.4

1. Compare the expected absolute deviation from the median to the expected absolute deviation from the mean in the Corner Grocery Store problem (section 6.2). Is the expected absolute deviation from the median still the lowest? Why?

2. Describe a random variable whose mean (expected value) is smaller than its median, and another whose mean is larger than its median. Are the distributions of the two random variables different in any other distinguishable way?

3. In part (b) of problem 1 of section 7.3, what is the median of the random variable?

4. In a toss of two fair, six-sided dice, what is the value of the random variable $X = $ sum of dots appearing on both dice that you will suggest as the standard if you wish to minimize the expected absolute deviation from this standard? What is your expectation about the size of the "average" absolute deviation?

5. What should you choose as the standard for raw material usage if from your experience you assess that the distribution of $X = $ raw material usage in pounds is as given by the table, and you wish to minimize the expected absolute deviation from the standard? What do you "expect" the "average" absolute deviation from the standard to be? What do you "expect" the "average" absolute deviation to be?

x_i	$P(x = x_i)$
3	.1
3.5	.15
4	.2
4.5	.25
5	.3

7.5 Expected Squared Deviation from the Mean

Suppose now you are the boss of Kipon Trucking, and would like your many terminal managers to shoot for the mean and not the median since you have found that on the whole the mean values of expenses are lower than the median values. Of course, you can impose this standard of expected value by fiat, but you prefer to get the approval of your employees before doing so. Even better, you would like them to suggest the mean and not the median as the standard. Can you accomplish this?

If you have managers who have read this text, it turns out that you can, by telling them that the deviations from the standard they choose will be *squared* for evaluation purposes. This, of course, differs from the last section in that it penalizes larger deviations more heavily.

If your terminal managers wish to find a standard which minimizes the *expected squared deviations*, the mean does the trick. In quantitative terms, if your future cost estimates are c_i, with probabilities $P(C = c_i)$, then $E[C]$ is the unknown M which minimizes

$$\sum_{\text{all } c_i} (c_i - M)^2 \times P(C = c_i)$$

Notice that $(c_i - E[C])^2$, the squared deviation of the random variable C from its mean, is also a random variable, N, say, with a probability distribution of its own. In Kipon Trucking, N can take on five values:

$$N = (300,000 - 397,500)^2 = \ \ 9,506,250,000 \quad \text{if } C = 300,000$$
$$N = (350,000 - 397,500)^2 = \ \ 2,256,250,000 \quad \text{if } C = 350,000$$
$$N = (400,000 - 397,500)^2 = \ \ \ \ \ \ \ 6,250,000 \quad \text{if } C = 400,000$$
$$N = (450,000 - 397,500)^2 = \ \ 2,756,250,000 \quad \text{if } C = 450,000$$
$$N = (600,000 - 397,500)^2 = 41,006,250,000 \quad \text{if } C = 600,000$$

and the distribution of N is

$$P(N = \ \ \ 9,506,250,000) = .2$$
$$P(N = \ \ \ 2,256,250,000) = .25$$
$$P(N = \ \ \ \ \ \ \ \ 6,250,000) = .1$$
$$P(N = \ \ \ 2,756,250,000) = .4$$
$$P(N = 41,006,250,000) = .05$$

Hence, the expected squared deviation from the mean is

$$E[N] = (300,000 - 397,500)^2 \times .2 + (350,000 - 397,500)^2 \times .25$$
$$+ (400,000 - 397,500)^2 \times .1 + (450,000 - 397,500)^2 \times .4$$
$$+ (600,000 - 397,500)^2 \times .05 = 5,618,750,000$$

which is less than the expected squared deviation from the median:

$$(300,000 - 400,000)^2 \times .2 + (350,000 - 400,000)^2 \times .25$$
$$+ (400,000 - 400,000)^2 \times .1 + (450,000 - 400,000)^2 \times .4$$
$$+ (600,000 - 400,000)^2 \times .05 = 5,625,000,000$$

Although we need the quantitative methods of chapter 11 to prove in general that the mean minimizes expected squared deviations, you can use this result if you'll trust us for now. The method of chapter 11 can also help us prove that the median is the minimizer of expected absolute deviations, which we claimed in the last section.

7.5.1 The Variance The expected squared deviation from the mean is also called the *variance*. In general, the variance of a random variable X which takes on values x with probabilities $P(X = x_i)$ is defined as

$$\sigma_x^2 = \text{Var } [X] = \sum_{\text{all } x_i} (x_i - E[X])^2 P(X = x_i)$$

The variance is commonly denoted either by the Greek symbol σ^2, read "sigma squared" or by Var [X].

For example, if your firm's annual profits are denoted by the random variable X, and the distribution of X is displayed in table 7.1, and you use the mean of $170,000 as the standard, then the variance of profits is

$$\text{Var } [X] = (100{,}000 - 170{,}000)^2 \times .2 + (150{,}000 - 170{,}000)^2 \times .3$$
$$+ (200{,}000 - 170{,}000)^2 \times .4 + (250{,}000 - 170{,}000)^2 \times .1$$
$$= 2{,}100{,}000{,}000$$

TABLE 7.1 Distribution of Profits

Profits in $1000 (x_i)	$P(X = x_i)$
100	.2
150	.3
200	.4
250	.1

7.5.2 The Variance as a Measure of Risk

Problem: Mississippi-Tahoe Corporation ⎯⎯⎯⎯⎯⎯⎯⎯⎯⎯⎯⎯

Your friend David Lamb, who is the investment analyst for Mississippi-Tahoe Corporation (MTC), has come to you for advice. He has been asked by the president of MTC to examine two investment opportunities that the company is considering and to recommend which of the two should be selected for implementation. Both projects require the same cash outlay. Project A is an investment in drilling and development of an oil field in the Mississippi Valley. Project B is land development in the Lake Tahoe area. After looking into the possible costs and benefits of each of the projects, David summarizes the information in tables 7.2 and 7.3, representing the rates of return, X and Y, and their probabilities. A "rate of return" is the percentage of the original investment that you make back in any one year.

TABLE 7.2   Project A Rates of Return

Rates of Return x_i	$P(X = x_i)$
−20%	.1
0%	.2
30%	.5
80%	.2

TABLE 7.3   Project B Rates of Return

Rates of Return y_i	$P(Y = y_i)$
−10%	.3
10%	.1
40%	.4
50%	.1
100%	.1

David has computed the expected value of the rates of return of each of the projects and it turns out that

$$E[X] = E[Y] = 29\%$$

That is, the expected rates of return of project A, $E[X]$, and project B, $E[Y]$, are identical. So he is about to go back and report to the president that there is no reason to prefer either project. But before actually doing so, he would like to consult with you on his recommendation. What should you advise David?

Analysis: Neither of the two projects seems "better" — MTC "expects" to make 29% profit on its investment regardless of which project it chooses. A reasonable suggestion in such a case is to select the project that is less "risky"; risk here can be measured in terms of the spread of the rates of return. Common sense tells you that one project is more risky than another if the spread of its possible rates of return is greater than the spread of the alternative project's rates of return. In practice, the variance of a random variable is used as a measure of the relative riskiness or spread. This is because of the fact that the variance does square the differences, thus heavily weighting large deviations representing outcomes which are seriously "off" the expected rate of return; a distribution centered closely around the mean will show low variance, indicating low risk, while a "risky" one, where you might gain or lose large amounts, has large variance. So you can tell David that if he uses the variance as the measure of risk for the rates of return of the two projects as follows

$$\text{Var } [X] = (-.2 - .29)^2 \times .1 + (0 - .29)^2 \times .2 + (.3 - .29)^2$$
$$\times .5 + (.8 - .29)^2 \times .2 = .0929$$
$$\text{Var } [Y] = (-.1 - .29)^2 \times .3 + (.1 - .29)^2 \times .1 + (.4 - .29)^2$$
$$\times .4 + (.5 - .29)^2 \times .1 + (1.0 - .29)^2 \times .1 = .1089$$

he should recommend drilling for the black gold in the Mississippi Valley.

The incorporation of risk considerations in decision making is something that you encountered before in the million-dollar coin flip of section 7.2. In a situation similar to that of your friend David, many of you would agree on the policy suggested – that is, to recommend the "less risky" project. But some who like risk might disagree with this suggestion. We will return to further analysis of different tastes for risk later in this chapter (section 7.10); we will discuss a quantitative language that incorporates both expected payoff and risk in measures of performance. But for now you should note that measures of spread can be very useful in decision making. Among these measures, the variance and its square root, called the *standard deviation*, are the most widely used. The standard deviation of a random variable X, denoted σ_x, is

$$\sigma_x = \sqrt{\sigma_x^2} = \sqrt{\sum_{\text{all } i} (x_i - E[X])^2 P(X = x_i)}$$

7.5.3 Other Important Uses of Variance and Standard Deviation

Suppose you manufacture steel bars, and the engineering design calls for a tensile strength of exactly 40 lbs. Small variations from this ideal or standard are tolerable, of course, but as the deviations increase, the cost of using the bars goes up. It may be reasonable to assume that the cost goes up in proportion to the *square* of the deviation from the normal or expected value, especially on the weak side. If so, the variance captures one essential feature of the quality control of the bars; the production objective then becomes one of minimizing variance (subject to technological constraints and resources available).

The variance, besides being conceptually convenient, is also used because it has some nice mathematical properties, which the other measures of spread do not. We will cite here without proof several of these properties starting with the following theorem:

THEOREM 7.2   The variance of a sum of n independent random variables is equal to the sum of the n individual variances of these random variables. That is, if the random variables $X_1, X_2, \ldots, X_n$ are independent with variances Var (X_1), Var(X_2), . . . , Var(X_n), respectively, then

$$Var \left[\sum_{\text{all } i} X_i\right] = \sum_{\text{all } i} Var \left[X_i\right]$$

Note the similarity of this theorem to the result of theorem 7.1, which is concerned with the expected value of the sum of random variables. The important difference between the two is that here we require the random variables to be *independent* (similar to independence of events), while in theorem 7.1 we didn't have any such restriction. This is worth noticing since it exemplifies what we have been saying all along — that before using a deductive quantitative method, you must be sure that the situation is right; that is, that the assumptions which are the basis of the quantitative method are satisfied. So, if you wish to compute the expected value of the sum of random variables, you can go ahead and use theorem 7.1, but if you wish to compute the variance of such a sum, you must be sure that the assumption about independence is met before using theorem 7.2.

You can now use the result of theorem 7.2 in easing the computation of the variance of the binomial distribution. Recall from section 6.1.3 that a binomial random variable can be viewed as the sum of n independent Bernoulli random variables. Hence, the variance of a binomial random variable is the sum of the variances of n Bernoullis. Now what is the variance of a Bernoulli random variable? For a random variable X that takes on the value 1 with probability p, 0 with probability $q = 1 - p$, and has expected value p (see section 6.1.2):

$$\begin{aligned} Var [X] &= (1 - p)^2 p + (0 - p)^2 q \\ &= (1 - p)^2 p + p^2(1 - p) \\ &= p(1 - p) \\ &= pq \end{aligned}$$

Therefore the variance of a binomial random variable,

$$Y = \sum_{i=1}^{n} X_i,$$

where each X_i is a Bernoulli random variable with probability of success p on each of n trials, is

$$Var [Y] = Var \left[\sum_{i=1}^{n} X_i\right] = \sum_{i=1}^{n} Var [X_i] = \sum_{i=1}^{n} pq = npq$$

Using this result, you can tell, for example, the management of Fun 'n Games in the More War problem (section 7.1) directly that the variance of the number of More War defectives this year is

$$10,000 \times \frac{1}{30} \times \frac{29}{30} = 322.2$$

and that the standard deviation is $\sqrt{322.2} \approx 18$.

For the management of Fun 'n Games to evaluate whether the deviation of the actual (290) from the expected (333.33) number of defective games is unusual, it needs some comparative reference, and the variance or the standard deviation can also serve in this capacity. In this case, the management can calculate that the actual deviation is 2.4 times the standard deviation $(333.33 - 290)/18 \approx 2.4$. Using the standard deviation to measure the significance of an actual result from the mean or expected value is quite appealing, since the standard deviation is a *relative* measure—that is, independent of the units of the random variable. If the units are "tens of games" (the expected number of defective "tens of games" is 33.333) the actual deviation (in units of standard deviation) would be 2.4, the observed value 29.0, and the standard deviation would still be 1.8. See the following example.

Problem: The Watergate Detergent Company (WDC) ——————————

As the manager of WDC, you receive a letter regarding a new type of machine for packing detergents in boxes. Currently you have two relatively old packing machines, one which packs 1000 one-pound packages per hour, and the other 750 24-ounce packages per hour. The specifications of both machines are such that the weight of packages packed by the one-pound machine is uniformly distributed with values ranging from 15/16 to 17/16 pounds, while the outputs of the second are uniformly distributed between 22 and 26 ounces. Recently you have received reports that the distribution is *not* uniform; practically all the packages packed by the one-pound machine are 1.0625 pounds, and packages from the other machine weigh 25 ounces. Since the price charged for the packages is according to the printed weight (one pound and 24 ounces, respectively) and repairing the machines is impractical, you've decided to replace only one machine by a new one (that's all the funds you have since you've apparently been undercharging!). The new one-pound machine costs the same amount as a new 24-ounce machine, and both produce at the same rate as the old machines with the same specifications. Which machine should you replace?

Analysis: The information that you have about the one-pound machine is in terms of pounds, while the information about the 24-ounce machine is in terms of ounces. Hence a comparison of the absolute deviations of these two machines may be misleading (clearly $1.0625 - 1 < 25 - 24$). You might want to equalize the units of the information about the two machines in some way for purposes of comparing the absolute deviations. If you convert the information about the first machine from pounds to ounces, you compute $17 - 16 = 1$ to be the deviation, and this is equal to the deviation of the other machine $(25 - 24 = 1)$. The implication of this comparison is that you should be indifferent about which machine to replace. But you probably can feel that you're somehow losing more percentagewise on the one-pound machine. That is, the comparison should be in *relative* rather than absolute terms. For this purpose you can use the *standard deviation* as a unit of comparison, which also takes care of the difference in units as well.

The original standard deviation of the one-pound machine based upon the uniform distribution is

$$\sqrt{\left(\frac{15}{16} - 1\right)^2 \times \frac{1}{3} + (1 - 1)^2 \times \frac{1}{3} + \left(\frac{17}{16} - 1\right)^2 \times \frac{1}{3}} \approx .05$$

and the original standard deviation of the second machine is

$$\sqrt{\begin{aligned} &(22 - 24)^2 \times \frac{1}{5} + (23 - 24)^2 \times \frac{1}{5} + (24 - 24)^2 \times \frac{1}{5} \\ &+ (25 - 24)^2 \times \frac{1}{5} + (26 - 24)^2 \times \frac{1}{5} \end{aligned}} \approx 1.414$$

The deviation of the first machine from the one-pound mean in terms of the number of *standard deviations* is

$$\frac{1.0625 - 1}{.05} = 1.25$$

and the deviation of the second machine in the same terms is

$$\frac{25 - 24}{1.414} \approx .7$$

which indicates that the one-pound packaging machine should be replaced, since you are losing more on the first machine *relative* to its output per package.

Changing the first machine's units to *ounces*, the exact same result occurs. The standard deviation of the first distribution is

$$\sqrt{(15 - 16)^2 \times \frac{1}{3} + (16 - 16)^2 \times \frac{1}{3} + (17 - 16)^2 \times \frac{1}{3}} \approx .8$$

and 17 ounces is

$$\frac{17 - 16}{.8} \approx 1.25 \text{ standard deviations away from the mean}$$

So, changing the units does not change the number of standard deviations from the mean.

To see why this is true of the standard deviations measure—that is, why it is in fact a "standard" for measuring "deviations" from the mean of a random variable—notice what happens to the units in the calculations. In the case of pounds, the units under the square root sign are (lbs/package)^2:

$$\sigma^2 = \left(\frac{15}{16} \text{ lbs/package} - 1 \text{ lb/package}\right)^2 \times \frac{1}{3}\frac{\text{package}}{\text{packages}} + \ldots$$

and when the square root is taken, the units are lbs/package.

$$\sigma = \frac{1.0625 \text{ lbs/package} - 1 \text{ lb/package}}{.05 \text{ lbs/package}} = 1.25 \text{ standard deviations}$$

Changing the units to ounces will result in no change in number of standard deviations, since a standard deviation will now be in terms of ounces/package and dividing by σ will again yield 1.25 standard deviations. The idea is that the standard deviations are *always* in the same units as the mean, so changing units won't affect the comparison of actual to expected value.

7.5.4 Chebyschev's Inequality   The important result above tells you that you can always trust the standard deviation to give you a good idea of how far your observed result is from the mean. But can you say whether "2.4 standard deviations away from the mean" is unusual? It turns out that you can, for *any* random variable,* based upon a theorem attributed to Pafnutry Chebyschev (1821–1894). This remarkable result tells you that the probability that your actual number of games in More War is 2.4 standard deviations away from the mean or more (that is, < 290 or > 376.66) is *at most* $(1/2.4)^2 \approx .175$. Since the distribution is *symmetric* in the binomial case, the probability that you get 290 or fewer defective games when the expected value is 333.33 is *at most* .0875. More formally, Chebyschev's result is:

> If you know the mean of any random variable X and its standard deviation, then for any number of standard deviations k, the probability that you'll get a number k standard deviations or further from the mean is at most

$$\frac{1}{k^2}$$

---

*The random variable must have a finite variance.

So you can refine your original advice to Fun 'n Games, Incorporated, in the More War problem, based upon your knowledge of Chebyschev's inequality. Perhaps they produce slightly fewer defectives than 1 in 30, based upon last year's results.

You can improve on Chebyschev's $1/k^2$ if you know exactly the distribution of the random variable, and you may wish to do so; we will do this in section 7.7. But knowledge of the inequality itself is often quite useful without further computation; for example, the probability of being 4 or more standard deviations away from the mean of *any* random variable is at most

$$\frac{1}{4^2} = \frac{1}{16}$$

Not a very high probability. So if you get an observation 4 standard deviations away from the supposed mean, you might want to question the validity of the estimated mean of the random variable!

PROBLEMS 7.5

1. What is the variance of X in problem 5 of the last section? What is its standard deviation?

2. Verify in problem 5 of the last section that the mean, and not the median, minimizes the variance.

3. For part (b) of problem 1 in section 7.3 compute the variance of the random variable.

4. What objections do you have to the variance as a measure of riskiness of an investment? What other measure might you suggest?

5. Would you choose X in the Mississippi–Tahoe Corporation problem even if $E(X)$ were a little smaller than $E(Y)$? Why?

6. You own a clothing store and have just received a lot of 1000 cloth shawls. If each shawl has a 4% chance of being defective, how many do you "expect" to have to sell at reduced price for defective? Suppose 60 are defective; how "abnormal" is this? How many standard deviations is this away from your expected number? At what level of defectives would you complain to the distributor? How did you choose that level?

7. How would your analysis change in problem 6 if you used X = "tens of defectives" as your random variable of interest? How many standard deviations away from the expected number of "tens of defectives" is 6? Is this unusual?

8. Using Chebyschev's inequality (ignoring the fact that you know the distribution is binomial), what is the lowest probability that you get between 30 and 50 defectives? Now using what you know about the variance of the binomial, what is the *actual* probability?

7.6 Characteristics of Distributions of Random Variables: An Overview

In sections 7.1–7.4 we've discussed several characteristics of probability distributions of random variables in their role as possible measures of performance for decisions. We looked at the *expected value* and the *median* as characteristics of the central (normal, usual) values of a random variable, and as standards to shoot for or have your subordinates shoot for. We also examined the *range*, the *absolute deviation from the mean and median*, and the *squared deviation from the mean*. These are measures of dispersion or spread. We saw that the *expected value of the absolute deviation* or the *expected absolute deviation* can be minimized by using the median as a standard. We then examined the *expected value of the squared deviation from the mean*, better known as the *variance*, and its square root, the *standard deviation*, as measures of spread (dispersion, scatter) which can be used as surrogates for risk or to measure deviations from standards. As you can imagine these are not all the characteristics of random variables, and even within the two classes of measures, centrality and spread, there are others besides those we discussed. For example, suppose you are in Las Vegas with $50 and you need about $100 to fly home. The only way available for you to get the extra $50 is to gamble in one of the games available and pray that you win. How might you choose among the games in which to participate? We will not go into an analysis of the problem but simply mention that in this case your objective seems to be to maximize the *likelihood* of obtaining an extra $50. This means that you might be interested in the game with the highest probability of $50 payoffs — that is, the game whose payoff random variable has a "mode" of $50. The *mode* of a random variable is that value of the random variable that has the highest likelihood (probability) of occurring.

We hope that you've gotten a feel for using characteristics of random variables like payoff as measures of performance in your decision-making life. Now it's time to turn to another important aspect of using the characteristics of distributions of random variables, namely, the reduction of informational overload.

7.7 Random Variables: Their Moments and Information

Your journey through decision making in the world of uncertainty began by spelling out each component of S, the set of states of the world. Soon you realized that in many cases such practices cause an overload of information which might distract you as the decision maker. Consequently, we suggested that S should be described by events that give rise to different outcomes, and we called these events "compound" since each way consists of more than one elementary event (state of the world). But even this method can be cumbersome, and hence we've described a way to express compound events concisely—via random variables. Thus you can express the behavior of

$$X = \text{the number of More War defective games}$$

by the concise notation $X \sim B$ (10,000, 1/30). However, this very compact notation is not altogether satisfactory, because it fails to do one important thing well: namely, to inform the decision maker economically about the probabilities of very unsatisfactory or unusual events. You can imagine the detailed work that either you or a computer would have to do in order to determine the probability that X is greater than 400, say.

We saw in the last section that Chebyschev's inequality can help in this regard, but we would like, if possible, to improve on that result when we know more about the distribution of the random variable. What is needed is a kind of super method which will classify probability distributions and tell us how to estimate what we need to know economically.

Those of you who have had some physics can easily see the analogy between some of the characteristics of probability distributions discussed earlier and the "moments" which are used in the description of the mass of a body. The mass of a body, like the earth, can be described in terms of

1. its center of gravity, which is the first moment,
2. the second moment around the center of gravity, which describes in part the scatter, and
3. higher moments.

Just as in physics, we can make many useful implications from a knowledge of the moments: if the probability distribution can be described, the moments can provide the MIS with very powerful and compact information about that distribution.

It was Karl Pearson (1885–1936) who showed that probability distributions of random variables can be described by moments. He identified the first moment to be the expected value or mean, the second moment to be the variance, and higher moments which we haven't discussed. Pearson saw the "complete" program to be one of classifying the different "masses" which the distributions represent and calculating the appropriate moments for any given distribution. Given the class and the moments, you can recreate the whole distribution—a very compact and economical information system!

To see how this idea works, suppose we return one more time to the coins, but now, sweeping modesty aside, we ask for the probability of 550 or more heads in a gleeful toss of $10 worth of pennies. If

$$X = \text{the number of heads}$$

then $X \sim B(1000,1/2)$, and you could spend the rest of this sunny weekend computing $P(X \geq 550)$. But it can be shown that $B(1000,1/2)$ very closely approximates a symmetric probability distribution in which X takes on any real-number values, called the *normal distribution*. This distribution was well known in Pearson's time and has been tabulated extensively. Appendix 7.1 shows the probability of deviating from the expected value of any normal distribution by more than k standard deviations, where k can be 1/2, 1, 2, 3, etc. For example, using appendix 7.1, the probability of a normal random variable deviating from its mean (in either a plus or minus direction) by more than

a.   1 standard deviation is .3174

b.   2 standard deviations is .0456

c.   3 standard deviations is .0026

d.   4 standard deviations is virtually zero

We have seen earlier that the variance of $B(n,p)$ is npq; hence the standard deviation is $\sqrt{npq}$. For the case of $B(1000,1/2)$, therefore, the standard deviation is $\sqrt{1000 \cdot 1/2 \cdot 1/2} \approx (32) \cdot 1/2 = 16$. To obtain 550 or more heads is to reach an event which deviates from the expected value (500) by about 50/16 standard deviations, or over 3 standard deviations. As you can see from appendix 7.1, the chances are very low that such an event will occur. You can also see that we reached this conclusion in a very few computational steps—that is, by a very compact information system.

Problem: Irish Red Winery ━━━━━━━━━━━━━━━━━━━━━━━

You have used your new-found knowledge of quantitative methods and probabilities so successfully that you've been able to purchase the Irish Red Winery from your earnings. You are interested in trying out a new advertising scheme in a region where there are normally 25,000 bottles of a standard wine sold each week, and where your "share of the market"—that is, the probability that your brand is sold—is about .20. You try the advertising scheme for a week and sell 5300 bottles. You wonder whether this result could be ascribed to usual random deviations, or whether the advertising scheme really helped.

Analysis: Your assumptions about how weekly sales usually occur can be represented by the compact assumption that they are distributed as $X \sim B(25,000,.20)$. The question posed is assumed to be equivalent to the question of whether the *observed* value, 5300, is an unusual deviation from the *expected* value, $np = (25,000)(.20) = 5000$ bottles.

Since np is large, you can use the normal distribution table. Since $\sqrt{npq} = \sqrt{25,000 \cdot 1/5 \cdot 4/5} \approx 64$, 5300 deviates from 5000 by 300/64 or over 3 standard deviations, indicating a very abnormal week. But in studies of this kind, beware! Perhaps there was a convention in town that week, or several big weddings, or whatever. Never get talked into a new advertising scheme, or any other deal, solely on the basis of one test, without examining alternative explanations. All you have to do is read about the confusing statistics on drugs and diets to see how faulty a study can become if the watchdog is asleep.

As a working rule, you can apply the method given above on a binomial random variable when n is reasonably large (say, 20 or more) and np is not too small (as a rule, greater than 30). So, in the More War problem the probability of 290 or less (2.4 standard deviations away from the mean of 333.3) is .0082 (1/2 of .0164). When np is small, you can approximate B(n,p) by another distribution, called the "Poisson" (after S. D. Poisson, 1781–1840). This distribution proves useful in a situation familiar in government and industry — when the inspection of items takes place.

Problem: An Inspector's Lot Is Not a Happy One ─────────────

As chief inspector of an army depot, you must certify that the tensile strength of the steel rods in a very large lot is high enough. You decide to randomly choose a sample of 100 rods from the lot, and find that all meet the required strength. You want to know if it's likely that such a sample came from a lot in which 1% or more of the rods are defective, since anything with over 1% defectives is an "unacceptable" lot. What are the chances that a lot with 1% or more defectives would yield no defectives in such a sample?

Analysis: Since you've examined 100 rods which can be either defective or not, the distribution of defective rods in samples of size 100 is approximately binomial. Strictly speaking, the distribution is not exactly binomial if you don't put the rods you've already tested back into the lot, but if the lot is large enough the binomial is a very close approximation. Suppose we assume that the lot is 1% defective, so that

$$p = .01, \ n = 100, \ np = 1$$

Now you can turn to the Poisson table in appendix 7.2, where np is symbolized by the letter m (for "mean" of the distribution). Since np = 1, look in the column in the Poisson table headed by m = np = 1.

The x-values on the left represent 0,1,2,3, . . . occurrences of a specified event, in this case, defective items. Hence you read the table as follows: the probability of finding 0 defects when the number of defects has a Poisson distribution with $m = 1$ is .3679. In other words, your chances are better than 1 in 3 of finding 0 defects if you sample only 100 and the probability is actually 1%. If the probability of a defective were .011 (1.1%) in the lot, the Poisson table tells you that your chances are .3329 of no defects if you randomly sample 100 rods. Even if the percentage defective were 3% ($p = .03$), the table shows that approximately 1 time in 20 (.05), you would not find a defective in a lot of 100. Hence your confidence in the sample result may be very weak, and you'd be tempted to sample some more rods, but this may be too costly or time consuming. Thus caution says you should inspect more but costs say you should not. Your problem as an inspector is therefore an ambiguous one, and this is why an inspector's lot is not a happy one! But don't forget the systems approach, which may lead you to seek some radically different and more powerful methods of inspection.

Problem: Asian Flu ────────────────────────────────

It is later than you think, and at last — at age 45 — you have become a medical statistician for a hospital. One of your duties is to alert the doctors about epidemics — of flu, for example. You have plenty of data, and you are reasonably sure that in your community of 100,000 persons, the incidence of Asian flu for any person in any one week is about one chance in 150,000. All of a sudden, there are five cases reported in one week. Should you alert the doctors that "there's a lot of Asian flu going around"?

Analysis: You may choose to assume that the nonepidemic situation is accurately described by $X \sim B(100{,}000, 1/150{,}000)$. But the mean $np = 100{,}000/150{,}000 = 2/3$ is small, and you should use the Poisson approximation to determine whether the deviation $5 - 2/3 = 4\text{-}1/3$ is unusual. From appendix 7.2, you can see that the probability of deviating to 5 or more when $np = 2/3$ is practically zero. So you'd better alert somebody! But you should also be aware that the assumptions of this analysis may be faulty, because the relevant events (getting-the-flu, not-getting-the-flu) may not be independent: given that one member of the community gets the flu, the probability that someone else will get the flu may go up significantly. Recall that the binomial distribution assumed independent trials, and if that assumption is violated, you can't use the Poisson distribution since the original distribution may not be binomial.

PROBLEMS 7.7

1. Using Chebyschev's inequality, what is the highest probability of being 1, 2, 3, or 4 standard deviations or more away from the mean? Compare this to the precise figures for the normal distribution.

2. What is the probability of 300 or fewer defective games if you sample 10,000 games and the probability of a game being defective is .05? .08? .12?

3. How would your analysis change if, in the Asian Flu problem, you had (incorrectly! Why?) used the normal approximation?

4. The latest hit on television is believed to be viewed in 50% of homes in Chicago. Recently, each of 600 Chicago homes, selected at random, was asked if the household was watching the program. 200 replied positively. How "safe" are you in quoting the 50% rating figure?

5. The agent for the Tankers Company in the Bay Area has asked you to help him estimate the weekly number of the company's ships expected to unload their crude oil in the Port of Richmond. He tells you that the Tankers own 50 ships and that there is a 10% chance for each ship to arrive at Richmond on any given week. (a) What should you tell him? (b) What are the chances that 20 or more ships arrive? (c) Twelve or more? (d) Fewer than 10?

7.7.1   Application of the Poisson Distribution to Waiting Lines   The Poisson distribution has a remarkable property which makes it extremely useful for studying service units like toll booths, barber shops, course registration, out-patient clinics, brothels, and the like. It turns out that for services where the client arrives "at random"—that is, not according to any schedule—the number of clients arriving in a specified time interval (for example, one minute or one hour) follows a "Poisson Law." If the average number of arrivals at a toll booth is 2.5 per minute, say, then (again consulting the Poisson table for $m = 2.5$), the probability of zero arrivals in a minute's time ($x = 0$) is .0821, of one arrival .2052, of two arrivals .2565, and so on. We say that the average number of arrivals in a time period is the *arrival rate*. It also frequently happens that there is a variation in the *service time* of clients (for example, at a toll booth, the busy executive quickly pays his 50 cents, the leisurely old gent wants to know the best place to eat in town). In many cases, the number of customers who can be served in a specified time interval also obeys the Poisson Law, though the mean arrival rate and the mean service rate are usually not the same. Indeed, if they are the same, and arrivals and service times both obey Poisson Laws, the *waiting lines* will keep increasing indefinitely or until the arrival rates begin to decline (for example, after the rush hour). One very common error that cost-conscious managers make is to try to minimize the idle time of the servers — that is, the time when they are waiting for the next customer. Such a policy tends to increase the waiting time of the clients, as you may have noticed in course registration lines or popular doctors' offices.

There is a whole branch of applied mathematics, called *waiting line*, or *queuing theory*, which provides a wide variety of models of service units, including many servers, balking customers (who walk away if the waiting line is too long), servers-in-sequence (as in a hospital), as well as arrivals and service times which are non-Poisson. The mathematics is beyond this text, but we have provided you with some fun in simulating service units in the exercises.

PROBLEMS 7.7.1

1. To simulate a very simple service unit, imagine that you run a one-man barber shop. Your customers are all men and want either a shave (service time 15 minutes) or a haircut (service time 30 minutes), but not both. The relative frequency of these two services is about the same, and follows no fixed pattern, so that you can assume that the probability of either service for an arriving customer is .5, and you can simulate the process by simply tossing a coin. Also, your past data indicates that the probability that zero customers will arrive in a ten-minute interval is .5, and that one customer will arrive is also .5. (You therefore never have more than one arrival in any ten-minute interval.) You can now simulate this service unit with the aid of your favorite coin. How? Write down the results in terms of (a) number of people waiting for a service (b) number of people who had a haircut between 9 A.M. and 12 noon; 3 P.M.; 5 P.M.

2. A somewhat more complicated simulation occurs when we use four different denominations of coins (penny, nickel, dime, quarter):
   0   Exactly three heads (HHHT, HHTH, HTHH, THHH) corresponds to no arrivals in the ten-minute intervals;
   1   Two heads and two tails, except for HHTT, corresponds to one arrival
   2   Exactly three tails (HTTT, THTT, TTHT, TTTH) corresponds to two arrivals
   3   All heads or all tails (HHHH, TTTT) corresponds to three arrivals
   4   HHTT corresponds to four arrivals

This scheme closely approximates a Poisson arrival with $m = 1.4$, as you can see if you calculate the probabilities of each case. Use the same service times as in problem 1, except that now you have *two* barber chairs. Note that if, say, three customers arrive, you flip the coin to determine type of service for each one.

7.8   A Function of a Random Variable

In many decision-making situations, you may be confronted with information in one form or scale and need to transform the unit of measurement to another scale. One example you've seen is in the Watergate Detergent Corporation, where we transformed pounds and ounces into number of standard deviations. Other examples are international corporations that must make transformations from francs to dollars or from dollars to lire. You also might be interested in using meters instead of feet or yards, or kilos when the data is in pounds.

We now want to see how to apply these transformations to probability distributions and their characteristics since this may prove very useful in many decision problems under uncertainty. Suppose you can safely assume the probability distribution of X, the number of dots showing as a result of the throw of two dice. X, of course, ranges from 2 to 12. Suppose you receive 12¢ times the number thrown (for example, if you throw a 5, you get 60¢); you might be interested in how much the game is worth to you in terms of, say, expected value. In this case, you know the distribution of the random variable X, and you can define a new random variable describing your reward, say Y, which is $12X$. Table 7.4 shows the values of X and the corresponding values of $Y = 12X$.

TABLE 7.4   Values of Random Variable $Y = 12X$

i	x_i: value of X	y_i: value of $Y = 12X$	$P(X = x_i) = P(Y = y_i)$
1	2	24	1/36
2	3	36	1/18
3	4	48	3/36
4	5	60	1/9
5	6	72	5/36
6	7	84	1/6
7	8	96	5/36
8	9	108	1/9
9	10	120	3/36
10	11	132	1/18
11	12	144	1/36

In general, you can define a new random variable $Y = g(X)$ for *any* function g of the random variable X that you desire. For example, if you are interested in the square of X, you can define $Y = X^2$. Or if you are interested, say, in the possible profit B, which is sales revenue minus a constant cost figure $50,000, you might define $B = \$3.25S - \$50,000$, where $3.25 is the price of a unit, S is the number of units sold (a random variable), and therefore $3.25S is the total revenue.*

7.8.1 Transformation and the Expected Value of Random Variables

In the above example where $Y = 12X$ you can receive 24¢ only when you throw 2; so the probability of $Y = 24$ is identical to the probability of $X = 2$. Similarly $P(Y = 36) = P(X = 3)$, $P(Y = 48) = P(X = 4)$, and so on. So the expected value of Y is

$$E[Y] = \sum_{\text{all } i} y_i P(Y = y_i) = \sum_{\text{all } i} y_i P(X = x_i)$$

$$= 24 \times \frac{1}{36} + 36 \times \frac{1}{18} + 48 \times \frac{3}{36} + \cdots + 132 \times \frac{1}{18} + 144 \times \frac{1}{36}$$

$$= 84$$

What we've done here is to use the knowledge about the variability of the number of dots in the throw of two dice to deduce the variability of the reward. The knowledge about X is the only thing you need to know because it is the only reason for the variability of the reward; the other component is a constant: 12¢ per dot showing. This suggests that instead of computing $E[Y]$ directly you could first compute $E[X]$ and multiply it by the 12¢ constant, and indeed

$$E[Y] = E[X] \times 12 = 7 \times 12 = 84$$

We can state this and a more general property of expected values in the following theorems:

THEOREM 7.3   The expected value of the random variable $Y = cX$, where X is some random variable and c is a constant, is c times the expected value of X; that is,

$$E[Y] = E[cX] = cE[X]$$

THEOREM 7.4   The expected value of the random variable $Y = cX + d$, where X is a random variable and c and d are constants is

$$E[Y] = E[cX + d] = cE[X] + d$$

Theorem 7.4 is a direct result of theorem 7.3 and the fact that the expected value of a constant is the constant itself; that is,

$$E[d] = d \times 1 = d$$

---

*You've already seen other examples in this chapter: $A = |c_i - E[C]|$, $D = (c_i - E[C])$, and $N = (c_i - E[C])^2$.

We will make use of these theorems shortly, but first you need to equip yourself with some additional tools.

7.8.2   Distributions of Functions of Random Variables

We said that you can define any new random variable $Y = g(X)$ for any function g of the random variable X that you desire. For example, if your friend Mike, who is an insurance salesman, asks you to help him in getting a better picture about his possible annual profit figures, you could do it by defining profits as a function of the sales and costs. Thus, if Mike's rewards are in terms of percentage commission on the amount of insurance he sells, 5% say, his costs are fixed at $5000, and he knows the distribution of his possible sales, then

$$\text{Return} = R = .05S - \$5000$$

is the random variable describing profits as a function of the random variable S describing sales, and the probability of any value of R is the probability of the respective value of S.

Sometimes, in defining random variables as a function of others, this direct relationship of probabilities doesn't hold. For example, if you are interested in the random variable $Y = X^2$ and X can take on two values, -1 and 1, with probabilities 1/3 and 2/3, respectively, the random variable Y can take on only one value, 1, with probability $= 1$. Verify it! (This was also true of the absolute deviation A of section 7.3.3.) We will contrast the two cases in the next problem.

Problem: Nick Numbers

Nick Numbers is in town with his favorite coin flip games. This time he offers you two alternative bets:

1. You choose any coin from your pocket and flip it three times. He will pay you a dollar for each show of heads, and you pay two dollars to play the game.
2. As before, you flip a fair coin three times and receive (or pay) according to the following payoff function:

$$W = (X - .50)^2$$

where X is the number of heads that appear in three flips; for example, if there are two heads in three flips, $X = 2$, then your payoff is $(2 - .50)^2 = \$2.25$.

What bet, if any, should you accept if you regard sure and expected dollars as being equivalent?

Analysis: The random variable of interest to you in both bets is net payoff. The random variable that determines your payoff is $X =$ the number of heads in three flips of a fair coin. The probability distribution of this random variable has been given several times earlier; that is,

x = value of X	P(X = x)
0	1/8
1	3/8
2	3/8
3	1/8

In the first bet, the payoff (which we denote by R) is a function of X. The value of R is determined by the value of X and a constant number, the $2 you pay to enter the game: $R = g(x) = X - 2$. Thus the values that R can take on are:

x = value of X	r = value of R = x − 2
0	0 − 2 = −2
1	1 − 2 = −1
2	2 − 2 = 0
3	3 − 2 = 1

The probabilities of the values of R can be deduced from the probabilities of the values of X. Since each value of R is associated with a unique value of X, you know that the probability of $R = 0$ is 3/8 because $R = 0$ corresponds to $X = 2$, whose probability is 3/8. With this reasoning you can deduce the probability distribution of R as follows: as follows:

x = value of X	r = value of R	P(R = r) = P(X = x)
0	−2	1/8
1	−1	3/8
2	0	3/8
3	1	1/8

and the expected value of bet 1 is

$$\frac{1}{8} \times (-2) + \frac{3}{8} \times (-1) + \frac{3}{8} \times 0 + \frac{1}{8} \times 1 = -50¢$$

which clearly indicates your refusal to take the bet. You could have used the rule for expected value (theorem 7.4) and deduced $E[X - 2] = E[X] - 2 = \$1.50 - \$2 = -\$.50$.

The analysis of the second bet offer is similar, though not identical, because the values of the payoff function W are not only determined by the random variable X and a constant, $-.50$, but the squaring operation is also present this time. If, for example, $X = 0$, then the payoff is $(0 - .50)^2 = \$.25$, which is the same as the payoff for $X = 1$: $(1 - .50)^2 = .25$. So two different values of X determine the same value of W.

Therefore, the probability of the event associated with $W = .25$ is the sum of the probabilities of the events $X = 0$ and $X = 1$; that is,

$$P(W = .25) = P(X = 0 \text{ or } X = 1) = P(X = 0) + P(X = 1) = \frac{1}{8} + \frac{3}{8} = \frac{1}{2}$$

When $X = 2$, $W = (2 - .50)^2 = \$2.25$ with probability 3/8, and for $X = 3$, $W = (3 - .50)^2 = \$6.25$ with probability 1/8. So the distribution of W is

$w =$ value of W	$x =$ value of X associated with w	$P(W = w)$
.25	0, 1	1/8 + 3/8 = 1/2
2.25	2	3/8
6.25	3	1/8

and the expected value of bet 2 is

$$\frac{1}{2} \times .25 + \frac{3}{8} \times 2.25 + \frac{1}{8} \times 6.25 = \$1.75$$

which means you gladly accept the bet.

PROBLEMS 7.8

1. A random variable X can take on the values 2, 3, 4, 5, 6 with probabilities .1, .3, .2, .15, .25, respectively.
    a. What is the expected value of $5X$?
    b. What is the expected value of $3 + X$?
    c. What is the expected value of $3 + 5X$?

2. The gross profit before concession fees on a beer can is 30¢. Do you expect to profit from a beer stand concession in the county fair if the distribution of sales is 1000 cans with probability .3, 2000 cans with probability .45, and 3000 with probability .25, and the concession fees are $200? What is the distribution of profits?

3. The probability of a defective game is .05. What is the distribution of repair costs of a lot of 10 if repairing a defective game costs $3? What if there are fixed costs of $10 to set up the repairing operations?

4. You have been presented with the following assessment of demand distribution for a new product you are considering:

Demand (in units)	Probability
10	.1
20	.25
30	.35
40	.15
50	.1
60	.05

The promotion and advertising costs to introduce the product are estimated at $500, and the profit per unit sold (before the above costs) is $100. Do you anticipate making profits on this new product?

5. In preparing the earnings forecast of your firm for the next meeting of the board of directors, you realize that independent of general economic conditions, an increment of $1.20 per share in earnings over this year can be expected for next year. The earnings per share are also expected to go up by an additional amount equal to 1% of the change in "GNP per capita" occurring next year. The present year earnings are $3.40 per share. How much would you forecast the earning per share for next year to be if the distribution of changes in the "GNP per capita" is as follows:

−$500	.05
−$250	.25
0	.3
+$250	.2
+$500	.15
+$750	.05

6. In problem 5, what is the distribution of the absolute deviations of earnings per share from the expected value? What is the expected absolute deviation from the median?

7. What is the expected absolute deviation in problem 6 if you forecast $4.60 per share for next year?

7.9   The Variance of Functions of Random Variables and Riskiness of Investments

You should recall that the *variance* of a random variable X can be interpreted as the expected value of some random variable Z, say, which is a function of X, where $Z = (X − E[X])^2$. So,

$$E[Z] = \sum_{\text{all } i} z_i P(Z = z_i)$$

$$= \sum_{\text{all } i} (X_i - E[X])^2 P(X = x_i)$$

$$= \text{Var}[X]$$

We can use this observation to deduce several useful properties of the variance.

THEOREM 7.5   The variance of a constant is zero. This is true since if the random variable X is a constant, say, K, then

$$E[X] = E[K] = K$$

and letting $Z = (X - E[X])^2$

$$\begin{aligned} E[Z] &= E[X - E[X]]^2 \\ &= E[K - K]^2 \\ &= E[0] = 0 \end{aligned}$$

This result is actually very intuitive; if the larger the variability of a random variable, the greater the value of the variance, then when there is no variability as is the case with a constant, the variance should be zero.

THEOREM 7.6   The variance of a random variable $Y = aX$ where a is a constant and X is another random variable is

$$\text{Var}[Y] = \text{Var}[aX] = a^2 \text{Var}[X]$$

What this theorem says is that the effect on the variance of multiplying a random variable by a constant is quite significant. If, for example, you change the units of measure of a random variable from pounds to ounces, the variance is $16^2 = 256$ larger. But if you transform from inches to feet, say, then the variance in terms of feet is $(1/12)^2 = 1/144$ the variance in inches. Since the standard deviation is the square root of the variance, changing the units of a random variable X by a also changes the standard deviation by the same factor a:

$$\sigma_Y = \sigma_{ax} = \sqrt{a^2 \text{Var}[X]} = a\sigma_x$$

7.9.1   Riskiness of Investments: Diversifying Your Portfolio   There is a very interesting application of theorem 7.6 involving the riskiness of investments. Financial managers have been taking advantage of this very property in suggesting that clients diversify their capital holdings. Their reason for "not putting all the eggs in one basket" can be represented deductively by a combination of theorems 7.1, 7.2, 7.3, and 7.6.

If you agree to use the variance—that is, squared deviations from the mean—as a measure of risk, then the risk associated with an investment is measured by the variance of the rate of return from the investment denoted by $Var[R_i]$. For example, if you put all your money in a *single* investment which has rate of return R_1, say, your risk is $Var[R_1]$. If you now split your money between two independent investments, with rates of return R_1 and R_2, which have the same *expected* rates of return (that is, $E[R_1] = E[R_2]$) and the same risk (that is, $Var[R_1] = Var[R_2]$), your total risk is reduced by 1/2, since

$$Var\left[\frac{1}{2}R_1 + \frac{1}{2}R_2\right] = \left(\frac{1}{2}\right)^2 Var[R_1] + \left(\frac{1}{2}\right)^2 Var[R_2]$$

$$= \frac{1}{4}Var[R_1] + \frac{1}{4}Var[R_2] = \frac{1}{2}Var[R_1] \quad \text{or} \quad \frac{1}{2}Var[R_2]$$

by theorems 7.6 and 7.2. So, your risk now is exactly 1/2 the risk you would have if you put all your money in either investment only.

The *expected* rate of return remains the same as if you invested in R_1 only. By theorems 7.1 and 7.3

$$E\left[\frac{1}{2}R_1 + \frac{1}{2}R_2\right] = \frac{1}{2}E[R_1] + \frac{1}{2}E[R_2] = E[R_1]$$

since

$$E[R_1] = E[R_2]$$

This is the idea behind what is called by Wall Streeters "building a diversified portfolio." By the same reasoning a portfolio of three investments with identical risk and mean return is 1/3 less risky than a portfolio of one, and so on.

7.9.2 Eliminating Inefficient Portfolios
Why, then, don't all the investors have the same portfolio, one that consists of all the possible investments? The reason is that reduction of risk is not the only concern of investors; they also want to make varying amounts of money! So there is a two-dimensional measure of performance consisting of returns which you wish to maximize and risk that you probably wish to minimize. Realistically, you cannot expect to find investments which have high expected rates of return and low risk.

For example, government bonds, which are very safe, have low returns (interest rate), while investment in drilling an oil well is very risky but this risk is compensated by high expected returns. In between these two extremes there are investments with moderate expected value of rate of return and moderate variance (risk). It is reasonable to

assume that you would reject any investment that has the same expected return as another potential investment but a higher variance.
Likewise you might not consider an investment that is inferior in its
expected returns to another investment with identical variance. So
when you are presented with investment opportunities, each with an
expected rate of return and a variance, you would immediately eliminate from the desirable investment list those for which there are
superior investments; that is, when there are alternatives with the
same mean and a smaller variance, or the same variance and a greater
expected return. All the investment opportunities that remain can be
classified into classes whose members share approximately the same
mean and variance. To each class you can apply the idea of diversifica-
tion we've discussed earlier; that is, reducing the risk without losing
expected returns by constructing a portfolio of opportunities all from
the same class. The end result of this process is a list of portfolios each
having its own expected returns and risk such that if one class is higher
in its expected return, it also has a higher risk, or if one has a higher risk
than the other, the former is compensated by higher expected returns.

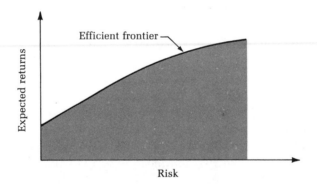

Figure 7.1 Portfolio Efficient Frontier

This can be seen by the curve in figure 7.1. In this figure you can
see the tradeoff between the risk and expected returns; all the portfolios which are the result of the above process are on the curve. That
is, the opportunities that are inferior in either the expected return for a
given level of risk or in risk for a given level of expected return are below the curve (in the shaded area) and are not considered as candidates
for your portfolio selection. Therefore the curve is called the efficient
frontier—since investments on the curved line or "frontier" are "more
efficient" or "better," according to the expected value-variance measures. But remember that both expected return and variance ("risk")
are measures of performance based on assumptions and may not correctly reflect your own value system.

Problem: Babahana Portfolio ━━━━━━━━━━━

Your good friend's grandma, Babahana, who has recently lost her husband, asks you to help her with investing the sum of $10,000 that she received from the life insurance company. Her friends and family have been bombarding her with investment ideas, talking to her about returns and risk, and she is at a loss. She has given you all the data, which is summarized in table 7.5, and is waiting for your recommendation. What can you say to her?

TABLE 7.5   Babahana's Investment Opportunities

	Investment	Expected Rate of Return	Variance
1	Government bonds	6%	0
2	Explore the Oceans stocks	50%	25
3	Lose in the Pacific stocks	60%	200
4	Safe & Co. bonds	8%	2
5	Kelley Beach stocks	50%	35
6	Mendocino Sauna bonds	8%	1
7	Competitive Cycling stocks	30%	10
8	Kauai Horses stocks	30%	10
9	Deb's Massage Parlors	50%	70
10	Martin International bonds	8%	1
11	Rishpon Land stocks	60%	30
12	Steinman Brush Co. bonds	10%	5
13	Curry Marketing bonds	10%	3
14	Abed Rugs	10%	3
15	Vodnoi's Vehicles stocks	60%	30
16	Ruth Piano Co. bonds	8%	1
17	Hershel's Mausoleum stocks	50%	25

Analysis: Your first task is to get rid of inferior investments. You can do it by comparing investments pairwise and eliminating those which are inferior in either the expected rate of return for the same variance, or in the risk for the same expected rate of return. For example, investments 2, 5, and 17 are all in the 50% expected rate of return class, but investment 5 has a higher variance than either number 2 or 17 (35 > 25). Therefore, 5 should be eliminated from the list of investments that are worth serious consideration. The result of such a process is given in table 7.6. Note that the government bonds which form class 1 have variance 0 which means that the rate of return of 6% is certain. In general, every investor can find an opportunity like this one which yields some (relatively small) rate of return and is a sure thing; a passbook account in a large commercial bank, government bonds, and the like. For this reason the curve in figure 7.1 doesn't start at the origin.

TABLE 7.6   Investments Worth Considering

Class	Expected Rate of Return	Variance	Investment Number
1	6%	0	1
2	8%	1	6, 10, 16
3	10%	3	13, 14
4	30%	10	7, 8
5	50%	25	2, 17
6	60%	30	11, 15

Now that you have reduced the list to 12 investments you can explain to Babahana that she must choose among the classes; that is, based on her preferences she can decide for herself which class fits best her "taste" in terms of the combination: expected rate of return and risk. You also ought to tell her that she should not choose any single investment out of the class she likes but construct a portfolio consisting of all the investments in the group, as we've seen earlier.

How should Babahana select the class? Of course, you cannot impose your own ideas on her, but you can explain to her that what she needs to decide is the way she feels about the tradeoff between expected rate of return and risk; that is, if she selects any class higher than number one, it means that the additional expected rate of return compensates for the additional risk (for example, moving from 0 to 1% variance is compensated by additional 2% return as we go from class 1 to 2). So what she actually needs is to state for herself a measure of performance which incorporates both returns and risk. A discussion of an attempt to construct such a measure is the subject of the next section.

PROBLEMS 7.9

1. Suppose you invest in a savings account with 5% interest. What are the expected value and variance of your return?

2. Suppose you invest $10,000 in "6% riskless government bonds," $10,000 in stocks with expected return of 18% but variance of 19%, and $10,000 in commodities with 30% expected return, 40% variance. All are independent investments. What is your expected return and risk (variance) of the total investment? Can you reduce the variance?

3. Are investment returns ever really independent?

4. What assumptions are made about your attitude towards risk in the discussion on constructing and selecting diversified portfolios?

Why would you prefer an investment with the same expected value, but lower risk?

5. Draw the "efficient frontier" for the Babahana problem, identifying those investments which are "below" the frontier.

6. If you were to draw an efficient frontier for your own investment opportunities, where should the curve intersect the "return" or y-axis?

7. How would you determine which investment to choose in the Babahana problem? Would you diversify? Why?

8. Mr. Pepler, the financial vice president, hands to you the following list of investment opportunities and their characteristics:

Investment Opportunity	Expected Return	Variance
Government bonds	5%	0
Paper plant in Africa	25%	20
Forest plantation in Brazil	30%	40
Paper plant in France	25%	25
Pulp plant in Brazil	30%	40
Paper plant in Brazil	30%	50
Pulp plant in Sweden	25%	20
Eurodollar deposits	9%	0

He indicates that the different investment plans are mutually independent. He would like from you a report on the plans that should be considered and recommendations on how to present them to the board of directors. What should your reply be?

7.10   The Utility Function as Measure of Performance

In the last section we left Babahana with the question of how to choose among the six portfolios so that she would "make the most she can." In order to make this decision, we said, she has to decide on how she wishes to evaluate the tradeoff between additional expected gains and increasing risk (as measured by the variance). That is, she has to construct for herself a measure of performance which takes into consideration both gains and risk, and she can then use this measure to select the "best" deal. Of course, such a measure is individualistic and manifests the individual's value system; if we ask you to choose between two bets which have identical expected value and differ in their variance, and you choose one over the other, this choice represents your preference and manifests your individual way of evaluating risk based on your own value system. If you are indifferent between the two bets, it can be explained by saying that you disregard risk as a factor in measuring performance. If you choose the bet with the smaller variance, it can be said that you are not fond of risk for the sake of risk, and try to avoid it. Finally, if you choose the bet with the higher variance, you are apparently a risk lover and Las Vegas is your dream place. The general idea behind choices of this kind can sometimes be explained by the economist's concept of utility.

Utility, measured in "utiles," is used for measuring the relative values of objects, including money. You may have already seen the basic preparation for this method of measuring values in the section on the axioms of preference (chapter 3). There we assumed you could make legitimate assumptions about preferences between discrete objects. Now we assume something even stronger—namely, that an individual has a preference between any given amount of money and something else of value (like risk) that can be expressed quantitatively. The basic idea behind this measure of relative values is the problematic "tradeoff"—that is, how much of one value (for example, low risk) you are willing to give up in order to attain a certain level of another value (for example, money). Suppose you are a daredevil risk seeker. Then you probably prefer a bet with high variance to one with low variance. The utility question then becomes: How much do we have to increase the expected dollar value of the low-variance bet for you to become indifferent between the games?

You should note that the term "measurement" has a different meaning depending on whether we are using the deductive or inductive or systems approach. In the deductive method, the measurement of utilities consists of finding some assumptions about tradeoffs that we feel are reasonably safe to make and then deducing the utility measure implied. In the inductive method, we try to observe a person's behavior and induce a generalization about it which expresses the tradeoff principle he apparently adopts in a consistent manner, thus inferring his utility measure by observation. In the systems approach, we try to study the meaningfulness of measures such as utility with respect to the larger social system or the individual soul.

Thus, from a systems point of view, you don't have to believe in the existence of utility measures as a manifestation of your value system any more than you have to believe in dollars as a basis. Indeed, if decisions are based on assumptions about utilities described in this section, then there is a simple logical manipulation which can convert the basis to adjusted dollars, so that utility theory does not avoid measuring lives and loves in monetary terms. But in the spirit of this deductive effort, we ask you to go along with the assumption of this section, namely, "act so as to maximize expected utility." To make this idea explicit, we introduce the *expected utility* of some discrete random variable X

$$E[U(X)] = \sum_i U(x_i)P(X = x_i)$$

where U is your utility function, which measures your utility if x_i occurs.

Suppose now that in a bet offer, bet I is a fair coin flipped, and if heads comes up you win $12, but if tails comes up you win $8. Bet II is a fair die thrown and if a 1 comes up you win $100; if a 2 occurs you win $50; if a 3 comes up you win $10; if a 4 comes up you win $10; if a 5 occurs you *pay* $30; and if a 6 occurs you *pay* $80. The two bets have the same expected value, $10, and variance 4 and 3233 respectively. If you choose bet II over I, we can interpret that for you:

$$U(\$12) \times \frac{1}{2} + U(\$8) \times \frac{1}{2} < U(\$100) \times \frac{1}{6} + U(\$50) \times \frac{1}{6}$$

$$+ U(\$10) \times \frac{2}{6} + U(-\$30) \times \frac{1}{6}$$

$$+ U(-\$80) \times \frac{1}{6}$$

This may seem strange to you since the expected return (in dollars) of both games was equal, but your *utility function* takes into consideration the value of money *to you*. If you prefer bet I, you are saying that either the value to you of $100 is not ten times that of $10 (but less) or paying $80 reduces your utility more than the gain of $80 increases it. Or perhaps both of these are true.

To see graphically what the above paragraph says, assume both of these are true and look at figure 7.2, representing your utility function with respect to money.

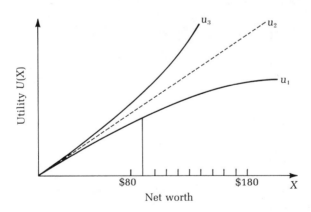

Figure 7.2   The Shape of Your Utility Function If You Prefer Bet I (u_1), If You Are Linear in Money (u_2), and If You Prefer Bet II (u_3)

Figure 7.2 has your "net worth," which is called X on the horizontal axis, and "your utility as a function of your net worth," U(X), measured on the vertical axis. It is assumed that before choosing the bet, you have $80 net worth so that you are able to play. The worst off you could be is $0 net worth at the end. By selecting the relevant points on the net worth scale for outcomes of the two games, you can verify that the utility of bet I is greater than that of bet II if u_1 represents your utility function. If we look at the shape of the curve, "maximizing expected utility" tells us that you would prefer a sure $10 win (yielding a net worth of $90) to either bet. This can be verified graphically for bet I, as shown in figure 7.3, where the expected utility of a sure $10, U($90), is greater than

$$\frac{1}{2} U(\$88) + \frac{1}{2} U(\$92)$$

which is the expected utility of bet I. A person who is a risk-averter has a utility function of this shape since he would rather avoid risk and have the sure money.

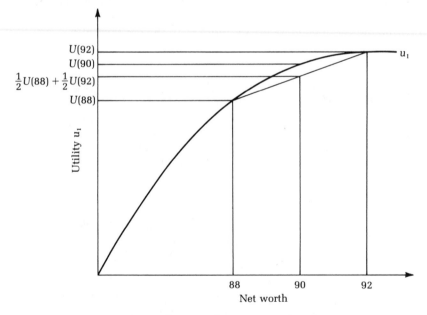

Figure 7.3 $U(90) > \frac{1}{2}U(88) + \frac{1}{2}U(92)$ for Utility Function u_1

The dashed line in figure 7.2 represents the utility function of a person whose utility is called *linear in money*. In other words, an expected dollar and a sure dollar yield the same utility to such a person.

You should be able to see that bet I, bet II, and $10 yield the same utility for him. In most of the problems discussed thus far, we assumed you had this type of utility function when we equated sure and expected dollars.

If you prefer bet II, your utility function probably looks like u_3. This means that your utility *increases* with money at an *increasing* rate. Translated into marginal terms (studied in chapter 3) as you move to the right on the graph, the *marginal* utility of money is increasing. For example, the additional utility of $1 at $0 net worth is less than the change in utility going from $80 to $81 net worth. You would have a utility function like u_3, if you are a *risk lover* who prefers a risky bet with an expected value of, say, $50 to $50 for sure.

We should note that this discussion of utility is based on one way of characterizing risk, namely, in terms of the variance of the amount of money one is willing to try for. But risk may have other meanings which cannot be translated either into variance or into dollar terms. It can be argued that the definition of utility can be extended to cover anything of value, but there are also strong arguments against this point of view.

In practice we may not be able to measure utilities, but it is important to notice that in principle they often explain what appears to be "irrational" behavior. For example, a friend of ours went around to his mathematician friends offering to pay them $100,000 if they guessed the telephone number (7 digits) he had written down on a slip of paper, but if they failed they had to pay him $1. He had many takers among the experts, even though the expected dollar value of the bet was about −99 cents. Although we will be using expected monetary value as the measure of performance in many of the future examples, as we have in the previous chapters, you should keep in mind that your attitude toward risk may play an important role in actual decision making.

Problem: The Insurance Salesman ▬▬▬▬▬▬▬▬▬▬▬▬

As the new manager of the Arcata Paper Mill Corporation warehouse, you are visited by a salesman from Clark Insurance. The warehouse normally holds $100,000 worth of flammable material, which would quickly be destroyed in the case of a flash fire. Although you have an automatic sprinkler system, Mr. Michaels, the salesman, has shown you figures which lead you to believe that the probability of a flash fire on your premises in any given year is .036. He has asked if you wish to renew the $100,000 insurance coverage at the same premium of $4500 per year that your predecessor had been paying. Was your predecessor a fool to have taken it in the first place?

Analysis: Analyzing the insurance problem in terms of the expected value of money involved, you observe that the expected insurance costs are $4500 if you buy; while if you don't buy, the expected costs are

$$\$100,000 \times .036 + \$0 \times .964 = \$3600$$

which is less than the $4500. However, there is obviously great risk involved in not buying insurance, as is indicated by the variance of the random variable,

$X =$ net worth of the flammable warehouse material less insurance

If you buy,

$$E[X] = \$95,500$$

and

$$Var\ (X) = 0$$

If you don't buy the insurance,

$$E[X] = \$96,400$$

and

$$Var\ (X) = (\$100,000 - \$96,400)^2 \times .964 + (\$0 - \$96,400)^2 \times .036$$
$$= 44,000,000$$

approximately.

Your predecessor's behavior can be explained by the fact that he was a risk-averter. He did not mind incurring the "loss" of $900 in

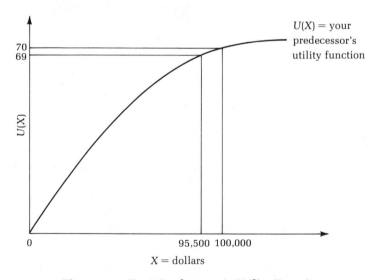

Figure 7.4   Your Predecessor's Utility Function

expected value compared to the "benefit" associated with the reduction of the risk. He passed this risk on to the insurance company. To
analyze this graphically, let's presume that your risk-averting predecessor's utility function looked like figure 7.4.

Suppose $U(95,500)$ is 69 utiles, $U(100,000)$ is 70 utiles, and $U(0)$ is
0 utiles; then, deciding to buy insurance:

$$E[U(X)] = U(\$95,500) \times 1 = 69 \text{ utiles}$$

Deciding not to buy insurance:

$$E[U(X)] = U(\$100,000) \times .964 + U(\$0) \times .036$$
$$= 70 \times .964 = 67.48 \text{ utiles}$$

So your predecessor was simply acting so as to maximize his
expected utility. Think about why you buy collision insurance for
your car, even if it's not required by law!

PROBLEMS 7.10

1. Could you explain, with the aid of utility analysis, why your friend
   entered the casino in Las Vegas and bet $10 on the number 7 in a
   roulette turn when in fact he knew that his chances of winning
   were 1/38 and his net gain would amount to $360 if indeed the
   number 7 appeared?

2. How stable is your utility function over time and place? Does it
   look like u_1, u_2, u_3, or something else?

3. Would you buy the fire insurance from Mr. Michaels (The Insurance Salesmen problem) if you are a risk lover? Support your
   conclusion with a pictorial analysis.

4. Using the same data as in figure 7.3, analyze the choice between
   a sure $10 win and bet I for (a) a risk lover; (b) a person with a
   linear utility function.

5. What are your objections to utility as a measure? Does it exist? What
   does it measure? Can you measure it?

6. Design a method for deriving the utility function of a manager,
   assuming you are free to ask him any questions you like without
   mentioning the word "utility."

7.11 Summary

In this chapter you have seen the usefulness of measures of performance other than expected payoff. The following points are worth
repeating:

a. Some important information about the distribution of a random variable can be captured in measures of the center and spread of the distribution; these measures (for example, expected value, standard deviation, variance) are also convenient in measuring the performance of a decision, or in representing the adherence to standards, as well as indicating the degree to which a given performance can be considered unusual.

b. Historically, Karl Pearson classified distributions according to some of these measures, specifically the moments of distributions (for example, mean, variance); if you can approximate the distribution of a random variable by some tabulated distribution such as the normal distribution, you can improve the accuracy of your estimate of the degree to which a result is unusual.

c. The Poisson distribution may prove very useful in describing the behavior of service units, especially the waiting times (or lines) and idle times.

d. You can use the results (theorems) about the transformation of random variables to improve your risk position by "not putting all your eggs in one basket."

e. One way of discussing behavior in risky situations is to use the concept of utility, which combines expected value and risk into one measure.

Throughout all of this analysis, you should be fully aware of all the assumptions. But even more importantly, expected value, variance, and utility may not really capture at all the way you actually or ideally make decisions. As with all quantitative methods, these are available as analytical tools to aid you in decision making. They are not, however, the Gospel according to Churchman, Auerbach, and Sadan.

In the next chapter, we will turn to the question of the value of information for decision making under uncertainty. When is information really "new," and how can you measure whether it's worth the cost of obtaining?

Appendix 7.1

Standard Normal Probability Distribution (Probability of k or more standard deviations from the mean in one direction. For negative values of k, areas are found by symmetry.)

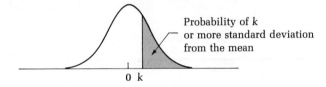

Probability of k or more standard deviation from the mean

0 k

k	.00	.01	.02	.03	.04	.05	.06	.07	.08	.09
				Second decimal place of k						
0.0	.5000	.4960	.4920	.4880	.4840	.4801	.4761	.4721	.4681	.4641
0.1	.4602	.4562	.4522	.4483	.4443	.4404	.4364	.4325	.4286	.4247
0.2	.4207	.4168	.4129	.4090	.4052	.4013	.3974	.3936	.3897	.3859
0.3	.3821	.3783	.3745	.3707	.3669	.3632	.3594	.3557	.3520	.3483
0.4	.3446	.3409	.3372	.3336	.3300	.3264	.3228	.3192	.3156	.3121
0.5	.3085	.3050	.3015	.2981	.2946	.2912	.2877	.2843	.2810	.2776
0.6	.2743	.2709	.2676	.2643	.2611	.2578	.2546	.2514	.2483	.2451
0.7	.2420	.2389	.2358	.2327	.2296	.2266	.2236	.2206	.2177	.2148
0.8	.2119	.2090	.2061	.2033	.2005	.1977	.1949	.1922	.1894	.1867
0.9	.1841	.1814	.1788	.1762	.1736	.1711	.1685	.1660	.1635	.1611
1.0	.1587	.1562	.1539	.1515	.1492	.1469	.1446	.1423	.1401	.1379
1.1	.1357	.1335	.1314	.1292	.1271	.1251	.1230	.1210	.1190	.1170
1.2	.1151	.1131	.1112	.1093	.1075	.1056	.1038	.1020	.1003	.0985
1.3	.0968	.0951	.0934	.0918	.0901	.0885	.0869	.0853	.0838	.0823
1.4	.0808	.0793	.0778	.0764	.0749	.0735	.0722	.0708	.0694	.0681
1.5	.0668	.0655	.0643	.0630	.0618	.0606	.0594	.0582	.0571	.0559
1.6	.0548	.0537	.0526	.0516	.0505	.0495	.0485	.0475	.0465	.0455
1.7	.0446	.0436	.0427	.0418	.0409	.0401	.0392	.0384	.0375	.0367
1.8	.0359	.0352	.0344	.0336	.0329	.0322	.0314	.0307	.0301	.0294
1.9	.0287	.0281	.0274	.0268	.0262	.0256	.0250	.0244	.0239	.0233
2.0	.0228	.0222	.0217	.0212	.0207	.0202	.0197	.0192	.0188	.0183
2.1	.0179	.0174	.0170	.0166	.0162	.0158	.0154	.0150	.0146	.0143
2.2	.0139	.0136	.0132	.0129	.0125	.0122	.0119	.0116	.0113	.0110
2.3	.0107	.0104	.0102	.0099	.0096	.0094	.0091	.0089	.0087	.0084
2.4	.0082	.0080	.0078	.0075	.0073	.0071	.0069	.0068	.0066	.0064
2.5	.0062	.0060	.0059	.0057	.0055	.0054	.0052	.0051	.0049	.0048
2.6	.0047	.0045	.0044	.0043	.0041	.0040	.0039	.0038	.0037	.0036
2.7	.0035	.0034	.0033	.0032	.0031	.0030	.0029	.0028	.0027	.0026
2.8	.0026	.0025	.0024	.0023	.0023	.0022	.0021	.0021	.0020	.0019
2.9	.0019	.0018	.0017	.0017	.0016	.0016	.0015	.0015	.0014	.0014
3.0	.00135									
3.5	.000 233									
4.0	.000 031 7									
4.5	.000 003 40									
5.0	.000 000 287									

Appendix 7.2

Poisson Probabilities: $P(X = x)$ (To use an approximation to binomial, use $m = np$.)

					m					
x	0.1	0.2	0.3	0.4	0.5	0.6	0.7	0.8	0.9	1.0
0	.9048	.8187	.7408	.6703	.6065	.5488	.4966	.4493	.4066	.3679
1	.0905	.1637	.2222	.2681	.3033	.3293	.3476	.3595	.3659	.3679
2	.0045	.0164	.0333	.0536	.0758	.0988	.1217	.1438	.1647	.1839
3	.0002	.0011	.0033	.0072	.0126	.0198	.0284	.0383	.0494	.0613
4	.0000	.0001	.0002	.0007	.0016	.0030	.0050	.0077	.0111	.0153
5	.0000	.0000	.0000	.0001	.0002	.0004	.0007	.0012	.0020	.0031
6	.0000	.0000	.0000	.0000	.0000	.0000	.0001	.0002	.0003	.0005
7	.0000	.0000	.0000	.0000	.0000	.0000	.0000	.0000	.0000	.0001

					m					
x	1.1	1.2	1.3	1.4	1.5	1.6	1.7	1.8	1.9	2.0
0	.3329	.3012	.2725	.2466	.2231	.2019	.1827	.1653	.1496	.1353
1	.3662	.3614	.3543	.3452	.3347	.3230	.3106	.2975	.2842	.2707
2	.2014	.2169	.2303	.2417	.2510	.2584	.2640	.2678	.2700	.2707
3	.0738	.0867	.0998	.1128	.1255	.1378	.1496	.1607	.1710	.1804
4	.0203	.0260	.0324	.0395	.0471	.0551	.0636	.0723	.0812	.0902
5	.0045	.0062	.0084	.0111	.0141	.0176	.0216	.0260	.0309	.0361
6	.0008	.0012	.0018	.0026	.0035	.0047	.0061	.0078	.0098	.0120
7	.0001	.0002	.0003	.0005	.0008	.0011	.0015	.0020	.0027	.0034
8	.0000	.0000	.0001	.0001	.0001	.0002	.0003	.0005	.0006	.0009
9	.0000	.0000	.0000	.0000	.0000	.0000	.0001	.0001	.0001	.0002

					m					
x	2.1	2.2	2.3	2.4	2.5	2.6	2.7	2.8	2.9	3.0
0	.1225	.1108	.1003	.0907	.0821	.0743	.0672	.0608	.0550	.0498
1	.2572	.2438	.2306	.2177	.2052	.1931	.1815	.1703	.1596	.1494
2	.2700	.2681	.2652	.2613	.2565	.2510	.2450	.2384	.2314	.2240
3	.1890	.1966	.2033	.2090	.2138	.2176	.2205	.2225	.2237	.2240
4	.0992	.1082	.1169	.1254	.1336	.1414	.1488	.1557	.1622	.1680
5	.0417	.0476	.0538	.0602	.0668	.0735	.0804	.0872	.0940	.1008
6	.0146	.0174	.0206	.0241	.0278	.0319	.0362	.0407	.0455	.0504
7	.0044	.0055	.0068	.0083	.0099	.0118	.0139	.0163	.0188	.0216
8	.0011	.0015	.0019	.0025	.0031	.0038	.0047	.0057	.0068	.0081
9	.0003	.0004	.0005	.0007	.0009	.0011	.0014	.0018	.0022	.0027
10	.0001	.0001	.0001	.0002	.0002	.0003	.0004	.0005	.0006	.0008
11	.0000	.0000	.0000	.0000	.0000	.0001	.0001	.0001	.0002	.0002
12	.0000	.0000	.0000	.0000	.0000	.0000	.0000	.0000	.0000	.0001

					m					
x	3.1	3.2	3.3	3.4	3.5	3.6	3.7	3.8	3.9	4.0
0	.0450	.0408	.0369	.0334	.0302	.0273	.0247	.0224	.0202	.0183
1	.1397	.1304	.1217	.1135	.1057	.0984	.0915	.0850	.0789	.0733
2	.2165	.2087	.2008	.1929	.1850	.1771	.1692	.1615	.1539	.1465
3	.2237	.2226	.2209	.2186	.2158	.2125	.2087	.2046	.2001	.1954

Table 7.2 is used by permission from *Handbook of Probability and Statistics with Tables*, by Burlington and May. Copyright, 1953. McGraw-Hill Book Co.

Appendix 7.2 (continued)

4	.1734	.1781	.1823	.1858	.1888	.1912	.1931	.1944	.1951	.1954
5	.1075	.1140	.1203	.1264	.1322	.1377	.1429	.1477	.1522	.1563
6	.0555	.0608	.0662	.0716	.0771	.0826	.0881	.0936	.0989	.1042
7	.0246	.0278	.0312	.0348	.0385	.0425	.0466	.0508	.0551	.0595
8	.0095	.0111	.0129	.0148	.0169	.0191	.0215	.0241	.0269	.0298
9	.0033	.0040	.0047	.0056	.0066	.0076	.0089	.0102	.0116	.0132
10	.0010	.0013	.0016	.0019	.0023	.0028	.0033	.0039	.0045	.0053
11	.0003	.0004	.0005	.0006	.0007	.0009	.0011	.0013	.0016	.0019
12	.0001	.0001	.0001	.0002	.0002	.0003	.0003	.0004	.0005	.0006
13	.0000	.0000	.0000	.0000	.0001	.0001	.0001	.0001	.0002	.0002
14	.0000	.0000	.0000	.0000	.0000	.0000	.0000	.0000	.0000	.0001

m

x	4.1	4.2	4.3	4.4	4.5	4.6	4.7	4.8	4.9	5.0
0	.0166	.0150	.0136	.0123	.0111	.0101	.0091	.0082	.0074	.0067
1	.0679	.0630	.0583	.0540	.0500	.0462	.0427	.0395	.0365	.0337
2	.1393	.1323	.1254	.1188	.1125	.1063	.1005	.0948	.0894	.0842
3	.1904	.1852	.1798	.1743	.1687	.1631	.1574	.1517	.1460	.1404
4	.1951	.1944	.1933	.1917	.1898	.1875	.1849	.1820	.1789	.1755
5	.1600	.1633	.1662	.1687	.1708	.1725	.1738	.1747	.1753	.1755
6	.1093	.1143	.1191	.1237	.1281	.1323	.1362	.1398	.1432	.1462
7	.0640	.0686	.0732	.0778	.0824	.0869	.0914	.0959	.1002	.1044
8	.0328	.0360	.0393	.0428	.0463	.0500	.0537	.0575	.0614	.0653
9	.0150	.0168	.0188	.0209	.0232	.0255	.0280	.0307	.0334	.0363
10	.0061	.0071	.0081	.0092	.0104	.0118	.0132	.0147	.0164	.0181
11	.0023	.0027	.0032	.0037	.0043	.0049	.0056	.0064	.0073	.0082
12	.0008	.0009	.0011	.0014	.0016	.0019	.0022	.0026	.0030	.0034
13	.0002	.0003	.0004	.0005	.0006	.0007	.0008	.0009	.0011	.0013
14	.0001	.0001	.0001	.0001	.0002	.0002	.0003	.0003	.0004	.0005
15	.0000	.0000	.0000	.0000	.0001	.0001	.0001	.0001	.0001	.0002

m

x	5.1	5.2	5.3	5.4	5.5	5.6	5.7	5.8	5.9	6.0
0	.0061	.0055	.0050	.0045	.0041	.0037	.0033	.0030	.0027	.0025
1	.0311	.0287	.0265	.0244	.0225	.0207	.0191	.0176	.0162	.0149
2	.0793	.0746	.0701	.0659	.0618	.0580	.0544	.0509	.0477	.0446
3	.1348	.1293	.1239	.1185	.1133	.1082	.1033	.0985	.0938	.0892
4	.1719	.1681	.1641	.1600	.1558	.1515	.1472	.1428	.1383	.1339
5	.1753	.1748	.1740	.1728	.1714	.1697	.1678	.1656	.1632	.1606
6	.1490	.1515	.1537	.1555	.1571	.1584	.1594	.1601	.1605	.1606
7	.1086	.1125	.1163	.1200	.1234	.1267	.1298	.1326	.1353	.1377
8	.0692	.0731	.0771	.0810	.0849	.0887	.0925	.0962	.0998	.1033
9	.0392	.0423	.0454	.0486	.0519	.0552	.0586	.0620	.0654	.0688
10	.0200	.0220	.0241	.0262	.0285	.0309	.0334	.0359	.0386	.0413
11	.0093	.0104	.0116	.0129	.0143	.0157	.0173	.0190	.0207	.0225
12	.0039	.0045	.0051	.0058	.0065	.0073	.0082	.0092	.0102	.0113
13	.0015	.0018	.0021	.0024	.0028	.0032	.0036	.0041	.0046	.0052
14	.0006	.0007	.0008	.0009	.0011	.0013	.0015	.0017	.0019	.0022
15	.0002	.0002	.0003	.0003	.0004	.0005	.0006	.0007	.0008	.0009
16	.0001	.0001	.0001	.0001	.0001	.0002	.0002	.0002	.0003	.0003
17	.0000	.0000	.0000	.0000	.0000	.0001	.0001	.0001	.0001	.0001

Appendix 7.2 (continued)

					m					
x	6.1	6.2	6.3	6.4	6.5	6.6	6.7	6.8	6.9	7.0
0	.0022	.0020	.0018	.0017	.0015	.0014	.0012	.0011	.0010	.0009
1	.0137	.0126	.0116	.0106	.0098	.0090	.0082	.0076	.0070	.0064
2	.0417	.0390	.0364	.0340	.0318	.0296	.0276	.0258	.0240	.0223
3	.0848	.0806	.0765	.0726	.0688	.0652	.0617	.0584	.0552	.0521
4	.1294	.1249	.1205	.1162	.1118	.1076	.1034	.0992	.0952	.0912
5	.1579	.1549	.1519	.1487	.1454	.1420	.1385	.1349	.1314	.1277
6	.1605	.1601	.1595	.1586	.1575	.1562	.1546	.1529	.1511	.1490
7	.1399	.1418	.1435	.1450	.1462	.1472	.1480	.1486	.1489	.1490
8	.1066	.1099	.1130	.1160	.1188	.1215	.1240	.1263	.1284	.1304
9	.0723	.0757	.0791	.0825	.0858	.0891	.0923	.0954	.0985	.1014
10	.0441	.0469	.0498	.0528	.0558	.0588	.0618	.0649	.0679	.0710
11	.0245	.0265	.0285	.0307	.0330	.0353	.0377	.0401	.0426	.0452
12	.0124	.0137	.0150	.0164	.0179	.0194	.0210	.0227	.0245	.0264
13	.0058	.0065	.0073	.0081	.0089	.0098	.0108	.0119	.0130	.0142
14	.0025	.0029	.0033	.0037	.0041	.0046	.0052	.0058	.0064	.0071
15	.0010	.0012	.0014	.0016	.0018	.0020	.0023	.0026	.0029	.0033
16	.0004	.0005	.0005	.0006	.0007	.0008	.0010	.0011	.0013	.0014
17	.0001	.0002	.0002	.0002	.0003	.0003	.0004	.0004	.0005	.0006
18	.0000	.0001	.0001	.0001	.0001	.0001	.0001	.0002	.0002	.0002
19	.0000	.0000	.0000	.0000	.0000	.0000	.0000	.0001	.0001	.0001

					m					
x	7.1	7.2	7.3	7.4	7.5	7.6	7.7	7.8	7.9	8.0
0	.0008	.0007	.0007	.0006	.0006	.0005	.0005	.0004	.0004	.0003
1	.0059	.0054	.0049	.0045	.0041	.0038	.0035	.0032	.0029	.0027
2	.0208	.0194	.0180	.0167	.0156	.0145	.0134	.0125	.0116	.0107
3	.0492	.0464	.0438	.0413	.0389	.0366	.0345	.0324	.0305	.0286
4	.0874	.0836	.0799	.0764	.0729	.0696	.0663	.0632	.0602	.0573
5	.1241	.1204	.1167	.1130	.1094	.1057	.1021	.0986	.0951	.0916
6	.1468	.1445	.1420	.1394	.1367	.1339	.1311	.1282	.1252	.1221
7	.1489	.1486	.1481	.1474	.1465	.1454	.1442	.1428	.1413	.1396
8	.1321	.1337	.1351	.1363	.1373	.1382	.1388	.1392	.1395	.1396
9	.1042	.1070	.1096	.1121	.1144	.1167	.1187	.1207	.1224	.1241
10	.0470	.0770	.0800	.0829	.0858	.0887	.0914	.0941	.0967	.0993
11	.0478	.0504	.0531	.0558	.0585	.0613	.0640	.0667	.0695	.0722
12	.0283	.0303	.0323	.0344	.0366	.0388	.0411	.0434	.0457	.0481
13	.0154	.0168	.0181	.0196	.0211	.0227	.0243	.0260	.0278	.0296
14	.0078	.0086	.0095	.0104	.0113	.0123	.0134	.0145	.0157	.0169
15	.0037	.0041	.0046	.0051	.0057	.0062	.0069	.0075	.0083	.0090
16	.0016	.0019	.0021	.0024	.0026	.0030	.0033	.0037	.0041	.0045
17	.0007	.0008	.0009	.0010	.0012	.0013	.0015	.0017	.0019	.0021
18	.0003	.0003	.0004	.0004	.0005	.0006	.0006	.0007	.0008	.0009
19	.0001	.0001	.0001	.0002	.0002	.0002	.0003	.0003	.0003	.0004
20	.0000	.0000	.0001	.0001	.0001	.0001	.0001	.0001	.0001	.0002
21	.0000	.0000	.0000	.0000	.0000	.0000	.0000	.0000	.0001	.0001

					m					
x	8.1	8.2	8.3	8.4	8.5	8.6	8.7	8.8	8.9	9.0
0	.0003	.0003	.0002	.0002	.0002	.0002	.0002	.0002	.0001	.0001
1	.0025	.0023	.0021	.0019	.0017	.0016	.0014	.0013	.0012	.0011
2	.0100	.0092	.0086	.0079	.0074	.0068	.0063	.0058	.0054	.0050
3	.0269	.0252	.0237	.0222	.0208	.0195	.0183	.0171	.0160	.0150

Appendix 7.2 (continued)

x										
4	.0544	.0517	.0491	.0466	.0443	.0420	.0398	.0377	.0357	.0337
5	.0882	.0849	.0816	.0784	.0752	.0722	.0692	.0663	.0635	.0607
6	.1191	.1160	.1128	.1097	.1066	.1034	.1003	.0972	.0941	.0911
7	.1378	.1358	.1338	.1317	.1294	.1271	.1247	.1222	.1197	.1171
8	.1395	.1392	.1388	.1382	.1375	.1366	.1356	.1344	.1332	.1318
9	.1256	.1269	.1280	.1290	.1299	.1306	.1311	.1315	.1317	.1318
10	.1017	.1040	.1063	.1084	.1104	.1123	.1140	.1157	.1172	.1186
11	.0749	.0776	.0802	.0828	.0853	.0878	.0902	.0925	.0948	.0970
12	.0505	.0530	.0555	.0579	.0604	.0629	.0654	.0679	.0703	.0728
13	.0315	.0334	.0354	.0374	.0395	.0416	.0438	.0459	.0481	.0504
14	.0182	.0196	.0210	.0225	.0240	.0256	.0272	.0289	.0306	.0324
15	.0098	.0107	.0116	.0126	.0136	.0147	.0158	.0169	.0182	.0194
16	.0050	.0055	.0060	.0066	.0072	.0079	.0086	.0093	.0101	.0109
17	.0024	.0026	.0029	.0033	.0036	.0040	.0044	.0048	.0053	.0058
18	.0011	.0012	.0014	.0015	.0017	.0019	.0021	.0024	.0026	.0029
19	.0005	.0005	.0006	.0007	.0008	.0009	.0010	.0011	.0012	.0014
20	.0002	.0002	.0002	.0003	.0003	.0004	.0004	.0005	.0005	.0006
21	.0001	.0001	.0001	.0001	.0001	.0002	.0002	.0002	.0002	.0003
22	.0000	.0000	.0000	.0000	.0001	.0001	.0001	.0001	.0001	.0001

					m					
x	9.1	9.2	9.3	9.4	9.5	9.6	9.7	9.8	9.9	10
0	.0001	.0001	.0001	.0001	.0001	.0001	.0001	.0001	.0001	.0000
1	.0010	.0009	.0009	.0008	.0007	.0007	.0006	.0005	.0005	.0005
2	.0046	.0043	.0040	.0037	.0034	.0031	.0029	.0027	.0025	.0023
3	.0140	.0131	.0123	.0115	.0107	.0100	.0093	.0087	.0081	.0076
4	.0319	.0302	.0285	.0269	.0254	.0240	.0226	.0213	.0201	.0189
5	.0581	.0555	.0530	.0506	.0483	.0460	.0439	.0418	.0398	.0378
6	.0881	.0861	.0822	.0793	.0764	.0736	.0709	.0682	.0656	.0631
7	.1115	.1118	.1091	.1064	.1037	.1010	.0982	.0955	.0928	.0901
8	.1302	.1286	.1269	.1251	.1232	.1212	.1191	.1170	.1148	.1126
9	.1317	.1315	.1311	.1306	.1300	.1293	.1284	.1274	.1263	.1251

					m					
x	9.1	9.2	9.3	9.4	9.5	9.6	9.7	9.8	9.9	10
10	.1198	.1210	.1219	.1228	.1235	.1241	.1245	.1249	.1250	.1251
11	.0991	.1012	.1031	.1049	.1067	.1083	.1098	.1112	.1125	.1137
12	.0752	.0776	.0799	.0822	.0844	.0866	.0888	.0908	.0928	.0948
13	.0526	.0549	.0572	.0594	.0617	.0640	.0662	.0685	.0707	.0729
14	.0342	.0361	.0380	.0399	.0419	.0439	.0459	.0479	.0500	.0521
15	.0208	.0221	.0235	.0250	.0265	.0281	.0297	.0313	.0330	.0347
16	.0118	.0127	.0137	.0147	.0157	.0168	.0180	.0192	.0204	.0217
17	.0063	.0069	.0075	.0081	.0088	.0095	.0103	.0111	.0119	.0128
18	.0032	.0035	.0039	.0042	.0046	.0051	.0055	.0060	.0065	.0071
19	.0015	.0017	.0019	.0021	.0023	.0026	.0028	.0031	.0034	.0037
20	.0007	.0008	.0009	.0010	.0011	.0012	.0014	.0015	.0017	.0019
21	.0003	.0003	.0004	.0004	.0005	.0006	.0006	.0007	.0008	.0009
22	.0001	.0001	.0002	.0002	.0002	.0002	.0003	.0003	.0004	.0004
23	.0000	.0001	.0001	.0001	.0001	.0001	.0001	.0001	.0002	.0002
24	.0000	.0000	.0000	.0000	.0000	.0000	.0000	.0001	.0001	.0001

Appendix 7.2 (continued)

						m				
x	11	12	13	14	15	16	17	18	19	20
0	.0000	.0000	.0000	.0000	.0000	.0000	.0000	.0000	.0000	.0000
1	.0002	.0001	.0000	.0000	.0000	.0000	.0000	.0000	.0000	.0000
2	.0010	.0004	.0002	.0001	.0000	.0000	.0000	.0000	.0000	.0000
3	.0037	.0018	.0008	.0004	.0002	.0001	.0000	.0000	.0000	.0000
4	.0102	.0053	.0027	.0013	.0006	.0003	.0001	.0001	.0000	.0000
5	.0224	.0127	.0070	.0037	.0019	.0010	.0005	.0002	.0001	.0001
6	.0411	.0255	.0152	.0087	.0048	.0026	.0014	.0007	.0004	.0002
7	.0646	.0437	.0281	.0174	.0104	.0060	.0034	.0018	.0010	.0005
8	.0888	.0655	.0457	.0304	.0194	.0120	.0072	.0042	.0024	.0013
9	.1085	.0874	.0661	.0473	.0324	.0213	.0135	.0083	.0050	.0029
10	.1194	.1048	.0859	.0663	.0486	.0341	.0230	.0150	.0095	.0058
11	.1194	.1144	.1015	.0844	.0663	.0496	.0355	.0245	.0164	.0106
12	.1094	.1144	.1099	.0984	.0829	.0661	.0504	.0368	.0259	.0176
13	.0926	.1056	.1099	.1060	.0956	.0814	.0658	.0509	.0378	.0271
14	.0728	.0905	.1021	.1060	.1024	.0930	.0800	.0655	.0514	.0387
15	.0534	.0724	.0885	.0989	.1024	.0992	.0906	.0786	.0650	.0516
16	.0367	.0543	.0719	.0866	.0960	.0992	.0963	.0884	.0772	.0646
17	.0237	.0383	.0550	.0713	.0847	.0934	.0963	.0936	.0863	.0760
18	.0145	.0256	.0397	.0554	.0706	.0830	.0909	.0936	.0911	.0844
19	.0084	.0161	.0272	.0409	.0557	.0699	.0814	.0887	.0911	.0888
20	.0046	.0097	.0177	.0286	.0418	.0559	.0692	.0798	.0866	.0888
21	.0024	.0055	.0109	.0191	.0299	.0426	.0560	.0684	.0783	.0846
22	.0012	.0030	.0065	.0121	.0204	.0310	.0433	.0560	.0676	.0769
23	.0006	.0016	.0037	.0074	.0133	.0216	.0320	.0438	.0559	.0669
24	.0003	.0008	.0020	.0043	.0083	.0144	.0226	.0328	.0442	.0557
25	.0001	.0004	.0010	.0024	.0050	.0092	.0154	.0237	.0336	.0446
26	.0000	.0002	.0005	.0013	.0029	.0057	.0101	.0164	.0246	.0343
27	.0000	.0001	.0002	.0007	.0016	.0034	.0063	.0109	.0173	.0254
28	.0000	.0000	.0001	.0003	.0009	.0019	.0038	.0070	.0117	.0181
29	.0000	.0000	.0001	.0002	.0004	.0011	.0023	.0044	.0077	.0125
30	.0000	.0000	.0000	.0001	.0002	.0006	.0013	.0026	.0049	.0083
31	.0000	.0000	.0000	.0000	.0001	.0003	.0007	.0015	.0030	.0054
32	.0000	.0000	.0000	.0000	.0001	.0001	.0004	.0009	.0018	.0034
33	.0000	.0000	.0000	.0000	.0000	.0001	.0002	.0005	.0010	.0020
34	.0000	.0000	.0000	.0000	.0000	.0000	.0001	.0002	.0006	.0012
35	.0000	.0000	.0000	.0000	.0000	.0000	.0000	.0001	.0003	.0007
36	.0000	.0000	.0000	.0000	.0000	.0000	.0000	.0001	.0002	.0004
37	.0000	.0000	.0000	.0000	.0000	.0000	.0000	.0000	.0001	.0002
38	.0000	.0000	.0000	.0000	.0000	.0000	.0000	.0000	.0000	.0001
39	.0000	.0000	.0000	.0000	.0000	.0000	.0000	.0000	.0000	.0001

Conditional Probability and the Value of Information   8

8.1 Introduction

The role of information is central in our lives, since we use various types of information for almost everything we do: dressing, bathing, eating, commuting, doing our business, entertainment, and in these days love making. It might generally be assumed that all information is valuable, but of course this is not so: it may be just as well that you don't know you have bad breath. But even when information is clearly advantageous, it does not follow that you should obtain it, since there is usually a cost involved in doing so. Therefore, one of the pervasive problems of our lives is the determination of whether to "buy" more information or not. This chapter will be concerned with questions of this type. In the next section we examine one rather simple but revealing example of this kind of decision, based upon the assumption that you want to maximize expected value.

8.2 Value of Perfect Information

Throughout our examination of deductive quantitative methods, we have been considering situations in which all relevant information is embedded in the statement of the problem. In some cases the information was *perfect* in the sense that before making the decision you knew the state of the world that prevailed and thus could pass from the known state of the world plus a decision, to a known outcome. When uncertainty prevails, the information has been given in the form of a probability distribution of the states of the world that might affect pay-offs, in which case the information is sometimes called *imperfect*. The decision maker's question is: What is it worth to acquire perfect information—that is, to know the state of the world with certainty? One answer is to use the familiar tactic of determining expected payoffs.

Problem: Crazy Bill Insurance Company ━━━━━━━━━

You are going on a trip abroad and you have decided to take your new $250 camera with you. Knowing your habits, you estimate that the probability of losing the camera during the trip is .10, so you consider buying an insurance policy to cover this possibility, at a cost of $10. Should you buy the policy?

Analysis: The problem by now should be very familiar to you. You can summarize the problem in a payoff table (as first introduced in section 1.4)

TABLE 8.1   Crazy Bill Insurance

DECISION	STATE OF THE WORLD (with probability)		EXPECTED PAYOFF
	Camera is lost	You return with camera	
	.1	.9	
Buy insurance	$250 - 10 = 240$	$250 - 10 = 240$	$.1 \times 240 + .9 \times 240$ $= 240$
Don't buy insurance	0	250	$.1 \times 0 + .9 \times 250$ $= 225$

The assumption that your measure of performance is to achieve the highest possible expected payoff dictates that you should choose to buy the insurance policy ($240 > $225).

━━━━━━━━━━━━━━━━━━━━━━━━━━━━━━━━━━━━

For the sake of exposition and understanding, suppose for a moment that you are clairvoyant and can tell *before* boarding the plane for your trip what will happen to your camera. If you know that you are about to lose your camera, the best decision remains "buy insurance" since you will return home with $240 rather than nothing. However, if you "see" that your camera will *not* be lost, your decision should become "don't buy insurance" ($250 > $240). Your ability to prophesy has eliminated all uncertainty, since your choice of the best act depends on what state of the world you *know* will occur. This knowledge of all the relevant facts with certainty, we said, is *perfect information*.

Suppose now that, instead of being clairvoyant, you are offered the following deal by the Crazy Bill Insurance Company: upon your return from the trip abroad you can choose whether or not to purchase the insurance policy. This is an unbeatable offer and therefore you should accept it since you get the best of two worlds. Your decision upon return will depend on whatever happens to your camera: If it is lost you buy the insurance for $10 and collect $250 on the policy; if you return with the camera you are not interested in any insurance.

Although you are delighted with the generosity of this offer you are still curious to know how much you expect to end up with, by the time you come home. If the camera is lost (probability .1) you will have $240; if not (probability .9) you will have a $250 camera (no premium payments); therefore your expected value is

$$.10 \times 240 + .90 \times 250 = 24 + 225 = \$249.$$

This last sum is called the *expected value with perfect information*, since your action will come *after* all the facts are known — that is, you make the decision to purchase insurance after you know the state of the world that prevails.

Now you receive a letter from the Crazy Bill Insurance Company telling you that they have decided for obvious reasons to change this policy: you can either buy the regular insurance for $10 before you start the trip, or pay $5 for the privilege to take the "Crazy" deal. Which of the two is better?

Your expected value based on the "Crazy" deal is $249, and you already know that the expected value of the $10 insurance offer is $240. The former increases your expected gain by $249 − $240 = $9, which is the most you should be willing to pay for the privilege of accepting the crazy after-the-fact deal. This value of $9 is called the *expected value of perfect information*, because it is the value which can be directly attributed to the removal of all uncertainty at the time you must make the final decision (to buy or not to buy the insurance). The insurance company asks you to pay $5, which gives you a net expected value of $249 − $5 = $244 for taking the "Crazy" deal. Since $244 > $240, you conclude that paying $5 for the "Crazy" deal is better. Equivalently, you could have used the fact that $9 was the expected value of perfect information, and it was being offered to you for $5, so you should take the deal since $9 > $5.

In general, under the principle of "make the most," if the *value of perfect information is greater than its cost to you, you should exercise the option of obtaining the information at that price* (unless better options exist). There is nothing new in this prescription; what we have done is to show how to use your newly acquired knowledge of probability theory to apply it.

Of course, you will never receive offers like the one above in reality, but we presented this example to give you an intuitive feel for the "value of perfect information." The point to be learned here is that knowing what is going to happen (or sometimes what already has occurred) can be of value to you in decision making. Information about what has happened or will occur may sometimes be available to you only at a certain cost, and the decision is whether or not to pay the price necessary to obtain that information. The following problems will elaborate on this point.

Problem: Ecological Oil Drilling Corporation ▬▬▬▬▬▬

The board of directors of the Ecological Oil Drilling Corporation is considering whether or not to drill a well in a new concession area. The cost of drilling is estimated at $50,000, and the company experts agree that the probability of a discovery of an oil field is .15 and a discovery of a gas field is .25; there is a .60 probability of a dry well. If oil is discovered, the net profit (after all costs, including drilling cost) is estimated to be $250,000, while a gas field will yield $100,000 net profit. As a special analyst you are asked to make a recommendation to the board on whether to drill. What should it be?

Analysis: Again, this is a familiar problem. The payoff table associated with the problem is table 8.2.

TABLE 8.2   Ecological Oil Drilling Corporation

DECISION	STATE OF THE WORLD probability			EXPECTED PAYOFF
	Oil field	Gas field	Dry well	
	.15	.25	.60	
Drill	250,000	100,000	−50,000	.15 × 250,000 + .25 × 100,000 + .60 × (−50,000) = $32,500
Don't drill	0	0	0	0

So, if you believe that the board's measure of performance is expected payoff, you recommend drilling.

Problem: Ecological Oil Revisited ━━━━━━━━━━━━

What if you are now offered the opportunity to gain perfect information about the concession area? Specifically, suppose that you have read in the *Oil and Gas* magazine that Debi's Instruments Company has invented a new device which can disclose the contents of a well without drilling. The cost of this device is $40,000 and it can be used only once. You must now decide whether to recommend that the board drill the well or purchase the device. What should you do?

Analysis: If the signal generated by the device indicates oil, you will recommend drilling ($250,000 profits); if gas is indicated, drilling is again your advice; but if the reading is "dry hole" the company will save the $50,000 drilling costs. So with perfect information you expect the value of the well to be

$$.15 \times 250,000 + .25 \times 100,000 + .60 \times 0 = \$62,500$$

Thus, the increase in expected value contributed by using the informational device is $62,500 - 32,500$, which is $30,000. But since the cost of the device is $40,000 you decide against it.

━━

What you have done is use the fact that employing the device eliminates uncertainty about what state of the world you expect when you make the final decision on drilling. Thus, this device is a producer of perfect information. The value added by using this device is the value of perfect information ($30,000). But, as your common sense tells you, when the cost of the information ($40,000) is greater than the benefit of the information ($30,000), you should reject the opportunity to "purchase" the information.

The moral of this little tale is that removing "all" uncertainty is sometimes a very inefficient way to manage affairs. This is especially relevant to auditors, accountants, and bureaucrats whose business it is to estimate "what really went on," since to find out "for sure" sometimes costs a great deal more than it's worth. It is also important for police departments, FBI, CIA, and other information-gathering agencies, since the "cost" of obtaining information about people's behavior may very well include invasion of privacy and reduction of freedom. To paraphrase Pope, "A little knowledge is a dangerous thing"; so, very often, is a lot of knowledge.

PROBLEMS 8.2

1.   What is the value of complete information in the Lottery problem of chapter 1?

2. What is the value of complete information in the SF Steel Works problem of appendix 2.1?

3. Write down, in words, the definition of the expected value of complete information using w_i, s_i, d_i, probabilities of s_i, and the conditional payoffs.

4. Do you have any objection to using the expected value of complete information as a measure of performance in, say, the Ecological Drilling problem?

5. You have received an order for 1000 toys at $5 per unit. The cost of producing a unit is $4.50. However, if the unit turns out to be defective it costs an additional $2 to replace it. Being concerned with these high costs of defective replacement and knowing that any of 1%, 5%, 10%, or 25% defectives may occur with probabilities .6, .3, .08, and .02, respectively, you consider one of the following three actions:
    a. leave the process as it is
    b. make a minor adjustment at the cost of $25, which will reduce a defective percentage of 10% or 25% to 5% but will not affect the 1% and the 5% rates
    c. make a major adjustment, at the cost of $100, which will guarantee exactly 1% defectives

    You recall an advertisement you've seen about a new device capable of detecting at once the precise percentage of defectives of any machine. The price of the device is $10, and it can be used only once. Should you invest the $10 in the device? What measure of performance did you use?

6. You have received a letter from the procurement department of the A.S.U. government requesting you to supply army jackets. You know that due to the end of the draft in the United States, there are 50,000 new jackets declared as surplus selling for 50¢ a unit. You estimate that the order you will receive from A.S.U. will be for 1000, 3000 or 5000 jackets at the price of $1 per jacket. You assess the chances of the three demand figures as 60%, 30%, and 10%, respectively. You also know that any jacket that you will not be able to sell to the A.S.U. government you can sell to the local army surplus store for 20¢ per jacket. You are pressed to make a decision on the purchase of the surplus and you wonder whether you should take a trip to A.S.U., where you are sure you can obtain the amount of the order immediately. You estimate the trip's expenses at about $1500. Should you take the trip?

7. Your friend E. John, who has recently established the Plumbers Information Corp., asks you for advice. He is requested by the president of Fashion, Inc., to quote a fee for a snooping operation

that will take him into the offices of Fashion's major competition to check whether this company is coming out with a revolutionary new line or just making minor adjustments to the present line. Fashion estimates that the chances of a new line by the competition is 60% and that its own profits will be affected by the competitor's policy as well as by Fashion's own advertising strategy, as the following payoff table portrays:

Ad Strategy	Competitor's Policy	
	Competitor introduces new line	Competitor does not introduce new line
No advertising	$100,000	$700,000
Minor ad campaign	$300,000	$600,000
Major ad campaign	$400,000	$500,000

What is your advice to E. John if Fashion, Inc., is a strict maximizer of expected payoffs?

8. Your neighborhood baker has come to you for help. He tells you that his most important customer, the Kawii Hotel, which purchases 10 to 15 cakes daily, has offered to inform him 24 hours in advance on the exact number of cakes they will need on the following day. In return they ask for a discount on orders. After a brief inquiry you obtain the following information: Presently the daily order of the hotel is being telephoned in every morning for a delivery within two hours from the time the order is placed. Therefore, the baker must decide on the daily baking before he knows the day's exact order. To make this decision he uses the demand information given below.

Number of cakes demanded: 10   11   12   13   14   15

Probability: .10   .15   .25   .35   .10   .05

The cost of baking a cake is $10, and cakes which are not sold must be disposed of at the end of the day. The selling price of a cake is $15. What is your advice to the baker?

8.3 Conditional Probability and Independence of Events*

The previous section indicated a somewhat new feature of the MIS based on uncertainty; we indicated how the uncertainty might be

---

*The student should review set theory (appendix 2.1) before reading this and the following sections.

removed and the exact nature of the state of the world revealed, but at a price. We now examine a more general version of this same design idea, wherein you know or assume with certainty a *part* of S, and where a knowledge of this part changes the *probabilities* of the uncertain parts of S. For example, if you toss three coins, you know that S consists of eight states of the world (HHH, HHT, HTH, THH, HTT, THT, TTH, TTT), each having a probability of 1/8. If you are interested in the compound event "exactly two heads," then the probability is 3/8. But now suppose you learn (at a price) that the first coin has fallen heads, but the fate of the other two is unknown. Then the probability of "exactly two heads in three tosses" depends on the four "residual" events (HH, HT, TH, TT), and specifically the cases when there is exactly one additional head. Hence the new probability is 1/2, *not* 3/8.

A similar example occurs in the Route to Work problem of chapter 1, where if you drive to work, your arrival time depends on the heaviness of traffic or the occurrence of an accident. Knowledge of the traffic conditions beforehand would lead you to revise the probabilities of your arrival time, thus suggesting alternative routes, which is why we listen to traffic reports!

In all these cases, you change your probability estimates for the occurrence of certain events (for example, a backup in traffic on the freeway) because of the knowledge that some other event has occurred (for example, an accident on the freeway). The new probability estimates are called *conditional probabilities* since they are conditioned by the occurrence of some event. If the event occurring is an accident, and you are interested in the probability that heavy traffic results, we write P (heavy traffic | an accident has occurred) and read "the conditional probability of heavy traffic *given* an accident has occurred." We will discuss methods of arriving at this conditional probability, when you have enough information to do so, by elaborating on the coin-flipping example.

Problem: Tricking Nick Numbers ━━━━━━━━━━━━━━━━━━━━

Nick Numbers has offered you the following bet: If you pay a dollar to play, he will pay you four dollars if your friend flips exactly two heads in two tosses of a coin which you know to be fair. But you also know that your friend has a trick whereby he can assure you that the first coin will come up heads, while the other will come up heads or tails with equal probability. He is willing to pull the trick for a "side payment" of 50 cents. Should you take the bet and pay for the trick (in effect "buy" some information about S)?

Analysis: *Without* your friend's trick, you know by now (in your sleep, probably) that the four elements of S are

$$e_1 = HH, \ e_2 = HT, \ e_3 = TH, \ e_4 = TT$$

and each has probability 1/4. So with probability 1/4 you can gain $3 ($4 reward minus $1 payment for the game), and with probability 3/4 you lose your $1 payment. Therefore, the expected value of the bet *without* the trick is

$$\frac{1}{4} \, (\$4 - \$1) + \frac{3}{4} \, (-\$1) = \$0$$

So you refuse Nick's offer, based on expected payoff.

If the trick is used, however, and you *know* that the first coin will be H, then the probabilities of the four events change in the following way:

$$P(e_1) = \frac{1}{2}, \; P(e_2) = \frac{1}{2}, \; P(e_3) = 0, \; P(e_4) = 0$$

You can use set theory (appendix 2.1) to convince yourself that this is true: the universal set *of relevance* contains only the first two events since the first coin must be H. Hence e_3 and e_4 are impossible. We will call this new universal set K. This is depicted in figure 8.1.

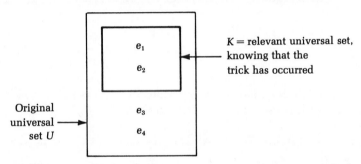

Figure 8.1   **Venn Diagram to Illustrate the Change in the Universal Set**

The universal set K corresponds to the event "the trick occurs," and the two elementary events included in K are equiprobable. Therefore, the probability of $e_1 = $ HH given K—that is, the probability that HH will appear when you know that there are only two equiprobable events that can occur—is $P(e_1 \mid K) = \frac{1}{2}$. This is illustrated in figure 8.2. Notice that the conditional probabilities of all the events, given K, still add up to 1, that is,

$$P(e_1 \mid K) = \frac{1}{2}$$

$$P(e_2 \mid K) = \frac{1}{2}$$

$$P(e_3 \mid K) = 0$$
$$P(e_4 \mid K) = 0$$

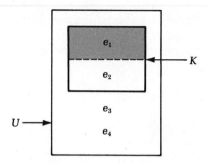

Figure 8.2   Venn Diagram to Illustrate $P(e_1 \mid K)$

So, with the knowledge of the trick, you now expect to make

$$\frac{1}{2}(\$4 - \$1) + \frac{1}{2}(-\$1) = \$1$$

Even with the "side payment" of $.50, the deal is worthwhile.

The example just given is a special case, because the event you were interested in, e_1, is completely contained in the new relevant universal set, K. This enabled you to adjust the probabilities in a relatively simple manner. We now want to examine the more general case, where the event of significance is not completely contained in K. The following problem illustrates this more general case.

Problem: Retricking Nick Numbers ━━━━━━━━━

Nick is now suspicious and offers you a new deal: he will pay $5 if your friend flips three heads or three tails in three tosses. Your friend offers to use his trick again for 50¢, and now promises that he can get at least two heads. Note that this is a different kind of assurance, since he does not specify which coins will come up heads. Should you take the deal if it costs you a dollar to play?

Analysis: The universal set U of the bet consists of the following elementary events:

$e_1 = \text{HHH}, \; e_2 = \text{HHT}, \; e_3 = \text{HTH}, \; e_4 = \text{HTT}, \; e_5 = \text{THH},$
$$e_6 = \text{THT}, \; e_7 = \text{TTH}, \; e_8 = \text{TTT}$$

You win if the compound event

$$A = \text{three heads or three tails} = e_1 \cup e_8$$

occurs. If your friend performs the trick, the relevant universal set K contains only elementary events that have at least two heads showing;

$K = e_1 \cup e_2 \cup e_3 \cup e_5$ becomes the relevant universal set. So if K occurs you know that e_8, which is one of the rewarding events, is impossible since $e_8 \cap K = \phi$. That is, $P(e_8 \mid K) = 0$. So, given that K occurs, you can win the \$5 only if e_1 occurs. That is, e_1 is the only element which is contained in both the relevant universal set K and the winning event A: $e_1 = A \cap K$. What is the probability of winning, $P(e_1 \mid K)$: Is it 1/8? If you didn't know about your friend's trick, then 1/8 is clearly the answer. But you know that the trick will occur, so the probabilities of the four mutually exclusive events contained in K must add up to one. (See chapter 5, assumption 2.) However, knowing that K occurs does not change the *relative* chances of the possible events. For example, knowing that K occurs does not change the fact that $P(e_1) = P(e_2)$. So to obtain the conditional probabilities you have to adjust the original probabilities of the relevant elementary events (e_1, e_2, e_3, and e_5) to add up to one to conform to probability assumption 2 (chapter 5) while at the same time keeping the relative probabilities the same.

Dividing (or multiplying) any set of numbers by a constant does not alter the relative magnitudes of the numbers. For example, the relative magnitudes of the numbers 2 and 3 is 2/3, and the relative magnitudes of $(\frac{1}{2}) \times 2$ and $(\frac{1}{2}) \times 3$ is $(2/2)/(3/2) = 2/3$. Hence you can divide the probabilities of the relevant elementary events by a constant and keep the relative probabilities the same. But you must choose the constant so that the sum of the adjusted probabilities of these events is *one* in order to satisfy probability assumption 2. The constant that will result in the adjusted (conditional) probabilities summing to one is exactly the probability of the conditional event. In this case it's $P(K)$:

$$P(K) = P(e_1) + P(e_2) + P(e_3) + P(e_5) = \frac{1}{2}$$

and therefore the probabilities which satisfy assumption 2 and keep the relative chances the same are

$$P(e_1 \mid K) = \frac{P(e_1)}{P(K)} = \frac{1/8}{1/2} = \frac{1}{4}$$

$$P(e_2 \mid K) = \frac{P(e_2)}{P(K)} = \frac{1}{4}$$

$$P(e_3 \mid K) = \frac{P(e_3)}{P(K)} = \frac{1}{4}$$

$$P(e_5 \mid K) = \frac{P(e_5)}{P(K)} = \frac{1}{4}$$

Note that you could also have arrived at this result by arguing that the possible elementary events are equiprobable, and since there are four of them, the probability of each is 1/4.

The general formula for the *conditional probability that an event A will occur given that K has occurred is*

$$P(A \mid K) = \frac{P(A \cap K)}{P(K)} \tag{1}$$

To see this pictorially, consider the Venn diagram in figure 8.3. In the

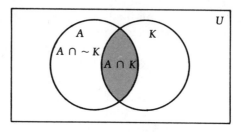

Figure 8.3   Venn Diagram to Illustrate $P(A \mid K)$

figure the original (unconditional) probability of A can be thought of as the proportion of U, the original universal set, taken up by the event A, and the probability of K is the proportion of U taken up by K. When you know that K has occurred, K becomes the relevant universal set whose probability of occurrence is 1. Thus, the part of A which is not in K cannot occur; that is, $P(A \cap \sim K \mid K) = 0$, and only the part of A which also belongs to K (represented by the shaded area) can occur. So the probability of A given K is the proportion of K taken up by $A \cap K$, or

$$\frac{P(A \cap K)}{P(K)}$$

To complete the problem's analysis you want to know the probability of winning given that the trick will be performed, $P(A \mid K)$, and the probability of losing (not winning) under the same condition, $P(\sim A \mid K)$. Using formula (1):

$$P(A \mid K) = \frac{P(A \cap K)}{P(K)} = \frac{P(e_1)}{P(e_1 \cup e_2 \cup e_3 \cup e_5)} = \frac{1/8}{1/2} = \frac{1}{4}$$

$$P(\sim A \mid K) = \frac{P(\sim A \cap K)}{P(K)} = \frac{P(e_2 \cup e_3 \cup e_5)}{P(e_1 \cup e_2 \cup e_3 \cup e_5)} = \frac{1/8 + 1/8 + 1/8}{1/2} = \frac{3}{4}$$

Knowing the relevant probabilities you can now compute the amount you expect Nick to pay:

$$\frac{1}{4} \times (\$5 - \$1) + \frac{3}{4} \times (-\$1) = \$.25$$

But if you are obliged to make the 50¢ "side payment" to your friend, the bet is not worthwhile.

The conditional probability formula is portrayed in another way in the Venn diagram in figure 8.4.

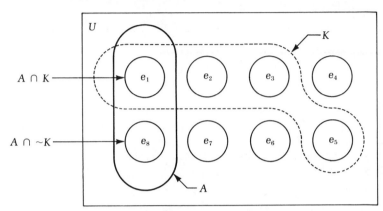

Figure 8.4   Venn Diagram for $P(A \mid K)$

In the figure the elementary events e_1, e_2, . . . , e_8, each of which has probability 1/8, constitute U. The winning event A consists of e_1 and e_8 (bounded by the heavy line) while the event K = at least two heads in three tosses is composed of e_1, e_2, e_3, and e_5 (bounded by the broken line). Once you know that K has occurred, the relevant elementary events are those which are contained in K, and the only way you could win is if $e_1 = A \cap K$ occurs. The probability of this event is the proportion of $P(K)$ taken up by $P(A \cap K)$; expressed otherwise, $P(A \mid K)$ = $P(A \cap K)/P(K)$.

We can use this general formula for computing conditional probabilities whether or not the elementary events are equiprobable. The formula may also be expressed as

$$P(A \cap K) = P(A \mid K)P(K) \qquad (2)$$

by cross-multiplying $P(K)$, assuming (all along!) that $P(K) > 0$. The derived formula reads: "The probability that both events, A and K, occur is the probability that A occurs *given* K times the probability that K occurs." Let us see how this helps in a practical example.

Problem: Eddie's Toy Company ──────────────────

You are the manager of the parts department for Eddie's Toy Company. There are three possible defects that can occur in the production of plastic wheels: insufficient strength to support the toy, a wheel diameter outside the tolerance limits, or broken spokes. In a lot of 1000 wheels, you feel safe in inferring from the engineering design and experience that:

> 120 are of insufficient strength,
> 80 have unacceptable diameters,
> 60 have broken spokes,
> 22 are of insufficient strength and unacceptable diameter,
> 16 have unacceptable diameter and broken spokes,
> 20 are of insufficient strength and have broken spokes,
> 8 have all three defects.

You have chosen a wheel at random from the 1000 pieces. What is the probability that it has insufficient strength if you know that:
a. It has broken spokes?
b. It has broken spokes *and* a diameter defect?
c. It has neither?

Analysis: To begin the analysis, it is often useful to list all of the probabilities of the various events that are given as information in the problem. Let us designate the events as follows:

$$B = \text{broken spokes} \qquad X = B \cap I$$
$$D = \text{diameter defect} \qquad Y = D \cap I$$
$$I \ = \text{insufficient strength} \qquad Z = B \cap D \cap I$$
$$W = B \cap D$$

You are given that:

$$P(B) \ = \frac{60}{1000} = .06 \qquad P(X) = P(B \cap I) = \frac{20}{1000} = .02$$

$$P(D) \ = \frac{80}{1000} = .08 \qquad P(Y) = P(D \cap I) = \frac{22}{1000} = .022$$

$$P(I) \ \ = \frac{120}{1000} = .12 \qquad P(Z) = P(B \cap D \cap I) = \frac{8}{1000} = .008$$

$$P(W) = P(B \cap D) = \frac{16}{1000} = .016$$

Part (a) asks for $P(I \mid B)$. Using formula (1) for conditional probability:

$$P(I \mid B) = \frac{P(I \cap B)}{P(B)} = \frac{P(X)}{P(B)} = \frac{.02}{.06} = \frac{1}{3}$$

Part (b) asks for:

$$P(I \mid B \cap D) = \frac{P(I \cap (B \cap D))}{P(B \cap D)} = \frac{P(Z)}{P(W)} = \frac{.008}{.016} = \frac{1}{2}$$

Part (c) asks for $P(I \mid$ neither B nor $D)$, for which you need to know $P(I \cap$ neither B nor $D)$ and $P($neither B nor $D)$.

To get the probability of the event "neither B nor D," which we will call A, recall from theorem 5.1 that $P(\sim (B \cup D)) = 1 - P(B \cup D)$. Also it can be proved that

$$P(B \cup D) = P(B) + P(D) - P(B \cap D) = .06 + .08 - .016 = .124$$

So, $P(\sim(B \cup D)) = 1 - .124 = .876$.

This calculation can also be seen in figure 8.5.

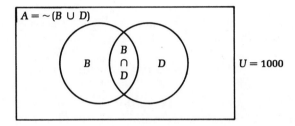

Figure 8.5   Venn Diagram for the Event A

The universal set is 1000 wheels, of which 80 are in D, 60 are in B, and 16 are in $B \cap D$. Therefore $(B \cup D)$ contains $60 + 80 - 16 = 124$ wheels and $\sim (B \cup D)$ contains $1000 - 124 = 876$ wheels. Thus, $P(A) = 876/1000 = .876$ as before.

To compute $P(I \mid A) = P(I \cap A)/P(A)$ you still need $P(I \cap A)$, which you can also get using the Venn diagram in figure 8.6. As can be seen

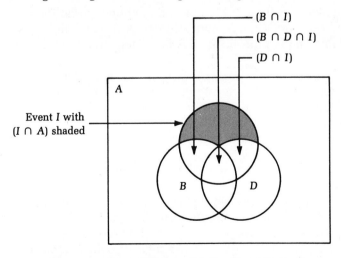

Figure 8.6   Venn Diagram for the Event $(I \cap A)$

in the figure, $(I \cap A)$ = number of wheels in I − number of wheels in $(B \cap I)$ − number of wheels in $(D \cap I)$ + number of wheels in $(B \cap D \cap I)$ since $(B \cap D \cap I)$ was subtracted twice. Therefore $(I \cap A)$ has $120 - 20 - 22 + 8 = 86$ wheels, and $P(I \cap A) = 86/1000 = .086$. You can now compute $P(I \cap A) = P(I \cap A)/P(A) = .086/.876 \approx .1$.

8.3.1 Independence of Events We have stated in probability assumption 4 of chapter 5 that if two events are independent, the probability that both events occur is the product of their respective probabilities. This is written as

$$P(A \cap B) = P(A)P(B) \qquad (3)$$

You can now see that independence is a special case of conditional probability. From the previous section you know that

$$P(A \cap B) = P(A \mid B)P(B) \qquad (2')$$

Equality $(2')$ is identical to (3) except for one term − in $(2')$ $P(A)$ is replaced by $P(A \mid B)$. Therefore, we could have introduced independence of events by *defining* it as a special case of conditional probability, replacing assumption 4 of chapter 5 by:

DEFINITION: If for any two events A and B

$$P(A \mid B) = P(A) \qquad (4)$$

then the two events are said to be *independent*.

If you look carefully at (4), you see that knowing that the event B has occurred does *not* change your estimate of the probability that A will occur − that is, the probability of A is "independent" of the occurrence of B.

In informational language, if A is the event of interest, then a knowledge of B is irrelevant to the decision maker; if you are wondering whether to invest in a certain stock, and I tell you that in my expert opinion the moon will be full tonight, my knowledge is worthless relative to your problem − that is, P(successful investment | full moon) = P(successful investment).

Intuitively, you can see what independence means in terms of Venn diagrams in figure 8.7.

The event A has probability $1/2$, represented as the left half of the universal set U. The event B, the lower half of the universal set also has probability $1/2$. The event $(A \cap B)$ is shown in the shaded area. You can see that $(A \cap B)$ is $1/2$ of the total area in B − that is, $P(A \mid B)$

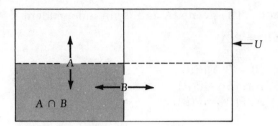

Figure 8.7 Independent Events

$= P(A \cap B)/P(B) = 1/2 = P(A)$. Thus, the two events are independent by (4). In terms of the diagrams, two events, A and B, are independent if the proportion of B taken up by A is equal to the proportion of U taken up by A.

You probably noticed that we have said "the two events A and B are independent" as opposed to "the event A is independent of B." This is because of the fact that if A is independent of B, B is also independent of A. This can be shown as follows.

From (4) and (2), if A and B are independent

$$P(A \mid B) = P(A)$$

and

$$P(A \cap B) = P(A)P(B)$$

and since $P(B \cap A) = P(A \cap B)$ and $P(A)P(B) = P(B)P(A)$ it follows from (2') that

$$P(B \cap A) = P(B)P(A) \tag{2''}$$

Consequently,

$$P(B \mid A) = \frac{P(B \cap A)}{P(A)}$$

and from (2'')

$$= \frac{P(B)P(A)}{P(A)} = P(B) \tag{4'}$$

That is, A is independent of B whenever B is independent of A. So we could have defined independence in any one of the following ways:

DEFINITION   The events A and B are independent if

a. $P(A \mid B) = P(A)$
b. $P(B \mid A) = P(B)$
c. $P(A \cap B) = P(A)P(B)$
d. $P(A \cap B)/P(B) = P(A)$
e. $P(B \cap A)/P(A) = P(B)$

Your knowledge about the union and intersection of events can now be summarized in table 8.3.

TABLE 8.3   Summary of Operations on Events

	$P(A \cup B)$	$P(A \cap B)$
General Case	$= P(A) + P(B) - P(A \cap B)$	$= P(B)P(A \mid B) = P(A)P(B \mid A)$
Special Case	$= P(A) + P(B)$ if A and B are exclusive events i.e., if $P(A \cap B) = 0$, or equivalently $(A \cap B) = \phi$	$= P(A)P(B)$ if A and B are independent i.e., if $P(A \mid B) = A$, or equivalently $P(B \mid A) = B$

PROBLEMS 8.3

1. In the Eddie's Toy Company problem, what is the probability that a wheel has broken spokes if you know that
    a. it has a diameter defect?
    b. it has no other defect?
    c. it has a diameter defect and insufficient strength?
    d. it has insufficient strength?

2. Are any two events really independent? Reflect on your assumptions.

3. Nick Numbers is back in town, and this time he proposes bets based on the outcomes of throwing one die and two coins. In all these bets heads is equivalent to 1 and tails to 0. Which of the following bets are profitable for you?
    a. He offers to pay you $10 if the sum of the number of dots plus the number of heads that show up is 7 while you pay $5 if any other number is the outcome.
    b. Seven is again the magic number, but the die and the coins are thrown sequentially, in that order; after the die is cast if 5 appears you can bet a dollar in return for $5 if you win; if 6 shows up you can gain $10 for a bet of $3.

4. Balls and boxes are Nick's new discovery. He has three boxes which contain red and black balls as follows:

> Box 1 contains 3 red and 7 blacks.
>
> Box 2 contains 6 red and 4 blacks.
>
> Box 3 contains 8 red and 2 blacks.

Nick offers to design bets which are based on first drawing a ball from box 1; if it is red, a ball from box 2 will be drawn; if not, a ball from box 3 will be drawn. Since this is a new structure he wishes to know some of the probabilities so he can pursue the design. He comes to you to help him out. What would you tell him is
a. the probability of drawing a red ball from box 1?
b. the probability of a second red ball given that a red ball is drawn from box 1?
c. the probability of a red ball provided the draw from box 1 is a black ball?
d. the probability of two red balls at the outset?

5. You compile the following data for your firm: among any 100 people who enter the store 10 are men over 40 years of age; 10 are men under 40; 50 are women over 40; and 30 are women under 40. A man over 40 enters the store and makes a purchase in one out of 100 cases; two men under 40 out of 100 enter the store and are actual buyers; the chances that a woman under 40 enters and makes a purchase is 9%, and a woman over 40 is 12.5% likely to enter and make a purchase.
a. What is the probability that a man under 40 who has entered the store will make a purchase?
b. What is the probability of a purchase being made by a woman over 40 who has entered the store?
c. What is the probability that a man over 40 who has entered the store will make a purchase?
d. What is the probability of a woman under 40 making a purchase if she has entered the store?
e. What is the probability that any customer who has entered the store will make a purchase?

6. You are requested to prepare the expenditures budget for the auto insurance department of the insurance company in which you serve as an analyst. The department has sold 100,000 policies, of which 10,000 have been sold to drivers who are expected to have at least one accident. You know that 1.1% of all policy owners are expected to be involved in two successive accidents this year. An average claim after a first accident is estimated to be $300, and after a second accident $500. What should be your *expected* budget?

7. On a vacation trip to Las Vegas you have chosen two slot machines on which you concentrate your attention. Your strategy is to flip a quarter before each play and to insert the quarter in machine I if heads show up or in machine II if tails is the outcome. You know that the probability of hitting the jackpot is .05 on machine I and .1 on machine II.
   a. What is the probability that you hit a jackpot on any one play?
   b. If the jackpots are equal, what do you think of this strategy? Why?

8.4 Bayes' Theorem

You have just seen how the ideas of conditional probability enable you to reverse some decision-making questions. We began by asking the probability that event A will occur, given B, $P(A \mid B)$ — for example, the probability of three heads in a toss of three coins, given that at least one coin is a head. But you can reverse the question and ask the probability that at least one head must occur, given that three heads did occur, $P(B \mid A)$.

The reverse question may seem rather odd, but consider the following very practical example. You go to a doctor because you have a temperature of 102°. Suppose that this evidence and other matters lead the doctor to believe that you have either flu A or flu B. He will give you a different shot, depending on which it is, but he is disinclined to give you both shots. Flu A frequently produces temperatures of 102° or higher, while flu B rarely does. Also, flu A is "all around," while flu B is not. Assuming that all the information is in, what should the doctor do? Common sense says that the cause of your trouble is "more likely" to be flu A than flu B; that is, in the language of the last sections, $P(\text{flu A} \mid 102°) > P(\text{flu B} \mid 102°)$. But notice what we have done: We have started with $P(102° \mid \text{flu A})$, the probability of 102° temperature given flu A, and then reversed the question to ask for the probability of flu A given 102° temperature, $P(\text{flu A} \mid 102°)$. Also notice that the doctor needs two things to make his diagnosis: the probability that each flu occurs and the probability of 102° temperature given flu A or B. That is, he needs $P(\text{flu A})$, $P(\text{flu B})$, $P(102° \mid \text{flu A})$ and $P(102° \mid \text{flu B})$.

One of the most important jobs of any manager, be he doctor, policeman, corporate head, whatever, is to make estimates of the causes of events, so that he can remove the causes if he doesn't like the consequences or create the causes if he likes the consequences. The example just given *seems* therefore to be one helpful answer to any manager's prayer. A policeman doesn't know whether Basil Baseheart or Sampson Strongbody did the crime, but he may have some good ideas of the probability that Basil or Sampson would commit a crime of this sort and the likelihood that Basil or Sampson could have had the opportunity. A decision maker may not understand why one of his subsidiaries is in trouble, but he may suspect it is either because the top manager is incompetent, or because he didn't supply the subsidiary with sufficient capital. He will also have to judge the likelihood of either of these prior events. If he is willing to make these *prior probability* judgments, he may then be able to estimate the *posterior* probabilities, P(subsidiary failure | poor management) or P(subsidiary failure | poor capital funding). In these examples, as before, he needs *both* P(cause) *and* P(event | cause) to find P(cause | event).

Now very often there are a whole lot of candidate causes for the events we observe. Furthermore, some candidates may seem promising because when they occur they are likely to cause the event to happen, but the candidate cause may not itself occur often. For example, a temperature of 102° is likely to be caused by flu A, but there isn't much flu A around right now. In these cases, it is far less obvious which is the culprit (or helper), and we have to begin to develop a quantitative technique to take care of the matter. The credit for the technique goes to Thomas Bayes (1702–1760) and is called Bayes' Theorem after him. Although the theorem is often useful, you should be aware all along that its usefulness is restricted to the manager's capability of assessing the prior probabilities (for example, the doctor's ability to judge the probability of flu A and the probability of 102° given flu A). From a systems point of view, there are also some other criticisms; for example, the relevant "cause" may be neither bad management nor poor funding, but some deeper reason that caused either one of these to happen. However, in this case, you still may find the revised posterior probabilities of the event useful, given the information about the occurrence of something you are not sure is actually causing the event. There has also been a philosophical controversy about the "meaning" of probability when we talk of the "probability that flu A occurs," since the prior cause either happened or it didn't, and its probability is therefore 1 or 0. But this is more a question of the reliability of empirical information, and in this deductive text "probability" can mean anything, including a subjective judgment, as long as the axioms of probability hold.

To present Bayes' Theorem in a general form, before examining some problems to clarify its meaning, suppose there are a whole set of "candidate prior causes," $C_1, C_2, \ldots, C_n$ for some event (effect) E that has occurred, and you are seeking the values of $P(C_1 \mid E)$, $P(C_2 \mid E)$, etc. You know the conditional probabilities $P(E \mid C_1)$, $P(E \mid C_2)$, $\ldots$, $P(E \mid C_n)$, which are the probabilities that E occurs, given C_i has occurred. You also know the probabilities of the causes C_i, $i = 1, \ldots, n$, which are assumed to be *mutually exclusive* and *collectively exhaustive*. This situation is depicted in figure 8.8 for $n = 14$.

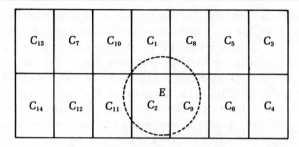

Figure 8.8   Venn Diagram for a Set of 14 Mutually Exclusive and Collectively Exhaustive Events (causes), and Event (effect) E.

$$\text{Bayes' Theorem: } P(C_i \mid E) = \frac{P(E \mid C_i)P(C_i)}{\sum\limits_{\text{all } j} P(E \mid C_j)P(C_j)} \tag{5}$$

$$\text{which is equivalent to: } P(C_i \mid E) = \frac{P(E \mid C_i)P(C_i)}{P(E)} \tag{6}$$

These $P(C_i)$'s are often called *a priori*, or prior probabilities, obviously referring to the idea that the C_i's come before and "cause" the event E. The probability of interest, $P(C_i \mid E)$, is often called the *a posteriori* or *posterior* probability of the event C_i, since it is the probability of the event (cause), C_i, which occurred *after* the information that E has occurred is known.

Before showing the proof of the theorem, which consists of algebraic manipulations of the definition of conditional probability, let's examine a gambling problem which will help to clarify the relationship among the components of the theorem.

Problem: The Sophisticated Nick Numbers ━━━━━━━━━

Your old friend Nick Numbers has shown up again. This time he is equipped with quite a sophisticated bet. The game involves a fair die and two urns. The first urn contains two red balls and three green, while the second contains five red balls and one green ball. Nick tells you that the die will be tossed and if 1, 2, 3, or 4 appears, the first urn will be selected, while if a 5 or 6 shows the second is chosen. Then a ball is drawn at random from the urn chosen. You are allowed to see the ball and then decide whether to bet. He will conduct the selection and drawing in the presence of your friend, who will tell you the color of the ball drawn. If the ball comes from the first urn you get $10; otherwise you pay $5. Should you accept the bet if the drawn ball is red?

Analysis: Assuming that you have no preference between a sure dollar and expected dollar, you would like to calculate the expected value of the bet for determining whether or not to accept it. For this you need the probability that the ball was drawn from the first urn given that a red ball was drawn, and/or the probability that the ball was drawn from the second urn given that a red ball was drawn (the two must sum to 1, of course). In other words, what are the probabilities that the "effect" that the ball is red was "caused" by its coming from the first urn or the second?

From the information Nick has provided, you know that the prior probability of the event C_1 = "the ball was drawn from the first urn" is 2/3, since the selection of this urn is associated with obtaining 1, 2, 3, or 4 in one toss of the fair die; that is, $P(C_1) = 2/3$. By the same token the prior probability of choosing urn two (C_2) is $P(C_2)$ = P(5 or 6 occur) = 1/6 + 1/6 = 1/3.

But you have some additional information besides the two priors. You know that each urn contains balls of two colors, red and green. You also know the composition of the two types of balls in each urn, and since the drawing of a ball from an urn is made at random, you can assume that the likelihood of any ball being drawn from the urn is equiprobable. Thus, if the drawing is from urn one, the probability of a red ball (denoted by R) is 2/5 since there are two reds out of five balls, and the probability of a green ball (denoted by G) is 3/5. If, on the other hand, the ball is selected from urn two, the probability of red is 5/6, while the probability of a green ball is 1/6. These possibilities with their appropriate probabilities are depicted in figure 8.9.

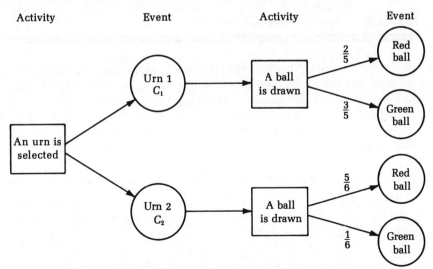

Figure 8.9 Nick Number's Sophisticated Gamble

In our conditional probability notation we write these last four probabilities as follows: $P(R \mid C_1) = 2/5$, $P(G \mid C_1) = 3/5$, $P(R \mid C_2) = 5/6$, and $P(G \mid C_2) = 1/6$.

Now, you know that a red ball has been drawn, and having this piece of information you would like to calculate the probability that the ball comes from urn one, $P(C_1 \mid R)$, and the probability that it comes from urn two, $P(C_2 \mid R)$. These two probabilities are the *posterior* probabilities of the events "urn one was selected" and "urn two was selected," respectively, since they use the information that the red ball was drawn. In other words, before knowing anything about the selected ball you had the prior probabilities $P(C_1) = 2/3$ and $P(C_2) = 1/3$, but now you can use the fact that a red ball was drawn to revise these probabilities. This revision can be done by using Bayes' Theorem:

$$P(C_1 \mid R) = \frac{P(R \mid C_1)P(C_1)}{P(R \mid C_1)P(C_1) + P(R \mid C_2)P(C_2)}$$

$$= \frac{2/5 \times 2/3}{2/5 \times 2/3 + 5/6 \times 1/3} = \frac{24}{49}$$

$$P(C_2 \mid R) = \frac{P(R \mid C_2)P(C_2)}{P(R \mid C_1)P(C_1) + P(R \mid C_2)P(C_2)}$$

$$= \frac{5/6 \times 1/3}{2/5 \times 2/3 + 5/6 \times 1/3} = \frac{25}{49}$$

Therefore, the expected value of Nick's new bet is

$$\frac{24}{49} \times \$10 + \frac{25}{49}(-\$5) = \$2.34,$$

which makes you accept his offer.

You will note in this example that the "prior cause" is the urn that was used for the draw. There is nothing odd about the example, but there is the question whether identifying the cause of a high fever is like identifying the urn in this example. But whether you think of the identification of the urn as a "cause" or just "new information," it still allows you to revise your probabilities and thus use Bayes' Theorem.

Problem: Harry's Beer Vending Company. ━━━━━━

Harry Harrison, a good friend of yours, sells beer and umbrellas at the 49'er football games on Sundays. He has three possible options available to him:

d_1 Sell only umbrellas

d_2 Sell umbrellas and beer

d_3 Sell only beer

If he chooses d_1 and it rains, he makes $200, but if it shines, he makes only $10. If he chooses d_2 or d_3, his profits are also affected by the weather, as given in table 8.4.

TABLE 8.4   Harry's Payoff Table

DECISION	STATE OF THE WORLD	
	R = rain	S = shine
d_1	$200	$10
d_2	$100	$100
d_3	$20	$250

Harry knows from long experience that there is a 40% chance of rain (a priori) on a given football Sunday in San Francisco; that is, $P(R) = 40\%$, $P(S) = 60\%$. He comes to you on Sunday morning with the problem of what he should sell if he wants to maximize his expected profits. You have a barometer, which you suggest might help, and you know the conditional probability of barometer readings given the actual state of the world that occurs, summarized in table 8.5.

TABLE 8.5   Conditional Probabilities of Barometer Readings; for example, $P(x_1 \mid R) = .9$

READING	STATE OF THE WORLD	
	R = rain	S = shine
x_1 = rain	.9	.2
x_2 = shine	.1	.8

What should you recommend to Harry if:

1. Your barometer is broken?
2. It reads "Rain" (x_1)?
3. It reads "Shine" (x_2)?

Analysis: 1. If the barometer is broken, you can use the unconditional probabilities ("prior" probabilities) multiplied by the profits to get the expected profit W.

If d_1 is chosen, $E(W) = .4 \times \$200 + .6 \times \$10 = \$86$

If d_2 is the decision, $E(W) = .4 \times \$100 + .6 \times \$100 = \$100$

If d_3 is the decision, $E(W) = .4 \times \$20 + .6 \times \$250 = \$158$

So you tell Harry to sell only beer.

2. If the barometer predicts "Rain," (x_1), you want $P(R \mid x_1)$ and $P(S \mid x_1)$, and since you know $P(R)$, $P(S)$, $P(x_1 \mid R)$, and $P(x_1 \mid S)$, you can use Bayes' Theorem.

$$P(R \mid x_1) = \frac{P(x_1 \mid R)P(R)}{P(x_1 \mid R)P(R) + P(x_1 \mid S)P(S)} = \frac{.9 \times .4}{.9 \times .4 + .2 \times .6}$$

$$= \frac{.36}{.36 + .12} = \frac{3}{4}$$

From probability assumption 2 (or 4) of chapter 5, $P(S \mid x_1) = 1 - P(R \mid x_1) = 1/4$. You could also have calculated this directly:

$$P(S \mid x_1) = \frac{.2 \times .6}{.36 + .12} = \frac{.12}{.48} = \frac{1}{4}$$

Harry's expected profits for the three decisions, then, are

$$d_1 \colon E(W) = \frac{3}{4} \times \$200 + \frac{1}{4} \times \$10 = \$152.50$$

$$d_2 \colon E(W) = \frac{3}{4} \times \$100 + \frac{1}{4} \times \$100 = \$100.00$$

$$d_3 \colon E(W) = \frac{3}{4} \times \$20 + \frac{1}{4} \times \$250 = \$77.50$$

So you tell Harry to sell umbrellas only.

3. If your barometer reads "Shine," (x_2):

$$P(R \mid x_2) = \frac{P(x_2 \mid R)P(R)}{P(x_2 \mid R)P(R) + P(x_2 \mid S)P(S)} = \frac{.1 \times .4}{.1 \times .4 + .8 \times .6}$$

$$= \frac{.04}{.52} = \frac{1}{13}$$

therefore $P(S \mid x_2) = 1 - 1/13 = 12/13$ by theorem 5.1, and after recalculating the three expected values, you will find that the best decision is again (d_3), sell beer only.

The example of selling beer and umbrellas should show you the practical difficulties of applying Bayes' Theorem once you go beyond coins, urns, and dice. But the point is that you may be able to combine some experience with some judgment and guesswork to come up with the required estimates. Techniques for generating these estimates belong under the general area of inductive quantitative methods, and are sometimes called Bayesian statistics. The systems approach goes far beyond any simple statement of cause-effect relations of the type represented by Bayes' Theorem.

∗8.4.1 Proof of Bayes' Theorem The theorem states that when you know that the event (effect) E has occurred, the posterior probability (of the cause) $P(C_i \mid E)$ can be obtained by either (5) or (6), where the C_i's in (5) are both mutually exclusive and collectively exhaustive events. We will first show that (6) holds, and then use that fact to show that (5), the theorem, is also true.

You know from the definition of conditional probability that

$$P(C_i \mid E) = \frac{P(C_i \cap E)}{P(E)}$$

For (6) to hold we need to show that $P(C_i \cap E) = P(E \mid C_i)P(C_i)$. But this also follows directly from the definition of conditional probability:

$$P(E \mid C_i) = \frac{P(E \cap C_i)}{P(C_i)} = \frac{P(C_i \cap E)}{P(C_i)}$$

where we use the fact that $P(C_i \cap E) = P(E \cap C_i)$.

After cross-multiplying, we get

$$P(E \mid C_i)P(C_i) = P(C_i \cap E)$$

as desired. So equation (6) holds.

For equation (5) to hold, we must show that $P(E) = \sum_{\text{all } j} P(E \mid C_j)P(C_j)$. From our definition of conditional probability, again,

$$P(E \mid C_j) = \frac{P(E \cap C_j)}{P(C_j)}$$

So,

$$P(E \mid C_j)P(C_j) = P(E \cap C_j)$$

and to sum the left-hand side over all j is the same as to sum the right-hand side over all j; that is,

$$\sum_{\text{all } j} P(E \mid C_j)P(C_j) = \sum_{\text{all } j} P(E \cap C_j)$$

So, equation (5) holds, if

$$P(E) = \sum_{\text{all } j} (E \cap C_j)$$

Since the C_j's are mutually exclusive, the right-hand side sum counts each part of E only once, and since the C_j's are collectively exhaustive, each part of E gets counted. Thus, $P(E) = \sum_{\text{all } j} P(E \cap C_j)$ and equation (5) holds.

PROBLEMS 8.4

1. In the Sophisticated Nick Numbers problem, should you accept the bet if the ball is green?

2. In Harry's Beer problem, suppose his priors were .3 for rain and .7 for shine. What should you tell him in the three cases now?

3. As the controller of your firm you've received the last month's report, which indicated a large unfavorable deviation of the actual performance from the standard. You know from experience that such a deviation is not always caused by the production process being out of control. More specifically, you assess the probability of a large deviation when, in fact, the process is out of control to be .7, and .3 to be the probability of a small deviation, under the same conditions. You also estimate that the chances of a large deviation when the process is in control is 20%. Before receiving the report your priors were .1 that the process is out of control and .9 in control. You have adopted a rule of thumb that every time you receive new deviation information you use it to revise your prior probabilities, and if you then assess that there are more than 15% chances for the production process to be out of control, the process should be halted and investigated to determine the cause of the deviation. What should be your decision this time?

4. Your friend, a public health official, is concerned about the possible outbreak of a flu epidemic. He must decide on the issuance of instructions on mass vaccination, which he will do in case his estimate that an epidemic is inevitable exceeds 20%. His current assessment is that there is .1 probability that the flu will reach epidemic proportion. But recent reports about the prevalence of certain symptoms among an increasing proportion of the city's population have indicated perhaps he should revise this probability. He asks you to assist him in this task, and tells you that his staff estimates that
    a. The probability of flu symptoms when an epidemic actually prevails is .85, and there is .15 probability that flu epidemic symptoms are not observed while such epidemics prevail.
    b. The probability of the epidemic symptoms when, in fact, there is no such epidemic is 10%, and in 90% of the times epidemic symptoms don't prevail if there is no epidemic.
       Does the new report of flu epidemic symptoms warrant the instructions for mass vaccination?

5. Your firm buys a certain part from two suppliers, Mr. Complainer and Mr. Quiet. Recently Mr. Complainer has come to you complaining that your quality control department has been slandering

his product. You promise to look into the problem, and you begin by collecting some information. You learn that of all incoming lots of this part, 3/10 are received from Mr. Complainer and 7/10 from Mr. Quiet. Past experience has shown that the quality control department rejects 5% of all Mr. Complainer's lots, while the rejection rate for lots received from Mr. Quiet is only half of that. You are also informed that Mr. Complainer is upset since in his recent visit with the quality control people they classified a lot that was rejected as coming from him without checking this fact. What is the probability that the rejected lot was indeed supplied by Mr. Complainer?

6. Nick Numbers has new urns and balls. Urn A contains 700 red balls and 300 green balls, urn B contains 700 green and 300 red balls, and urn C contains 500 green and 500 red balls. Nick offers you the following bet: He will flip a fair die and select urn A if 1 or 2 shows, B if 3 or 4 shows, and C if 5 or 6 shows. Then he will choose, at random, a ball from the selected urn, record its color, replace it, and thoroughly mix the balls again. This sequence of actions will be repeated three times. You will receive $5 if you guess correctly the sequence of the selected urns, while you pay $1 for an incorrect guess. You ask him to conduct the game, and he tells you that the ball selected each time is red. What is your expected reward if you bet that the urn chosen is urn A in all three times?

7. Suppose now that you play the same game as in problem 6 except that the selection of an urn is done only once. That is, after an urn is selected according to the face of the die that shows, Nick chooses, three times, at random, a ball from the urn, records its color, and returns the ball to the urn. He tells you that he has recorded the selection of three red balls. What is your expected reward if you bet that the urn selected is A?

8. Explain the difference in your answers to problems 6 and 7.

9. If C_i is a cause, and E a resulting event, "the probability of the cause given the result is the proportion of the time that the result is caused by the event." Is this what problems 5 and 6 say?

8.5 Two Random Variables

8.5.1 Joint Probability Distributions When you make a simple choice like how to dress for work in the morning, your decision may depend upon the value of more than one random variable. For example, although the random variables "temperature" and "precipitation" can be classified under the heading "weather," you might want to separate the two to make your decision. If it is raining and the temperature is below fifty degrees, you may want to put on a warm jacket and a raincoat. If the temperature is going to be warmer, you may skip the warm jacket, or if the rain stops, you might skip the raincoat. Sometimes the uncertainty involved in such situations can be described by a probability distribution which is joint to the two (or more) random variables of interest.

For each possible combination of value (x and y) of two random variables (X and Y) there is a probability that the combination will occur. Symbolically, this probability is written $P(X = x, Y = y)$ or $P(x,y)$. In the above example, suppose that you are interested in four values of the random variable,

$X =$ temperature: 1. temperature in the 40's or lower

2. temperature in the 50's

3. in the 60's

4. in the 70's or higher

Also, suppose that you classify precipitation into only two categories, "rain" and "no rain," corresponding to a random variable,

$Y =$ precipitation,

taking on the values 0 and 1, respectively. Then you can describe the *joint distribution of the random variables X and Y* as in table 8.6. For

TABLE 8.6   Joint Probability of X and Y

Y \ X	1	2	3	4	$P(Y = y)$
0	.15	.15	.10	.01	$\sum_{\text{all } x} = .41$
1	.05	.10	.25	.19	$\sum_{\text{all } x} = .59$
$P(X = x)$	$\sum_{\text{all } y} = .20$	$\sum_{\text{all } y} = .25$	$\sum_{\text{all } y} = .35$	$\sum_{\text{all } y} = .20$	$\sum = 1$

example, the probability of rain, $Y = 0$, and temperature in the 50's, $X = 2$, denoted by $P(X = 2, Y = 0), = .15$, and P(temperature in the 70's and no rain) $= P(X = 4, Y = 1) = .19$.

This joint probability distribution of the two random variables can be represented geometrically by figure 8.10, where the size of the dot corresponds to the size of the probability.

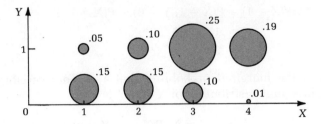

Figure 8.10   Geometric Representation of a Joint Distribution

8.5.2   Marginal Distributions Sometimes you may have at your disposal the joint probability distribution of two random variables and may be interested in the distribution of one of the two random variables separately. In the above example, for instance, having the joint distribution of temperature and precipitation, you may want to know the probability distribution of precipitation; that is, the probabilities of "rain" $(Y = 0)$, or of "no rain" $(Y = 1)$.

To get the probability of rain, $P(Y = 0)$, you simply use common sense and table 8.6. The event "rain" consists of all the following mutually exclusive events:

$$\text{Rain and } 40° = (X = 1, Y = 0)$$
$$\text{Rain and } 50° = (X = 2, Y = 0)$$
$$\text{Rain and } 60° = (X = 3, Y = 0)$$
$$\text{Rain and } 70° = (X = 4, Y = 0)$$

Since the values are exclusive, you simply add (probability assumption 3, chapter 5) the probabilities of the four events to get the probability of rain:

$$P(Y = 0) = P(X = 1, Y = 0) + P(X = 2, Y = 0) + P(X = 3, Y = 0)$$
$$+ P(X = 4, Y = 0)$$
$$= .15 + .15 + .10 + .01$$
$$= .41$$

We can place this sum in the *margin* of row 1 of table 8.6, since the probabilities of the four events come from row 1. For this reason, it is commonly called the *marginal probability of rain*. Similarly, $P(Y = 1)$ $= .59$. Notice that $.59 + .41 = 1$ as required by assumption 2 for the distribution of Y.

If you want to get the distribution of X alone, called the *marginal distribution of X*, add up the probabilities for a particular value of X over all possible values of Y. The probability of temperatures in the 40's, for example, *regardless* of whether it rains or not, is

$$P(X = 1) = P(X = 1, Y = 0) + P(X = 1, Y = 1)$$
$$= .15 + .05$$
$$= .20$$

In general, the *marginal probability* that a random variable, $X = x$, taken from a joint distribution of X and Y is

$$P(X = x) = \sum_{\text{all } y} P(X = x, Y = y)$$

(Recall that $\sum_{\text{all } y} P(X = x, Y = y)$ means you take the sum over all the possible values y of $P(X = x, Y = y)$.)

Similarly, the marginal probability that a random variable $Y = y$ is

$$P(Y = y) = \sum_{\text{all } x} P(X = x, Y = y)$$

Some simple applications of the marginal probability distributions can be seen in the following problems.

Problem: Heads and Changes ───────────────

Suppose that the persistent Nick Numbers offers you the following bet: He will pay you three dollars if, on three flips of a fair coin, exactly two heads occur *and* the number of changes is exactly one in the sequence of heads and tails (for example, HTH has two changes, HHH has none, THH has one). If it costs a dollar to play, should you?

Analysis: Call the random variable X = number of heads and Y = number of changes in the sequence. You can use table 8.7 to carry out the analysis.

In the table the event corresponding to $X = 2$ is bounded by the heavy line, while the event "one change" ($Y = 1$) is shown within the broken-line boundaries. What you are looking for is the probability that the random variable X is equal to two and Y is one, $P(X = 2, Y = 1)$. That is, the event of interest is the *intersection* of the two events $X = 2$ and $Y = 1$. This event contains two elementary events e_2 and e_5.

You can read from the table that

$$P(X = 2, Y = 1) = P(e_2 \cup e_5) = \frac{1}{8} + \frac{1}{8}$$

since elementary events are mutually exclusive. Since the probability is 2/8 that you will win,

TABLE 8.7 The Values of the Random Variables X and Y

Elementary event		Probability	x-value	y-value
e_1	HHH	$\frac{1}{8}$	3	0
e_2	HHT	$\frac{1}{8}$	2	1
e_3	HTH	$\frac{1}{8}$	2	2
e_4	HTT	$\frac{1}{8}$	1	1
e_5	THH	$\frac{1}{8}$	2	1
e_6	THT	$\frac{1}{8}$	1	2
e_7	TTH	$\frac{1}{8}$	1	1
e_8	TTT	$\frac{1}{8}$	0	0

$X = 2$

$Y = 1$

$$1 - \frac{2}{8} = \frac{6}{8}$$

is the probability that you will lose (by probability assumption 3 of chapter 5), and your expected earnings are

$$\$3 \times \frac{2}{8} + \$0 \times \frac{6}{8} = \$.75$$

Since you pay a dollar to play, you tell Nick to get lost if you are an expected dollar maximizer.

You may notice from this example that you have already studied "joint probability distributions" in an earlier context, when you were considering games that involved both coins and dice. Hence, you could have solved the problem given above without the explicit concept of joint distributions. But the joint probability distribution is a more general concept in which more complicated problems can be solved.

The probability of interest in this example, $P(X = 2, Y = 1)$, is a particular value of the joint probability of X and Y, and we can represent the entire joint probability distribution by table 8.8.

TABLE 8.8   The Joint and Marginal Probability Distributions
of X and Y in the Heads and Changes Problem

X \ Y	0	1	2	$P(X = x)$
0	1/8	0	0	1/8
1	0	2/8	1/8	3/8
2	0	2/8	1/8	3/8
3	1/8	0	0	1/8
$P(Y = y)$	2/8	4/8	2/8	1

As you would expect, when you sum over all the possible values of
X and Y, you get 1. This conforms to assumption 2 of our deductive
probability system in chapter 5. A geometric way of representing the
joint distribution of the two random variables is in figure 8.11, where,
as before, the size of the dot corresponds to the weight of the probability.

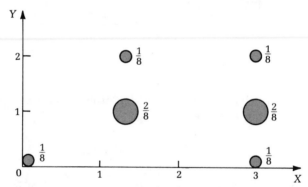

Figure 8.11   Geometric Representation of $P(X = x, Y = y)$

Problem: Changes Only ─────────────────────────────

Nick Numbers now offers you a bet that pays $1 if there is only one
change ($Y = 1$) in three tosses of a fair coin, $5 if there are no changes
($Y = 0$), and you pay $10 if there are two changes ($Y = 2$). Should you
accept the bet?

Analysis: For the purpose of analyzing this bet you are not interested
in the random variable X (the number of heads). What you are looking
for is the probability distribution of

$$Y = \text{number of changes}$$

since this is the relevant random variable for making the current decision. Of course, you can start from scratch, list all the possible elementary events associated with the different values that Y can take on, and obtain the distribution of Y. However, having the joint probability distribution of X and Y you can easily derive from it the individual distribution of Y by adding up each *column* of table 8.8 and obtaining the marginal probability distribution of Y. Thus, the probability of the number of changes being zero $(Y = 0)$ regardless of the number of heads in three flips of a fair coin is

$$P(Y = 0) = \sum_{\text{all } x} P(X = x, Y = 0) = P(X = 0, Y = 0) + P(X = 1, Y = 0)$$

$$+ P(X = 2, Y = 0) + P(X = 3, Y = 0)$$

$$= \frac{1}{8} + 0 + 0 + \frac{1}{8} = \frac{2}{8} \text{ (bottom of column 1)}$$

and $P(Y = 1) = \sum_{\text{all } x} P(X = x, Y = 1) = 0 + \frac{2}{8} + \frac{2}{8} + 0 = \frac{4}{8}$
(bottom of column 2)

and $P(Y = 2) = \sum_{\text{all } x} P(X = x, Y = 2) = 0 + \frac{1}{8} + \frac{1}{8} + 0 = \frac{2}{8}$
(bottom of column 3)

The marginal probability distribution of Y is summarized in table 8.9.

TABLE 8.9

y = value of Y	P(Y = y)
0	2/8
1	4/8
2	2/8

The expected value of the new bet is $2/8 \times \$5 + 4/8 \times \$1 + 2/8 \times (-\$10) = -\$.75$, and you again ask Nick to leave the premises.

Problem: Seattle Discount Bank

You are receiving a visit tomorrow from the board of directors of Discount Bank, who wish to look over the operations of the data processing department which you manage. You have been having a problem with employee absenteeism and do not wish to be embarrassed by the absence of a large number of employees during this visit. You have been diligently trying to solve this problem, and to test out a theory of yours you have requested and just received data on the joint distribution of absenteeism and rain, where the weather conditions have been divided into "rainy days," "misty days," and "clear days." The information is given in table 8.10. You are deciding whether to call your employees and ask them to please come tomorrow, but your time is limited because of the important expected guests.

If five or more employees don't show, you feel that this will be noticed by the board members. Based on the table, what is the probability that five or more employees will not show tomorrow?

TABLE 8.10   Number of Days in the Last 150 That $Y =$ Weather Condition and $X =$ Number of Absentees Has Occurred

X \ Y	Rain	Mist	Clear
0	0	13	9
1	3	4	7
2	2	2	0
3	5	1	2
4	6	7	0
5	8	2	3
6	12	3	2
7	7	5	1
8	14	5	2
9	3	3	1
10 or more	9	6	3

TABLE 8.11   Joint Distribution of X and Y

X \ Y	Rain	Mist	Clear	$P(X = x)$
0	0	13/150	9/150	22/150
1	3/150	4/150	7/150	14/150
2	2/150	2/150	0	4/150
3	5/150	1/150	2/150	8/150
4	6/150	7/150	0	13/150
5	8/150	2/150	3/150	13/150
6	12/150	3/150	2/150	17/150
7	7/150	5/150	1/150	13/150
8	14/150	5/150	2/150	21/150
9	3/150	3/150	1/150	7/150
10	9/150	6/150	3/150	18/150

Analysis: Your first assumption is that the data given in table 8.10 is reasonably representative of the whole situation, and therefore you can use the table to construct the joint probability distribution for X and Y. This is done by dividing the figures of table 8.10 by 150. The results are given in table 8.11. You also can get the marginal distribution of X by adding up each individual row of table 8.11 as in the last column of the table.

From table 8.11 it is clear that

$$P(X \geq 5) = \sum_{x \geq 5} P(X = x) = \frac{13 + 17 + 13 + 21 + 7 + 18}{150} = \frac{89}{150}$$

Alternatively, by theorem 5.1,

$$P(X \geq 5) = 1 - P(X < 5) = 1 - \sum_{x < 5} P(X = x)$$

$$= 1 - \frac{22 + 14 + 4 + 8 + 13}{150} = 1 - \frac{61}{150} = \frac{89}{150}$$

8.5.3 Conditional Distributions of Random Variables

Having the joint distribution of two random variables, you may also be interested in the probability of one of them conditioned by your knowledge that the other has taken on some value. For example, you know that $Y = 0$ (rain has occurred), and you want to know the distribution of the temperature given this knowledge.

In the example given above, you might have wanted to use the information in table 8.11 to answer a question like "If it rains tomorrow, what is the probability that exactly five employees won't show?" In our conditional probability language, what is $P(X = 5 \mid Y = \text{Rain})$?

Just as in the case of conditional probability of events, the universal set becomes restricted to include only absenteeism on rainy days ($Y = \text{Rain}$), which is represented by column 1 of table 8.11. As before, we want

$$\sum_{x} P(X = x \mid Y = \text{Rain})$$

to equal 1, satisfying assumption 2 of chapter 5. We therefore use

$$P(Y = \text{Rain})$$

as the constant to divide by (adding up the elements in column 1 yields $P(Y = \text{Rain})$). Thus, using the fact that

$$P(Y = \text{Rain}) = \frac{69}{150}$$

you can calculate the conditional probabilities given in table 8.12. For example,

$$P(X = 5 \mid Y = \text{Rain}) = \frac{P(X = 5, Y = \text{Rain})}{P(Y = \text{Rain})} = \frac{8/150}{69/150} = \frac{8}{69}$$

TABLE 8.12   The Conditional Probabilities of X Given Y = Rain

X	Column I of Table 8.11 $P(X = x, Y = \text{Rain})$	$P(X = x \mid Y = 1)$
0	0	0
1	3/150	3/69
2	2/150	2/69
3	5/150	5/69
4	6/150	6/69
5	8/150	8/69
6	12/150	12/69
7	7/150	7/69
8	14/150	14/69
9	3/150	3/69
10	9/150	9/69
	Sum = $P(Y = \text{Rain})$ = 69/150	Sum = 69/69 = 1

In general, the rule for the conditional probability of random variables is identical to the rule for events, with the substitution in formula (1) of $X = x$ for A and $Y = y$ for K:

$$P(X = x \mid Y = y) = \frac{P(X = x, Y = y)}{P(Y = y)} \tag{7}$$

Sometimes you may be interested in the conditional probability of $X = x$ given that Y takes on one of several possible values $a \le Y \le b$ (that is, the values that Y takes on are greater than or equal to a but smaller than or equal to b). Then formula (7) can be extended to cover this case:

$$P(X = x \mid a \le Y \le b) = \frac{P(X = x, a \le Y \le b)}{P(a \le Y \le b)}$$

For example, you may be interested in the probability that the level of absenteeism will be three given that $Y = \text{Rain}$ or (union) $Y = \text{Mist}$. From table 8.11,

$$P(X = 3, Y = \text{Rain or } Y = \text{Mist}) = P(X = 3, Y = \text{Rain})$$

$$+ P(X = 3, Y = \text{Mist}) = \frac{5}{150} + \frac{1}{150} = \frac{6}{150}$$

and

$$P(Y = \text{Rain} \cup Y = \text{Mist}) = P(Y = \text{Rain}) + P(Y = \text{Mist}) = \frac{69}{150}$$

$$+ \frac{51}{150} = \frac{120}{150}$$

since rain and mist are mutually exclusive. Therefore,

$$P(X = 3 \mid Y = \text{Rain} \cup Y = \text{Mist}) = \frac{P(X = 3, Y = \text{Rain} \cup Y = \text{Mist})}{P(Y = \text{Rain} \cup Y = \text{Mist})}$$

$$= \frac{.6/150}{120/150} = \frac{6}{120}$$

8.5.4 Bayes' Theorem for Random Variables As in the case of conditional probability of events, you can extend Bayes' Theorem to cover random variables. By this time, you know that the values of random variables are associated with the occurrence of events, so the restatement of the theorem is straightforward.

BAYES' THEOREM If X and Y are random variables,

$$P(X = x_i \mid Y = y) = \frac{P(Y = y \mid X = x_i)P(X = x_i)}{\sum_{\text{all } x_j} P(Y = y \mid X = x_j)P(X = x_j)}$$

where y is a typical value of the random variable Y, and the x_j's, of which x_i is one, are the values taken on by the random variable X.

We need not stipulate that the random variable values of X are mutually exclusive and collectively exhaustive, since the events for which a random variable takes on two different values are exclusive, and summing over all the values of the random variable $\left(\sum_{\text{all } x_j} \right)$ exhausts all the possible events.

8.5.5 Independence of Random Variables You can also define the independence of two random variables by using the independence of events as the basis. X and Y are said to be *independent random variables* if for every value x of X and every value y of Y the *events* represented by these values are independent. This is equivalent to saying that X and Y are independent random variables if

$$P(X = x, Y = y) = P(X = x)P(Y = y) \tag{8}$$

for every x and y. When feasible, you can then test for independence by testing every (x, y) combination, and if equation (8) does not hold for some x and y, then the random variables are not independent.

Problem: Discount Bank Revisited _____

The absenteeism problem has subsided somewhat in your department, but you are still searching for ways to cut it down further. You have collected data on 50 employees, relating their age to the number of days absent per month. You have completed a summary table of this data, table 8.13. Are Y = age and X = number of days absent independent random variables, based upon the data?

TABLE 8.13   Data on Absenteeism and Age

Y / X	15–25	25–40	40–65
0 – 3	5	5	0
4 – 6	5	20	5
7 – 10	0	5	5

Analysis: If you can assume that the data of table 8.13 are truly representative of the future situation, so that you can transform the data into a joint probability distribution, you can test for independence.

The transformation of table 8.13's entries into probabilities is accomplished by dividing through by the total number of employees, 50. The results are given in table 8.14. From this table,

$$P(X = 0, Y = 15 \text{ to } 25) = .1$$

but

$$P(X = 0)P(Y = 15 \text{ to } 25) = (.2) \times (.2) = .04$$

using the marginal probabilities. Since $.1 \neq .04$, you can conclude that X and Y are *not* independent random variables.

TABLE 8.14   Joint Distribution of Y = Age and X = Number of Days Absent

Y / X	15–25	25–40	40–65	$P(X = x)$
0	.1	.1	0	.2
1	.1	.4	.1	.6
2	0	.1	.1	.2
$P(Y = y)$	.2	.6	.2	$\Sigma = 1$

8.5.6 Conditional Expected Value of a Random Variable You have already examined many situations in which you are interested in finding the expected return for some decision, and you represented your return by a random variable. You have also seen that your assessment of the probability distribution of the random variable of interest may be affected by your knowledge that some event has occurred. You can now combine these two ideas to describe a way of computing the expected value of a random variable, conditioned on the occurrence of some event A, denoted by $E[X \mid A]$. The event A may represent a single value of some other random variable, in which case you want

$$E[X \mid Y = y]$$

or A may represent a compound event involving several values of the random variable, in which case you are interested in

$$E[X \mid Y = a \cup Y = b \cup Y = c]$$

Problem: Hiring a Bus on Wet Days ─────────────────────

Recalling the original Seattle Discount Bank problem, suppose you have the data given in table 8.15 on absenteeism. You are considering hiring a bus to pick up your employees from their homes on misty and rainy days, which, as before, you predict will cut down absenteeism on

TABLE 8.15   Joint Probability Distribution of Absenteeism
(X) and Precipitation (Y)

X	Wet rain	Wet mist	Clear
0	0	13/150	9/150
1	3/150	4/150	7/150
2	2/150	2/150	0
3	5/150	1/150	2/150
4	6/150	7/150	0
5	8/150	2/150	3/150
6	12/150	3/150	2/150
7	7/150	5/150	1/150
8	14/150	5/150	2/150
9	3/150	3/150	1/150
10	9/150	6/150	3/150

those days by half. Since the bus costs quite a bit, you want to know, "What is the expected number of absentees on a wet (rainy or misty) day if you *don't* use the bus?" to see if the bus is worth it.

Analysis: You can rephrase the question as: "What is the expected number of absentees given a wet day occurs?" That is, what is $E[X \mid Y = \text{Rain} \cup Y = \text{Mist}]$. For purposes of brevity, let us denote the event "a wet day occurs" which is equivalent to $(Y = \text{Rain or } Y = \text{Mist})$ by A; then you are looking for $E[X \mid A]$. To get the conditional expectation, you need to first get the conditional probabilities of the values of X (the conditional distribution of X), and then use these probabilities as weights for the values of X. To get the conditional probability of a value of X, given A, use an extension of formula (7):

$$P(X = x \mid A) = \frac{P(X = x \cap A)}{P(A)}$$

To use the formula, you need to get the probability of A, which you can obtain from table 8.15 by adding up the first two columns; that is,

$$P(A) = P(Y = \text{Rain}) + P(Y = \text{Mist}) = \frac{69}{150} + \frac{51}{150} = \frac{120}{150}$$

$P(X = x \cap A)$ is obtained for each value x of X by adding the first two elements in the appropriate row; for example,

$$P(X = 5 \mid A) = P(X = 5, Y = \text{Rain}) + P(X = 5, Y = \text{Mist})$$

$$= \frac{8}{150} + \frac{2}{150} = \frac{10}{150}$$

These probabilities are given in table 8.16.

TABLE 8.16 $P(X = x \cap A)$		**TABLE 8.17** $P(X = x \mid A)$	
X	$P(X = x \cap A)$	X	$P(X = x \mid A)$
0	13/150	0	13/120
1	7/150	1	7/120
2	4/150	2	4/120
3	6/150	3	6/120
4	13/150	4	13/120
5	10/150	5	10/120
6	15/150	6	15/120
7	12/150	7	12/120
8	19/150	8	19/120
9	6/150	9	6/120
10	15/150	10	15/120
		$\Sigma = 120/120 = 1$	

Finally, the distribution of X given A is given in table 8.17 by using

$$P(X = x \mid A) = \frac{P(X = x \cap A)}{P(A)}$$

For example,

$$P(X = 3 \mid A) = \frac{6/150}{120/150} = \frac{6}{120}$$

You can now compute the conditional expectation of X given A by weighing values of X by their probabilities.

$$E[X \mid A] = 0 \times \frac{13}{120} + 1 \times \frac{7}{120} + 2 \times \frac{4}{120} + \cdots + 10 \times \frac{15}{120}$$

$$= \frac{665}{120} = 5\tfrac{13}{24}$$

So the expected number of employees absent if it is wet outside is $5\tfrac{13}{24}$. Therefore, if you use the bus, you reduce the expected number of absent employees by half to $2\tfrac{37}{48}$.

In general, for any random variable X, the *conditional expected value of X given an event A has occurred* is

$$E(X \mid A) = \sum_{\text{all } x} xP(X = x \mid A),$$

and the conditional expected value of X given that another random variable Y has taken on a value y is

$$E(X \mid Y = y) = \sum_{\text{all } x} P(X = x \mid Y = y)$$

PROBLEMS 8.5

1. In the Heads and Changes problems
   a. what is the probability of "at least one change"?
   b. what is the probability of "at most one change"?
   c. what is the probability of "at most one change *and* at most two heads"?
   d. what is the probability of "at least one change *and* at least one head"?
   e. what is the probability of "at least one change *and* at most one head"?

2. Suppose you assign the value 1, in the Seattle Bank problem, to represent the event "Rain," the value 2 to represent the event "Mist," and the value 3 to the event "Clear." What is the marginal distribution of the random variable Y which corresponds to the "weather"?

3. X and Y are random variables whose joint probability distribution is given in the following table.

X＼Y	−2	−1	0	1	2	3
10	.02	.03	.01	0	.09	.001
11	.1	0	.03	.04	.06	.01
12	.003	.11	.005	.02	0	.09
13	.015	.08	.08	.05	.004	.01
14	.002	.04	0	.06	.01	.03

a. What is the marginal probability of X?

b. What is the marginal probability of Y?

c. What is the probability that Y is negative and X is greater than 12?

d. What is the probability that regardless of the value of X, Y is nonnegative?

e. What is the probability of X and Y both having negative values?

4. Recently your firm, which includes both your division and one other division, has commissioned a market research study so that better demand information is available to the various managers in the firm. In their report, the researchers tabulated the number of customers in the sample that purchased the two products produced by the two divisions as follows.

Weekly Quantity Purchased of the Other Division's Product	Weekly Quantity Purchased of Your Division's Product						
	0	1	2	3	4	5	6
0	10	15	17	11	9	6	3
1	5	12	19	14	11	10	7
2	7	15	22	20	17	14	10
3	9	18	25	20	10	5	2

(For example, 19 customers purchase a weekly supply of two units of your division's product and one unit of the other division's product.) The report discusses the problems associated with generalizing on such sample information and concludes that based on sensitivity tests the numbers in the table represent the distribution of purchases fairly accurately.

a. For your own division's benefit, you need the probability distribution of the demand for your product. How would you go about obtaining it?

b. What is the distribution of the other division's sales?

5. In the Seattle Discount Bank problem, what is the conditional probability distribution of
   a. number of absentees given the weather is misty?
   b. number of absentees given the weather is clear?
   c. the weather given four absentees?
   d. the weather given nine absentees?

6. In problem 3 above calculate the following:
   a. $P(X = 10 \mid Y = 0)$
   b. $P(X = 13 \mid Y = -1)$
   c. $P(Y = 3 \mid X = 14)$
   d. $P(Y = -2 \mid X = 11)$
   e. conditional probability distribution of X given $Y = -2$
   f. conditional probability distribution of Y given $X = 12$

7. In problem 4 above suppose you know that next week's demand for the other division's product will be either one or two units. Based on the sample information as given in the table, what is your assessment of the probability distribution of next week's demand for your division's product?

8. Suppose your physician assesses that the probability of having flu A is .3 and flu B is .7. Knowing something about quantitative methods, he defines a random variable $X =$ type of flu, and assigns to it the value 0 for flu A and the value 1 for flu B. He also knows that the random variable $Y =$ temperature can take on the values 98, 99, 100, 101, and 102, and that if a patient has flu A, he has a temperature above 100 65% of the time, and that if he has flu B, he has a temperature 35% of the time, if those are the two choices for diagnosis. A patient has just come into the physician's office with the flu, running a temperature of 101. Using the random variables, what are the chances that she has flu B?

9. Your firm is considering establishing a new plant 500 miles away from the present location. An important consideration in the decision is the availability of workers in the new location. Since this will be relevant only in another year or so when the plant is completed, you are asked to assess the probabilities of unemployment $(X = 0)$, partial employment $(X = 1)$, and full employment $(X = 2)$ in the region. From recent conversations with people from the region you estimate the probability distribution of X as $P(X = 0) = .3$, $P(X = 1) = .5$, and $P(X = 2) = .2$. But the president of your company has just handed you a report he received from an economic forecasting service which provides regional economic indicators including "housing starts." The housing starts indicator, Y, can take on the value of $Y = 2000$, $Y = 1000$. You know that there is a relationship between current housing starts and future level of employment. This relationship, however, is not always the same, as can be seen from the following information:

$$P(y_1 \mid x_1) = .2 \qquad P(y_1 \mid x_2) = .4 \qquad P(y_1 \mid x_3) = .9$$
$$P(y_2 \mid x_1) = .8 \qquad P(y_2 \mid x_2) = .6 \qquad P(y_2 \mid x_3) = .1$$

    a. Would you revise your prior probabilities on the state of employment if you know that the economic service has informed you that $Y = 2000$?

    b. What if $Y = 1000$?

10.   In the context of problem 9, suppose that the profits of your firm will change according to the following table, if you decide to build the new plant in the new location:

State of the World	Unemployment	Partial Employment	Full Employment
Change in profits	200,000	75,000	−20,000

If you decide, however, to construct the plant in the present location, you expect $100,000 increase in profits.

    a. What should your decision be if you have no knowledge about the value of the housing starts indicator?

    b. What should your decision be if you know that the indicator is 2000?

    c. Will you change your decision if the indicator's value is 1000? Why?

11.   In the Seattle Bank problem, section 8.5.2, what is the conditional expected number of absentees given a clear day? Given a misty day? Given that it is not raining?

8.6   Relevant Information in Decision Making

In our journey through the world of preparing for decisions we have used quite extensively the MIS framework first introduced in section 1.4. You recall that four sets, D (decisions), S (states of the world), O (outcomes), and W (payoffs), have been the basic building blocks of this MIS. As a decision-maker, you have control over which decision d in D to choose so that "you make as much as you can," while the components of S are beyond your control. For any decision d in D and state of the world s in S there is an outcome; that is, an element d and an element s jointly determine the outcome o of O with which a payoff w of W is associated. In case you are uncertain about what state of the world prevails we assume in this text that you can describe your uncertainty by a probability distribution of the possible elements of S. Thus the probability distribution, which we have called the *prior*, is an integral part of the MIS. We have devoted the last three chapters to this uncertainty aspect of decision problems. We started with problems in which only prior probabilities are available; then we introduced a refinement in the form of a set of *informational signals* Y, which indicate what state of the world is about to prevail or what outcome will obtain. We first discussed the case of perfect information, in section 8.2, where a signal received reduces all uncertainty about the situation and indicates accurately and uniquely the state of the world which occurs. Such was the case in the Ecological Oil Drilling Corporation problem, where the reading of the device discloses with certainty the content of the well. If X denotes the contents of the well ($X = 1$ is the event "oil field," $X = 2$ is "gas field," and $X = 3$ is "dry well"), and Y the reading of the device with the same values as for X, the elimination of uncertainty can be written as

$$P(X = 1 \mid Y = 1) = 1$$
$$P(X = 2 \mid Y = 2) = 1$$
$$P(X = 3 \mid Y = 3) = 1$$

In reality, however, the elimination of *all* uncertainty, on the basis of information obtained, is quite rare. The more common case is where the information helps you to *reduce* the uncertainty somewhat, which in the deductive probability system means that the information provides you with a probability distribution (posterior) of the states of the world or outcomes which is *different from* the original (prior) distribution. But not all information results in such a change. In other words, you should distinguish between *relevant* and *irrelevant* information. The former contributes to the knowledge of decision makers about the possible states that will prevail, while the latter may overload the decision maker with data which doesn't change his uncertainty about what might occur. If you translate these ideas into probability concepts, "the set of information signals Y are irrelevant" is equivalent to saying that the information signals y_j and the states of the world s_i are independent, since independence tells us

$$P(s_i \mid y_j) = P(s_i)$$

for all i and j. This says that the posterior probability of any state of the world s_i given an irrelevant information signal y_j remains unchanged.

For example, suppose you are interested in the occurrence of the event "an ace" in a draw from a 52-card bridge deck. Since there are four aces in the deck, if the draw is at random, the prior probability of a_1, an ace, is

$$\frac{4}{52} = \frac{1}{13}$$

Suppose now that you are told the suit (spade, heart, diamond, club). The information signals are then

$$y_1 = \text{spade} \qquad y_3 = \text{diamond}$$
$$y_2 = \text{heart} \qquad y_4 = \text{club}$$

But the probability of an ace, given the information signal (say, spade), is still 1/13 since there are 13 spades and only one ace of spades:

$$P(a_1 \mid y_1) = \frac{1}{13}$$

In fact,

$$P(a_1 \mid y_2) = \frac{1}{13}, \qquad P(a_1 \mid y_3) = \frac{1}{13}, \qquad P(a_1 \mid y_4) = \frac{1}{13}$$

You could have also used Bayes' Theorem and the independence assumption to calculate these probabilities. In fact, it can be proven by Bayes' Theorem that the independence of random variables implies that the associated posterior and the prior are equal.*

As another example, suppose the accurate forecast of the weather bureau is that the chance of rain tomorrow morning is 40%, $P(R) = .4$, and the chance of not rain is 60%, $P(\sim R) = .6$. Suppose now that there is an earthquake in the region, an event which we denote by C, and yet the weather bureau doesn't alter the original probabilities; that is,

---

*1. If Y and S are independent random variables, then by definition: $P(y_j \mid s_i) = P(y_j)$ for any signal y_j and state s_i.

2. Bayes' Theorem, recall, says that

$$P(s_i \mid y_j) = \frac{P(y_j \mid s_i)P(s_i)}{\sum\limits_{\text{all } k} P(y_j \mid s_k)P(s_k)}$$

3. But since Y and S are independent, $P(y_j \mid s_i) = P(y_j)$. So Bayes' Theorem now says

$$P(s_i \mid y_j) = \frac{P(y_j)P(s_i)}{\sum\limits_{\text{all } k} P(y_j)P(s_k)}$$

4. We can divide both numerator and denominator of the right-hand side by $P(y_j)$ which yields

$$P(s_i \mid y_j) = \frac{P(s_i)}{\sum\limits_{\text{all } k} P(s_k)}$$

5. But $\sum\limits_{\text{all } k} P(s_k) = 1$, so $P(s_i \mid y_j) = P(s_i)$

$P(R \mid C) = P(R) = .4$ and $P(\sim R \mid C) = P(\sim R) = .6$; the prior probabilities are identical to the posterior probabilities. Then we say that information about the earthquake is *irrelevant* with respect to tomorrow's weather since it has not provided us with any new knowledge about the state of the world (weather) that will prevail tomorrow morning. Formally, if S is the set of states of the world, and Y is the set of informational signals, then if

$$P(s_i \mid y_j) = P(s_i)$$

we say that the informational signal y_j is irrelevant. On the other hand, if

$$P(s_i \mid y_j) \neq P(s_i)$$

then we say that the signal is relevant, since when you receive the signal your estimate of the likelihood of the occurrence of a state of the world is changed.

Let us review the examples given in section 8.3 in the context of informational relevancy when the prior probabilities are known. In the Tricking Nick Numbers problem the prior probabilities of urn 1 being selected, C_1, and urn 2 being selected, C_2, were $P(C_1) = 2/3$ and $P(C_2) = 1/3$. You obtained a new piece of information: a red ball was drawn. Is this signal relevant? The answer is yes, since

$$P(C_1 \mid R) = \frac{24}{49} \neq \frac{2}{3} = P(C_1), \qquad P(C_2 \mid R) = \frac{25}{49} \neq \frac{1}{3} = P(C_2)$$

So knowing that a red ball is drawn changes the probabilities about what urn (state of the world) prevails.

In Harry's Beer Vending Company, the prior probabilities of "rain," R, and "shine," S, are .4 and .6, respectively, while the posterior probabilities, if the reading is x_1, are

$$P(R \mid x_1) = \frac{3}{4}, \qquad P(S \mid x_1) = \frac{1}{4}$$

and if the reading is x_2:

$$P(R \mid x_2) = \frac{1}{13}, \qquad P(S \mid x_2) = \frac{12}{13}$$

So, both signals, x_1 and x_2, are relevant.

PROBLEMS 8.6

1. In Harry's Beer problem, is the signal "your barometer is broken" relevant?

2.   In problem 8 of section 8.5, is the temperature 101 a relevant signal?

3.   In problem 9 of section 8.5, is the value of the "housing starts" indicator relevant?

8.7   Value of Information in Decision Making

Is it worthwhile to obtain relevant signals when they are available? As with the case of perfect information, the answer depends on the contribution of the relevant information to the decision maker; that is, if the cost of obtaining the signals exceeds their gross value, then although the information might be relevant, you will be better off without them. Similarly, if their gross value is higher than the cost, you should obtain them. We now turn to an example which requires a bit of computation.

Problem: Bay Area Savings and Loan Association ————

As a department head for Bay Area Savings and Loan you are in charge of approving loans to land developers in San Mateo county. You are considering three alternative policies for the coming year:

d_1 = extend a \$10,000,000 loan at 7% interest rate

d_2 = extend a \$4,000,000 loan at 9% rate

d_3 = extend no loans for next year

You have asked your staff to prepare for you a forecast of profits and losses for each of these alternatives. After an elaborate analysis, they have classified all the relevant factors (for example, unemployment, new industry moving into the area, average salaries) that will affect the outcomes, and thus your expected payoff, into four mutually exclusive and collectively exhaustive categories (states of the world):

s_1 = depression in San Mateo county

s_2 = recession

s_3 = stable conditions

s_4 = economic growth

They estimate that these states will occur with the probabilities

$$P(s_1) = .25, \ P(s_2) = .30, \ P(s_3) = .35, \ P(s_4) = .10$$

The forecast payoff for the various combinations of states of the world and alternative decisions is submitted to you in table 8.18.

Since you plan to base your decision on the expected values of the alternatives, you compute $E(W_1)$, $E(W_2)$, and $E(W_3)$ where W_i is the random variable describing payoff associated with decision i:

TABLE 8.18 Payoff

DECISION	STATE OF THE WORLD			
	s_1	s_2	s_3	s_4
d_1	−600,000	100,000	300,000	500,000
d_2	−250,000	150,000	280,000	300,000
d_3	0	0	0	0

$$E(W_1) = .25 \times (-600,000) + .30 \times 100,000 + .35 \times 300,000$$
$$+ .10 \times 500,000 = \$35,000$$
$$E(W_2) = .25 \times (-250,000) + .30 \times 150,000 + .35 \times 280,000$$
$$+ .10 \times 300,000 = \$110,500$$
$$E(W_3) = \$0$$

The maximum is $110,500, which suggests the extension of $4,000,000 at 9% rate, d_2, as the best decision. However, you are not completely satisfied with this analysis, since your staff's estimates are based on data that are two years old. Consequently, you consider hiring a consulting firm which promises to provide you with an updated report to assist you in making the required decision. You have invited a representative of the consulting firm to talk this idea over and he offers to conduct a socio-economic survey of the county that will give you a better indication (*informational signals*) about the probable occurrence of the states of the world. He also tells you that after reviewing the report prepared by your staff he has concluded that the probabilities and payoffs estimated by your staff are reasonable, so that they can be regarded as accurate.

He expects the survey to yield one of three signals:

y_1 = prospects for the county are very good

y_2 = prospects are reasonably good

y_3 = prospects are not good

He warns you that these signals don't remove all the uncertainty about what state will actually prevail; for example, it is possible that you will receive y_3 while the actual state of the world will be s_4, that of economic growth: that is,

$$P(y_3 \mid s_4) \neq 0$$

He explains to you that this is so because the survey methods which he uses are not perfect, and therefore sometimes the results are erroneous.

However, he can provide you with probabilistic estimates about the relationship between the occurrence of the states of the world and the signals. For example, based on his experience he estimates that $P(y_1 \mid s_4) = .8$, which means that if "economic growth" prevails there is an 80% chance that you will receive a report stating that "prospects for the county are very good." His estimates for the state of the world-signal relationships are as follows:

$P(y_1 \mid s_1) = 0$	$P(y_1 \mid s_2) = .15$	$P(y_1 \mid s_3) = .3$	$P(y_1 \mid s_4) = .8$
$P(y_2 \mid s_1) = .3$	$P(y_2 \mid s_2) = .75$	$P(y_2 \mid s_3) = .5$	$P(y_2 \mid s_4) = .15$
$P(y_3 \mid s_1) = .7$	$P(y_3 \mid s_2) = .1$	$P(y_3 \mid s_3) = .2$	$P(y_3 \mid s_4) = .05$

Note that for each state of the world the conditional probabilities of the three possible signals add up to one, since regardless of the state of the world you will receive some signal; for example,

$$P(y_1 \mid s_1) + P(y_2 \mid s_1) + P(y_3 \mid s_1) = 0 + .3 + .7 = 1$$

The study will cost $5000. Should you commission the consulting firm to conduct the study?

Analysis: The questions you must answer are how the information obtained by the study will improve your decision, and whether or not the expected additional benefits will exceed the potential cost of $5000 for hiring the consulting firm. You first must establish how to measure improvements which are solely attributable to the information provided by the consulting firm.

One criterion which we have already discussed is relevancy; that is, whether or not the posterior probabilities of the states of the world (based on the information signal received) are different from the prior probabilities of these states. However, it is possible that you may receive relevant information which is so costly that it makes the informational deal undesirable. If you measure desirability by expected dollars and adopt the prescription "you ought to make as much as you can," then you should calculate the expected values associated with each decision, d_i, and informational signal, y_k, and make the informational choice on the basis of these expected values.

Your common sense probably tells you that the optimal decision depends on what signal the survey will yield; that is, the expected value associated with each decision is not independent of the informational signal if the signals are relevant. Therefore, your analysis of the situation must be first in the context of each of the signals followed by an evaluation of the whole survey based on these separate results. So, the first step is to obtain the posterior probabilities of the various states given each signal by using Bayes' Theorem; for each signal then choose the best decision if that signal occurs; then calculate the probability of each signal, and finally, the total expected payoff with the information.

You can start by analyzing the problem under the assumption that y_1 will be the signal received. Having received y_1, you can revise your probabilities of the states of the world by computing the posterior probabilities using Bayes' Theorem:

$$P(s_1 \mid y_1) = \frac{P(y_1 \mid s_1)P(s_1)}{\sum\limits_{i=1}^{4} P(y_1 \mid s_i)P(s_i)}$$

$$= \frac{0 \times .25}{0 \times .25 + .15 \times .30 + .3 \times .35 + .8 \times .10} = 0$$

$$P(s_2 \mid y_1) = \frac{P(y_1 \mid s_2)P(s_2)}{\sum\limits_{i=1}^{4} P(y_1 \mid s_i)P(s_i)}$$

$$= \frac{.15 \times .30}{0 \times .25 + .15 \times .30 + .3 \times .35 + .8 \times .10} = \frac{.045}{.23} = .20$$

$$P(s_3 \mid y_1) = \frac{P(y_1 \mid s_3)P(s_3)}{\sum\limits_{i=\infty}^{4} P(y_1 \mid s_i)P(s_i)} = \frac{.3 \times .35}{.23} = .46$$

$$P(s_4 \mid y_1) = \frac{P(y_1 \mid s_4)P(s_4)}{\sum\limits_{i=1}^{4} P(y_1 \mid s_i)P(s_i)} = \frac{.8 \times .10}{.23} = .34$$

If you now make the comparison between the prior and posterior probabilities of the s_i's given that y_1 has been received, $(P(s_1) = .25 \neq 0 = P(s_1 \mid y_1)$; $P(s_2) = .30 \neq .20 = P(s_2 \mid y_1)$; $P(s_3) = .35 \neq .46 = P(s_3 \mid y_1)$; $P(s_4) = .10 \neq .34 = P(s_4 \mid y_1))$, you conclude that y_1 is a relevant signal.

You can now compute the expected values associated with each of the three possible decisions using the revised (posterior) probabilities. If you denote these expected values by $E(W_i \mid y_1)$, then

$$E(W_1 \mid y_1) = 0 \times (-600,000) + .20 \times 100,000 + .46 \times 300,000$$
$$+ .34 \times 500,000 = \$328,000$$

$$E(W_2 \mid y_1) = 0 \times (-250,000) + .20 \times 150,000 + .46 \times 280,000$$
$$+ .34 \times 300,000 = \$260,800$$

$$E(W_3 \mid y_1) = \$0$$

So if you receive y_1, you choose to extend $10,000,000 at 7% interest rate, which yields an expected value of payoff of $328,000, which is different from the expected payoff based on the prior probabilities.

But before you take the survey (that is, when you must make your decision) you are not yet assured of the results of the survey. It may yield, for example, the signal

$$y_2 = \text{prospects are reasonably good}$$

so you must repeat the above analysis to see what will happen in case y_2 is the signal.

The posterior probabilities of the states of the world given that y_2 has been received are

$$P(s_1 \mid y_2) = \frac{P(y_2 \mid s_1)P(s_1)}{\sum\limits_{i=1}^{4} P(y_2 \mid s_i)P(s_i)}$$

$$= \frac{.3 \times .25}{.3 \times .25 + .75 \times .30 + .5 \times .35 + .15 \times .10} = \frac{.075}{.49} = .15$$

$$P(s_2 \mid y_2) = \frac{P(y_2 \mid s_2)P(s_2)}{\sum\limits_{i=1}^{4} P(y_2 \mid s_i)P(s_i)} = \frac{.75 \times .30}{.49} = .46$$

$$P(s_3 \mid y_2) = \frac{P(y_2 \mid s_3)P(s_3)}{\sum\limits_{i=1}^{4} p(y_2 \mid s_i)P(s_i)} = \frac{.5 \times .35}{.49} = .36$$

$$P(s_4 \mid y_2) = \frac{P(y_2 \mid s_4)P(s_4)}{\sum\limits_{i=1}^{4} P(y_2 \mid s_i)P(s_i)} = \frac{.15 \times .1}{.49} = .03$$

which indicate y_2 is also a relevant signal (compare these posteriors to the priors). The expected values associated with the three decisions if the signal is y_2 are:

$$E(W_1 \mid y_2) = .15 \times (-600{,}000) + .46 \times 100{,}000 + .36 \times 300{,}000$$
$$+ .03 \times 500{,}000 = \$79{,}000$$
$$E(W_2 \mid y_2) = .15 \times (-250{,}000) + .46 \times 150{,}000 + .36 \times 280{,}000$$
$$+ .03 \times 300{,}000 = \$141{,}300$$
$$E(W_3 \mid y_2) = 0$$

So you choose to allocate four million dollars at 9%.

Finally, there is still the possibility that you might obtain the signal y_3. Under this assumption the revised probabilities are:

$$P(s_1 \mid y_3) = \frac{P(y_3 \mid s_1)P(s_1)}{\sum\limits_{i=1}^{4} P(y_3 \mid s_i)P(s_i)}$$

$$= \frac{.7 \times .25}{.7 \times .25 + .1 \times .3 + .2 \times .35 + .05 \times .1} = \frac{.175}{.28} = .62$$

$$P(s_2 \mid y_3) = \frac{P(y_3 \mid s_2)P(s_2)}{\sum\limits_{i=1}^{4} P(y_3 \mid s_i)P(s_i)} = \frac{.1 \times .3}{.28} = .11$$

$$P(s_3 \mid y_3) = \frac{P(y_3 \mid s_3)P(s_3)}{\sum\limits_{i=1}^{4} P(y_3 \mid s_i)P(s_i)} = \frac{.2 \times .35}{.28} = .25$$

$$P(s_4 \mid y_3) = \frac{P(y_3 \mid s_4)P(s_4)}{\sum\limits_{i=1}^{4} P(y_3 \mid s_i)P(s_i)} = \frac{.05 \times .1}{.28} = .02$$

The expected values of the decisions associated with the signal y_3 are

$$E(W_1 \mid y_3) = .62 \times (-600,000) + .11 \times 100,000 + .25 \times 300,000$$
$$+ .02 \times 500,000 = -\$276,000$$

$$E(W_2 \mid y_3) = .62 \times (-250,000) + .11 \times 150,000 + .25 \times 280,000$$
$$+ .02 + 300,000 = -\$62,500$$

$$E(W_3 \mid y_3) = 0$$

and you decide to deprive San Mateo county of any funds for the next year.

You can summarize your analysis in table 8.19.

TABLE 8.19   Signal, Optimal Decision, and Payoff in BASL

If the signal received is:	y_1	y_2	y_3
Then the optimal decision is:	d_1	d_2	d_3
Associated with the payoff:	$328,000	$141,300	$0

So, should you commission the survey?

If you do not hire the consulting firm you expect to make $110,500 by extending four million dollars at 9% rate. How much do you expect to make on the basis of the survey? Is it $328,000, $141,300, or $0? Since you don't know in advance what signal will be the result of the survey and since the dollar figures above represent your expected payoff conditioned upon receiving a particular signal, you cannot consider any of them as your unconditional expected payoff. However, if you knew the chances of receiving each of these signals, $P(y_1)$, $P(y_2)$, and $P(y_3)$, you could compute the expected payoff (with the information which takes into consideration the possible signals of the survey), as follows:

$$P(y_1) \times 328{,}000 + P(y_2) \times 141{,}300 + P(y_3) \times 0$$

How can you obtain these probabilities? Going back several sections to 8.3, recall that

$$P(y_k \cap s_i) = P(y_k \mid s_i) \, P(s_i) \quad \text{for} \quad i = 1, 2, 3, 4; \; k = 1, 2, 3 \qquad (9)$$

Also, recall from section 8.5 that if you have the joint distribution, the $P(y_k \cap s_i)$'s, and want to calculate the marginal probabilities,

$$P(y_k) \quad \text{for} \quad k = 1, 2, 3$$

then you can do it by

$$P(y_k) = \sum_{i=1}^{4} P(y_k \cap s_i) \qquad (10)$$

You can combine (9) and (10), yielding

$$P(y_k) = \sum_{i=1}^{4} P(y_k \mid s_i) P(s_i), \; k = 1, 2, 3 \qquad (11)$$

which are the desired probabilities. So let's get to work:

$$P(y_1) = \sum_{i=1}^{4} P(y_1 \mid s_i) P(s_i) = 0 \times .25 + .15 \times .30 + .3 \times .35$$
$$+ .8 \times .10 = .23$$

$$P(y_2) = \sum_{i=1}^{4} P(y_2 \mid s_i) P(s_i) = .3 \times .25 + .75 \times .30 + .5 \times .35$$
$$+ .15 \times .10 = .49$$

$$P(y_3) = \sum_{i=1}^{4} P(y_3 \mid s_i) P(s_i) = .7 \times .25 + .1 \times .30 + .2 \times .35$$
$$+ .05 \times .10 = .28$$

which are the probabilities of the three possible survey results. Hence, you can compute the gross expected payoff if you commission the survey:

$$.23 \times 328{,}000 + .49 \times 141{,}300 + .28 \times 0 = \$144{,}677,$$

which is

$$144{,}677 - 110{,}500 = \$34{,}177$$

higher than your expected payoff without the survey. This $34,177 expected dollars can be directly attributed to the information (the survey); therefore it is called the gross value of information. The net value of the information is the difference between the gross value and the cost of obtaining the information (the $5000 survey cost):

$$\$34,177 - \$5000 = \$29,177$$

Since you want to maximize expected value, you decide to hire the consulting firm to conduct the survey, which makes you $29,177 happier and the representative happy as well—unless a better job offers itself.

As you may have noticed there are several probability distributions playing roles in this decision problem:

1. the prior probability of the states of the world, $P(s_i)$
2. the probabilities of the possible signals, $P(y_k)$
3. the conditional probabilities of a signal given that a state of the world prevails (or will prevail)

At about this time, you might be asking yourself the question, "Is it very realistic to assume that I, as a decision maker, know so much (all these distributions), and if not, why should I go through such an elaborate analysis to solve problems on the basis of unrealistic assumptions?" We shall discuss this important question more fully in chapter 12, when we suggest the expansion of the analysis to include inductive systems and the systems approach.

For now we will examine how we might use the above type of analysis in a familiar context, the presidential elections in the U.S. This will help to clarify the nature of the assumptions behind this quantitative method.

Suppose that two candidates, Mr. United and Mr. States, are the contenders for the presidency, and that the elections will be held on November 3. Also, suppose that today is Labor Day and while picnicking with friends you discuss the possible results of the presidential elections. One of your statements might be: "The chances of Mr. United are 60% while those of Mr. States are 40%." From the point of view of our MIS, this is equivalent to assessing the prior probability of the states of the world (1) Mr. United will be the next President, and (2) Mr. States will be the next President, which you estimate to be .6 and .4, respectively. You also might discuss the possible results and validity of the opinion polls which will be held next week. Since you have been misled quite a number of times by polls, you state that you cannot rely solely on their results. On the basis of past experience and feelings about the current presidential race, you can make a guess as to the accuracy of the poll results with respect to the actual states of the world (the election results in November). This is equivalent to assessing the

conditional probabilities of each signal given that each state of the world
will occur. By your earlier analysis, once you have assessed these conditional probabilities and the priors of the states of the world you can
obtain the probabilities of the possible poll results (the signals) as
in (11).

Our basic premise in this review has been that somehow (by using
experience and feel of the situation) you can quantify chances of things
you are uncertain about. We have not specified in this chapter how it is
that you use reason and/or experience to arrive at these prior probabilities. Of course, you may still wish to decide whether it is worthwhile
to obtain information without resorting to the methods used in this
section, because estimating prior and conditional probabilities may
appear to be a tenuous endeavor. However, as you refine your ability
to estimate such probabilities based on reason and experience you may
find the quantitative techniques discussed above worthwhile in many
situations.

8.7.1 A Formal Summary of Value of Information

In this section, as
in the Bay Area Savings and Loan problem (see p. 290), we assume
that in the context of your decision problem you know all the components which constitute the MIS described in section 1.4. That is, you
know the set of states of the world, $S = (s_1, s_2, \ldots s_n)$, the set of alternative decisions available to you, $D = (d_1, d_2 \ldots d_m)$, and the payoff
associated with each decision, d_j, and state of the world, s_i, which we
denote by

$$W(s_i, d_j),$$

where $W(s_i, d_j)$ is an element of W, the set of payoffs. In addition, we
assume that you can obtain further information about the occurrence
of the states of the world in the form of informational signals, $Y = (y_1,$
$y_2, \ldots, y_l)$. We also assume you can assess the prior probabilities of
each state of the world and the conditional probabilities of each signal
for any given state of the world. Thus, we assume that you know
$P(s_i), i = 1, \ldots, n$, and $P(y_k \mid s_i), k = 1, \ldots, l, i = 1, \ldots, n$. These
sets $(D, S, W, \text{and } Y)$ and the probabilities $(P(s_i)\text{'s and } P(y_k \mid s_i)\text{'s})$ are
then the components of an extended MIS associated with your de-
cision problem.

Under these assumptions the method which calculates the value of
the information signals Y works as follows:

STEP 1   For each signal y_k, compute the posterior probabilities of the
states of the world using Bayes' Theorem:

$$P(s_i \mid y_k) = \frac{P(y_k \mid s_i)P(s_i)}{\sum\limits_{j=1}^{n} P(y_k \mid s_j)P(s_j)}$$

STEP 2   Based on these posterior probabilities, compute for each signal the expected value associated with each decision:

$$E[W(d_j) \mid y_k] = \sum_{i=1}^{n} P(s_i \mid y_k)W(s_i, d_j)$$

STEP 3   For each possible signal choose the decision which has the highest conditional expectation. We call this the "optimal" decision with respect to the given signal y_k, and denote it by $d(y_k)$. Place these results in a table of the form of table 8.20 (see page 300).

STEP 4   The expected values associated with the possible signals (given in line (3) of the table) depend on the occurrence of the signals. Therefore, in order to compute your gross expected payoff, $E(W(Y))$, which takes into consideration all these signals, you must have the probabilities of each signal. You can obtain these probabilities by using the definitions of conditional probability and marginal probability as follows: For any signal y_k

$$P(y_k) = \sum_{i=1}^{n} P(y_k \mid s_i)P(s_i)$$

STEP 5   Now you can compute $E[W(Y)]$,

$$E[W(Y)] = \sum_{k=1}^{l} P(y_k)E[W(d(y_k) \mid y_k)]$$

STEP 6   The gross value of information, denoted by $G(Y)$, is the expected payoff which can be directly attributed to receiving the information (one of the signals that belong to Y). Since, without the signals, you can expect

$$E[W(d^*)] = \sum_{i=1}^{n} P(s_i)W(s_i, d^*)$$

(where d^* is some decision d_j, for which the expected value without information is the highest), the difference between $E[W(Y)]$ and $E[W(d^*)]$ is the gross value of the information; that is,

$$G(Y) = E[W(Y)] - E[W(d^*)]$$

STEP 7   If $C(Y)$ denotes the cost of obtaining the information, then the net value of information $N(Y)$ is

$$N(Y) = G(Y) - C(Y)$$

This review may have shocked you into realizing how much you have learned by now. If you still feel a bit of uneasiness about the nota-

TABLE 8.20 Summary of Information – Optimal Decision Relationships

If the signal received is:	y_1	$y_2 \cdots$	y_l
Then the optimal decision is:	$d(y_1)$	$d(y_2) \cdots$	$d(y_l)$
For which the expected payoff is:	$E[W(d(y_1) \mid y_1)]$	$E[W(d(y_2) \mid y_2)] \cdots$	$E[W(d(y_l) \mid y_l)]$

TABLE 8.21 Payoff Table

DECISION	STATE OF THE WORLD	
	s_1	s_2
d_1	$W(s_1, d_1) = 200$	$W(s_2, d_1) = 10$
d_2	$W(s_1, d_2) = 50$	$W(s_2, d_2) = 50$
d_3	$W(s_1, d_3) = 20$	$W(s_2, d_3) = 250$

TABLE 8.22

If the signal (reading) received is:	y_1	y_2
Then the optimal decision is:	$d(y_1) = d_1$	$d(y_2) = d_3$
For which the expected payoff is:	$E[W(d_1) \mid y_1] = \$152.50$	$E[W(d_3) \mid y_2] = \$232.31$

tion, however, we hope that the following review of Harry's Beer Vending Company of section 8.4 will serve as a means for translation of the symbols into action.

Problem: Harry's Beer Vending Company Revisited ——————

The extended MIS of Harry's problem consists of the following:

1. The set of states of the world S ($s_1 =$ Rain, $s_2 =$ Shine)
2. The set of decisions D ($d_1 =$ Sell Only Umbrellas, $d_2 =$ Sell Umbrellas and Beer, $d_3 =$ Sell Only Beer)
3. The set W of payoffs given in table 8.21
4. The set of signals $Y = $ ($y_1 =$ Barometer Reading of Rain, $y_2 =$ Barometer Reading of Shine)
5. The prior probabilities of the states of the world $P(s_1) = .4$, and $P(s_2) = .6$
6. The conditional probabilities of each signal given a state of the world:

$$P(y_1 \mid s_1) = .9 \qquad P(y_1 \mid s_2) = .2$$
$$P(y_2 \mid s_1) = .1 \qquad P(y_2 \mid s_2) = .8$$

To compute the gross value of the information supplied by your barometer, use the above procedure:

STEP 1   If the reading is y_1, the posterior probabilities of s_1 and s_2 are

$$P(s_1 \mid y_1) = \frac{P(y_1 \mid s_1)P(s_1)}{\displaystyle\sum_{i=1}^{2} P(y_1 \mid s_i)P(s_i)} = \frac{.9 \times .4}{.9 \times .4 + .2 \times .6} = \frac{3}{4}$$

$$P(s_2 \mid y_1) = \frac{P(y_1 \mid s_2)P(s_2)}{\displaystyle\sum_{i=1}^{2} P(y_1 \mid s_i)P(s_i)} = \frac{.2 \times .6}{.9 \times .4 + .2 \times .6} = \frac{1}{4}$$

If the reading is y_2, the posterior probabilities of s_1 and s_2 are

$$P(s_1 \mid y_2) = \frac{P(y_2 \mid s_1)P(s_1)}{\displaystyle\sum_{i=1}^{2} P(y_2 \mid s_i)P(s_i)} = \frac{.1 \times .4}{.1 \times .4 + .8 \times .6} = \frac{1}{13}$$

$$P(s_2 \mid y_2) = \frac{P(y_2 \mid s_2)P(s_2)}{\displaystyle\sum_{i=1}^{2} P(y_2 \mid s_i)P(s_i)} = \frac{.8 \times .6}{.1 \times .4 + .8 \times .6} = \frac{12}{13}$$

STEPS 2 AND 3   If the reading is y_1 and Harry chooses d_1, his expected payoff is

$$E[W(d_1) \mid y_1] = \sum_{i=1}^{2} P(s_i \mid y_1)W(s_i, d_1) = \frac{3}{4} \times 200 + \frac{1}{4} \times 10 = \$152.50$$

If the reading is y_1 and Harry's decision is d_2, his expected payoff is

$$E[W(d_2) \mid y_1] = \sum_{i=1}^{2} P(s_i \mid y_1)W(s_i, d_2) = \frac{3}{4} \times 50 + \frac{1}{4} \times 50 = \$50$$

If his decision is d_3, given the reading is y_1, Harry expects to make

$$E[W(d_3) \mid y_1] = \sum_{i=1}^{2} P(s_i \mid y_1)W(s_i, d_3) = \frac{3}{4} \times 20 + \frac{1}{4} \times 250 = \$77.50$$

So, as we concluded before, if y_1 is the reading, Harry's optimal decision is d_1 associated with \$152.50 payoff.

If the reading is y_2 and the choice is d_1:

$$E[W(d_1) \mid y_2] = \sum_{i=1}^{2} P(s_i \mid y_2)W(s_i, d_1) = \frac{1}{13} \times 200 + \frac{12}{13} \times 10 = \$24.62$$

For the same signal, y_2, and decision, d_2:

$$E[W(d_2) \mid y_2] = \sum_{i=1}^{2} P(s_i \mid y_2)W(s_i, d_2) = \frac{1}{13} \times 50 + \frac{12}{13} \times 50 = \$50$$

Finally, for y_2 and d_3:

$$E[W(d_3) \mid y_2] = \sum_{i=1}^{2} P(s_i \mid y_2)W(s_i, d_3) = \frac{1}{13} \times 20 + \frac{12}{13} \times 250 = \$232.31$$

and the optimal decision is d_3 with payoff \$232.31. The summary table is therefore table 8.22 (see page 300).

STEP 4   The probabilities of the two possible signals are

$$P(y_1) = \sum_{i=1}^{2} P(y_1 \mid s_i)P(s_i) = .3 \times .4 + .2 \times .6 = .48$$

$$P(y_2) = \sum_{i=1}^{2} P(y_2 \mid s_i)P(s_i) = .1 \times .4 + .8 \times .6 = .52$$

STEP 5   So Harry's expected payoff, which takes into consideration the two possible signals, is

$$E[W(Y)] = \sum_{k=1}^{2} P(y_k)E[W(d(y_k)) \mid y_k)]$$
$$= P(y_1)E[W(d(y_1)) \mid y_1)] + P(y_2)E[W(d(y_2)) \mid y_2)]$$
$$= .48 \times 152.50 + .52 \times 232.31 = \$194.00$$

Harry's expected payoff without information (the barometer is broken) is $E[W(d_3)] = \$158$, which you have computed in section 8.4. So, $d^* = d_3$.

STEP 6 Therefore, the additional payoff that can be directly attributed to the use of the barometer (the gross value of information) is

$$G(Y) = \$194.00 - \$158 = \$36.00$$

STEP 7 Since Harry is a friend of yours and you don't charge him anything for reading your barometer or calculating the optimal decision, $C(Y) = 0$. So the net value of information in Harry's case is

$$N(Y) = G(Y) - C(Y)$$
$$= \$36.00 - \$0 = \$36.00$$

PROBLEMS 8.7

1. Suppose, in the Savings and Loan problem, that the survey can yield only two results:

$$y_1 = \text{prospects are good}$$
$$y_2 = \text{prospects are not good}$$

which are related to the states of the world as follows:

$$P(y_1 \mid s_1) = 0 \quad P(y_1 \mid s_2) = .5 \quad P(y_1 \mid s_3) = .4 \quad P(y_1 \mid s_4) = 1$$
$$P(y_2 \mid s_1) = 1 \quad P(y_2 \mid s_2) = .5 \quad P(y_2 \mid s_3) = .6 \quad P(y_2 \mid s_4) = 0$$

Should you commission the survey?

2. Suppose that in the Ecological Oil Revisited problem of section 8.2 the oil-detecting device is not perfect. That is, it can indicate the existence of oil or gas (y_1) or dry well (y_2) according to the following probability specifications:

$$P(y_1 \mid s_1) = .9 \quad P(y_1 \mid s_2) = .7 \quad P(y_1 \mid s_3) = .2$$
$$P(y_2 \mid s_1) = .1 \quad P(y_2 \mid s_2) = .3 \quad P(y_2 \mid s_3) = .8$$

where $s_1 = $ oil field; $s_2 = $ gas field; and $s_3 = $ dry well. Should you recommend the purchase of the device?

3. As manager of High Fashion, Inc., you are considering the introduction of a new High line next season. You estimate the success of the line (s_1) to have 40% chance, and failure (s_2) 60%. Also you assess the change in the profitability of High Fashion to be according to the following payoff table:

DECISION	STATE OF THE WORLD	
	s_1	s_2
d_1 = introduce new High line	100,000	−50,000
d_2 = don't introduce	0	0

So you decide to go ahead with the new line. But before you act your assistant suggests that you might consider conducting a customer survey to gain information about the possible success or failure of the line. He gathers the following data about the survey:
a. it will cost $4000
b. it will yield one of two signals

$$y_1 = \text{survey predicts success}$$
$$y_2 = \text{survey predicts failure}$$

c. its reliability can be measured by the following probabilities:

$$P(y_1 \mid s_1) = .9 \qquad P(y_1 \mid s_2) = .1$$
$$P(y_2 \mid s_1) = .1 \qquad P(y_2 \mid s_2) = .9$$

Should you conduct the survey?

4. To improve the control system at the plant the board of directors is considering establishing a variance reporting scheme which provides management with information about deviations of the actual performance from the planned level. The board has asked you to prepare a recommendation on the establishment of the reporting scheme. You collect the following data:
a. The production process can be in control (s_1) or out of control (s_2). The probabilities of these two states for the coming period are assessed by the plant manager to be .8, and .2, respectively.
b. The cost of investigating the process for a possible irregularity is $5000.
c. The cost of correcting the process if in fact it is investigated and found to be out of order is $3000.
d. The periodic loss associated with the process being out of control and not corrected is estimated at $25,000.
e. The process cannot be corrected without prior investigation.

f. The reporting scheme contemplated will generate two signals:

$$y_1 = \text{normal deviation} \qquad y_2 = \text{large deviation}$$

g. The relationships between the signals and the actual states of the process can be summarized by the following:

$$P(y_1 \mid s_1) = .9 \qquad P(y_1 \mid s_2) = .3$$
$$P(y_2 \mid s_1) = .1 \qquad P(y_2 \mid s_2) = .7$$

h. The period cost of operating such a reporting scheme is estimated to be $2000. What should your recommendation be?

5. What are your reservations about evaluating information using the measure of performance "expected value of information"?

6. How would your analysis change in problems 1 through 4 above if you were a risk averter? a risk lover?

7. Prepare an example in your life where the quantitative method of this section might apply.

8.8   Summary

In this chapter we have examined preparation for decision making under uncertainty, when new information becomes available or can be bought at a price. Hopefully, you will have added some tools for revising probability estimates and evaluating new information. A few points are worth repeating:

a. You are said to have perfect information when you know the state of the world with certainty; one way to measure the value of perfect information to you is to use the expected value criteria.

b. Conditional probabilities of events and random variables are ways of expressing how your probability estimates change if you are given information about an event or about the value of a random variable.

c. Some events or random variables are independent, meaning the knowledge of one does not change the probability of the other.

d. Bayes' Theorem is useful in revising prior probability estimates of the "causes" of events, after having observed an "effect."

e. You can use Bayes' Theorem to determine whether information you have received is relevant, and, using the expected value criteria, whether it is worth the cost of obtaining even if it does not give you perfect knowledge of the state of the world.

⑨ The Use of Lines in Decision Making

9.1 A Shift Toward Complexity

In the last part of this book, we shall examine decision making in which the size and complexity of the problem are greatly increased. In most of the problems we've discussed, you could look in detail at each alternative decision and assess its potential value to you.

For the present, we'll say that a decision-making problem becomes more complicated as the sizes of S and D increase, provided that there is no trick which, when revealed, solves the problem immediately. Thus tic-tac-toe is simpler than chess according to this criterion. In tic-tac-toe, if you play first, you have nine choices, your opponent then has eight, you then have seven, and so on; there are "only" 9! (9 factorial $= 9 \times 8 \times 7 \times 6 \times 5 \times 4 \times 3 \times 2 \times 1$) possible games of tic-tac-toe. But in chess you have 20 possible beginning moves, your opponent then has 20 replies, you have at least 20 second moves (probably more), he at least 20 replies. There are at least $(400)^3$ ways in which the first three moves of chess can be played, a number which far exceeds 9!.

You should be aware that defining complexity is itself a tricky and complicated matter; it's probably safe to say that most people who feel that we live in a far more complex world than did our ancestors don't really have a criterion for complexity! In any event, the one we have suggested is clearly not the only one, because there are other ways that a problem can be complicated even though S and D are small; for example, when the mathematical functions connecting the elements of

S and D are beyond your comprehension. But, also, the criterion we've suggested may not work, if there's an underlying "trick" or insight that simplifies everything, as the following problem shows.

Problem: Connie's Con Game _____

Nick Numbers's girl friend, Connie, runs a private game for bored customers at the back of Nick's emporium. She has a perfectly round table top, and there are two cans of small round chips, colored white and green. The first player places his chip anywhere on the table, but it must lie wholly within the table top. The second player places his chip anywhere on the table, provided it lies wholly within the table top and does not touch the other chip. Play continues until a player cannot play his chips without either going over the edge of the table or touching another chip. At this point he loses and must pay $10 to the other player. Figure 9.1 gives an example of the play in progress. Connie gives you the choice of first or second move. How should you play?

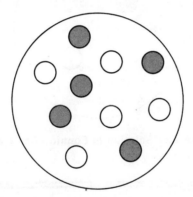

Figure 9.1 Connie's Con Game after Five Moves

Analysis: Assuming you want to play the game, your decision set D of how to play is very large, especially if the chips are small relative to the table. Think of all the possible spots you can place your first chip. Indeed, D is *infinitely* large, in the sense that its membership, in principle, exceeds any positive constant, no matter how large. S, too, is both very large and very uncertain, because S includes the possible moves your opponent can make on the second and subsequent moves; there are "infinitely" many such moves, and it is very unclear (to you at the outset) which move will be made. Hence, you might be inclined to say that Connie's game presents you with a very complicated problem; at least it does according to the criterion of size of S and D.

But geometrical insight clarifies the whole problem and makes it very simple. You tell Connie you want the first move, and you place your chip right in the center of the table. Then, in your mind's eye, you draw two perpendicular lines, as shown in figure 9.2, so as to divide the table into four "quadrants." Now, when your opponent plays his chip, you simply place your next one in the symmetrical position in the opposite quadrant, as shown in the figure. Thus you can always be sure of placing your chip in a legal position (not protruding over the edge, not touching another piece), provided your opponent has made a prior legal move. Hence your opponent must eventually lose, by the principle of symmetry: whatever opponent move is made, you can reply symmetrically.

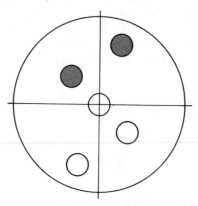

Figure 9.2   Solution to Connie's Con Game

Before leaving the problem, we should point out that the symmetry principle has wide applicability in games and other competitive situations; for example, at the end of chess games, the so-called "principle of opposition" of the kings is based on the symmetry principle. Once you know you have a sure way of replying successfully to every conceivable choice of your opponent, you've got it made.

Thus there may be insights which transform complexity into simplicity. There may also be events which do the same thing. For example, suppose you and your friend are stewing over all the possible entertainment spots you could visit on New Year's Eve, not to mention the sequence of your visits (which, you may dimly recall from chapter 5, gets you into factorials). So D is very large. But then one of you gets very sick at the stomach in all the excitement, and suddenly D is practically nonexistent and the problem has become very simple, at least for the sick one!

In this chapter we examine what is probably the simplest of complicated problems: where the decision maker has specified an exact list of requirements from which only one decision can be deduced that is satisfactory. The requirements can all be stated in terms of equations, and specifically, *linear equations*. A linear equation, you will recall, is one in which the variables appear only in the first power. Thus

$$3x + 7 = 12$$

is a linear equation; whereas,

$$3x^2 + x = 7$$

is nonlinear (it is a "quadratic" equation).

As we shall see, linear equation problems reduce to problems of computation only, and these, in principle at least, could be given to a computer to solve. You don't need to know very much about computers to understand the rest of the chapter, because you can safely take it for granted that a computer "knows how to" add, subtract, multiply, and divide, and will do all these things with a high degree of accuracy once it's instructed to do so.

But beware of the power that is now placed in your hands. So fascinating is the computational beast that you're apt to be impressed by its sheer capability of computing, without asking whether the results are meaningful (that is, whether the assumptions make sense).

Recall from chapter 1 that the formulation of a problem into mathematical or computer language is called a "model" of the problem situation, provided you can use the language to help determine the best choice. Since all of the relationships in this chapter can be expressed in linear equations, the mathematical representations of the problems are called *linear models*. So, as with all the decision problems in previous chapters, the first task will be to represent the problem in a mathematical model, and the second task will be to see how to use the appropriate method to find a *D* which satisfies your measure of performance.

9.2 Introduction to Linear Models with Equalities

All of you have had experience in decision making which can be represented by models consisting of one linear equation. In such cases the decision to be made depends on the determination of the value of one variable which satisfies a single equality relationship; for example, suppose it is 600 miles from your home to Yosemite. You have a half tank of gas left and wonder whether you should buy at the expensive station ahead. Then you might check your odometer and find that you have gone 478 miles. How many miles are left before the cheaper station at Yosemite? Well, the remaining number of miles, x, must satisfy

$$600 - x = 478 \qquad (1)$$

and the solution is $x = 122$ miles left. You might then figure: Half a tank means about seven gallons, 20 miles per gallon on the road, perhaps I'll chance it. For this calculation, the model is

$$20y = 122 \qquad (2)$$

So

$$y = 6.1$$

is the number of gallons you'll need (at 20 miles per gallon) to get you to Yosemite. So, you might chance it.

Now you may have been able to solve all this "in your head." But if you wrote it down, you probably solved the first equation by putting the x "on one side" and the numbers "on the other," arriving at the solution that way. Such a procedure (set of rules) for finding solutions to a model is called an *algorithm* and is the basis on which computers can find solutions, since each step can be represented as an instruction to a computer.

We should pause for a moment to say something about the very simple MIS entailed in this example, which is characteristic of decision making based on linear equation models. Here there is one desired outcome (to arrive at Yosemite without having to hitchhike). Furthermore, the states of the world S are all known; S consists of the stipulations about gas stations, distances, miles per gallon. D consists of two choices: to stop for gas or not. W, the payoff, is very simple: the inconvenience of hitchhiking is a much greater loss than the inconvenience of stopping. Hence the sole deductive question is whether or not stopping implies hitchhiking, given S. If so, then stop; if not, then go on. The only complication of the problem is the structure of S, with infinitely many possible implications, only one of which satisfies all the conditions.

Of course, the linear equation model can become more complicated by involving more than one linear equation in more than one decision variable. For example, you may be shooting for an exact "target" profit, and would like to know exactly how much of each of several products to produce. Or you might want to know how to combine possible activities to reach the point at which you "break even."

Perhaps you wish to achieve a profit goal while at the same time meeting sales contracts.

As the relationships and variables become more numerous, finding the solution becomes more complicated than "taking variables to one side," and methods precise enough to be implemented on high-speed computers become desirable; as it turns out, such explicit procedures (algorithms) often can provide other information about the problem at hand than just the "solution" to the model. This chapter concerns itself with problems which can be approximated by models consisting of a series of linear equations; an algorithm will be presented by which *any size system of linear equations* can be solved.

You should be aware that often the equality represented by an equation may not be possible or even desirable; you may not be able to achieve exactly $30,000 profit, or hit your "target" budget on the nose. In the next chapter we will relax such strong equality requirements by considering inequalities. But for now, we turn to exacting equality problems both to examine situations where equality does make sense, and to appreciate one algorithm, readily adapted to computers, for solving large-scale problems.

9.3 Two Equations with Two Unknowns

You probably recall having solved models of two equations with two decision variables or "unknowns" in high school. We will begin our discussion of the solution of equation systems with this simple model.

Problem: Kathy's Kona Koffee _____

You work for Kathy's Kona Koffee Company, and your division, which produces Kathy's Freeze-Dried and Instant Koffee, is $10,000 short of its production target for the current quarter. You have 15,000 pounds of beans with one week left in the quarter. It takes 1.5 pounds of beans to produce one pound of freeze-dried, which Kathy's sells for $.90 per pound. You also can produce a pound of instant out of 1.25 pounds of beans, but the price has just risen to $1/pound for the final product. You would like to hit your production target on the nose. Can you do it?

Analysis: As we suggested in the *D-S-O-W* MIS, it often proves useful to begin the analysis of a problem by identifying the decisions (variables) which are under your control. You can produce freeze-dried or instant with the remaining beans, so let

x = number of pounds of freeze-dried produced

y = number of pounds of instant produced

Note that x and y are your "decision variables" and, in principle, can take on an infinity of values, so that the set D is very large, and the problem is thus "complicated." S, on the other hand, is very simple, since the technology and price of coffee are exactly specified and known.

You wish to produce exactly $10,000 of final product, so

$$.90x + 1.00y = 10,000 \qquad (3)$$

since you get $.90 and $1 per pound, respectively. You have only 15,000 pounds of beans to work with; and if you want to use them all (why?) to produce the final products, then

$$1.5x + 1.25y = 15,000 \qquad (4)$$

since each pound of freeze-dried uses 1.5 pounds of beans, and each pound of instant uses 1.25 pounds of beans.

In modeling it is always wise to make sure you have translated the situation correctly. Here we ask whether equation 3 makes sense. The right-hand side says "15,000 pounds of beans"; hence the left-hand side must also be talking in terms of "pounds of beans" or else the

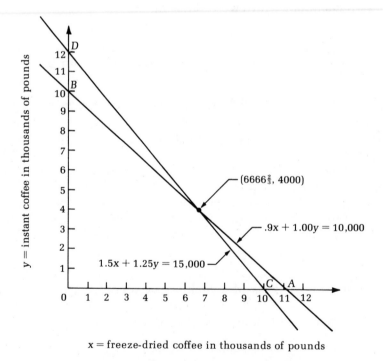

x = freeze-dried coffee in thousands of pounds

Figure 9.3   Graphical Solution to Koffee Problem

equation is nonsense. A little reflection will show you that 1.5x and 1.25y do in fact represent "pounds of beans."*

You now have a two-equation, two-decision-variable model representing your decision problem. You probably recall that such a model can be solved graphically, as in figure 9.3. One way to draw figure 9.3 is to set x to zero in one of the equations, and solve for y. This will result in one point on the line representing that equation. Setting y to zero and solving for x will yield a second point, and connecting these two points gives a graphical representation of the "set of solutions" to the equation. For example, in equation (3), setting y to zero (that is, eliminating instant coffee entirely) gives you

$$.9x = 10,000$$

or

$$x = 11,111.11$$

which says that the point A, where $x = 11,111.11$ and $y = 0$, is on the line representing the set of points satisfying the first equation; if you make only freeze-dried, then to come up to the quota you should make 11,111.11 pounds of it. We write $A = (11,111.11, 0)$. Setting $x = 0$ (make only instant) yields $B = (0, 10,000)$ as a second point on that line, which indicates that you need to make 10,000 pounds of instant to satisfy the quota when you eliminate freeze-dried. If we connect A and B, the graphical representation of the set of solutions to equation (3) is complete. Similarly, setting x and y to zero in (4) yields C and D, and connecting the two points gives the graphical representation of the set of points satisfying (4). The point where the two lines meet represents the values of the decision variables which satisfy both equations simultaneously. This point is the solution to the system of two equations. So, you can meet your target by producing $x = 6666\frac{2}{3}$ pounds of freeze-dried and $y = 4000$ pounds of instant.

═══════════════════════════════════════

You can already see that although the graphical method is both simple and intuitively appealing, it is not very precise unless you are quite careful about drawing the lines. (Are you *sure* the solution isn't $x = 6668$?)

Also, it is a rather cumbersome method, since you have to get out graph paper and begin plotting lines. But, more to the point, when the

---

*One way of making sure is to "check the units":

$$\frac{1.5 \text{ lbs of beans}}{1 \text{ lb of freeze-dried}} \times x \text{ lbs of freeze-dried} = 1.5x \text{ lbs of beans}$$

variables become more numerous, graphs become harder to draw and interpret. Imagine a six-dimensional graph for a problem with six unknowns!

One of the world's mathematical greats, Carl Friedrich Gauss (1777–1855), developed an algebraic *algorithm for solving systems of equations* of any size. The method depends primarily upon the basic rule of equations: that you can add or subtract one equation from another and the equality will still hold. (See chapter 3, rules A and B.) The whole idea behind Gauss's algorithm is that it can be applied (as a set of computational instructions) to any set of linear equations. For small systems of equations, Gauss's algorithm may seem a bit cumbersome, but other methods you may have learned (like "substituting" for variables) become less efficient or manageable when there are many equations and unknowns.

9.4   Some Computational Instructions

In order to understand what follows, we need to introduce some fairly simple computational instructions. We assume that whoever or whatever does the computations, he/she/it knows how to obey the instructions to add, subtract, multiply, and divide. The last operation, division, does require some technical care in designing the computational system, because we have to design a "rounding-off" procedure. Thus, "divide 3 by 17" could result in a never-ending decimal, $0.176 \ldots$, so that the poor computer might never stop. Hence the instructions must include "stopping rules," not only for this instruction, but for others. The stopping rules for division are essentially based on carrying out the division just far enough so that "rounding off to the nearest digit" (for example, 0.176 rounds off to 0.18) does not significantly distort the desired result. We won't go any further into this tedious but important problem of computation in this book; if you are the computer, you'll have to rely on common sense (like using fractions) and maybe overkill (carrying out the decimal further than necessary) to guide you.

Next, since you'll be operating with equations, you need to understand the basic arithmetic operations applied to them. As an example, suppose you have these two equations:

$$5x + 7y = 3 \qquad\qquad (5)$$
$$x - 4y = 6 \qquad\qquad (6)$$

Note that we "line up" the variables in columns throughout, in order to make the arithmetical operations clearer.

To *add* equations (5) and (6), simply add the columns:

$$(5) + (6): (5x + x) + (7y - 4y) = 3 + 6$$

Hence

$$(5) + (6): \quad 6x \quad + \quad 3y \quad = 9$$

(Note that adding two equations always yields an equation.)

Similarly, to *subtract* equation (6) from equation (5), subtract the appropriate columns:

$$(5) - (6): (5x - x) + (7y - (-4y)) = 3 - 6$$

Hence

$$(5) - (6): \quad 4x \quad + \quad 11y \quad = -3$$

(Again, subtracting an equation from an equation always yields an equation.)

We are not interested in multiplying or dividing linear equations by each other in this chapter, since the results will generally be a *non-linear* equation, but we are definitely interested in multiplying or dividing an equation by a constant. For example, suppose you want to multiply equation (5) by the number 3:

$$3 \times (5): 3(5x) + 3(7y) = 3(3)$$

Hence

$$3 \times (5): \quad 15x \quad + \quad 21y \quad = 9$$

All you do is multiply each term of the equation by 3 (called "multiplying through"). The result, as before, is always an equation.

Similarly, dividing equation (6) by the number 3 results in

$$(6) \div 3: \frac{x}{3} - \frac{(4y)}{3} = \frac{6}{3}$$

Hence

$$(6) \div 3: \frac{x}{3} - \frac{4y}{3} = 2$$

You will next see why these operations on equations are useful, for they will enable you to find solutions to sets of linear equations.

9.5 Gauss's Elimination Algorithm

Gauss's method for solving systems of linear equations begins by moving all the *variables* to one side and the *numbers* (constants) to the other in each equation. Gauss's algorithm then "eliminates" each variable from all the equations save one until there are no more variables to eliminate or no more equations to eliminate variables from (or both). To see how this works in the Koffee problem, recall the equations displayed on page 312.

$$1.5x + 1.25y = 15,000 \qquad (4)$$
$$.9x + 1.00y = 10,000 \qquad (3)$$

(As mentioned before, write the equations so that the variables line up in columns.) The first variable to be "eliminated" is x, and you can do this by starting with equation (4). Gauss's first step is to get a 1 as a coefficient of x in equation (4). This is done by dividing equation (4) by 1.5, as explained in the previous section. The result is

$$x + .8333y = 10,000 \qquad (4')$$

Next, using (4'), "eliminate" x from (3). To do this, multiply (4') by .9, and get

$$.9x + (.9)(.8333)y = (.9)(10,000),$$

which simplifies to

$$.9x + .75y = 9000$$

Subtract the result from (3), yielding

$$.25y = 1000 \qquad (3')$$

(This may seem cumbersome in this case, but we are illustrating the general method which, in specific cases, can be simplified). Notice that $(3') = (3) - .9 \times (4')$.

Now x is eliminated from all save (4'), which has replaced (4) in the method, so the next step is to turn to y. Following the same procedure, get a 1 as the coefficient of y by multiplying (3') (which has replaced (3)) by 4:

$$y = 4000 \qquad (3'')$$

That is, $(3'') = 4 \times (3')$. Next, subtract $.8333 \times (3'')$ from (4'), thus "eliminating" y from (4'), yielding

$$x = 6666.67 \qquad (4'')$$

Since there are no more variables or equations, the Gaussian algorithm is done and the solution can be read off:

$$x = 6666\tfrac{2}{3}, \qquad y = 4000$$

So far, this algorithm of Gauss's may not seem very ingenious to you, but as we said, its beauty lies in the fact that it can be used to solve larger systems of equations. Let's see how it works on a problem involving three equations and three unknowns.

Problem: Uke's Ukelele Heaven ━━━━━━━━━━━━━━━━━━━━━

Uke, owner of Uke's Ukelele Heaven, has come to you for advice regarding his window display of ukes. He has categorized his customers into three types: "tourist," "novice," and "expert." For each type of customer he has a particular line of ukes, respectively,

a.   production line from his own factory for $25

b.   locally handmade for $50

c.   handmade from Hawaii for $100

Uke's son, York, has determined that for each type of ukelele placed in the window, the corresponding type of customer responds in the following way: each type (a) ukelele attracts 20 tourists per day; each type (b) ukekele attracts 3 novices per day; each type (c) ukelele attracts 2 experts per day.

Because of a personal superstition, Uke would like to sell four of his own ukes for every one of the other two types combined. Since the proportion of buyers is the same among all three types of customers, he would like to arrange his window to draw customers in this proportion. He would also like to draw his maximum capacity of 100 potential customers a day, and he can fit a total of 12 ukes in his window. How should he allocate his window space?

Analysis: Uke can start by defining his decision variables:

$$x_1 = \text{number of type (a) ukes in the window}$$
$$x_2 = \text{number of type (b) ukes in the window}$$
$$x_3 = \text{number of type (c) ukes in the window}$$

The first specification of his linear model is that he wants to attract four tourists for every two novices and every one expert combined; that is, the total number of tourists $(20x_1)$ should be four times the total number of novices and experts, so

$$20x_1 = 4(3x_2 + 2x_3)$$

or

$$20x_1 - 12x_2 - 8x_3 = 0 \qquad (7)$$

to get the variables "lined up." Second, he wants a total of 100 customers:

$$20x_1 + 3x_2 + 2x_3 = 100 \qquad (8)$$

Finally, he wants 12 ukes in the window:

$$x_1 + \quad x_2 + \quad x_3 = 12 \tag{9}$$

With (7), (8), and (9) as the equations, you can now use Gaussian elimination to get a solution. First, get a 1 as the coefficient of x_1 in (7) by multiplying (7) by 1/20:

$$x_1 - \frac{12}{20} x_2 - \frac{8}{20} x_3 = 0 \tag{7'}$$

Next, subtract (or add) appropriate multiples of (7') to (8) and (9) to eliminate x_1:

$$x_1 - \frac{3}{5} x_2 - \frac{2}{5} x_3 = 0 \qquad (7')$$

$$15x_2 + 10x_3 = 100 \qquad (8') = (8) - 20 \times (7')$$

and

$$\frac{8}{5} x_2 + \frac{7}{5} x_3 = 12 \qquad (9') = (9) - (7')$$

Next, get a coefficient of 1 for x_2 in (8') by multiplying (8') by 1/15:

$$x_2 + \frac{2}{3} x_3 = \frac{100}{15} \qquad (8'') = \frac{1}{15} \times (8')$$

Now, "eliminate" x_2 from (7') and (9') by adding or subtracting appropriate multiples of (8''):

$$x_1 = 4 \qquad (7'') = (7') + \frac{3}{5} \times (8'')$$

$$\frac{5}{15} x_3 = \frac{20}{15} \qquad (9'') = (9') - \frac{8}{5} \times (8'')$$

The next variable to work on is x_3; get a 1 as its coefficient in (9''):

$$x_3 = 4 \qquad (9'') = \frac{15}{5} \times (9'')$$

Now, eliminate x_3 from (8'') and (7'')—only (8'') is necessary since x_3 is already eliminated from (7''):

$$x_2 = 4 \qquad (8'') = (8'') - \frac{2}{3} \times (9'')$$

$$x_1 = 4 \qquad (7'')$$

So he should put four of each in the window.

Notice that it was lucky for Uke that the solution came out in whole numbers, since half a uke is no uke at all! We'll consider shortly the question of getting solutions in whole numbers, when fractions don't make sense. But you may begin to see now why Gauss's idea is so marvelous; it works for *any* number of equations and unknowns by simply adding equals to equals in a specified fashion. This is particularly useful since a computer can be easily programmed to perform Gaussian elimination on any number of linear equations.

As for yourself, you may either understand the general idea of Gaussian elimination, or you may want to make sure that you can act like a computer. In the latter case, you'll find that the computational process is tedious though straightforward, but if you make computational errors you may have to work a long problem through to the end before you discover your mistake (for example, by finding that the solution, when put back in the original equations, doesn't make sense). This can be frustrating during the busy season, and you may yearn for a computer to be your slave.

9.6   When Is a Model Not a Model?

The problem of Uke's Ukelele Heaven is reminiscent of the old Navy yarn in which the chief asks the recruit what he'd do if an east wind came up. "Throw an anchor eastward," says the lad. "What if a north wind suddenly came up?" "Throw an anchor to the north." "What if the wind shifted to the west?" "Throw an anchor westward." "Say, where are you getting all these anchors from?" "Same place you're getting your winds from."

There's a great temptation in modeling to toss in a lot of stipulations you or the manager think desirable or necessary, like selling four times as many of Uke's own as the other two combined, or having only 12 ukes in the window. The question that naturally occurs to a thinking type is whether all these stipulations together form a coherent story.

In the case where the model is made up of a set of linear equations, there are three conditions where things can "go wrong." These are, in ascending order of importance: (1) two or more of the equations are redundant — that is, say the same thing (in the language of chapter 8, an additional equation provides no additional information); (2) the equations are not sufficient to imply a unique solution, in which case there are an "infinity" of solutions; and (3) two or more of the equations are inconsistent, in that they imply contradictory solutions (for example, $3x = 7$ and $3x = 8$).

Another elegant feature of Gaussian elimination is that in each case the algorithm will reveal the trouble: for (1) it will end up with something like $0 = 0$; for (2) it will stop before the final elimination with something like $x_1 + x_2 = 6$; and for (3) it will end up with an absurdity, like $0 = 5$. Hence the algorithm has additional power; it tells you whether you've been stipulating winds and anchors sensibly!

To see how this works for redundancy, suppose, in the Ukes problem, Uke specified in some conversation: "I want eight out of every ten ukes sold to be our own kind." Using the variables from the analysis, the equation representing his request is

$$(20x_1) = \frac{8}{10}(20x_1 + 3x_2 + 2x_3) \tag{10}$$

That is, the number of tourist customers should be 8/10 of the total number of customers. At first glance, this may seem like new information; but it turns out, as you can see, that this request is identical to "I want four of my own ukes to every one of the other two types combined." To see what happens in the process of Gaussian elimination, consider now the *four* equations in three unknowns, with the variables "lined up":

$$20x_1 \quad -12x_2 \quad -8x_3 = 0 \tag{7}$$
$$20x_1 \quad +3x_2 \quad +2x_3 = 100 \tag{8}$$
$$x_1 \quad +x_3 \quad +x_3 = 12 \tag{9}$$
$$4x_1 \quad -2.4x_2 \quad -1.6x_3 = 0 \tag{10}$$

The first step is the same:

$$x_1 - .6x_2 - .4x_3 = 0 \tag{7'}$$

but when x_1 is to be eliminated from (10), the result is

$$0 + 0 + 0 = 0, \qquad (10') = (10') - 4 \times (7')$$

That is, $0 = 0$!!! Well, what else is new? The point is that you already knew that $0 = 0$, which tells you that you already knew the information in (10) from the other equations; in this case, $(10) = \frac{1}{5} \times (7)$ — that is, (10) was just a multiple of (7) to begin with.

When an equation in a linear system provides no new information — that is, when it is somehow a multiple of some other equation or equations — it is called *linearly dependent* on the other equation(s). Whenever a system of equations has one or more linearly dependent equations, Gaussian elimination will result in a $0 = 0$, which says that that equation can then be *dropped* from the system. The decision maker is thus alerted to the fact that some equation(s) or requirements are *redundant*, or provide no new information.

When equations *do* provide new information, they are called *linearly independent*. The decision maker as well as the solver of a system of equations is interested in the number of such independent equations as compared to the number of unknowns. If the number of *linearly independent equations* is *equal* to the number of unknowns, *one* solution will result from Gaussian elimination, as above in Uke's problem.

But suppose the number of linearly independent equations is *less* than the number of unknowns. Then the second condition applies, where the equations are not sufficient to imply a unique solution. Here the Gaussian elimination will stop with some expression like $x_1 + 3x_2 = 5$, and will not be able to proceed further. In this case, any values of x_1 and x_2 which satisfy the equation $x_1 + 3x_2 = 5$ are "satisfactory," and in the real number system there are an infinite number of these. But, of course, the problem does not end at this point, since there may be other stipulations which you or the decision maker wish to add.

For example, Uke clearly did not intend to display $3\frac{1}{2}$ ukes of any type in his window. He implicitly meant that only *whole* ukes were permitted. When you are interested only in whole-number solutions to a set of linear (or nonlinear) equations, you require an additional technique called Diophantine analysis after Diophantus (1st century A.D.), who contributed the early foundations of the method. Even Diophantine analysis (also called "integer solution technique") does not end in a unique solution, since there are still an infinite number of integers satisfying $x_1 + 3x_2 = 5$; but if you specify that x_1 and x_2 must be positive integers (greater than zero), then there is only one solution: $x_1 = 2$ and $x_2 = 1$.

Alternatively, the decision maker may have some additional preferences he's willing to add, which will narrow the number of possible decisions.

Finally, and most serious, is the case where two or more of the equations contradict each other. For example,

$$3x + 6y = 24 \tag{11}$$
$$x + 2y = 10 \tag{12}$$

are contradictories, since they cannot both be true; if you divide (11) by 3, you get $x + 2y = 8$, which contradicts (12). If you were to try Gaussian elimination to this pair, you'd proceed with a straight face to derive (11'):

$$x + 2y = 8 \tag{11'}$$

Then you'd subtract (11') from (12) and get

$$0 + 0 = 2$$

or $0 = 2$, which is absurd. This means that the information provided to you in (11) and (12) is contradictory, and you'd better check either your assumptions or your information source!

In general, if there are any number of linear equations with at least one pair of contradictories, Gaussian elimination will result in a "reduction to the absurd"—that is, to something like $0 = 2$, $0 = 10$.

9.7   When Is a Model Really a Model?

But none of these technical flaws in modeling is nearly as difficult as the basic issue, already discussed in section 1.8: Is the model any good? What is the criterion of goodness? There seems to be a great temptation on the part of many writers to say that a model is a "representation of reality," and that a model is good if it represents reality accurately. But if we took this criterion seriously, we'd have to say that there are no good models, since no model, either of the stars or the earth, ever portrays the multiplicity of the hidden secrets of Nature. Besides, the criterion really tells us nothing, since to apply it we must know what reality is, which we don't or we wouldn't be modeling in the first place.

From the point of view of this text, there is already a more satisfactory criterion of the goodness of a model—namely, whether the model helps you prepare well for decision making compared to other ways of preparing. The model doesn't have to be "accurate" and may leave out large aspects of the situation that are largely irrelevant from the point of view of your goals. (See chapter 8 as an example: not all "signals," even though they are accurate, are worthwhile receiving.)

Note that a model may be good for many reasons other than directing you to a decision. When you list the assumptions of the model, you then have a chance to ask yourself, "Do I really want to make these assumptions?" For example, you can ask Uke whether he "really" wants to sell four times as many of his own ukes as the other two combined. He may reply, "That was the sales figure on the luckiest day of my life, when I met my wife, Luvlik." A little discussion about life and symbols might lead Uke to drop his mystic requirement; if so, you'd have to judge whether Uke is better off on the whole without his pet superstition. If you judge "yes," then the model, or modeling process, is "good."

If you are philosophically inclined, you will recognize that the decision-based criterion of the goodness of a model simply carries the decision-making philosophy up one level, so to speak. First, there is the decision maker with a problem, and you with your model trying to help him make the right decision, based, say, on the prescription "to make the most." When you ask how "good" your modeling is, you ask whether the manager could have made more without your modeling. If so, then your modeling was not so good, and if it caused him to make much less than he would have otherwise, your modeling was very bad. If you are very philosophically inclined, you will see that this account of the goodness of a model, in principle, requires a third-level judgment that judges the goodness of the second-level judgment about the first-level modeling. This whole situation delights philosophers because it is so nicely paradoxical, but seems to frustrate the nonphilosophical types; so, in deference to their feelings, we'll let the matter drop. After all, you can have faith in your own common sense without getting into a philosophical "infinite regress."

You should note that in this discussion we have gone from "model" to "modeling," from the *thing* called a model to the *process* or *activity* called modeling. This is proper to do, because throughout this text you are interested in decisions, which are actions, not things. Hence the goodness of modeling, as we said, depends on how well the actions are taken, and not just on one product of the actions called a model.

A very significant aspect of these actions lies in the relationship between the modeler and the decision maker. If they understand each other well, then the chances of good modeling are vastly increased. One homely yarn will illustrate the point. In Maine, if you ask a farmer how far it is to the nearest town, he may answer laconically, "'bout a mile." After you've gone three miles and no town appears, your strict mind might judge that the farmer's model is "inaccurate." But once you get to know a Maine farmer, you'll understand that he doesn't want to fuss with quantitative concepts like 3.2 miles, so that any place that's quite a piece down the road is "'bout a mile." After that, you can use his model quite successfully.

Off and on, in this book, we've mentioned the "systems approach," which, we said, goes far beyond deductive or inductive methods. If you're willing to judge modeling in the context described above, you're on your way to a systems approach to modeling, which is both frustrating and rewarding. It's a way of asking "What's it all about?"

9.8   Summary

In this chapter we have made a shift toward complexity, in which we examine linear equation models, where the number of possible decisions D can be very large. Several points are worth repeating:

a. The "complexity" of any problem may disappear if you can find a trick to cut down the size of the problem.

b. Linear equation models, when they involve two unknowns, can be solved graphically; when the number of unknowns gets larger, algebraic techniques become necessary.

c. The elimination algorithm of Gauss "solves" linear systems of equations of any size; the basis of the algorithm is to manipulate equations algebraically; a computer can be programmed to carry out the steps of the algorithm.

d. The algorithm also provides information about redundancy or inconsistency in a linear model.

e. Even though you may reach a solution to the model you have constructed, the criterion for the goodness of the model, and thus the usefulness and meaningfulness of the solution, is a whole systems' question.

PROBLEMS 9

1. Solve the following algebraically for x:

  a. $32x + 7 = 20$

  b. $\dfrac{3x}{4} = 25$

  c. $\dfrac{x-22}{3} = 0$

  Solve the following algebraically *and* graphically for x and y:

  d. $x + y = 10$
  $x - y = 0$

  e. $3x + 4y = 2$
  $.4x - y = 7$

  f. $x = 4$
  $-x + 3y = 0$

2. An investor with $10,000 wishes to invest part of it at 5 1/2% and the rest at 6%, for tax purposes. How much should he invest at 5 1/2% if he wishes to receive a total of $557.50 interest per year?

3. A producer knows that he can sell as many items at 20¢ per item as he can produce in a day. His fixed costs are $50 per day. If each additional item costs him 10¢, how many items must he produce to break even? How many must he produce to make $50 per day?

4. You own a roadside nut stand at which you are currently selling cashews at $1.50 a pound, and peanuts for 60¢ a pound. Cashews are proving too expensive for your potential customers, so you want to mix the two together and sell the mixture for a more reasonable price than the pure cashews. You think the "traffic" will bear 90¢, and you have decided to start with a sample batch of mixed nuts totaling 100 pounds. You would like to conduct this marketing experiment while achieving the same income from the 100 pounds as you did selling each nut separately. How many pounds of each nut should you mix to meet these requirements?

5. You are manager of the transportation division of an oil company, and U.S. President Mull T. Phasic has just instituted profit controls. Under the new controls, your division is permitted profits

of $30,000 per week. You are under contract to Yasmimin Oil of Iran to receive 50,000 barrels of oil per week, and it is very expensive to store, so you are unwilling to wait for the freeze to be lifted. You can send the oil to your outlets in Richmond, California, or Seattle, Washington, on your tankers, and you know that you'll make a profit of 50¢ a barrel on oil sent to California and 75¢ a barrel on oil sent to Seattle. How could you "make the limit" on the 50,000 barrels?

6. Tomcat Clothes, Inc., has 80 items in inventory at their San Leandro store (inventory includes items on the floor). They sell pants and shirts only, and for their current sale, all pants cost $7 and all shirts are priced at $5. Because of previous records on amount sold, Sam Slick, owner of Tomcat, knows that he has $524 of inventory left, but he has not kept records on pants versus shirts. He does not want to count his pants and shirts, but would like to know how many of each he has left. Can you help him?

7. A ticket to see "Do You Love Your Mother" costs $1.25 for adults and 50¢ for children. During an afternoon showing, a total amount of $221 was received.

   a. What is the number of adults and the number of children attending the evening showing if during the evening performance twice as many adults attended and one-half as many children attended as watched the afternoon show, and the amount received was $373?

   b. What is the number of adults and number of children attending the afternoon show if prior to the evening show you learn that a total of 232 people attended the show?

   c. What if your cashier reports to you that he received only $220 during the afternoon show and your usher reports on 232 people attending the show?

8. Irene Cohn and her brother, "Ice Cream," want to invest, and are arguing over the risks and percentages. They have $8000 between them and can invest at 5%, 5 1/2%, or 6%. If they wish to receive $455 per year, which they have agreed upon as a reasonable amount, how much should they invest at 5% and how much at 6%, if Irene insists on investing $2000 at 5 1/2%?

9. What if Uke had wanted a capacity of 120 instead of 100 customers? Resolve the equations and see if it makes sense, using Gaussian elimination. What does 4/5 of a ukelele mean?

10. Suppose you make 50¢ a barrel on oil to California and 50¢ on oil to Seattle in problem 5. What is the new equation model? What kind of an inconsistent equation does Gaussian elimination lead to? Draw the two equations graphically.

11. Find the solution (or solutions) to the following systems of equations—if they exist.

a. $2X_1 + 3X_2 \qquad = 3$

b. $2X_1 \qquad\qquad = 4$
$\ X_1 + 2X_2 \qquad = 6$
$\ 3X_1 - \ X_2 + \ X_3 = 5$

c. $\ X_1 + 2X_2 + \ X_3 = 4$
$\ 2X_1 + \ X_2 + \ X_3 = 4$
$\ X_1 - \ X_2 + \ X_3 = 1$

d. $X_1 + \ X_2 + \ X_3 = 3$
$\ 2X_1 + 3X_2 + 3X_3 = 8$
$\ 3X_1 + 4X_2 + 4X_3 = 11$

12. Every day you delight in lunch at Misako's Restaurant. Your friend Misako is having a problem getting enough meat for her Teriyaki burgers (which you cannot live without) due to both personal difficulties and a beef shortage. She tells you that she needs 1500 pounds of beef per week, and she blends three grades of meat in her burgers. Due to the meat shortage, she must use 1000 pounds of grade B and grade C combined. She also wants, if possible, to use 2 ounces of grade A and 4 ounces of other grades (combined) in each burger. How much of each grade should she order? Using Gaussian elimination, you should come up with at least two meaningful solutions (there are many).

13. In the process of planning for your budget next year for Avigdor's Wineries you have gathered the following information:

a. You produce only one product, Ilene Wine.

b. You have four departments in the firm: manufacturing, water, steam generation, electricity.

c. Each gallon of Ilene Wine requires .6 gallons of water, .9 cubic feet of steam, and 4.8 kilowatt-hours of electricity.

d. To generate one kWh of electricity requires an input of .15 cubic ft of steam.

e. To pump one gallon of water requires .8 kWh of electricity.

f. To produce one cubic foot of steam requires .5 gallons of water.

g. The costs in the three departments are: $1 per 75 gallons of water, 1¢ per cubic foot of steam, and $20 per 1000 kWh.

h. It is expected that 100,000 gallons of wine will be produced this year, each gallon requiring direct cost (in addition to the cost accumulated by nonmanufacturing departments) of $2.

What should the budget figures be for the four departments?

14. You have been appointed to the antitrust division of the government to look into possible violations of the law in several industries. You have decided to ask your staff to gather information regarding the supply and demand in each of these industries so

that you can estimate the competitive equilibrium price and quantity and use it as a reference to evaluate the actual figure (equilibrium price is that price for which the quantity demanded is equal to the quantity supplied). In the directions you've given to the staff you have explained that as a first approximation you would ask for linear approximations to the supply and demand functions. These are given to you for the oil industry as follows:

$$D = -50p + 250 \qquad S = 25p + 25$$

where D is the quantity demanded; S is the quantity supplied; p is the price.

What are your reference price and quantity figures in the industry?

15. How would you evaluate the model in problem 14? What would be your next step?

16. Before completing the investigation in problem 14, you receive a note that the Treasury Department has imposed a 90¢ sales tax per unit on oil (suppose the units are barrels of oil). Does this information change your reference price and quantity?

17. Set up a model of three equations and three unknowns which has a unique solution. Solve by Gaussian elimination. Do the same with a model of three equations and two unknowns. Two equations and three unknowns.

18. Set up and solve a three equation–three unknown model which has many solutions.

19. Set up and solve a three equation–three unknown model which has no solution.

20. a. Set up the equations to solve the following problem, with some indication as to what your variables represent. DO NOT SOLVE. A company buys three brands of fuel, each in 100-gallon drums. The fuel is a blend of ethanol, methanol, and propanol. The

	Percent by Volume		
	Methanol	Ethanol	Propanol
Brand A	10%	80%	10%
Brand B	15%	75%	10%
Brand C	15%	60%	25%

company wishes to make 5000 gallons of fuel with the following specifications in percent by volume: methanol 13%, ethanol 70%, propanol 17%.

How many barrels of each brand should be mixed? Assume
that fractional barrels can be used and that there is unlimited
supply of barrels.

b. If Brand C were not available, can you take a guess whether
the required blend is possible? Support your answer.

Appendix 9.1   Review of Slopes and Intercepts of Lines; Marginal Analysis for Linear Functions

Problem: Susie's Razor Company ━━━━━━━━━━━━━━━

As owner-manager of Susie's Razor Company, you produce
triple-edged long-lasting razor blades for distribution to retail outlets.
This is your only product, and last year you produced and sold 80,000
packages of blades. The total expenses of your firm for last year are
summarized in the table below.

TABLE 9.1

Total Variable Costs		Total Fixed Costs	
Steel for blades	$ 5,000	Rent	$ 3,600
Packaging and shipping	1,000	Telephones, etc.	400
Labor	10,000	Executive salary	10,000
Total variable costs	$16,000	Total fixed costs	$14,000

Fixed costs are costs you incur even if you produce nothing. Fixed
costs remain constant, regardless of the level at which you produce.
Variable costs are costs which vary with the level of production. In
this case, you can safely assume that as production increases, so does
the total variable cost, and in a linear fashion; that is, if you produce
twice as many blades next year, your total variable costs will double.
This year your projected sales are 120,000 packages. What do you expect your costs will be for the year?

Analysis: You have one data point with which to work—last year's
total costs were $16,000 + $14,000 = $30,000 and you produced 80,000
packages. You also know that if you produce nothing in any year you
will still incur a total cost of $14,000—the fixed costs. The two points
appear as point A and point B in the graph of figure 9.4 with total cost
as a function of volume. Since you assume that your total cost is a
linear function of volume, you can connect points A and B to get the
general relationship between the number of units produced and total
costs. In order to answer the question posed in this problem, you now
must find the point on the line which corresponds to 120,000 volume
and read off its total cost. This can be done geometrically by carefully

constructing a graph as in figure 9.5 and drawing a line perpendicular to the horixontal axis where volume is 120,000 (point C), finding the point D where it intersects with the total cost line, and then drawing a horizontal line from point D perpendicular to the total cost axis and reading off the total cost at the point of intersection E, which is $38,000.

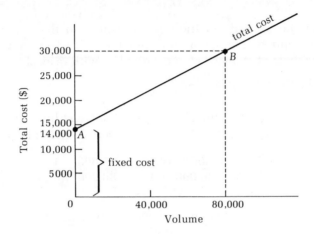

Figure 9.4

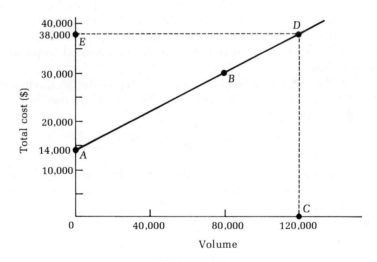

Figure 9.5

But it is probably simpler and certainly more accurate to use another method — namely, to solve this problem algebraically by developing the equation for the total cost line using the *slope* and *intercept*.

Alternative Analysis:

DEFINITION   Let (x_1, y_1) and (x_2, y_2) be two points on a straight line of the form $y = ax + b$. Then the slope a of the line is defined to be

$$a = \frac{y_2 - y_1}{x_2 - x_1} \quad \text{or} \quad a = \frac{y_1 - y_2}{x_1 - x_2}$$

Note that the second equation is equivalent to the first with both numerator and denominator multiplied by -1. This slope is often called the "rate of change" of one variable y with respect to the other x and can be thought of as $\dfrac{\text{the change in } y}{\text{the change in } x}$.

In Susie's problem the *slope* of the total cost line can be derived from the two points $(0, \$14{,}000)$ and $(80{,}000, \$30{,}000)$ by

$$a = \frac{30{,}000 - 14{,}000}{80{,}000 - 0} = \frac{16{,}000}{80{,}000} = \frac{1}{5}$$

or

$$a = \frac{14{,}000 - 30{,}000}{0 - 80{,}000} = \frac{-16{,}000}{-80{,}000} = \frac{1}{5}$$

as shown in figure 9.6. In other words, when volume increases five units, the total cost increases by one dollar, or when volume increases by one unit, total cost increases by 20¢ ($\$1/5$). (This 20¢ is called the *unit* variable costs, since it is the costs directly related to producing any one unit.)

Using the *slope* as a tool, it is an easy step to derive the equation for a line *if you have one other point on the line*. If you use the general equation for a straight line

$$y = ax + b$$

then the slope is given by a since changing x by 1 unit should change y by a units. In this problem $a = 1/5$. The point you have is $x = 80{,}000$, $y = 30{,}000$. You can just plug the x and y values of the point into the equation and then solve for b. In Susie's problem

$$30{,}000 = \frac{1}{5} \times 80{,}000 + b$$

and solving for b gives you

$$b = 14{,}000$$

There is a general term for the point b, where a line meets the vertical axis.

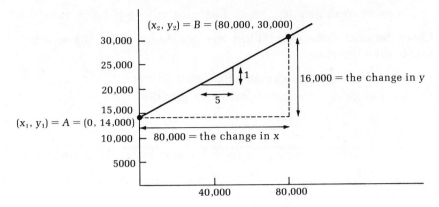

Figure 9.6   Slope of the Line *AB*

DEFINITION   Let

$$y = ax + b$$

be the equation of a straight line. If x = 0, then y = b. We call b the *intercept* of the line since (0, b) is the point at which the line "intercepts" the y-axis.

Now that you have derived the equation for the total cost line, you can use the technique of solving one equation with one "unknown" variable to answer the question: What will the total cost be if Susie's Razor Company produces 120,000 packages of blades? Since total cost is a linear function of production, the equation for total cost can be written

$$TC = a \times V + b$$

where

$$TC = \text{total cost} \quad \text{and} \quad V = \text{volume}$$

You know that *a* is 1/5 and *b* is 14,000, so the equation for total cost in Susie's problem is

$$TC = \frac{1}{5}V + 14,000$$

You know that volume is going to be 120,000; you need only solve for the "unknown" *TC*. Therefore

$$TC = \frac{1}{5} \times 120,000 + 14,000 = \$38,000$$

So you expect that next year's total cost will be $38,000 as before.

Computational Examples: Find the equations of the lines which satisfy the following:

1.   has a slope of 3 and contains the point (2, −1)
2.   has a slope of −1/3 and contains the point (4, 3)
3.   contains the points (2, 1) and (−1, 4)
4.   has a slope of 4 and a y-intercept of 4
5.   has the same slope as 2y = 6x + 1 and contains the point (−1, 1)

Analysis: Since you are looking for equations of *straight lines*, they all have the form $y = ax + b$.

1.   Using the slope 3 and plugging in the point for y and x: $-1 = 3 \cdot 2 + b$. Solving for b, $b = -7$, and the equation for the line is $y = 3x - 7$.
2.   Using the same analysis as in example 1, $3 = -\frac{1}{3} \times 4 + b$ and $b = 4\frac{1}{3}$, so $y = -\frac{1}{3}x + 4\frac{1}{3}$.
3.   Using the same method as in Susie's Razor Company, the slope of the line is

$$a = \frac{4 - 1}{-1 - 2} = \frac{3}{-3} = -1$$

Using their slope and the point (2,1) — you could have used (−1,4) — we get: $1 = -1 \times 2 + b$ and, therefore, $b = 3$. The equation for the line is, therefore $y = -x + 3$.

4.   You can write down directly $y = 4x + 4$ or equivalently derive this from the slope of 4 and the point (0,4).
5.   Solving for y will give you $y = 3x + 1/2$, so the slope of the line is $y = 3$. Equivalently, you could have arbitrarily chosen two values for x and used the two points to get the slope. The line with slope 3 containing the point (−1,1) has intercept $1 = 3(-1) + b$ or $b = 4$, and equation $y = 3x + 4$.

Linear Programming Models 10

10.1 From Equations to Inequalities

You may have developed an uneasy feeling about some of the problems discussed in the last chapter, since the decision maker always specified a "target profit" or "desired number" of customers or sales per day. In real decision-making situations, such specifications can sometimes be met, but more often than not these tight restrictions are neither reasonable nor desirable. For example, as the Kona Koffee manager, you might be satisfied to come as close to the target as possible, or to use up less than all the coffee beans if necessary.

The point is that you would, in reality, loosen the tight restriction of equality if necessary and specify that pounds of beans used "not exceed" 15,000 pounds, or that profit be "at least" $30,000. Inequalities (first introduced in chapter 3) describe these new restrictions in a mathematical model. In decision models, an inequality is a model for a relationship in which the variables take on a range of values which is *bounded* by some upper or lower limit.

Problem: Belinda's Beauty Products ━━━━━━━━━━━━━━━━

As marketing manager for Belinda's Beauty Products, you have been given an advertising budget of $100,000. You are considering your options in media advertising. Your experience tells you that newspaper advertisements reach 20 people per dollar spent, while TV reaches 15 per dollar spent. Because of contractual obligations, you must spend at least $35,000 on TV. You also know that "oversaturation" sets in after $70,000 in each media, so you don't want to put more than that amount into either. You want to make sure to reach at least a million people (combined). How should you allocate your $100,000 budget?

Analysis: Ignoring the larger systems question of how else you might spend your advertising dollars, you have two ways to spend the money. Let

$$x_1 = \text{dollars spent on TV advertising}$$
$$x_2 = \text{dollars spent on newspaper advertising}$$

Your budget *constraint* is

$$x_1 + x_2 \leq 100,000$$

since you cannot spend more than you have! You wish to reach at least one million potential customers. You assume that separability (section 3.7) holds – that is, that the same person is not reached by both media; hence

$$15x_1 + 20x_2 \geq 1,000,000$$

You also must spend at least $35,000 on TV advertising:

$$x_1 \geq 35,000$$

but no more than $70,000 on any one medium:

$$x_1 \leq 70,000$$
$$x_2 \leq 70,000$$

Finally, since you are using inequalities, you can specify explictly that spending "negative" dollars on either medium makes no sense:

$$x_1 \geq 0$$
$$x_2 \geq 0$$

The entire model for Belinda's problem then looks like:

$$
\begin{array}{ll}
x_1 + x_2 \leq 100,000 & (1) \\
15x_1 + 20x_2 \geq 1,000,000 & (2) \\
x_1 \geq 35,000 & (3) \\
x_1 \leq 70,000 & (4) \\
x_2 \leq 70,000 & (5) \\
x_1 \geq 0 & (6) \\
x_2 \geq 0 & (7)
\end{array}
$$

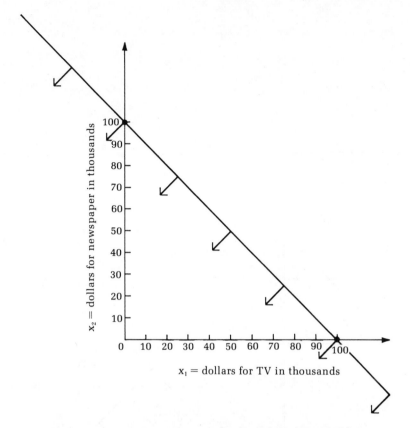

Figure 10.1   First Constraint in Belinda's Beauty Problem

The model is represented geometrically in figures 10.1 through 10.5. In figure 10.1, the first constraint ($x_1 + x_2 \leq 100{,}000$) divides the plane into two areas. The line dividing the plane is $x_1 + x_2 = 100{,}000$; all the points *below* or on the line satisfy (1); that is, all the points (x_1, x_2) in the shaded region satisfy $x_1 + x_2 \leq 100{,}000$. For example, in figure 10.2 points (60,000, 20,000), (30,000, 10,000) and (20,000, 80,000) satisfy the inequality since $60{,}000 + 20{,}000 < 100{,}000$; $30{,}000 + 10{,}000 < 100{,}000$; and $20{,}000 + 80{,}000 \leq 100{,}000$. On the other hand, the point (90,000, 40,000) does not satisfy the inequality since $90{,}000 + 40{,}000 > 100{,}000$.

In figure 10.3 the second constraint, $15x_1 + 20x_2 \geq 1{,}000{,}000$ is included; all points *above* $15x_1 + 20x_2 = 1{,}000{,}000$ satisfy the second constraint. The shaded area in figure 10.3 satisfies both (1) and (2). Looking at figure 10.4, you can see that in addition to point (90,000, 40,000), point (30,000, 10,000) is outside the area that satisfies the *two* constraints, since $15 \times 30{,}000 + 20 \times 10{,}000 < 1{,}000{,}000$. Points (20,000, 80,000) and (60,000, 20,000) meet the two requirements.

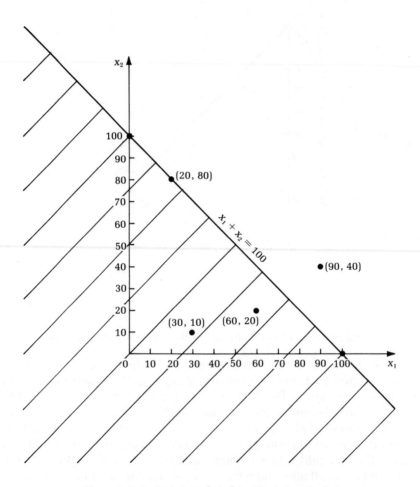

Figure 10.2   Points Related to First Constraint

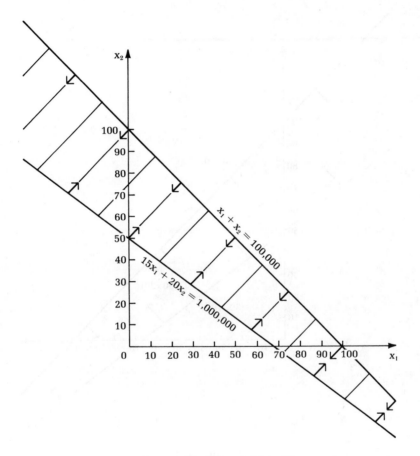

Figure 10.3   Constraints (1) and (2) in Thousands

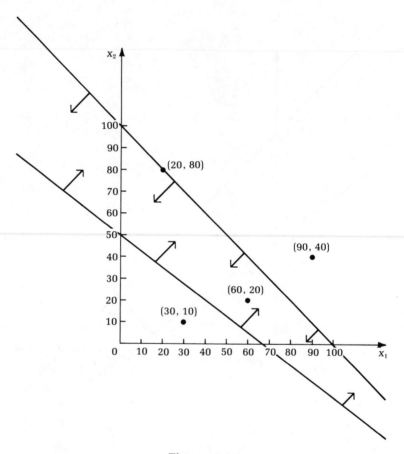

Figure 10.4

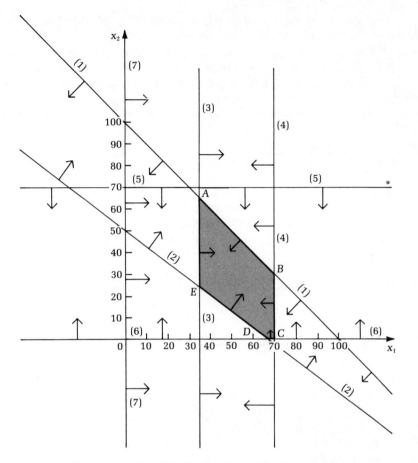

Figure 10.5   Feasible Region for Advertising Decision

Adding the rest of the constraints and carefully noting the *direction* (less than or greater than) of the inequalities, we derive the *feasible region*, or set of solutions which satisfy all the constraints simultaneously, as represented by the shaded area in figure 10.5. The last two constraints, (6) and (7), specify that the feasible region is restricted to the positive quarter of the plane, and are called *nonnegativity constraints*, which keep you from including solutions which you assume make no sense.

As figure 10.5 suggests, there are *many* solutions to Belinda's problem. For example, you could spend $70,000 on TV advertising and nothing on newspaper, or $70,000 on TV and $30,000 on newspaper, or $45,000 on each, or many, many other combinations of x_1 and x_2 which satisfy all the constraints.

You may now expect us to tell you how you should allocate the budget—that is, which one of the *feasible solutions* is "the best." But with the information given so far, we cannot! The problem statement has not specified an explicit or implicit measure of performance; there are no directions as to how to choose between any of the feasible solutions! In reality, though, you probably would have a way of choosing between solutions in this problem. For example, your measure of performance might have been to minimize total expenditures on TV and newspaper while satisfying the constraints. This would provide the most money for alternative advertising expenditures mentioned at the start of the analysis. Or, you might want to maximize exposure—that is, reach the most people—again subject to the constraints. It is to this type of "constrained optimization" problem that we now turn; we will impose a measure of performance on the problem, while at the same time satisfying equality or inequality constraints.

PROBLEMS 10.1

1. Draw the feasible region for the following sets of inequalities (constraints):

    a. $4x_1 + 3x_2 \leq 12$
        $2x_1 + 5x_2 \leq 10$
        $x_1 \geq 1$
        $x_1 \geq 0, x_2 \geq 0$

    b. $x_1 - x_2 \leq 1$
        $4x_1 + 6x_2 \geq 24$
        $x_1 \geq 2$
        $x_1 \geq 0, x_2 \geq 0$

    c. $x_1 + x_2 \geq 5$
        $8x_1 - 7x_2 \leq 0$
        $2x_1 + 3x_2 \leq 18$
        $x_1 \leq 6$
        $x_2 \leq 4$
        $x_1, x_2 \geq 0$

2. Your firm produces three textile products for which it uses two major resources: man hours and machine hours. For each blouse (product 1) it uses two man hours and one-half machine hour; for a pair of pants (product 2) it uses three man hours and one machine hour; and for a pair of shorts it uses 1.5 man hours and .75 machine hour. Blouses and pants are sold together in sets only (one blouse and one pair of paints = one set). Presently you have a commitment for 500 such sets to be supplied in 30 days. You have 10,000 man hours and 8000 machine hours at your disposal for each month.

    a. Set up the constraints which limit your production plans.

    b. Suppose shorts are dropped from production. Draw the new feasible production set for your firm.

3. Set up your own constraints on time, money, and library hours for the following activities: preparing for this course exam; writing a paper for another course; considering time needed with your coperson, and other responsibilities.

10.2 A Linear Programming Problem

Suppose now that you *do* want to minimize your advertising expenditures while at the same time satisfying the constraints (1) through (7). The mathematical model for your problem is

$$\text{Minimize } x_1 + x_2$$

$$\text{subject to} \quad x_1 + x_2 \leq 100{,}000$$
$$15x_1 + 20x_2 \geq 1{,}000{,}000$$
$$x_1 \geq 35{,}000$$
$$x_1 \leq 70{,}000$$
$$x_2 \leq 70{,}000$$
$$x_1 \geq 0$$
$$x_2 \geq 0$$

The new model has in it the criteria for choosing between the feasible solutions based upon your measure of performance — that is, an *objective function* (chapter 3). The above problem is called a *linear programming* problem; "linear" since the measure of performance (objective function) is linear and so are all of the constraints (when you draw any of them, they are straight lines).

How would you go about "solving" such a problem? Unfortunately, Gaussian elimination will not work by itself since you cannot assume that all of the constraints are equalities, and even if you could, what about the objective function, $x_1 + x_2$, which is not an equation at all? This problem can be solved in several ways, but one of the most powerful is the *simplex method* developed in the 1940's by George Dantzig, which, like Gauss's method for equations, systematically finds the solution to any linear programming (LP) problem. The method is based upon a very fundamental result, which says that if you examine all of the "corners" in the feasible region of any LP problem, one of the "corners" will be an *optimal* solution; that is, it will maximize or minimize the objection function. In Belinda's problem, the feasible corners (see figure 10.5) are

$$x_1 = \$66{,}667, \quad x_2 = 0$$
$$x_1 = \$70{,}000, \quad x_2 = 0$$
$$x_1 = \$70{,}000, \quad x_2 = \$30{,}000$$
$$x_1 = \$35{,}000, \quad x_2 = \$65{,}000$$
$$x_1 = \$35{,}000 \quad x_2 = \$23{,}750$$

The fundamental result says that one of these is the optimal solution to Belinda's problem; that is, one of these corner points minimizes $x_1 + x_2$ subject to the constraints. To see graphically that this result holds in the current problem, you should observe that equal values of the objective function $x_1 + x_2$ can be represented by the parallel lines in figure 10.6. For example, the topmost line ($x_1 + x_2 = 90,000$) represents all the decisions that cost \$90,000—for example, (80000, 10000) and (20000, 70000). Since your objective is to minimize costs while satisfying the constraints, your goal, graphically, is to find the *lowest* parallel cost line which has at least one point inside the feasible region. As you can see in figure 10.7, this is the "corner" point ($x_1 = 35000, x_2 = 23750$).

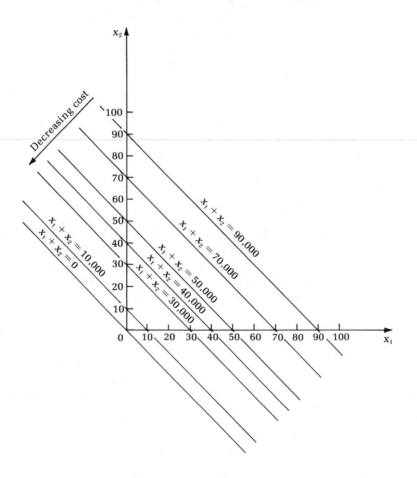

Figure 10.6   Equal Values of the Objective Functions

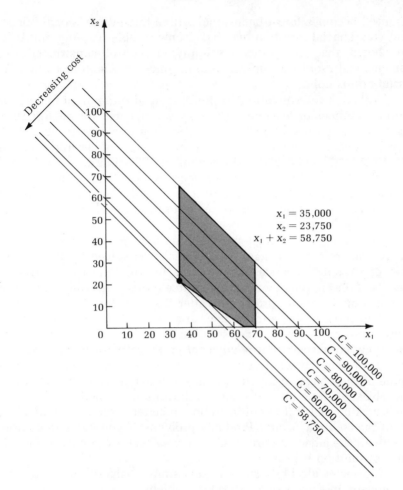

Figure 10.7   Optimal Solution to Minimum Cost Problem Where
$C = $ Cost

Another way to use your spacial intuition is to think of the objective function $x_1 + x_2$ as forming an absolutely flat but slanting roof over the whole x_1, x_2 plane as x_1 and x_2 increase, so that the parallel lines shown in figure 10.6 indicate the height of the flat roof. You should then see that the lowest height of the roof must occur at one of the corners just as the highest height must occur at some other corner, so that intuitively you can see why the search for the minimum or maximum need only examine the corners. Obviously, there are pitfalls in any spacial intuition, so that these statements need to be backed up by clear-cut deductive reasoning. Also, when there are more than three variables, so that, say, $2x_1 + 3x_2 + x_3$ is the objective function, then the "house" becomes four-dimensional with a three-dimensional "floor," and your spacial intuition may have some trouble working. But it can be shown that the principles applying to well-constructed two-dimensional problems apply also to *n* dimensions so long as linearity assumptions hold.

With this interpretation in mind, instead of having to check the infinite number of feasible solutions that appeared inside *ABCDE* in figure 10.5, you need check only the five feasible corners, *A, B, C, D,* and *E.* Thus, a problem with an infinite number of feasible decisions can be solved by checking a finite number of feasible corner solutions! The simplex method of Dantzig does exactly that; it algebraically searches the corner solutions until it reaches the one which optimizes the objective function. (The corner solutions are called "basic" solutions in algebra.)

With the use of high-speed computers, problems with many, many constraints and many variables can be solved by the simplex method. It is not necessary, at this time, for you to learn the algebraic details of the simplex method; but suffice it to say that the method uses the idea of Gaussian elimination, after first transforming the inequalities into equalities by adding new variables. The simplex method then goes from one feasible corner solution to the next in such a way that each new corner solution is *adjacent* graphically to the previous one examined. The adjacent solution is chosen so that it gives a *better* value of the objective function than the previous solution. That is, if the objective function calls for maximization, a "better value" is a higher value, but if it is minimization, a better value is a smaller one, as in the Belinda Beauty Products problem. If you come to a corner where all the adjacent corners give "worse" values, you stop since the current solution is best.

The major algebraic steps in this simplex algorithm can be seen graphically by means of another LP problem.

Problem: Poipu Sugar Company

As general manager of Poipu Sugar, you are trying to prepare for distribution of the current cane harvest. You make $6 profit on each ton of unrefined sugar, and $7 on each ton of sugar you refine at Poipu. You have 12,000 human work hours available and it takes 2 human work hours for each ton of unrefined sugar, and 3 for each refined ton. You also have limited packing facilities (8000 hours available) and a ton of unrefined sugar takes two hours to pack, while a ton of refined sugar takes an hour.

Your refinery facilities cannot handle more than 3000 tons of refined sugar during this harvest period. To maximize profits, how much of each should you produce?

Analysis: To formulate the mathematical model, you can begin as before with the decision variables:

$$x_1 = \text{number of tons of unrefined sugar}$$
$$x_2 = \text{number of tons of refined sugar}$$

The objective is to maximize your profit:

Maximize $6x_1 + 7x_2$

subject to the constraints

$$2x_1 + 3x_2 \leq 12,000 \qquad (1)$$
$$2x_1 + x_2 \leq 8000 \qquad (2)$$
$$x_2 \leq 3000 \qquad (3)$$
$$x_1, x_2 \geq 0 \qquad (4), (5)$$

where (1) represents the humanpower constraint, (2) is the packaging constraint, (3) is the limit on refining, and (4) and (5) are the usual nonnegativity constraints. The feasible region is depicted in figure 10.8.

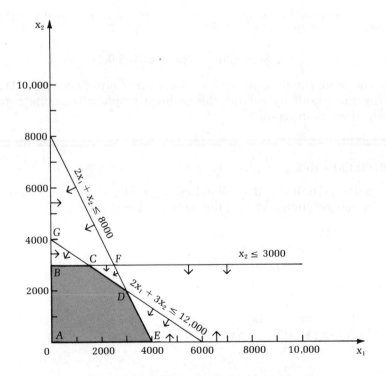

Figure 10.8 Feasible Region for Poipu Sugar

The simplex method starts with one of the *feasible* corners as its initial feasible corner solution. In this case, $x_1 = 0$, $x_2 = 0$ is an obvious starting point. Profits at (0, 0) are zero, since

$$6(0) + 7(0) = 0$$

The procedure then "moves" to point B, which is also a *feasible* corner solution whose profit is

$$\$6(0) + \$7(3000) = \$21,000$$

since at B, $x_1 = 0$, $x_2 = 3000$ tons. The next adjacent corner solution which improves the profit objective is C (G violates (3)) where $x_1 = 1500$ tons and $x_2 = 3000$ tons; so at C

$$\$6(1500) + \$7(3000) = \$30,000 \text{ profit}$$

Moving next to D (F is not feasible since it violates (1)), the solution is $x_1 = 3000$ tons, $x_2 = 2000$ tons, and profit is

$$\$6(3000) + \$7(2000) = \$32,000$$

The simplex method stops here, since moving to E would result in a *decrease* in profit:

$$\$6(4000) + \$7(0) = \$24,000$$

So you refine 2000 tons and package 3000 unrefined tons. Try to verify this result by solving the problem graphically, using parallel profit lines as in figure 10.7.

PROBLEMS 10.2

1. Solve graphically the following LP problems by (1) checking the corner solutions, and (2) the method of parallel lines.

   a. Maximize $x_1 + x_2$
      subject to $x_1 - x_2 \leq 1$
      $$4x_1 + 6x_2 \geq 24$$
      $$x_1 \geq 2$$
      $$x_2 \geq 0$$

   b. Minimize $x_1 + 3x_2$
      subject to $10x_1 + 15x_2 \leq 150$
      $$5x_1 + 10x_2 \geq 50$$
      $$x_1 - x_2 \geq 0$$
      $$x_1 \leq 6$$
      $$x_1 \geq 0, x_2 \geq 0$$

2. Gloria's Construction Corp. produces prefabricated housing units. She does it in two departments: casting and finishing. She can make two types of units: Mendocino and Bolinas, each of which requires processing in each of the two departments. The Mendocino units generate a $200 profit per unit; the Bolinas units, $250. The Mendocino requires 200 hours of casting time and 120 hours of finishing time. The Bolinas requires 100 casting hours and 200 finishing hours. Gloria has a 2000-hour daily capacity in the casting department and a 2400-hour capacity in the finishing department. Unfortunately, because of a severe materials shortage, Gloria must limit her production to a maximum of nine Bolinas units per day. How many units of each type should she produce?

3. Batami Software Corp. produces two kinds of software packages: Herzlia and Oded. The Herzlia contributes $600 profits per package sold while the Oded contributes $500. Both software packages require the time of Batami as well as the time of her lowly assistant Jean. The Herzlia requires 40 hours of Batami's time and 40 hours of Jean's time for implementation. The Oded requires 30 hours of Batami's time and 50 hours of Jean's. Batami has 400 hours available per month and lowly Jean is willing to work 600 hours. There is great demand for both packages so that they can sell as many of each package as they have time to implement. How many of each package should they sell each month to maximize profits?
   a. Solve this problem graphically by checking all the feasible corner solutions.
   b. Solve the problem graphically by using parallel profit lines.

4. Jackie's Publishing Company produces *Pet House* magazine. The magazine has been concerned about the quality of paper in their issues. Jackie uses pulp and ash as the basic ingredients for the magazine's paper. Each ounce of pulp costs 6¢ and each ounce of ash costs 10¢. An ounce of pulp contains 5 grams of fine paper material, 3 grams of medium paper material, and 5 grams of coarse paper material. Each ounce of ash contains 3 grams of fine, 6 grams of medium, and 2 grams of coarse material. To be safe Jackie feels she had better use at least 12 grams of fine, 12 grams of medium, and 10 grams of coarse material in each page. What is the lowest-cost mix of pulp and ash that will satisfy *Pet House* magazine demands?
   a. Solve the problem by checking the corner solutions.
   b. Solve the problem by using parallel cost lines.

10.3 Shadow Prices and Duality

10.3.1 Shadow Prices The decision maker in the above LP problems has had to decide the levels of various *activities* which are under his or her control: how much sugar to refine, how much TV advertising to purchase. The *resources* at the disposal of the decision maker have been a part of the state of the world he faces: 8000 human hours available, $100,000 budget. But quite often, particularly in long-range planning, the decision maker has the opportunity to alter his resources. For example, you may be able to obtain more human hours through hiring or get a larger advertising budget if you can justify it. In such cases, the "right-hand side" of the constraint inequality is a part of your decision, and it turns out that another aspect of the linear programming problem can aid greatly with these resource decisions.

Problem: Poipu Sugar Company Revisited ─────────────

Kapa Kapagamos has returned to Poipu for summer vacation from the University of Hawaii and offers to work for you for the summer for $4 per hour. Is her labor worth the cost to you?

Analysis: Again ignoring the larger systems questions (for example: How will a "college kid" affect morale? How does her pay rate compare with other salaries?), your problem is whether to buy an additional unit of the resource "human-hours" at $4 per unit. The question is equivalent to asking the value *to you* of an additional human-hour. Such a value is called a *shadow price* or *implicit price*. It is the highest "price" *you* should be willing to pay for the additional human-hour without losing on it. *It is not, in general, necessarily equal to Kapa's value on the open labor market*. This type of question may seem familiar to you if you read Marginal Analysis in chapter 3. This time, however, the answer is not as straightforward. One way to attack the problem is to solve the LP over again, changing constraint (1) to include an additional human-hour:

$$2x_1 + 3x_2 \leq 12,001$$

The new LP solution may have a new profit figure (perhaps not, since you may not be using all your human-power at 12,000), and the difference between the two is the value to you of one additional hour of labor.

───

But it can be shown that there is *another* LP problem, associated with the *original* LP problem, which reveals the shadow price of *all* the resources (not only labor). This associated problem is called the *dual*; and to distinguish, the original problem is called the *primal*.

10.3.2 The Dual Problem You can begin to understand the relationship between the primal and the dual if you consider two very simple problems.

Problem: Making Sleds ━━━━━━━━━━━━━━━━━━━━━━━

You make sleds in your garage and can make a sure profit of $4 on each one you make. It takes you an hour to make a sled, and you only have 100 hours per month available. How many sleds should you make each month in order to maximize your profit?

Analysis: In the LP format, this problem is

$$\text{Maximize } 4x$$

$$\text{subject to the constraints } x \le 100$$

$$x \ge 0$$

where x is the number of sleds you make per month. A little reflection will reveal that you should produce as many sleds as possible — that is, 100 — and you'll make $400 profit.

━━

Problem: The Cost of Making Sleds ━━━━━━━━━━━━━━━━━━━

Now suppose you realize that you have 100 hours available that you are spending by making sleds. You'd like to minimize the *cost* of making sleds, and since the garage is free, that means you'd like to minimize the cost of your total time spent. Since you can always make sleds with your time, you know your time is worth at least $4 per hour. What is the minimum cost to you of making sleds?

Analysis: This can be described by the LP

$$\text{Minimize } 100y \qquad \text{subject to } y \ge 4$$

where y is the (implicit) price of your time. The obvious solution is $y = 4$, and the minimum cost is $400. This new LP is the *dual* of the LP in the Making Sleds problem.

━━

What have the two problems to do with each other? In the first, the emphasis is on what you can make in the way of profit; in the second, the emphasis is on how you can minimize the cost of making the profit. The decision in the first is how many hours of your own time to spend on making sleds; in the second, it is how much an hour of your time is worth, or the "price" to you of using up your valuable resource of time (100 hours).

Interestingly enough, the solutions to the primal and dual problems yield equal values; the profit is equal to the cost. This may seem a little strange at first, but if you think like an accountant for a moment, and allocate a share of profits to all the resources (including, for example, the owner's time or his investment of capital), then it makes sense. The $400 is profit, but it costs you 100 hours to make the profit; if they are to balance, as all accounts must, then all the profits will be allocated to the various resources.

Of course, these two problems are a bit oversimplified, to say the least, since there are other resources involved and you can do other things with your time, which might be worth more than $4 per hour.

Problem: Super Sleds ──────────────────────────

Your sled business is growing, and you have discovered a market for "super sleds," on which you make $8 profit. But the "super sleds" take an hour and a half to make, and you can only sell 12 of these per month. How many of these (if any) should you make per month?

Analysis: This problem can also be solved as an LP:

Maximize $4x_1 + 8x_2$

subject to $x_1 + 1.5x_2 \le 100$, $x_2 \le 12$, $x_1 \ge 0$, $x_2 \ge 0$

where

$$x_1 = \text{the number of sleds}$$
$$x_2 = \text{the number of super sleds}$$

You can solve this graphically, if you like, by checking the corner points or using parallel profit lines. The solution is

$$x_1 = 82, \qquad x_2 = 12$$

and your profit is

$$4(82) + 8(12) = \$424$$

So, you make 12 super sleds, and spend the rest of your 100 hours making regular sleds.

Problem: The Cost of Making Sleds and Super Sleds ──────────

Now you want to know: "What is my time worth now? What is my time worth while I'm making sleds? And would it be worthwhile to go out and drum up some more business for my super sleds?" Again, you want to minimize the cost of getting business and making sleds in terms of your time; how can you do it?

Analysis: This can be described by the LP:

$$\text{Miminize } 100y_1 + 12y_2$$
$$\text{subject to } y_1 \geq 4$$
$$1.5y_1 + y_2 \geq 8$$
$$y_2 \geq 0$$

where y_1 is again the value of your time while making sleds, and y_2 is the value of drumming up additional super-sled business. The solution is

$$y_1 = 4, \qquad y_2 = 2$$

which means that getting one additional order for a super sled is worth only $2, while an additional hour making sleds is worth $4. So if you're going to put more time into your sled business, continue making regular sleds unless you can find more than two new super-sled customers in each hour you spend drumming up business.

You should again notice that $424 is the total current cost to you of your business, which is exactly equal to the profit in the Super Sleds problem.

What are these dual "shadow" prices, y_1 and y_2? They are exactly the value *to you* of changing the right-hand side of the primal constraints in the Super Sleds problem from 100 to 101, and from 12 to 13, respectively. Thus the dual "shadow" price of a human-hour in Poipu Sugar should tell you what the value of hiring Kapa's time is.

10.3.3 The Relationship Between the Primal and Dual Problems

The correspondence between the dual and primal problems in the Poipu Sugar problem can be seen in figure 10.9: the "dual" is a *new* LP problem; the dual objective is to minimize (the "primal" objective was to maximize), the right-hand side of the dual (dual resource constraints of six and seven dollars) are the primal objective coefficients, and the dual objective coefficients are the primal right-hand side (resource constraints of 12,000 hours, etc.). There are three dual variables (y_1, y_2, y_3) and two dual constraints ((D1), (D2)) besides the nonnegativity constraints; there are two primal variables (x_1, x_2) and three primal constraints besides the nonnegativity conditions. So everything is flipped around! Even the inequalities are in opposite directions (primal $\leq$, dual $\geq$)! And if you flip the dual (pretend for a moment that the dual is the original problem), you get the primal back again! So "*the dual of the dual is the primal*" (six and seven dollars become objective coefficients, you maximize instead of minimize, etc.).

Primal Problem		*Dual Problem*	
Maximize	$6x_1 + 7x_2$	Minimize	$12{,}000y_1 + 8000y_2$
			$+ 3000y_3$
subject to		subject to	
$2x_1 + 3x_2 \leq 12{,}999$	(1)	$2y_1 + 2y_2 \geq 6$	(D1)
$2x_1 + x_2 \leq 8000$	(2)	$3y_1 + y_2 + y_3 \geq 7$	(D2)
$x_2 \leq 3000$	(3)	$y_1, y_2, y_3 \geq 0$	
$x_1, x_2 \geq 0$			

Figure 10.9   Primal and Dual of Poipu Sugar

Well, all of this is perhaps interesting, perhaps a bit confusing; but what about all the information that's supposed to assist you in deciding on hiring Kapa? Let's examine the elements of Poipu's dual problem. First, the dual in this problem minimizes an objective function which is made up of three new variables, y_1, y_2, y_3. It turns out that when the dual problem is solved, the dual objective function has the same optimal value as the best primal objective function as in the various sled problems. So if you solve both, the optimal objective functions have the same value. In this light, the dual objective function can be thought of as the total *value* of the resources in the primal problem; at dual optimality this is equal to the optimal (primal) profit from (or cost of, if the primal minimizes cost) using these resources. In Poipu sugar, the dual problem is to find optimal *shadow prices* (y_1, y_2, y_3) of one unit of each resource (human-hours, packing facilities, refining facilities) so that you minimize the total cost of using these resources. At the minimum, the sum of the shadow prices of the resources (the dual objective function) is equal to the profit from those resources (the primal objective function). So solving the dual yields the optimal value of y_1, the value of one human-hour, which is the highest price you would be willing to pay young Ms. Kapagama. Solving the dual by the simplex method yields

$$y_1 = \$2$$

which is less than the \$4 asked, so you don't hire Kapa.

It turns out, however, that you need not solve the dual problem by the simplex method all over again once you have solved the primal problem. This is because of the relationship of the *constraints* in the dual to the *variables* in the primal, and vice versa. The dual variables, at optimality, give the value of the primal resources at optimality. If the primal optimal solution is such that you are not using up all of some resource, an additional unit must be worth nothing to you. For example, since $x_2 = 2000$ at optimality, adding extra refining facilities to the 3000 tons' capacity is not worth anything to you. In other words, y_3, representing the price or value to you of an additional unit of refining facility, is zero at dual optimality. Now recall that the primal is the dual of the dual. So x_1 and x_2, at primal optimality, represent the value of changing the right-hand side of constraints (D1) and (D2) by one unit. But, in the optimal solution, x_1 and x_2 are positive ($x_1 = 3000$, $x_2 = 2000$); whatever "resources" are represented by (D1) and (D2) must be of some positive value, so you must be using up all of the current "resources." In other words, since $x_1 > 0$ and $x_2 > 0$, the optimal solution to the dual problem *must* use up all of the right-hand sides of (D1) and (D2). So *equality* must hold in constraints (D1) and (D2). With the knowledge that $y_3 = 0$, you can now solve the two equations (D1) and (D2) in two unknowns, y_1 and y_2. Using Gaussian elimination of chapter 9, the solution is $y_1 = 2$, $y_2 = 1$, $y_3 = 0$. So the "shadow prices" are: $0 for additional refining facilities, $1 for additional packaging hours, and $2 for additional human-hours, as we said. We will see how to use this in a problem in a moment.

10.3.4 Summary and Extension of Duality

You've probably just had your mind blown by these revelations about the dual problem, the information it provides, and some of its interpretations and uses; there is even more to follow. But you can take a breath for the moment, and we'll review what's been said so far.

The original LP problem now has a name: the primal linear programming problem, called "the primal" for short. From it, you can write down a closely associated LP problem, called the dual LP problem, or just "the dual." The following relationships hold between the primal and dual problems:

1. The objective of the dual is opposite of that of the primal: if one maximizes, the other minimizes.

2. The constraints in one are associated with the variables in the other, excluding nonnegativity constraints. The dual has the same number of constraints as the primal has variables; the dual has the same number of variables as the primal has constraints.

3. The direction of the inequalities is opposite; for example, $\leq$ in the primal becomes $\geq$ in the dual.

4. The "right-hand side," or resources available, in one are the coefficients of the objective function in the other.

5. Both have nonnegativity constraints on all the variables.

6. At optimality, the primal and dual objective functions are equal. The dual objective function can be interpreted as the total cost of the primal resources.

7. The dual variables, at optimality, represent "shadow prices" on the primal resources; the primal variables are shadow prices on the dual "resources." Thus, the dual variables' optimal value tells you how much you'd be willing to pay for an additional unit of the corresponding primal resource.

8. The information from (7) can be used to solve one problem directly if the other has been solved by the simplex or graphically; for example, if a primal variable at optimality is positive, the corresponding dual constraint must be an equality. If a primal constraint is not "tight"—that is, if all of the primal resource is *not* being used at optimality and strict inequality holds—the corresponding dual variable or shadow price is zero. This reduces the solution of one of the problems to solving a system of equations. To check the solution, see if primal and dual objectives are equal.

9. The dual of the dual is the primal; that is, the two problems are completely symmetric, and what holds for a primal-dual relationship holds for a dual-primal relationship.

10. Finally, if you are just interested in solving the primal, you may find the dual easier to solve computationally, and then use its solution to solve the primal as indicated in (8).

As promised, there is even more. With the interpretation of dual variables as the shadow prices of the primal resources, the *dual constraints* can now be interpreted. First, the dual nonnegativity constraints simply say that the shadow prices cannot go below zero; at worst, an additional unit of a resource is worthless to you. Now look at constraint (D1) in figure 10.9:

$$2y_1 + 2y_2 \geq 6$$

Since the y's are shadow prices, and since their coefficients (2 and 2) are the amounts of the resources "human-hours" and "packaging hours" used up by activity x_1, (D1) says that prices y_1 and y_2 should be determined in such a way that "shadow cost" or "imputed cost" of activity x_1 should not be less than its profit, $6. In fact, at optimality, you have seen that in the case of the activity x_1, constraint (D1) is "tight" (equality holds) so the imputed price of the activity is *equal* to its profit contribution. Recall that the strict inequality holds if the primal activity level is zero; this makes sense, since the dual inequality says that the imputed cost of the activity is greater than the profit from the activity; so optimally it is not worth it to engage in such an activity. Let's reexamine all of these dual results with an example.

Problem: Truckin' Shoes ━━━━━━━━━━━━━━━━━━━━━━━━━━━━━━

Truckin' Shoes produces shoes and luxury slippers for sale to retailers. A pair of shoes yields $2 profit and a pair of slippers $6. There are three scarce resources involved in the production process: (1) There are 5000 cubic feet of warehouse space available and a pair of shoes takes up four cubic feet while a pair of slippers take up only one cubic foot on the average. (2) There are 7000 hours of machine time available. Two machine hours are needed per pair of slippers, while shoes take up three machine hours per pair. (3) You have hired 2000 hours of inspection and packing time, and each type of footwear takes one hour per pair. How should the firm split up its production so as to maximize its profit? What are the meaning and value of each of the dual constraints and variables?

Analysis: To answer the first question, you set up the problem as an LP by defining:

$$x_1 = \text{number of pairs of shoes produced}$$
$$x_2 = \text{number of pairs of slippers produced}$$

The "primal" problem is then:

$$\text{Maximize } 2x_1 + 6x_2$$

subject to $4x_1 + x_2 \leq 5000$	(1)
$3x_1 + 2x_2 \leq 7000$	(2)
$x_1 + x_2 \leq 2000$	(3)
$x_1 \text{ and } x_2 \geq 0$	

Solving the problem graphically or by the simplex, the optimal solution is

$$x_1 = 0, \ x_2 = 2000, \ \text{profit} = \$12,000$$

that is, produce 2000 slippers and no shoes! The graphical solution is portrayed in figure 10.10, where $ABCD$ is the feasible region, and B is the optimal profit point.

The "dual" problem is

$$\text{Minimize } 5000y_1 + 7000y_2 + 2000y_3$$

subject to $4y_1 + 3y_2 + y_3 \geq 2$	(D1)
$y_1 + 2y_2 + y_3 \geq 6$	(D2)
$y_1, y_2, y_3 \geq 0$	

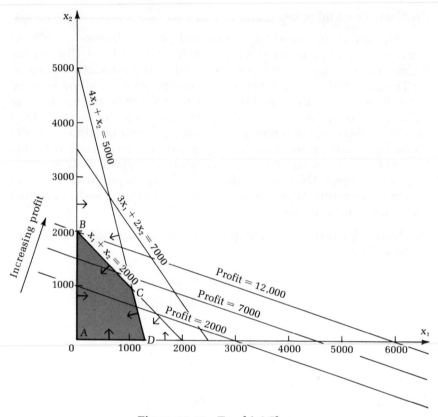

Figure 10.10   Truckin' Shoes

To solve the dual, using the primal solution, first use the fact that the only constraint which is "tight" at optimality in the primal is (3); therefore y_1 and y_2, corresponding to shadow prices on warehouse space and machine time, must be zero! So, looking at (D1) and (D2), you see that $y_3 \geq 2$, and $y_3 \geq 6$ are the effective constraints. But since $x_1 = 0$, (D1) must not be "tight," while $x_2 > 0$ means (D2) must be "tight"; that is, equality holds in (D2), so $y_3 = 6$. Thus, $y_1 = 0$, $y_2 = 0$, $y_3 \doteq 6$ is the solution to the dual. We can check this by the objective function:

$$5000(0) + 7000(0) + 2000(6) = 12,000$$

So the primal and dual optimal objective functions are equal.

What is the interpretation of all this? Well, to begin with, $y_3 = 6$ says that an additional hour of inspection and packaging time is worth $6; that is, you should be willing to pay that much to acquire more of it. (You already noted that you are not constrained by your warehouse or machine facilities—y_1 and y_2 are zero). In addition, using the shadow prices, you can interpret constraint (D1),

$$4(0) + 3(0) + 6 \geq 2$$

as saying that if you were to produce a unit of x_1 (shoes), you would *lose* $(6-2) = 4$ dollars, since the total shadow cost of shoes is \$6, while the profit is \$2. This is the *opportunity cost* or the cost of the lost opportunity (chapter 4) of producing shoes and not slippers. On the other hand, (D2) tells you, as it should, that the imputed cost of slippers is

$$0 + 2(0) + 6 = \$6,$$

which is equal to the price of slippers, \$6.

PROBLEMS 10.3

1. Interpret the meaning of the shadow price for the second primal constraint in the Poipu Sugar problem.

2. Interpret the meaning of the shadow price for the third primal constraint in the Poipu Sugar problem.

3. What are the shadow prices in Gloria's Construction Company (problem 2 of section 10.2)?

4. Set up the dual to the following problems:
   a. Maximize $12x_1 + 15x_2$
   subject to $4x_1 + 3x_2 \leq 12$
   $2x_1 + 5x_2 \leq 10$
   $x_1 \geq 0, x_2 \geq 0$
   b. Maximize $x_1 - 2x_2 + 3x_3$
   subject to $x_1 + x_2 + x_3 \leq 7$
   $x_1 - x_2 + x_3 \leq 2$
   $x_1 \geq 0, x_2 \geq 0, x_3 \geq 0$
   c. Maximize $5x_1$
   subject to $4x_1 - 2x_2 \leq 12$
   $x_1 + x_2 \leq 3$
   $x_1 \geq 0, x_2 \geq 0$

5. Solve graphically the primal and dual in problem 4 (a) and show that the optimal objective functions are equal.

6. Write down the dual to Batami's Software problem in the previous section (problem 3, section 10.2) and interpret:
   a. the dual variables
   b. the dual constraints
   c. the dual objective function

7. Show in problem 4 (a, b, c) above that "the dual of the dual is the primal."

10.4 Extensions of Linear Programming

Useful discoveries about LP problems did not end with duality. In fact, the dual problem and the nature of its relationship to the primal has led to the development of solution techniques which are sometimes computationally more efficient than the simplex method. As mentioned, you might want to solve the dual problem if it is easier; methods have been developed which alternately use interim corner solution in the primal and dual to arrive at optimality in fewer steps. Since problems involving transporting goods often have linear technologies (for example, it costs 10 times as much to transport goods 100 miles as 10), LP turns out to be a good model of many problems involving transportation of goods. The *primal* transportation problem minimizes the cost of a series of source locations to a series of destinations by choosing how much to send from and to each. The *dual* of a transportation problem turns out to have a special structure; it is quite easy to solve without going through the sometimes numerous simplex computations, and much computer space and time can be saved by using a technique called the "transportation method" on the dual problem. Some "transshipment" problems (transportation problems with intermediate destinations) can be put in LP form, and the dual is again easy to solve without resort to simplex. Other problems involving the assignment of, say, people to jobs can sometimes easily be solved by a technique called the "assignment method"; this method also exploits the special structures of the primal LP "assignment model" representing minimization of labor time or maximization of some measure of job efficiency.

Other developments in LP have organizational implications; a large-scale informationally decentralized organization's decision procedures can sometimes by approximated by "decomposing" an LP representation of the firm. The "central office" is assumed to know the objective function of the firm while "local" decentralized managers don't. Their knowledge consists of the availability of resources and technologies (coefficients) in their individual localities. The managers make local decisions on activity levels of the variables under their control and transmit tentative decisions (interim corner solutions) to the head office, which can force changes in the decisions by imposing "shadow prices" on the resources.

The important lesson from all this is that although at first a problem's solution may appear sufficient for decision-making purposes, there may be tremendous potential for information lurking in the problem itself or in the interpretation of some associated quantitative method like the dual. Further, computational efficiency may be saved by searching for more efficient solution techniques. But before over-zealousness about LP sets in, you should be aware of the strong assumptions of linear programming: linearity of the objective function and constraints; complete knowledge of the resource constraints, the technology, and the objective function—that is, the coefficients and the measure of performance; separability and additivity in the objective function and the constraints (see section 3.7). Not many situations satisfy all these assumptions, so despite the appeal of LP and duality, you should be careful about applying LP.

Furthermore, all the remarks about the reality of the model given at the end of the last chapter apply equally well to LP. The temptation to throw in another constraint "just to see what it means" may lead to ridiculous results masquerading as the truth.

But, more to the point, you should realize the tremendously strong assumptions which LP makes, which you can readily understand through the interpretation we have given of the dual. Consider the very simple example of the manufacture and sale of the sleds. Suppose that somewhere in your world a job awaits you which pays you $4.10 an hour. If so, to maximize profits you would produce *no* sleds, and the dual would show *not* a $4 shadow price for making sleds—but a zero price! The discovery of one more alternative changes the whole nature of the model. To use a more dramatic example, there exists an LP of an oil company which is reputed to involve 2,000,000 variables and over 35,000 constraint equations. Suppose now that engineers are able to tap solar energy for virtually all uses—heating, transportation, lighting, etc.—at a cost far less than the price of oil. Then, from a national-economy point of view, the shadow prices of all the two million variables might very well vanish to zero!

You should understand, therefore, that LP makes very strong "whole system" assumptions, and that a manager could very well get himself boxed into a model by assuming he knows all the alternative resources just because the model says so. This does not detract from the value of an LP, but the wise decision maker should not merely say "so that's what I should do," but rather "I suspect the result and wonder what's wrong with it."

Next, you should realize the strong causal assumptions in LP. If you write down max $z = 3x_1 + 7x_2 + x_3$, you are assuming that you as a decision maker can cause x_1, x_2, and x_3 to change, and that where you do cause a change, the change in turn causes the specified changes in z (for example, a one-unit change in x_1 *causes* a three-unit change in z). In the case of the sleds, this causal chain may have been more or less obvious, but often we try to infer the causal links from past data. For example, using data on a large number of communities, you may find a positive relationship exists between the dollars a community spends on education and the average income of the community (obviously using other variables such as location and ethnic mix). Thus if you plotted educational expenditure of each community versus average income, you might see an approximate straight-line relation: the higher the educational expenditure the higher the average income. If your aim is to maximize community income, you might then be tempted to use your graph in an LP model. But to do so, you'd have to assume that increasing educational funds in a community *causes* increased income. This might well be a fallacious assumption for at least two reasons: (1) you are injecting a sudden increase of funds, which none of the communities of your study had ever done before, so that your data tell you nothing about the causal effects of such an action; (2) your graph *aggregates* or averages over a great many communities and ignores the unique social and political forces that may occur in the specific community where you may want to place the educational funds. The point is that the relationship you have set up based upon the past data may completely miss any real causal linkages that exist. When constructing a model like LP, you must be very careful to realize that you are assuming causal relationships over the whole relevant range of the variables.

But above all you should understand the deep philosophical assumptions that lie behind the instructions "maximize z" and "minimize z." These instructions assume that there is one unifying "measure of performance" and that it is ethically right to make this measure as high (or as low) as possible. For example, in the case of a community, is it ethically correct to say that the community ought to maximize average income? Surely not, if it does so only by increasing the incomes of the wealthy. Besides, should we condone a wealthy, crooked community? Then what is the measure of performance of a community? No one knows, and many people doubt that there is one or should be one. LP assumes that such a measure exists, and that a reasonable approximation can be made to it. LP is therefore based on a philosophical assumption called "monism," whose deadly enemy is "pluralism," which sees a world of conflicting and irresolvable values. Of course, you may try to live in the best of the two worlds, using monism if you're the boss, pluralism if you're not. In any event, you should realize that philosophically speaking, applications of LP may be ethically wrong.

We should also point out that both the primal and the dual permit us to assess how critical the coefficients and constraints really are. To return (for the last time) to sleds, the dual may show that the coefficient of one dollar for making the "super" is not very critical, because if you're off even 100 percent (say it's really two dollars), it doesn't matter: the shadow price of the "super" is still zero. We call this assessment of the importance of the data "sensitivity analysis"; you should be able to see how sensitivity analysis could be used in larger LP. But no amount of sensitivity analysis will respond to the doubts raised above:

Is there another alternative, and does this alternative cause such-and-such a change?

You should also know that LP is a door to many other marvels of the kingdom of models. We can create curvaceous mathematical models, for example, in which either the objective function is nonlinear ($z = x_1^2 + 5x_1x_2 + x_2^2$) or the constraints are nonlinear ($\sqrt{x_1 + x_2} \leq 100$). We can also introduce probabilities by describing the probability distribution of either the coefficients or the constraints, or both. We can require that the assignment of a resource come out as a whole number, as in the sled example; we call this model "integer programming." It's a large and happy land, this kingdom of models; you can go live in it for your lifetime without once leaving it or worrying about the rest of the world "out there." Happy days!

PROBLEMS 10.4

1. Your efforts in advertising Belinda's Beauty Products have been very gratifying. Belinda is flooded with orders. The demand is concentrated in three regions: at least 5000 units in the Valley of the Mills, and at least 20,000 units in each of the regions Berkwii and Yorq. Belinda's manufacturing plants, however, are located in three other regions—Paul City, Susan Village, and Marshall Town—with production capacity of 20,000 units, 15,000 units, and 10,000 units, respectively. So you must decide on how to allocate the output of the plants to the three markets. You choose to adopt an allocation plan that minimizes the total cost of shipment. You know that the shipping costs per unit from the various plants to the three markets are as given in the table below.

    Prepare for your decision by setting up the problem as a linear program.

Plant / Market	Paul City	Susan Village	Marshall Town
Valley of the Mills	$ .90	$1.00	$1.00
Berkwii	$1.00	$1.40	$.80
Yorg	$1.30	$1.00	$.80

2. Suppose that Belinda owns two warehouses in Ware and in House and all its products to the three market-regions are transshipped through these warehouses. The shipping costs between the ware-

houses and the plants and markets are given in the table below. The capacity of each warehouse is 22,500 units. How should you decide on the shipping network now? Formulate the linear program of the problem to assist you in the decision.

Plant/Market — Warehouse	Ware	House
Valley of the Mills	$.40	$.50
Berkwii	.60	.25
Yorq	.80	.70
Paul City	.30	.55
Susan Village	.65	.75
Marshall Town	.50	.45

3. As an assistant to the dean you are in charge of assigning the 28 sections of courses to the 28 available classrooms. You know that certain assignments are ruled out because of large enrollment in some sections, schedule conflicts, etc. How can you prepare for your assignment decision? Formulate the problem.

4. Can you think of an organization which fits the information requirements of a "decomposed" linear program? Describe it in detail.

5. What causal and whole systems assumptions have been made in the Poipu Sugar problem and the associated problem brought on by Kapa Kapagamos?

10.5   Summary

In this chapter we have examined again problems with a linear structure; but inequalities described the constraints on your resources, and you had a linear objective function for choosing between alternatives. We should point out that the problems presented in the chapter were intentionally simple, for purposes of explanation; in reality, LP and the simplex algorithm are most useful in large-scale decision-making problems. The following points are worth repeating:

a. When the constraints on your resources are in the form of inequalities, there may be many "feasible" solutions to your decision problem.

b. In order to choose between these, you may be able to formulate an objective function, which specifies how your decision variables combine in a single measure of performance.

c. If the constraints and objective function are linear, the problem is called a Linear Programming problem, and you can use the simplex algorithm to solve it; if only two variables are involved, you can solve the problem graphically using parallel lines representing different values of the objective function.

d. Associated with every LP problem there is a dual problem, which provides a great deal of information about "shadow prices" on the resources and "opportunity costs" of various decisions; the dual can also be solved by means of the simplex method and then used to solve the primal by accounting for the relationships between the dual and primal variables and constraints.

e. There are many extensions of linear programming, and many uses in large-scale decision problems, but the assumptions of linearity, causality, and monism must be carefully scrutinized before you attempt to use the results.

11 The Use of Rates of Change in Decision Making: Calculus

11.1 Introduction

In order to appreciate the next step in using quantitative methods to prepare for decisions, you should realize something that we've already mentioned in earlier chapters: How one thing changes with respect to another often makes a big difference in your decision making.

One of the most common examples is how distance traveled changes with respect to time. If you have a date an hour from now which is twenty miles from your home, then you know that you'll have to average twenty miles an hour to make it; "twenty miles an hour" means that as your distance changes from twenty to zero miles, time will change from zero to one hour. The word for the change in distance relative to the change in time is "velocity." But, often, consideration of velocity is not enough to prepare for decisions about travel. Suppose your route involves a lot of stop signs though the traffic is light, If your car has a lot of pep, you can do much better than if it's sluggish. What does "pep" mean? It means you can get your velocity from zero up to the speed limit rather quickly. In this case, you're interested in the way in which velocity changes with time, and we call the relative change "acceleration." A sluggish car accelerates slowly.

An amazing amount of your decision making involves calculations about things like velocities and accelerations, but these are not the only relative changes that interest you. For example, costs vary with respect to changes in all kinds of things, like number of products, number of children, number of employees—and not necessarily linearly, as was the case in chapters 9 and 10. If it costs you $1000 to manufacture 100 ski boots, it may cost you only $1500 to manufacture 200, because the original costs for machinery can be spread more widely in the second case. Similarly, changes in revenue will vary depending on the size of the lot of goods you plan to sell. You may have read our discussion of such changes in chapter 3, where we confined ourselves to discrete units of change. There we used marginal analysis to describe changes in cost and revenue, relative to *unit* increases or decreases in items produced, boxes ordered, etc. In this chapter we consider relative changes in the continuous case, distance versus time, velocity versus time, pounds of sugar manufactured versus cost, hours of service rendered versus hours of labor time.

11.1.1 Continuous Decision Alternatives From time to time in this book we have introduced the idea that the set D of alternative decisions may be very large. Consider, for example, a fairly simple case of a manufacturer of pharmaceuticals. His equipment mixes various powders together and forms them into pills which are bottled and distributed. He orders the basic powders from other chemical companies. How much of each powder should be ordered at any given time?

If you think about this problem in the usual fashion, you can see that for each amount (for example, weight) of powder he orders, there are some relevant outcomes. If he orders a whole lot of a powder, then it may sit around for quite awhile before it is used. As a consequence, the outcome of ordering a large quantity may include spoilage; it also includes tying up his capital in idle inventory; it may also include taxes, storage costs, and other similar outcomes. On the other hand, if he orders a very little at a time, then the outcome will include the repeated cost of placing the order, increased transportation costs, and perhaps the danger of shortages. So the analytic problem is to find the right (optimal) middle ground between ordering too much and too little. But the set D contains as elements "order X pounds of this specific raw material (powder)," where X can be any number from 0 on up, including whole numbers, rationals, square roots, roots of polynomials, and so on (see the discussion of numbers in chapter 3). The only exceptions seem to be negative numbers and imaginaries! Thus, D contains a "whole lot" of choices. We say that D is "continuous," as opposed to "discrete."

If you have the same problem as the manufacturer with respect to buying sugar or salt for home consumption, the problem usually turns out to be discrete since sugar and salt are sold in boxes or bags that come in discrete steps (for example, one lb., two lbs., etc.). You might be inclined to regard the manufacturer's problem in the same way, arguing that it is "good enough" to examine a few discrete cases of amounts to be ordered, and you would be right in many cases. To resort to a quantitative technique for a continuous D may be a waste of time. But there are many cases where organizations lose large amounts of money by attempting to get along with crude approximations. In this chapter, as we did in chapters 9 and 10, we examine techniques of dealing with a continuous D.

PROBLEMS 11.1

1. Try to describe the changes in your knowledge of quantitative methods with respect to the time you may devote to the study of these materials.

2. How would your knowledge of quantitative methods change with respect to the amount of time you devote to extracurricular activities?

3. What is the direction of change in total production costs with respect to changes in total output? (State your assumptions explicitly.)

4. What is the direction of change you anticipate in government spending with respect to changes in the rate of inflation? (State your assumptions.)

5. If total cost of operations changes by $10 with respect to a one-hour change in machine utilization, and machine utilization changes by 30 minutes with respect to a one-unit change in production, what is the change of total costs with respect to a one-unit change in production?

11.2   The Derivative

Calculus has sometimes gotten a bad reputation among students, probably because it was taught primarily as a mathematical subject. Actually, its first use was in physics, and we will introduce you to it as a physical concept where it is perhaps easier to understand.

Galileo (1564–1642) argued deductively from first principles in his *Dialogues* that if you drop an object and it falls free, it will have constant acceleration. Acceleration, as we said, is the rate of change of velocity over time, and constant acceleration means that the velocity is increasing "steadily." Galileo's theory, which has been tested and confirmed many times, amounts to saying that the distance the object will fall is proportional to the square of the time of fall. We would say, therefore, that the distance d is a function of the time t; in free fall when d is expressed in feet,

$$d = 16t^2 \tag{1}$$

where 16 is approximate (if you want to be fussy, it is about 15.98). Thus after $t = 1$ second the distance is 16 feet, after 2 seconds 16×2^2

$= 16 \times 4 = 64$ feet, and after 3 seconds $16 \times 3^2 = 16 \times 9 = 144$ feet; in other words, if you fell freely from the top of a building 144 feet high, you would have about 3 seconds to enjoy the trip down.

Now think about the velocity of this freely falling object. At distance $d = 0$, it has zero velocity. At 1 second, it has fallen 16 feet. You might want to say that its "average" velocity during the first second was about 8 feet per second, but this would not be very helpful because it is obviously changing its velocity very rapidly. So let's try another approach to understanding the object's velocity still based on averages.

You would like to ask how fast the object is falling (what is its velocity) exactly 1 second after it has dropped. This seems like a sensible enough question as it did to Newton (1642–1727) and Leibniz (1646–1716), who independently studied it. Their idea of how to get an answer to it is extremely simple and ingenious. After 1 second the object has gone 16 feet. How far has it gone after 1.1 seconds? Well, using the function $16t^2$ to find out, we derive

$$16 \times (1.1)^2 = 16 \times (1.21) = 19.36$$

This means that in 1/10 of a second the object fell

$$19.36 - 16 = 3.36 \text{ feet}$$

Since velocity is distance over time, you calculate 3.36 divided by 1/10 and get

$$33.6 \text{ feet per second}$$

This is the velocity of the object at around 1 to 1.1 seconds.

You can refine this estimate by shortening the time to 1.01 seconds. How far did it fall in 1/100 of a second? Using the function (1) again, you get

$$16 \times (1.01)^2 = 16.3216$$

Hence, in the 1/100 of a second it fell $16.3216 - 16 = .3216$ feet, and its calculated velocity was, therefore, .3216 divided by 1/100, which is 32.16.

In 1/1000 of a second, it fell $16(1.001)^2 - 16 = .032016$ feet, and the calculated velocity is 32.016 feet per second.

Now you can see what is happening; you are exploring a series of numbers that begins 33.6, 32.16, 32.016, as you proceed from 1.1 to 1.01 to 1.001, and so on. Furthermore, carrying this a little bit further suggests that the series is approaching 32 very rapidly (try 1.0001 and 1.00001); so why not say that 32 *is* the velocity of the object at exactly 1 second?

Now if you wanted to do the same thing for 2 seconds and 3 seconds and so on, you could, but the calculations become tedious and, more to the point, unnecessary, because you can go into the general answer right away. Instead of talking about 1 second, 2 seconds, and so on, let's talk about t seconds, and instead of talking about 1.1, 1.01, 1.001 seconds, let's talk about $t + \Delta t$ seconds, where Δt (read "delta t") is an "increment" that takes you slightly beyond t, an increment you are going to allow to shrink towards zero. In this general mode, you do exactly what you did before. The distance the object has gone at time t is $16t^2$; the distance it has gone at $t + \Delta t$ is $16(t + \Delta t)^2$. But

$$(t + \Delta t)^2 = t^2 + 2(\Delta t)t + (\Delta t)^2$$

Therefore, the distance traveled in Δt is

$$16[t^2 + 2(\Delta t)t + (\Delta t)^2] - 16t^2 = 16[2(\Delta t)t + (\Delta t)^2]$$

Velocity is distance divided by time; in this case, the time elapsed is Δt. So the velocity over the incremental time Δt is

$$16[2(\Delta t)t + (\Delta t)^2]/\Delta t = 32t + 16\Delta t$$

But Δt is getting smaller and smaller, and "in the limit" the velocity is $32t$ when Δt reaches the limiting value of zero. So now you have a function which describes the velocity V, of the falling object at time t:

$$V = 32t$$

Hence, the velocity at 1 second is 32 feet per second, at 2 seconds 64 feet per second, at 3 seconds 96 feet per second, and so on. Since 96 feet per second is a bit less than 70 miles per hour, you can see why falling from a 144-foot building might not be very comfortable when you land.

You can proceed in the same manner to describe the acceleration of the falling body at a specific instant of time. Acceleration is velocity divided by time. At 1 second the velocity is 32 feet per second, and at 1.1 seconds $V = 32(1.1) = 35.2$ feet per second, an increase of 3.2 feet per second over 1/10 of a second, or an acceleration of 3.2 divided by $1/10 = (32$ feet per second) per second. If you generalize to any t, as you did above, you see that for an increment Δt the velocity increases from $32t$ to $32(t + \Delta t)$, or

$$32t + 32\Delta t - 32t = 32\Delta t$$

Hence, since acceleration is the increase in velocity over time, the acceleration is

$$32\Delta t/\Delta t = (32 \text{ feet per second}) \text{ per second}$$

for all times. This is just another way of stating Galileo's hypothesis that the acceleration of a freely falling body is constant, 32 feet per second per second, which is often written as 32 feet/second².

If the above has been reasonably clear, then you have acquired your first understanding of calculus. The ratios you have been dealing with, velocity and acceleration, are called *derivatives* because they are derived from a function; specifically, in this case, the derivatives of the function (16t²) with respect to time. Mathematicians like to generalize so they generalize on these very common-sense ideas of velocity and acceleration and speak of the derivative of any function with respect to a variable. In the above case, the function was

$$d = f(t) = 16t^2$$

What you did above was to take the ratio of $[f(t + \Delta t) - f(t)]$ to Δt and then let Δt approach zero (denoted $\Delta t \to 0$). Leibniz introduced the notation for the definition of a derivative that we use today: *the derivative of the function f with respect to the variable t is written*

$$\frac{df(t)}{dt} = \text{limit as } \Delta t \to 0 \text{ of } \frac{f(t + \Delta t) - f(t)}{\Delta t}$$

The notation could be confusing if you're used to thinking of letters like d as variables or constants; here d is used to represent the limiting values of Δt and $[f(t + \Delta t) - f(t)]$. You can sense why this generalized mathematical idea was bothersome, because Δt is going to zero, and we emphasized in chapter 3 that letting the denominator of a fraction be 0 is forbidden; you are not allowed to cancel out 0's in a fraction because nonsense may result. But we were cheerfully cancelling Δt above as it became smaller and smaller, even to the limit. All of this worry can be overcome by some ingenious mathematical theory, but this need not concern you further now.

11.2.1 Some Rules for Evaluating the Derivatives of Functions Using the definition of the derivative of a function and the same type of mathematical manipulations we used on the Δt's with the function $f(t) = 16t^2$, many general rules for evaluating the derivatives of functions can be deduced. For example, reconsider now the two functions discussed above, $16t^2$ and $32t$. The derivative of $16t^2$ was

$$\frac{d(16t^2)}{dt} = 32t = 2(16t)$$

This result can be generalized to any function of the form ax^2, where a is a constant and x is a variable:

$$\frac{d(ax^2)}{dx} = 2ax$$

Next, we took the derivative of 32t, which turned out to be

$$\frac{d(32t)}{dt} = 32$$

Using the definition of the derivative, we can generalize this to any function of the form ax, where a is a constant and x is a variable:

$$\frac{d(ax)}{dx} = a$$

In the case of 32t, $a = 32$ and as was shown,

$$\frac{d(32t)}{dt} = 32$$

If you like this game, you may want to go on and take the derivative of 32, but actually the game is about over since 32 is a constant and is not changing with time. By definition, we say that the derivative of a constant is zero to convey in this case the idea of zero change:

$$\frac{d(32)}{dt} = 0$$

and, in general,

$$\frac{d(a)}{dx} = 0$$

for any constant a and any variable x. This can be proven very easily · from the definition of the derivative, so we'll show you the proof.

Suppose the function is

$$f(t) = a$$

regardless of the value of t. Then

$$f(t + \Delta t) = a \quad \text{and} \quad f(t) = a$$

By the definition of derivative,

$$\frac{df(t)}{dt} = \text{limit as } \Delta t \to 0 \text{ of } \frac{f(t + \Delta t) - f(t)}{\Delta t} = \text{limit as } \Delta t \to 0 \text{ of } \frac{a - a}{\Delta t}$$

$$= \text{limit as } \Delta t \to 0 \text{ of } \frac{0}{\Delta t}$$

Without knowing the rules of limits, you can see that this last expression has value zero.

From the definition of derivative and rules of limits, derivatives of many other functions can be deduced directly. For example, we can derive a very useful rule about the derivative of functions that raise a variable to some power like ax^n, where n is 1, 2, 3, etc. This rule says that:

$$\frac{d(ax^n)}{dx} = nax^{n-1}$$

Thus:

$$\frac{d(ax^3)}{dx} = 3ax^2$$

$$\frac{d(ax^4)}{dx} = 4ax^3$$

and so on. This rule also works when the exponent is negative or a fraction (see chapter 3). Thus

$$\frac{d\left(\frac{a}{x}\right)}{dx} = \frac{d(ax^{-1})}{dx} = -ax^{-2} = -\frac{a}{x^2}$$

and

$$\frac{d(ax^{-2})}{dx} = -2ax^{-3}$$

We can also combine the powers of x, as in the function $ax^2 + bx + c$. To find the derivative of this function we require a rule that tells us we can find the derivative of each term and add them together. Thus

$$\frac{d(ax^2 + bx + c)}{dx} = 2ax + b + 0$$

and in general

$$\frac{d(f(x) + g(x) + h(x) + \cdots)}{dx} = \frac{df(x)}{dx} + \frac{dg(x)}{dx} + \frac{dh(x)}{dx} + \cdots$$

There is one very special function whose derivative is the function itself. This is the function

$$f(x) = e^x$$

where e is approximately 2.718281828. . . . Thus

$$\frac{d(e^x)}{dx} = e^x$$

e^x is the only nonzero function whose derivative is the function itself. Of course, we have not yet told you how to take the derivatives of other functions like e^{x^2}, but we'll examine such functions and their derivatives in the appendix to this chapter. For now, we can summarize the derivatives of some functions in table 11.1.

TABLE 11.1   Simple Derivatives of Functions of the Variable x;
a, c, and n Are Constants

Function $f(x)$	$\dfrac{df(x)}{dx}$	Example
1. ax^n	1. nax^{n-1}	1. $\dfrac{d(3x^2)}{dx} = 6x$
2. c	2. 0	2. $\dfrac{d(32)}{dx} = 0$
3. e^x	3. e^x	3. $\dfrac{d(e^x)}{dx} = e^x$
4. $g(x) + h(x)$	4. $\dfrac{d(g(x))}{dx} + \dfrac{d(h(x))}{dx}$	4. $\dfrac{d(3x^2 + 2x)}{dx} = 6x + 2$
5. $g(x) - h(x)$	5. $\dfrac{d(g(x))}{dx} - \dfrac{d(h(x))}{dx}$	5. $\dfrac{d(3x^2 - 2x)}{dx} = 6x - 2$

PROBLEMS 11.2

1. Calculate the derivatives of the following functions:
   a. $f(x) = x^3$
   b. $f(x) = ax + b$, a and b are constants
   c. $f(x) = e^x + ax + b$, a and b are constant
   d. $f(x) = \dfrac{1}{3}x^3 - x^2 - 2.5x + 10$
   e. $f(x) = e^4 + e^3$
   f. $f(x) = 3x^4 + 2x^5 + 7$
   g. $f(x) = \dfrac{a}{x} - \dfrac{2}{x^3}$, a is a constant
   h. $f(x) = \dfrac{1}{x}$
   i. $f(x) = \dfrac{ax^2 + bx + c}{5}$, a, b, and c are constants
   j. $f(x) = \dfrac{3}{x^2}$

2. Evaluate the derivatives of the following functions:
   a. $f(x) = x^2$, at $x = 5$
   b. $f(x) = x^4 + x^2$, at $x = 3$
   c. $f(x) = 5x + 8$, at $x = 35$
   d. $f(x) = e^x + 7x^2$, at $x = 4$
   e. $f(x) = \dfrac{a}{x} + \dfrac{a}{x} + x$, at $x = a$

3. If the total cost function of producing wheat is

$$f(x) = \frac{1}{2}x^2$$

where x is the output of wheat, what do you anticipate the increase in the cost per pound of wheat to be if you increase production from 100 to 101 pounds? Note that this is the marginal cost at 100 pounds output.

4.   In problem 3 above, what is the quantity of wheat that should be produced if you wish the marginal cost to be $150?

5.   The demand for your product can be approximated by the function

$$p = \frac{2}{q}$$

where p is the price per unit and q is the quantity demanded. What is your marginal revenue at q = 100?

11.3   Some Applications of the Derivative

We have indicated why physicists (and hence engineers) would have a strong interest in calculus, because it enables them to describe some very essential aspects of the physical world. But why should calculus interest you, a student of decision making?

Problem: Jack Pepper's Store ─────────────

Jack Pepper sells Yasmin tea in bulk in his grocery store in Bolinas. Since the cost to him of an ounce of Yasmin tea had gone up recently to 15¢ per ounce, Jack was wondering whether he could get away with raising the price of tea to his customers without losing profits. So Jack did a little experiment: He raised the retail price of tea from the current price of 15¢ per ounce to the price of 20¢ per ounce, then to 25¢ per ounce, to 30¢ per ounce, and finally, to 35¢ per ounce. Of course, as the price he charged went up, the quantity sold went down. In the language of functions (chapter 3), Jack found that the quantity sold is a function of the price he charges.

Jack's profits on tea are based upon the 15¢ cost to him, the price he charges, and the quantity he sells, which itself depends on the price he charges. After a little reflection Jack realized that the price to him is fixed at 15¢, and the only thing which he controls that changes his profits is the retail price of an ounce of Yasmin tea. Jack summarized the data from his experiment in table 11.2. (The last figure in the table

TABLE 11.2   Daily Profits for Various Prices of Tea
(in dollars)

Price	.15	.20	.25	.30	.35
Profits	0.00	2.25	3.75	2.25	0.00

shows that Jack "priced himself out of the market" at 35¢ and that there was no demand for his tea.)

Jack is currently charging 25¢ per ounce, and would like to know if raising the price a bit would increase his profits. What should he do?

Analysis: Based upon table 11.2 it is difficult to tell what Jack should do. However, if you plot the curve of profits versus price, the result is shown in figure 11.1. If you sketch in roughly the curve implied by the

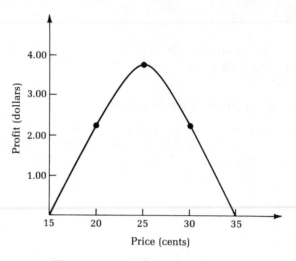

Figure 11.1   Jack Pepper's Profits

profit points as we did, you'll find that the smooth curve depicted in the figure might well represent Jack's profits for various price levels.

The algebraic function which describes the curve in figure 11.1 is

$$Y = f(p) = -3p^2 + 150p - 375$$

where $Y = f(p)$ represents Jack's profits when he charges price p. (This type of curve-fitting to data falls under inductive quantitative methods, so don't worry about it for now.)

Based upon $Y = f(p)$, you could try all of the (infinite) possible prices p to find which one gives Jack the most profit. However, this would take you quite a long time, to say the least. But, if

$$-3p^2 + 150p - 375$$

is an accurate description of Jack's profit function, it turns out that you can use the quantitative methods of the derivative and the slope of a line to solve Jack's problem. (For a review of slopes of straight lines, see the appendix to chapter 9.)

Just as every linear function has a slope, so does every nonlinear one, but the slope of a linear function is always the same while the slope of a nonlinear one keeps changing. The slope can now be generalized to mean the *rate of change of the function with respect to changes in the value of its variable (x)*; that is, the change in f(x) as x changes. This is exactly what we were observing in the physical example given earlier, where we described the rate of change in the distance fallen as the velocity, which was the first derivative. So, the first derivative is the slope of the function at each point! We can do exactly the same thing with Jack's profit function. Its rate of change with respect to increasing price is

$$\frac{dY}{dp} = -6p + 150$$

by the rules for calculating derivatives given in the last section. How does this help you? Well, if you look at figure 11.2, you will see the idea of slope represented by the straight line, $-6p + 150$, at the point where $p = 20$. There the slope is fairly steep, but as you approach the top of the curve, the slope decreases and at the peak, just before it starts down, it is zero. Far out! The slope is zero at the mountain peak, just where the profit is maximum! But the slope is always represented by $-6p + 150$, the first derivative. So if you set $-6p + 150$ equal to zero, and solve for p, you will have found the best price, the one that maximizes the profit:

$$-6p + 150 = 0, \quad \text{or} \quad p = 25$$

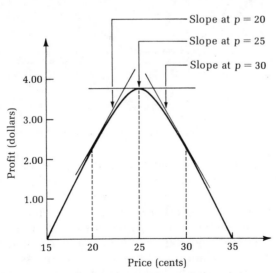

Figure 11.2   Slopes of Jack's Profit Function

Hence, Jack's current price is right after all; the best price is 25 cents. He cannot make any more than $3.75 per day on his exotic tea.

There are several words of caution and explanation about this method of setting the first derivative to zero and finding the "peak" or maximum of a function. First of all, on the technical side it should be noted that unless you are careful, you may end up with the *worst* rather than the best, because the slope is zero at the bottom as well as at the top. But you can check for this because if you are approaching the top of the mountain as you move towards the right (as in figure 11.2), then the slope is changing from positive to negative.

The rate of change of the first derivative (slope) is called the second derivative; that is, it is the derivative of the derivative. We have already seen this earlier: the "acceleration" or second derivative is the rate of change of the first derivative or velocity.

If the first derivative is changing from positive to negative, as in Jack's profits, its rate of change must be negative, so the second derivative is less than zero. As you approach a minimum, though, as in figure 11.3, the slope (first derivative) is changing from negative to positive, so the second derivative is positive.

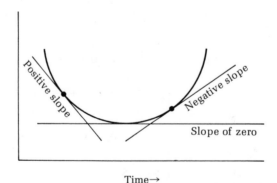

Time→

Figure 11.3   Slopes When You Are at the Minimum

In figure 11.3 as you move from left to right on the time axis, the slope goes from negative to zero to positive; that is, the slope is *increasing*. The test for the "top" (maximum) versus the "bottom" (minimum) is, therefore, to find the second derivative, which tells how the slope is changing, and see whether it is negative or positive. In Jack's case, the second derivative is the derivative of $(-6p + 150)$ or -6, which is negative; thus he has a maximum profit, not a minimum, as any fool could have seen in the first place by looking at figure 11.1. But in more complicated problems with lots of variables, it may not be possible to draw figures and it may not be obvious whether you have reached a max or a min value, so you'll need to resort to the second-derivative "test."

Second, as a word of explanation, the problem Jack posed and its solution is, in the sense of chapter 3, a "marginal profit" analysis since he found the price where an additional unit of price yields less profit. But clearly the method we have introduced has a great deal of power and can be generalized far beyond the *unit* marginal analysis of chapter 3. The point is that commodities like tea (sugar, salt, cereal) that can be sold in bulk rate take on continuous values: $1\frac{1}{2}$ ounces, 2.03 ounces, etc., and hence marginal *unit* analysis may not work. For example, consider the case where the cost of producing x pounds of sugar is given by

$$c(x) = k\sqrt{x} = kx^{1/2}$$

where k is a constant. If p is the price of a pound of sugar, and the cost of producing x is $c(x)$, then the net profit is

$$px - c(x) = px - kx^{1/2}$$

What value of x maximizes profit? Find the first derivative of

$$px - kx^{1/2}$$

and set it equal to zero:

$$p - k\left[\frac{1}{2}x^{-1/2}\right] = 0$$

or

$$\frac{kx^{-1/2}}{2} = p \qquad (2)$$

What this says in the language of marginal analysis is that profit is maximized when the "marginal revenue" p is equal to the marginal cost $kx^{-1/2}/2$. This makes sense when marginal costs are going up and marginal revenues are constant or going down as you sell additional units, since selling more will result in marginal costs which are greater than marginal revenues and thus a decrease in total profits. If you produce less, then you will not be maximizing since marginal revenues exceed marginal costs, and you can make more profit by producing additional units.

In this case marginal revenue equals marginal cost at

$$x = \frac{k^2}{4p^2},$$

which you can verify by solving equation (2) for x, and profits are maximized by producing $k^2/4p^2$ pounds.

Third, from a total systems point of view, Jack's "optimal" price of 25¢ may not be optimal at all since the demand for exotic tea may be competing with the demand for coffee, or other teas, or other groceries. Hence, what Jack may really need is an analysis of all his product lines and their demands and prices, which may not be feasible, and in any event is obviously costly.

Fourth, it appears that in cases like Jack's the "optimal" is somewhere "in between." Aristotle early recognized this idea of human values by offering us the prescription to choose the mean between the extremes: not too much or too little generosity, self-esteem, determination. Even killing is treated as a mean between extremes in our culture: in order to defend ourselves or to drive speedily on highways we believe the "optimal" amount of killings is between the extremes of zero and everybody. Calculus in some cases will help us find this optimal point.

Problem: O.K. Schmatte's Inventory ━━━━━━━━━━━━━━━

Your friend O.K. Schmatte is the purchasing manager for Chaim's Jeans. He has asked you to solve a problem for him. It seems that his inventory is tying up too much of his capital (money). He knows Chaim could make 10% per year in the stock market if the funds tied up in inventory were made available; so Schmatte uses this 10% as his "opportunity cost" of capital. He realizes that he cannot have too small an inventory either, since it costs him $20 in delivery fees and information processing (paperwork and accounting) each time he orders jeans from the warehouse. Based on years of experience, Schmatte also knows that weekly demand for jeans is approximately constant at 1300 pairs per week. Chaim pays $4 per pair from the warehouse. How often should Schmatte place an order for jeans, or equivalently, how much should he order each time?

Analysis: The problem faced by your friend is one faced by many firms which maintain large inventories. The question is, how to trade off the cost of holding large amounts of inventory with the cost of constantly reordering which results if you order small amounts and reduce inventory size. In this problem, the only "holding cost" attached to the inventory is the 10% cost of capital tied up in the jeans in stock, although in practice there are often many other costs: storage, deterioration, obsolescence, etc. This holding cost is to be "traded off" against the $20 reordering cost.

The question Schmatte faces is how much or how often to reorder. To show that these are equivalent, let's examine a fixed period of time for Chaim's Jeans, say, a year. Assume the year starts with no inventory; Schmatte places an order for, say, Q pairs of jeans at $4 a pair. The inventory level over time looks like figure 11.4.

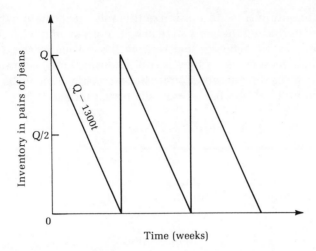

Figure 11.4   Inventory of Chaim's Jeans over Time

Since the demand is approximately constant, the inventory level drops in a straight line from Q to zero; at that point, Schmatte orders Q pairs again (we assume that the delivery is virtually immediate). In a year then, the total demand is

$$1300 \times 52 = 67{,}600 \text{ pairs of jeans}$$

How many times does Schmatte reorder in a year? Well, if he orders Q each time, he must reorder 67,600/Q times in a year. And how much does the inventory cost him in that time period? This can be computed by calculating the *average* amount of inventory Schmatte has on hand during the year and then multiplying the value of that average amount by 10%. If you think about it for a moment, it makes sense; if you have $20 in the bank for 6 months at 10% and $0 for the other 6 months, it's the same as having $10 (the *average* amount) all year.

For Schmatte, the *average* number of pairs on hand is Q/2 since the demand is constant. So his inventory holding cost is

$$(Q/2 \times \$4) \times 10\%$$

(Each pair costs $4, so Q/2 × $4 is the average amount of capital tied up in inventory all year.) So Schmatte's total cost of inventory for the year is the number of times he reorders times $20, plus the holding cost.

Suppose we call both Schmatte's costs, the ordering and the holding, his *total* (relevant) costs, TC. Then

$$TC = \frac{67{,}600}{Q} \times \$20 + (Q/2 \times \$4) \times 10\%$$

Since Schmatte wishes to minimize this total cost, the newly learned technique of finding the derivative can be applied, and we will do so in a moment. But first, notice that finding the optimal *amount* to order, Q^*, can also be seen as finding the optimal *time* between orders, since $67,600/Q^*$ gives the number of times Schmatte places an order in a year. To get the optimal number of *weeks* between orders, W^*,

$$W^* = \frac{52}{\frac{67,600}{Q}} = \frac{Q^*}{1300}$$

which makes sense since 1300 are demanded per week. So finding Q^* you also find the optimal timing of the orders,

$$W^* = \frac{Q^*}{1300}$$

The *optimal* reorder quantity Q^* is found when total cost is minimized. To do so, first find the derivative of the total cost function.

$$TC = \frac{\$1,352,000}{Q} + .2Q$$
$$= \$1,352,000Q^{-1} + .2Q$$

So,

$$\frac{d(TC)}{dQ} = -1,352,000Q^{-2} + .2$$

Now, setting $\frac{d(TC)}{dQ}$ to zero and solving for Q to find the minimum Q^* (where the slope of *TC* is zero):

$$-1,352,000\,(Q^*)^{-2} + .2 = 0$$
$$(Q^*)^{-2} = \frac{.2}{1,352,000} = \frac{1}{6,760,000}$$
$$(Q^*)^2 = 6,760,000$$

Taking the square root of both sides to get Q^*:

$$Q^* = \sqrt{676}\ \sqrt{10,000} = 26 \cdot 100 = 2600$$

So, Schmatte should order 2600 pairs each time. This is exactly twice his weekly demand, so in this case he'll place an order once every other week; that is,

$$W^* = \frac{2600}{1300} = 2$$

To check to see if Q^* minimizes cost, compute the *second derivative* of total cost.

$$\frac{d\left(\frac{d(TC)}{dQ}\right)}{dQ} = \frac{d}{dQ}(-1{,}352{,}000Q^{-2} + .2)$$

$$= (-2)(-1{,}352{,}000)Q^{-3}$$

$$= 2{,}704{,}000Q^{-3}$$

which is positive (> 0) as long as Schmatte orders a positive amount. Specifically, at $Q = 2600$,

$$\frac{2{,}704{,}000}{(2600)^3} > 0$$

So the second derivative is positive; thus $Q^* = 2600$ is a *minimum*.

Can you solve Schmatte's problem if his opportunity cost of capital is 15%? What if it costs only $5 to reorder? What if the weekly demand is 800? By using a little insight, you can get a *general* solution to Schmatte's problem for any cost of holding inventory per period, any reorder cost, and any periodic demand.

Let:

a = the periodic demand for the product (period, for example, could be a year or a week)

h = the cost of holding one unit of inventory for one period

k = the cost of placing an order (reorder cost)

Then the total cost for a period, if Q is ordered each time, is

$$TC = a/Q \times k + Q/2 \times h$$
$$\quad\;\; \text{reorder} \quad \text{holding}$$
$$\quad\;\; \text{cost} \quad\quad \text{cost}$$

since orders must be placed a/Q times per period and the average inventory is $Q/2$. Proceeding as before, to find the minimum cost quantity:

$$\frac{d(TC)}{dQ} = -akQ^{-2} + h/2$$

Setting $d(TC)/dQ$ to zero and solving for Q^*:

$$(Q^*)^{-2} = h/2ak$$

So,

$$(Q^*)^2 = 2ak/h$$

and

$$Q^* = \sqrt{2ak/h}$$

for any demand a, reorder cost k, and holding cost h. (Check this for Schmatte's problem.) Note that the second derivative is

$$+2akQ^{-3}$$

which is positive (denoting a minimum) as long as a, k, and Q are positive.

From a systems point of view, you should be aware that the formula $Q^* = \sqrt{2ak/h}$ does not apply in all cases, nor is it clear how the critical values of a, k, and h are to be obtained. The "solution" was obtained under the assumption that demand could be reasonably well predicted and is the same in each time period. Obviously, these assumptions often don't hold; if the exact demand is not known, then you run the risk of shortages and must estimate the cost of shortage; a large inventory mitigates against shortages, but again runs into larger holding costs. But also the demand, holding costs, and ordering costs cannot be based simply on historical data; perhaps advertising or pricing can be made to influence demand when inventories are too high or low, perhaps there is a better way of using extra capital so that the holding cost is higher, or perhaps ordering costs can be reduced. Thus, in order to obtain the data for the model of the inventory system, you must make some very strong assumptions about other systems of the firm, the marketing, financial, and purchasing systems, for example. Models like the one given above are widely used, but must be used with a great deal of caution.

11.3.1   Notation for Derivatives   Before we leave derivatives, we should introduce you to the common notation used to denote the second derivative of a function. We write the first derivative of a function like $f(t)$ as

$$\frac{df(t)}{dt}$$

and the second derivative of the function $f(t)$ as

$$\frac{d^2f(t)}{dt^2}$$

Here again the notation could be confusing if you were to think of d^2

as the square of d; it is used here to represent the operation of the derivative on a derivative. For example, in the O. K. Schmatte problem,

$$TC = f(Q) = \frac{1,352,000}{Q} + .2Q$$

$$\frac{df(Q)}{dQ} = -1,352,000Q^{-2} + .2$$

and

$$\frac{d^2f(Q)}{dQ^2} = 2,704,000Q^{-3}$$

Further, the first derivative of a function like $f(t)$ is also denoted by f', and the second derivative by f''.

PROBLEMS 11.3

1. Calculate the first and the second derivatives of the following functions:
   a. $f(x) = 3x + 5$
   b. $f(x) = x^2 - 5x$
   c. $f(x) = \frac{1}{3}x^3 - x^2 - 2x + 3$
   d. $f(x) = e^x$
   e. $f(x) = \frac{a}{x} + \frac{a}{x^3}$

2. For each of the following functions identify its point of maximum or minimum, whichever is applicable.
   a. $f(x) = -3x^2 + 6x + 1$
   b. $f(x) = 2x^2 - 9x + 3$
   c. $f(x) = -3x^2 - 10x + 4$
   d. $f(x) = x^3 - 3x$
   e. $f(x) = x^4 - 8x^2 + 8$

3. Suppose the relationship between a company's production volume and its profits is expressed by the following equation: $p = 96v - 24v^2$ where $p = $ profits in thousands of dollars, and $v = $ production volume in thousands of units. What is dp/dv? What is the value of dp/dv at $v = 1$? at $v = 2$? Is the value of the derivative increasing? What is happening to total profits at volumes of v greater than 2? Graph the function p. Graph dp/dv. What happens to the sign of dp/dv as v goes from 0 to 4? Where is the maximum profit achieved?

4. A whisky manufacturing firm faces a total cost function $C(X) = 5X^2 - 20X + 30$ and a total revenue function $R(X) = -5X^2 + 50X$ where X is the number of cases of whisky produced. The firm has a maximum capacity of producing 20 cases. (All cost, revenue, and capacity figures are on a per day basis).
    a. What is the cost per day when the plant is shut down? What does this cost figure represent?
    b. What are the cost and revenue at $X = -3$? (careful) Explain.
    c. At what production level should the firm operate if it wants to minimize costs?
    d. At what production level should it operate if it wants to maximize revenue?
    e. Where is it optimal if the firm is a profit maximizer?
    f. If for some reason your answer to (e) was $X = 27$, what do you have to say?

5. Mr. J. Wayne buys cattle weighing 500 pounds each, at 25¢ per pound to fatten for market. He estimated that each animal will gain 3/4 pound per day he owns them, at a cost of 9¢ per pound gained for feed and care. The selling price, starting at 25¢ per pound total, can be expected to decrease by .02¢ per day over the next six months. When should he plan to sell cattle in order to realize maximum profits? Answer this question if the cost of feeding is 9¢ per pound of animal per day for feed and care (for example, if it weighs 900 pounds, it costs 900 × 9¢)

6. Why would you want marginal revenue to equal marginal cost? What does this have to do with total profit? Why would we expect the second derivative of total profit to be negative at maximum in every case? Draw graphs, and rationalize these things to yourself.

7. What should be your order size of inventory if the demand for your product is 20,000 units per year, the inventory holding cost is $2 per year, and the cost of placing an order is $4.50?

8. The Quigley Company is attempting to determine the optimum order size for ordering a type of steel plate. The steel may be ordered by using three different-size orders.

Size of Order	Total Invoice Cost per Order
10 tons	$ 15,000
100 tons	$120,000
200 tons	$225,000

Other costs connected with ordering and storing inventory are as follows.

Cost of paperwork: $8 per order
Handling costs: $2 per order plus $12 per ton

Property taxes: $50 per ton of average inventory per year

Insurance: $10 per ton on average inventory per year

Interest on capital invested (use invoice cost and average inventory): 20 per cent per year

Risks of spoilage: $30 per ton of average inventory

Storage costs: $2000 per year (This covers the rent on a storehouse that will store 120 tons.), and $10 per ton per year for additional storage space (The cost is determined by maximum possible demand for space.)

Inventories for each of the three order sizes (in tons) would be

Size of Order	Average Inventory	Maximum Inventory
10	15.0	20
100	52.5	105
200	102.5	220

What do you recommend should be the order size, assuming the demand for this material is 300 tons in the next year?

11.4   Integration

We mentioned at the beginning of this chapter that you can use the information about relative changes in two ways: you can go from the relation between two variables to the rate of change, or from the rate of change to the relation. In this section we consider the second option. To do so suppose we return to Galileo. What he asserted was that the acceleration of a falling body is constant. We know that he also assumed that the distance fallen is a function of time: $d = f(t)$. But what function? By saying that the acceleration is constant, we know he meant that

$$\frac{d^2f(t)}{dt^2} = \text{constant}$$

Hence, proceeding in reverse, we know that the velocity, $df(t)/dt$, is assumed to be a linear function:

$$v = \frac{df(t)}{dt} = at + b$$

because only with such a function would he get

$$\frac{d^2f(t)}{dt^2} = \text{constant}$$

We also know that the constant $= a$. Finally, we know that the distance fallen must be a "quadratic" function,

$$f(t) = \frac{1}{2}at^2 + bt + c$$

because only with such a function would he get

$$\frac{df(t)}{dt} = at + b$$

You can see that we have been reversing the steps back from the derivatives to the functions. This process is called "integration," and for reasons we will soon explain, is symbolized by $\int f(t)dt$ called "the integral of the function $f(t)$." The following gives the basic idea:

$$\frac{d(ax^2 + c)}{dx} = 2ax; \text{ and } \int (2ax)dx = ax^2 + c$$

$$\frac{d(ax^n + c)}{dx} = nax^{n-1}; \text{ and } \int (nax^{n-1})dx = ax^n + c$$

You'll note that the reverse process, integration, is somewhat ambiguous. If we tell you that the derivative of a certain function is $3x^2$, then you can infer that the function (the integral of $3x^2$) is $x^3 +$ constant, but you cannot determine what this constant is since the derivative of $(x^3 +$ constant) is always $3x^2$ no matter what the constant is.

Returning to Jack Pepper, if we see him calculating the optimal price by dividing 6 into 150 from

$$-6p + 150 = 0$$

then we know that he thinks that the derivative of his profit function is

$$\frac{dY}{dp} = -6p + 150$$

Hence, he must assume by integration that

$$Y = -3p^2 + 150p + \text{constant}$$

since such a function is the only way in which he could have arrived at

$$\frac{dY}{dp} = -6p + 150$$

We do not know what constant he assumed, but in this case *it does not matter*. Such a constant in a profit function represents a fixed amount (usually fixed costs) which is independent of the decision about price, and therefore irrelevant for managerial decisions about price.

Now let's see a managerial application of the integral.

Problem: Slightly Risky Associates (SRA) ━━━━━━━━

SRA is a firm which publishes texts for colleges. A prospective author wants $18,000 in advanced royalties, and the question SRA faces is whether they should sign a contract with him. Past experiences with this type of text indicate that sales in the first year are generally low, then increase rapidly in the next two years, after which they decline to an insignificant figure at the end of the fifth year. Instead of forecasting total sales directly, SRA uses a "peak week" forecasting technique where they estimate the highest sales volume they expect in the middle of the five-year period and then fit an equation of the form

$$\text{Sales} = s = -at^2 + bt + c$$

where t is time in years, starting at 0 and ending at 5, and a, b, and c are coefficients that depend on the success of the book—that is, on the "peak week" estimate (figure 11.5). In this particular case, SRA's market projections based on a first draft the author has prepared are that the appropriate equation is

$$s = -2400t^2 + 12{,}000t$$

where s represents yearly rate of sales at any point in time t. In other words, if $s = 9600$ at $t = 1$, then if sales were to remain at exactly that rate for a whole year, SRA would sell 9600 books in the second year. Of course, the "smooth" curve is only approximate since books are sold in units and certainly not in a continuous stream. But SRA managers have found that the "peak week" approximation works reasonably well and gives a more accurate forecast of sales than an annual total forecast would do. The problem now is to determine what the predicted total sales will be for five years, and to see if this warrants the advance of $18,000.

Analysis: SRA could approximate total sales by observing that at the start when $t = 0$, $s = 0$, while a year later ($t = 1$),

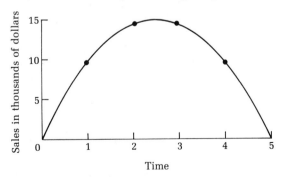

Figure 11.5   **Sales $s = -at^2 + bt + c = -2400t^2 + 12{,}000t$**

$$s = -2400(1^2) + 12,000(1) = 9600$$

The average sales in the first year can be approximated by taking sales at the end of the year (9600), and sales at the beginning (0), and averaging the two:

$$\frac{9600 + 0}{2} = 4800 \text{ average sales for the first year}$$

In this way, SRA can get an approximation for *total* sales by getting the average sales for each year, resulting in the building blocks of figure 11.6. For example, "average" sales for year 2–3 is

$$\frac{s(3) + s(2)}{2} = \frac{14,400 + 14,400}{2} = 14,400$$

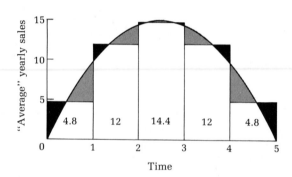

Figure 11.6   Approximate *Yearly* Sales in Thousands

The total "area" of the blocks in figure 11.6 adds up to 48,000, which is an approximation of the total sales. The "approximation" is not exact, since it leaves out the lightly shaded area and includes the darkly shaded areas, thus distorting the true area.

You could refine this process and reduce the error by taking half-year figures and constructing a similar graph as in figure 11.7, and the resulting total area of 49,500 is more accurate since you are adjusting more adequately for steep and flat sections of the curve and getting smaller areas of over- and underestimation. Similarly, you could take quarter-year figures as in figure 11.8 and be even more accurate (49,850).

If this process of systematically narrowing down the time interval seems vaguely familiar to you, it is because we did exactly the same thing when we were discussing velocities and accelerations of falling bodies. There we were interested in rates-of-change or, what is the same

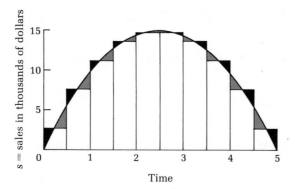

Figure 11.7

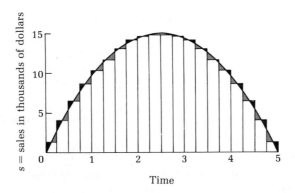

Figure 11.8

thing, "slopes" of lines, whereas here we are interested in areas. Note that here the area is represented as the "average" value of $s = f(t)$, times the time segment Δt, which may be one year, 1/2 year, 1/4 year, etc. If we let this time segment Δt become smaller and smaller, then its "limiting" value is represented as dt, and the area as $f(t)dt$; now we want to "add" all of these areas together as Δt becomes smaller and smaller. Previously, when we added terms, we symbolized the addition by Σ; here we are adding an infinity of terms, and use the symbol $\int$. So we represent the sum as

$$\int f(t)dt$$

Now you can see why this symbol for the integral was used. But we also have to indicate for what part of the curve we are calculating the area. We do this by the symbol

$$\int_0^5 f(t)dt$$

meaning that we are calculating the area under $f(t)$ from $t = 0$ to $t = 5$.
In general

$$\int_a^b f(t)dt$$

is the area under the curve representing the function $f(t)$ from point a
to point b, where $b \geq a$.

But how do you add an "infinite" sum of the areas $f(t)dt$? You do it
first by "taking the integral of $f(t)$"—that is, by finding the function
whose derivative is $f(t)$. In the SRA case, you want to know what function has the derivative

$$-2400t^2 + 12,000t$$

You know that integration must raise t^2 to t^3 and t to t^2, since the
reverse derivative process *lowers* the power by 1. Integration must also
compensate for the fact that the derivative process multiplies by the
original exponent; so it must divide through by the original exponents
in each term:

$$\int (-2400t^2 + 12,000t)dt = -\frac{2400t^3}{3} + \frac{12,000t^2}{2} + \text{constant}$$
$$= -800t^3 + 6000t^2 + \text{constant}$$

Note that the constant in this case is zero, because when t is zero there
are no sales. The integration process determines the numerical value
of the integral at the two extreme points of interest, 0 and 5, and sub-
tracts the first from the second. This step is represented by

$$(-800t^3 + 6000t^2) \Big|_0^5$$

At $t = 0$, the integral is

$$-800(0)^3 + (6000)(0)^2 = 0$$

At $t = 5$, the integral is

$$-800(5)^3 + (6000)(5)^2 = -(800)(125) + (6000)(25) = 50,000$$

Thus the forecasting formula SRA uses indicates that the total
sales will be $50,000 - 0 = 50,000$ books. If their net profit is one dollar
per book, say, then they can well afford to pay the author $18,000, even

if he delivers the manuscript three years hence, since the combined interest on 18,000, even compounded at 12% per annum (see chapter 4) is small compared to SRA's profit.

In general, if you want an area under a curve representing a function $f(x)$, from the point $x = a$ to the point $x = b$—that is, when you want to determine $\int_a^b f(x)dx$, you first integrate $f(x)$ (that is, determine $\int f(x)dx$) and then evaluate the integral to a and subtract this value from the value of the integral at b: $\int f(x)dx \mid_a^b$. Table 11.3, shown on the following page, contains some common integrals of functions.

Let's examine another managerial example of the use of integration.

Problem: Bruce's Garbage Dump

Bruce the garbage man owns a dump in Kailua, and since his current dump is filling rapidly, he would like to have an idea of when he's going to have to find a new area to dump his garbage. Because of the influx of people to the area and increased consumption, he has noticed that the amount of garbage he has to dump is proportional to the square of the amount of time in weeks he's been open. For example, when he opened his business ($t = 1$), he had 1000 cubic feet of garbage in the first week, and in the second week ($t = 2$), he had $1000(2)^2 = 4000$ cubic feet, while in the ninth week, he had 81,000 cubic feet. He has a total of 10 million cubic feet of space. If he estimates that the amount dumped will continue to grow at this rate, when will his current dump be full?

Analysis: Bruce's weekly amount dumped w in week t is

$$w(t) = 1000t^2$$

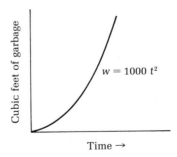

Figure 11.9   Weekly Garbage

TABLE 11.3 Some Integrals of the Function $f(x)$; a and c Are Constants

$f(x)$	$\int f(x)dx$	Example
1. x^n	1. $\dfrac{1}{n+1}x^{n+1} + c \ (n \neq -1)$	1. $\displaystyle\int_1^2 x^3 dx = \dfrac{x^4}{4} + c \Big|_1^2 = \dfrac{2^4}{4} + c - \dfrac{1^4}{4} - c = 3\tfrac{3}{4}$
2. a	2. $ax + c$	2. $\displaystyle\int_0^1 4dx = 4x + c \Big|_0^1 = 4 - 0 = 4$
3. e^x	3. $e^x + c$	3. $\displaystyle\int_2^4 e^x dx = e^x + c \Big|_2^4 = e^4 - e^2$
4. $g(x) + h(x) + \ldots$	4. $\displaystyle\int g(x)dx + \int h(x)dx + \ldots + c$	4. $\displaystyle\int_0^1 (x^{-3} + x^{1/2})dx = \dfrac{x^{-2}}{-2} + \dfrac{2}{3}x^{3/2} + c \Big|_0^1 = \dfrac{1}{-2} + \dfrac{2}{3} - 0 = 1/6$
5. $g(x) - h(x)$	5. $\displaystyle\int g(x)dx - \int h(x)dx$	5. $\displaystyle\int_{-1}^{+1} (x^2 - 7)dx = \dfrac{x^3}{3} - 7x + c \Big|_{-1}^{+1} = 1/3 - 7 + 1/3 - 7 = -13\tfrac{1}{3}$

where t is continuous and represents the number of weeks he's been open. The amount is graphed in figure 11.9. Assume that the stream of garbage into the dump can be approximated by the continuous curve, much like an inflow into a reservoir.

The *total* amount of garbage at a particular time T, representing the amount of space used up by that time, is just the sum of the amounts put into the dump up to time T, which under the assumption of continuous dumping can be approximated by the integral of the amounts dumped over time. So the area left for dumping is

$$10,000,000 - \int_0^T 1000t^2 dt$$

Bruce wants to know at what time T does the area reach 0—that is, when does

$$\int_0^T 1000t^2 dt = 10,000,000$$

You know that if

$$w(t) = 1000t^2$$

then

$$\int w(t)dt = \frac{1000t^3}{3}$$

and that

$$\int_0^T w(t)dt$$

is

$$\frac{1000t^3}{3}\Big|_0^T = \frac{1000T^3}{3} - 0$$

So you need only solve

$$\frac{1000T^3}{3} = 10,000,000$$

or

$$T^3 = 30,000$$
$$T = \sqrt[3]{30,000}$$

which is a little more than 31. So Bruce is going to run out pretty quickly (31 weeks from opening) if garbage continues to pile up at the currently alarming rate!

PROBLEMS 11.4

1. Integrate the following functions:

   a. 2

   b. x^4

   c. a, a is a constant

   d. $2x^3$

   e. $\dfrac{5}{x^2}$

   f. $\sqrt{x}$

   g. $\dfrac{2}{3}x^{n-1}$

   h. $2x^3 + 6x^2 - x + 3$

   i. $4x - \dfrac{1}{x^3}$

   j. $ax^2 + bx + c$

2. Integrate and evaluate the following functions:

   a. $3x^2 - 4x + 2$ between $x = 0$ and $x = 2$

   b. e^x between $x = 0$ and $x = 1$ (See page 371.)

   c. $x^2 - \dfrac{1}{x^2}$ between $x = -5$ and $x = 5$

   d. $\sqrt[3]{x^2}$ between $x = 0$ and $x = 1$

   e. x^n between $x = a$ and $x = b$

3. The daily profits of your company follow a pattern approximated by

$$p(t) = t^3 - 50t^2 + 30t - 5000$$

   where t takes on the values 25 for the year start and 265 for year end. Each month is assumed to have 20 working days.

   a. What are your anticipated profits for the year?

   b. What are your anticipated profits for the month of January?

   c. What are your anticipated profits for the month of April?

4. The weekly demand for your company's product follows the pattern

$$d(t) = 500 + 300t + 2500t^2$$

   where t takes on the value 0 indicating Monday morning and 6 indicating Friday at closing time. The product is perishable, hence you wish to produce the exact quantity in order to meet the total weekly demand. How many units should you produce every week?

5. You have received an order of 10,000 candles at 75¢ per candle. The price is about 25% lower than what you normally charge, but the

size of the order is very large. You know that your efficiency increases with the size of the production batch, and you approximate that the total cost changes with respect to changes in the size of the production batch are

$$1.5 - .0002x$$

where x is the size of the batch. Should you accept the order?

11.5   Caution: Possibly Poisonous

You should be aware that the technique of estimating the maximum (or minimum) by means of calculus, while similar to other techniques we have described for "making the most," is much more powerful than these and therefore potentially more dangerous.

The point is that we have shown you how to construct a function that hopefully "describes reality" in a fairly rich way and then "deduces" the decision that produces the best outcome. But the function may be wrong, of course, as in the "peak week" example where we forecast the whole lifetime of a book from some strong assumptions. One may be swept away by the relative ease with which the maximum is reached, without worrying about the strong assumptions that were the basis for the analysis.

As in the case of linear equations and inequations, so here the functions we use to infer the maximum are a part of a "model." A model is sometimes defined as a "representation of reality," but this is in fact a very deceptive expression. A model is more aptly defined as a technique for estimating a correct decision based on a set of assumptions about reality. This definition has the advantage of emphasizing the importance of the assumptions in model building. The set of assumptions about reality can be called a "world-view" (borrowed from the German "Weltanschauung"). So if someone tells you he has a model of a firm, or a city, or the world, you should immediately ask yourself: What is his world-view? Specifically, what has he assumed to be relevant, what has he assumed to be irrelevant, and how has he combined the relevant variables into a function? Then, how is each of these sets of assumptions justified? If you exercise your critical powers in this way, you will usually find that other plausible assumptions could have been made, and that therefore modeling requires the use of sound judgment, a faculty that is by no means easy to define or acquire. To illustrate these remarks, let's reexamine Mr. Schmatte's problem.

Problem: O. K. Schmatte Revisited ━━━━━━━━━━━━━

Mr. Schmatte has been promoted to production manager for the supplier of Chaim's Jeans because of his previous cleverness with inventory problems. He now considers himself a "model-builder" of sorts and comes to you as a *consultant* because he thinks you are more than a mere quantitative expert; you know the deductive methods as well as the inductive *and* the systems approach.

Schmatte the "model-builder" explains his model to you. "We order all the denim we use. The question I considered was how much denim to order at a time. Call the size of the order Q, measured, say, in square yards. Now when the cloth is sitting in inventory, there are certain costs that arise, all of which depend on the amount of inventory. Thus there are storage costs, deterioration costs, taxes, and the cost of tying up funds in inventory (which is in effect an interest rate on these funds). I labeled these holding costs (denoted h) and assumed that for a specified time period this total holding cost is proportional to the size of my inventory.

"I realized that this cost alone would suggest that we order small amounts since if Q is small, then so is $h \cdot Q$. But then I realized that small orders result in frequent placing of orders with all the additional paperwork, postage, handling, and so on. I assumed that this ordering cost k can be represented by k/Q, since if Q is large, then k/Q is small, and if Q is small, k/Q is large.

"Then I realized that both the holding cost and the ordering cost depend on how rapidly the cloth is used in manufacturing. Hence I picked a time period, say a week, and found the rate of consumption of the cloth, which was pretty constant. Call this

$$a = \text{number of square yards used per week}$$

Hence if Q is the quantity ordered, then this quantity will be held in inventory for Q/a weeks, at the end of which period a new order will be placed. Figure 11.10 shows how the inventory is reduced due to constant demand. I read the first part of chapter 11 in this new book, which told me that for any period like a week, my total cost is

$$TC = a/Q \times k + Q/2 \times h$$

and that my best choice for Q would be

$$Q^* = \sqrt{2ak/h}$$

"What do you think of this model and its solution, Mr. Consultant?"

Analysis: You might tell Mr. Schmatte that the evaluation of a model takes place at several levels, which depend on the scope of the system being modeled.

At the first level, you accept the assumption that the relevant system is the specific one chosen for study (in this case the inventory of the raw materials), and accept the goal Schmatte has chosen. Hence the

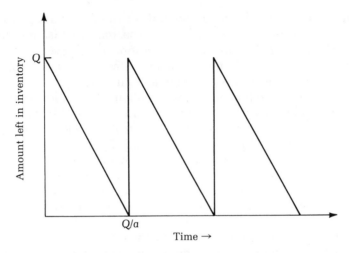

Figure 11.10

goal is to minimize costs of carrying inventory and placing orders. At this level, the primary·basis of evaluation is to determine whether the model is reasonably accurate, within the boundaries you, the consultant, have chosen.

This determination is made by asking three questions: Does the model include all the relevant variables? In this case, Schmatte, the modeler, has assumed that Q, the quantity ordered, is the only relevant variable. In more complicated inventory problems, one has to consider other variables; for example, the time it takes to receive the goods once an order has been placed (called the "lead time") may be a decision variable if, for example, the manager can influence the lead time by occasionally paying for a "rush order."

Now whenever you feel justified in doubting an assumption, you should ask yourself: how important is the possible error? The point is that in decision making the assumptions do not have to be absolutely accurate, and there is no point arguing about a possible inaccuracy if the inaccuracy doesn't alter the value of the payoff significantly. Ideally, you should investigate the question of the significance of inaccuracy by three steps. First, estimate the payoff, assuming that the original assumption is correct. Second, estimate the payoff, assuming that the assumption is incorrect and changing it to another version, in this case adding a second variable. Third, compare the two results to determine whether they are "significantly" different. "Significant" means "large enough to indicate that further investigation of the assumption is warranted in terms of total payoff of the research study." If the answer is "yes," then the assumption will need investigating; if "no," then the original assumption (which is the simpler of the two) will be made without further investigation. This method of studying assumptions we called *sensitivity analysis* in chapter 10, and it is, in effect, a way of conducting research on research — that is, of evaluating a research method, in this case assumption making. Obviously, the ideal procedure is usually not attainable, either because of cost or lack of data, and one has to use judgment as a substitute.

The second question to be raised about the model is: Does the model accurately describe the *appropriate* relationship between the objective and the decision variables? Schmatte's objective is to minimize total cost TC, so that TC is a "measure of performance" of the system: the lower TC, the better the system works. The question to ask Schmatte therefore is whether TC is appropriately represented as a function of the decision variables. "Appropriately" is meant to imply that you are not interested merely in a model that describes the system, but one that tells us how the system *ought* to work. Questioning the model in these terms means reviewing the assumptions that went into the model construction. For example, the model assumes that storage costs are proportional to the amount of cloth that is stored. But often companies rent space for storage; they can't rent an additional square foot, but have to rent, say, by rooms which are 144 square feet. In this case, the storage costs go up in steps, and are not linear in the amount of cloth stored. If you have reason to suspect the linearity assumption, then you may choose to go through the same "sensitivity" analysis described above: for example, does approximating a "step function" by a straight line significantly lessen the value of the model to the decision maker? If "yes," then you may recommend altering the model, even though it then becomes more complicated; if "no," then you accept the linear relation, even though it is not completely accurate.

The third, and often the most difficult, question is: Are the data accurate? The data are the numbers used in the model to describe such things as demand, costs, prices, etc. For example, the demands for items in inventory are obviously important data in this instance. The question is whether Schmatte has used the appropriate demand data.

At first blush, it would seem obvious how to collect such data: simply look over some past records of withdrawals from inventory. But it is astonishing how often organizations lack such data, either because they never collect it or because they record it in an unusable manner (for example, by years or months, when the model calls for daily usage).

But even when the data are available in the form required by the model, they may be wrong. For one thing, the data at best describe the past demands, whereas the model is to be applied to future demands. There is the question, then, of whether the future will be like the past. But more to the point, *should* future demand follow past policies? For example, in the case of raw material usage, possibly the manufacturing end of the business has ignored the inventory problem and placed unexpected demands on inventory when it would be simple enough to adjust their requirements in order to create a "smoother" demand. The point is an important one, because it shows that all data used in building decision-making models are based on a judgment about how a part of the total system ought to operate—in this case, the demand system. In effect, the data are the linkages between subsystems of the total system, and questions about demands and costs reflect the nature of these linkages.

Consider, as another example, the cost of holding inventory, and specifically the cost of capital tied up in idle inventory. Here you can be sure that the organization will have no records, since this cost is almost never collected by accountants or others. What the cost means is that the organization is losing some money it could make if its dollars were not tied into inventory; hence the cost is sometimes called an "opportunity cost," since it represents a lost opportunity for making money. The cost of capital tied up in inventory is a linkage between the inventory system and the financial system of the company, and the numerical value of the cost depends on how the financial system should use liquid capital: what should the financial system do if, say, $100,000 were released from the inventory system? It might be appropriate for it to do nothing but put the money into a no-interest bank account; the cost would then be zero. Or the correct action might be to put the money in a savings account at 5% interest; the cost would be $5000 per year. Or it might be right to invest the money in a new enterprise; the cost might then be 15% per year. Note that the cost—just like the demand above—is estimated by asking how another subsystem should behave under such-and-such conditions. Note also that this other subsystem may not be changeable in its policies: perhaps the financial subsystem is stupidly conservative with liquid capital but no one can change its policies. If so, then Mr. Schmatte must decide to base his estimate of the cost of capital on these inflexible policies.

Most often, cost data for decision-making models of the type we are considering are based on the experience and judgment of those who manage. The analyst should try to learn how the managers run their business, and hence infer how the subsystems should operate. Of course, if he has no confidence in management's judgment, he may want to ask advice outside the organization, or else quit.

The discussion of the data collection problem has really taken us beyond the original system to consideration of the role of the system in the larger system. This is the "second level" question of modeling. In one of its strongest forms, it asks whether the inventory system should exist at all—that is, whether the company should be making the clothing in the first place. A more likely question is whether the "solution" recommended by Schmatte would cause more problems than it solves. Very often, what seems to be optimal in the narrower scope turns out to require system changes that are extremely disruptive. Perhaps the little old man who really knows the business of making and selling clothes will quit when the boss takes away his powers to decide on order quantities.

The point about the larger system is an important one in today's complex society, where we are living through the ill effects of solving problems piecemeal. On the other hand, there is a limit to which one can go in looking into larger and larger systems. The artistry of model building and evaluation consists of deciding how broadly to view a problem.

What we have been saying in this section relates to the whole of the book and to "quantitative methods" in general. In most of the "problems" we have purposefully built you into a narrow system, and given you the data and enough guidance to formulate the model for a "solution." We did this to improve your piano playing capability. But in the real world out there, no one wants to hear finger exercises. No one will give you data, or tell you exactly what function describes how the system works; you're going to have to compose your own music.

To summarize, one should evaluate a model both at the very specific level, by determining whether the model includes all the relevant, important decision variables, and whether the content (form) of the model is correct, and also at the very general level, by determining how the system being modeled is linked to other systems, such linkages being the basis for estimating costs, demands, etc.

11.6 Summary

In this chapter you have been introduced to the basic techniques of calculus: integration and finding the derivative. The following points are worth repreating:

a. Both the derivative and the integral are useful notions with which you are already familiar; velocity is the derivative of distance with respect to time, acceleration is the derivative of velocity with respect to time, and an integral is just a sum of a function over many values.

b. Rules for evaluating derivatives and integrals of functions can be deduced directly from their definitions.

c. You can use the fact that a function reaches its "peak" or "ebb" where the slope or derivative becomes zero to find the maximum or minimum of the function; this is done by setting the first derivative to zero and solving the resulting equation.

d. You can check for the maximum versus the minimum by checking the change in the slope or "second derivative"; if the second derivative is negative, you're at a maximum, and if it's positive, you're at a minimum.

e. The integration process can be thought of as the reverse of taking the derivative; the integral can be used to calculate the area under a curve to evaluate total sales, for example.

f. The techniques of the calculus, like all quantitative methods, are powerful but dangerous if you don't ask yourself carefully whether your model accurately captures *all* of the important aspects of reality.

Appendix 11.1 Chain Rule Operations

We promised earlier in the chapter that we would tell you how to take the derivative of functions like e^{x^2}. This is done by means of another rule of derivatives, called the "chain rule." The rule uses the fact that you can look at the expression

$$e^{x^2}$$

as a "double function" or "function of a function," $f[g(x)]$, where

$$g(x) = x^2$$
$$f[g(x)] = e^{g(x)}$$

To get the derivative of e^{x^2}, you can evaluate the derivative of $f[g(x)]$, acting as though first $g(x)$ were a variable and then using x as the variable. The chain rule (which can be derived from the definition of the derivative) says that you do this by multiplying the derivative of $f[g(x)]$ by the derivative of $g(x)$:

$$\frac{df[g(x)]}{dx} = \frac{df[g(x)]}{d[g(x)]} \cdot \frac{dg(x)}{dx}$$

or

$$\frac{df}{dx} = \frac{df}{dg} \cdot \frac{dg}{dx}$$

In this case:

$$\frac{df[g(x)]}{dg} = \frac{d[e^{g(x)}]}{dg} = e^{g(x)}$$

since the derivative of e^y is e^y for any variable like y or $g(x)$. Also

$$\frac{dg(x)}{dx} = \frac{d(x^2)}{dx} = 2x$$

So,

$$\frac{df[g(x)]}{dx} = \frac{df}{dg} \cdot \frac{dg}{dx} = e^{g(x)} \cdot 2x = 2xe^{x^2}$$

In trying to apply the chain rule, the main trick is to express a function in the form $f[g(x)]$. The chain rule can also be applied when there are three "levels" — that is, where the expression can be given the form of $f\{g[h(x)]\}$. For example, consider

$$e^{(x+a)^2}$$

Here

$$f(x) = e^{(x+a)^2}$$
$$g(x) = (x + a)^2$$

and

$$h(x) = x + a$$

Then

$$f(x) = e^{g(x)} = e^{(h(x))^2}$$

and

$$g(x) = (h(x))^2$$

so

$$\frac{df(x)}{dx} = \frac{df}{dg}\frac{dg}{dh}\frac{dh}{dx} = [e^{(x+a)^2}][2(x + a)][1]$$
$$= 2(x + a)e^{(x+a)^2}$$

The chain rule can also be used to take the derivative of any complicated function to a large power without multiplying out the power of the functions. For example,

$$f(x) = (3x^2 + 2x)^7$$

Let

$$g(x) = (3x^2 + 2x),$$
$$f(g(x)) = g(x)^7$$
$$\frac{df}{dg}\frac{dg}{dx} = [7g(x)^6][6x + 2]$$
$$= 7[3x^2 + 2x]^6[6x + 2]$$

Appendix 11.2 Product and Quotient Rules for Derivatives

We showed you earlier how to find the derivative of a function which is the sum of other functions. There is also a rule for finding the derivative of a function that is a product of two other functions, which is given by:

If

$$h(x) = f(x)g(x)$$

then

$$\frac{dh(x)}{dx} = \frac{d[f(x)g(x)]}{dx} = f(x)\frac{dg(x)}{dx} + g(x)\frac{df(x)}{dx}$$

For example, if

$$h(x) = (3x + 7)(x^2 + 4)$$

then

$$f(x) = 3x + 7$$
$$g(x) = x^2 + 4$$

and

$$\frac{dh(x)}{dx} = f(x)\frac{d(g(x))}{dx} + g(x)\frac{d(f(x))}{dx}$$

$$= (3x + 7)\frac{d(x^2 + 4)}{dx} + (x^2 + 4)\frac{d(3x + 7)}{dx}$$

$$= (3x + 7)2x + (x^2 + 4)(3)$$

$$= 9x^2 + 14x + 12$$

as you can check by first multiplying $(3x + 7)(x^2 + 4)$ out, and then finding the derivative. Note that though the derivative of a sum is the sum of the derivatives, the derivative of a product is *not* necessarily the product of the derivatives.

There is a similar rule for finding the derivative of a function which is a quotient of two other functions. The rule goes as follows: If

$$h(x) = \frac{f(x)}{g(x)}$$

then

$$\frac{d(h(x))}{dx} = \frac{d[f(x)/g(x)]}{dx}$$

$$= \frac{g(x)\frac{df(x)}{dx} - f(x)\frac{dg(x)}{dx}}{[g(x)]^2}$$

For example, if

$$h(x) = \frac{2x^2 + x}{x^3 - 3}$$

then

$$f(x) = 2x^2 + x$$
$$g(x) = x^3 - 3$$

and

$$h(x) = \frac{f(x)}{g(x)}$$

So

$$\frac{dh(x)}{dx} = \frac{(x^3 - 3)\dfrac{d[2x^2 + x]}{dx} - (2x^2 + x)\dfrac{d[x^3 - 3]}{dx}}{(x^3 - 3)^2}$$

$$= \frac{(x^3 - 3)(4x + 1) - (2x^2 + x)(3x^2)}{(x^3 - 3)^2}$$

$$= \frac{-2x^4 - 2x^3 - 12x - 3}{(x^3 - 3)^2}$$

Appendix 11.3   Minimizing Functions of Several Variables; the Partial Derivative

Of course, not all measures of performance depend on the value of only one variable. Suppose, for example, that your costs depend on *two* variables, x and y. You want to minimize

$$f(x, y) = x^2 + y^2 - x - y$$

where $f(x, y)$ is your cost function. What values of x and y minimize this function? You can get a sense of how this function behaves if you think in three dimensions. Imagine four people holding a blanket by its corners so that it sags. The surface of the blanket would then represent a function of two variables that give the location of a point on the blanket with respect to the floor of a room, say, and the function itself gives the height of that point from the floor. The minimum point on the blanket is at the bottom of the sag, as in figure 11.11.

Note that at the minimum, both the slope in the direction parallel to the x-axis and the slope in the direction parallel to the y-axis are zero. You can calculate the slope of the function in the "x-direction" by regarding y as a constant for the time being, and taking the derivative "with respect to x." We call this the partial derivative with respect to x and write it as

$$\frac{\delta f(x, y)}{\delta x}$$

which, in this case, equals

$$2x - 1$$

since y^2 and $-y$ are now being treated as constants whose derivatives are zero.

Similarly, the slope in the y-direction is obtained by taking the derivative with respect to y and regarding x as a constant:

$$\frac{\delta f(x, y)}{\delta y} = 2y - 1$$

Now set the two partial derivatives equal to zero, and solve for x and y:

$$2x - 1 = 0$$
$$2y - 1 = 0$$

which yields $x = y = 1/2$, or the point (1/2, 1/2). As before, when minimizing a function of one variable, you can't be sure that this point is the minimum, since there may be other minimums or the point may actually be a maximum. In this case these fears are pretty well resolved by common sense and a little testing. Common sense indicates that (1/2, 1/2) is surely not a maximum, since as x and y increase, $x^2 + y^2$ becomes increasingly larger than x and y. A bit of testing of other x and y values near 1/2 will show you that the function keeps increasing as you move away from (1/2, 1/2). Thus at (1/2, 1/2), $x^2 + y^2 - x - y$ is $-1/2$; at (0, 0) and (1, 1), it is 0. At (1/4, 1/4), it is $-3/8$; and so on.

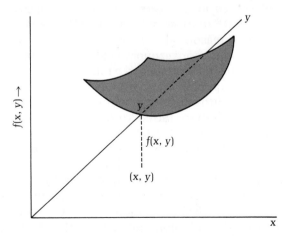

Figure 11.11

There exist second-derivative tests, as in the one-variable case, to tell you whether the point determined by the partial derivatives is a minimum or a maximum, and also whether there are other minima or maxima, and you can consult these tests in any standard calculus book if the need ever arises. The need probably won't arise in the real managerial world, since if you ever do get around to modeling a real managerial situation, you'll find that there are far more than two variables. You could proceed as we did above, and take the partial derivative of each variable, set all the results to zero and solve, but even with 30 or 40 variables you'd be a pretty busy kid for several days, and God knows how many mistakes you'd make. So what would you do? You'd ask your boss for some computer time, of course. Let the computer "take the partials" and solve the system of equations. And while it's at it, it might just as well check for maximum versus minimum, and for other minima or maxima.

Appendix 11.4   Continuous Probability Distributions (for those who have read chapters 5 and 6)

The calculus can aid in understanding another natural phenomenon of importance in decision making: continuous probability distributions. In chapters 5–8 we concentrated our attention on the probability of events which were discrete, like heads, tails, aces, kings, dots on a die, and so on. But often in the real world there are events which can only be described by a continuous measure: length of life of a person or machine parts, weights, energy, and so on. For example, the length of a life is described in terms of time, but the exact time can be any real number between 0 and 150 years, say. In management we often find it important to consider the probability that someone or something will last so many years. To keep the discussion from becoming too personal, suppose we consider fluorescent tubes in an office building. The reason why their "life expectancy" may be important is that it is often more economical to replace all the tubes in an office at the same time, rather than make repeated trips to replace single tubes. Hence it is important to know the probability distribution of failures, so as not to throw away too many good tubes.

We can begin by drawing the curve shown in figure 11.12, which is an example of a life-expectancy curve, and shows the probability of failure before time t (in hours). Obviously, if the tubes are any good, the probability is virtually zero of failing in a very small number of hours, but eventually failures occur, and the probability curve begins rising, until it approximates one, when virtually all tubes will have failed. We call this probability function a "cumulative probability function" (chapter 6) and represent it by $P(t)$. $P(t)$ can have many different forms, depending on what our *empirical* tests tell us: often there is no deductive method of inferring the form of P(t) from first principles, as we did in the case of heads and tails.

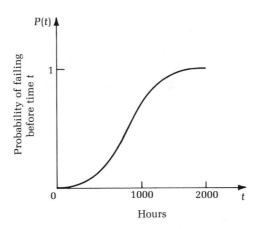

Figure 11.12   Cumulative Distribution for Life of Fluorescent Tubes

Suppose we are reasonably confident from our tests that the cumulative function shown in figure 11.12 is a good estimate of the life expectancy of the tubes. Then, as we shall see, it is useful to consider the slope of this cumulative function; in other words, if we know P(t), we can take its first derivative with respect to t:

$$\frac{dP(t)}{dt} = p(t)$$

The term p(t) represents the rate of change in P(t) at any moment t; if you like, it can be called the "probability" of failure at the moment t. Calculus has again enabled us to handle a paradoxical situation quite sensibly. It was (perhaps) strange to talk of the velocity of a falling body at a moment of time (when it is really not "moving"), but we saw how this strangeness could be removed by thinking of the velocity at a moment as the limit of a series of average velocities over smaller and smaller time segments Δt. Similarly, it may sound strange to talk of the probability of a tube's failing at *exactly* time t (when the chances of failing at a precise moment seem virtually nil), but we can always think of the probability of failing over some interval Δt, and hence of the limit as Δt approaches zero. If we were to plot p(t) for the curve given in figure 11.12 we would get a curve like the one shown in figure 11.13, which we call the "probability density."

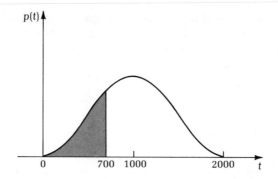

Figure 11.13   Probability Density for Life of Fluorescent Tubes

Now, if $p(t)$ is the derivative of $P(t)$, then $P(t)$ + constant is the integral of $p(t)$:

$$P(t) + \text{constant} = \int p(t)dt$$

But the constant is zero, since in this case $P(t) = 0$ when $t = 0$:

$$P(t) = \int p(t)dt$$

Specifically, if we take the area under the curve up to 700 hours, then

$$P(700) = \int_0^{700} p(t)dt$$

as is shown by the shaded portion in figure 11.13.

We can note that the area under the whole curve in figure 11.13 is 1, because the span 0 to ∞ takes care of all possible lifetimes:

$$\int_0^{\infty} p(t)dt = 1$$

Note that this integral "goes to infinity"; that is, it is unbounded on the upper side.

Finally, we can represent the mean of the distribution (mean lifetime of a tube) by following the same rules we used in chapter 6. There we calculated the mean — or "expected" — value by multiplying each possible value times its probability and adding all the results. Here we replace Σ by ∫ and do the same thing:

$$\text{mean} = \int_0^{\infty} tp(t)dt$$

This result is often symbolized by the Greek letter μ (mu).

To summarize thus far, we assume that there exists a very large class of items, called a *population*, each member of which can take on a value x from some continuous measure (age, weight, tensile strength, etc.); we also assume that there exists a cumulative probability distribution P(x) which is a function that goes from x to the probability that items from the population have measurements less than or equal to x. Finally, we assume we can take the derivative of P(x), symbolized p(x), and that p(x) can be used to determine the mean:

$$\mu = \int_a^b xp(x)dx$$

where a and b are the extreme values that x can take on.

To see how all this works in a specific instance, we can begin with a very simple example, which rarely occurs in reality, where the probabilities p(t) are equal over an interval of time and zero outside this interval. This is called the continuous uniform probability distribution (see discrete uniform in chapter 6) and is shown in figure 11.14. Within the interval a to b, p(t) is constant $= c$; otherwise, $p(t) = 0$. Hence the cumulative probability is

$$P(t) = \int_a^t p(t)dt = (t - a)c$$

as is shown in figure 11.15. But there is a relationship between a, b, and c, since

$$\int_a^b p(t)dt = 1 = ct \Big|_a^b = bc - ac$$

or

$$c(b - a) = 1 \quad \text{and} \quad c = \frac{1}{b - a}$$

Hence $p(t) = \frac{1}{b - a}$ in the interval a to b. Finally,

$$\text{mean} = \int_a^\infty tp(t)dt = \int_a^b t\frac{1}{(b-a)}dt = \frac{t^2}{2(b-a)}\Big|_a^b$$

$$= \frac{b^2 - a^2}{2(b-a)} = \frac{(b-a)(b+a)}{2(b-a)} = \frac{b+a}{2}$$

which is not very surprising if you think about it.

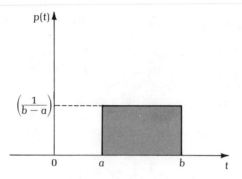

Figure 11.14   Continuous Uniform Probability Distribution

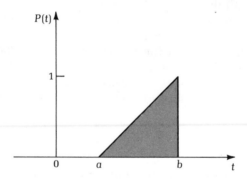

Figure 11.15   Cumulative Probability for Continuous Uniform Probability Distribution

A great many probability distributions are "exponential," meaning that $P(t)$ and $p(t)$ are represented by some constant which is raised to the power x or some function of x. The constant is usually expressed by e, which we have seen before. Recall that e has the property

$$\frac{de^x}{dx} = e^x$$

That is, e^x is the only nonzero function which is its own derivative. It follows that

$$\int e^x dx = e^x + \text{constant}$$

Also,

$$\frac{de^{-x}}{dx} = -e^{-x}$$

and

$$\int e^{-x}dx = -e^{-x} + \text{constant}$$

A fairly simple example of an exponential probability distribution is

$$p(x) = e^{-x} \quad \text{and} \quad P(x) = 1 - e^{-x}$$

This distribution often describes the distribution of "service times" at toll booths, information desks, and the like, as in figures 11.16 and 11.17. If x is very near zero, then p(x) is very near one, and as x increases, p(x) becomes smaller and eventually approaches zero. When applied to service stations like toll booths, this means that the service time is most likely to be extremely short (virtually zero), since many customers smoothly pay their fare and are on their way. But there are

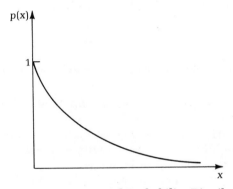

Figure 11.16   Exponential Probability Distribution

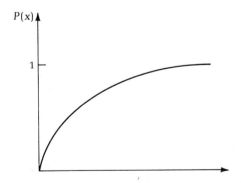

Figure 11.17   Cumulative Exponential Probability Distribution

customers who fumble for their change, stall their motors, stop and ask for directions, have no money and haggle for a free ride; in each case the service time is increasingly long. One can imagine the scene when the auto blows up itself and the toll booth, thereby creating a service time of eternity.

The most common exponential probability distribution, called the "normal," is given by

$$p(x) = \frac{1}{\sqrt{2\pi}\sigma} e^{-(x-\mu)^2/2\sigma^2}$$

where μ and σ (sigma) are constants which describe the mean and standard deviation spread of the probability density function, and π is the constant 3.14159 — the ratio of the circumference of a circle to its diameter. Its "bell-shaped" picture is shown in figure 11.18. It can be shown that

$$\mu = \int_{-\infty}^{+\infty} xp(x)dx$$

for this particular $p(x)$, though finding the value of this integral may be beyond your present knowledge. If you'll look back at the function for the normal distribution you'll see that the exponent of e is raised to the power $-(x - \mu)^2/2\sigma^2$ — that is, to a minus squared deviation from the mean in units of $2\sigma^2$. When $x = \mu$, this exponent is zero; but a constant raised to the zero power is one. Hence $p(x) = 1/\sqrt{2\pi}\sigma \, e^{-0} = 1/\sqrt{2\pi}\sigma$ when $x = \mu$. This is also the highest point of the bell-shaped curve. Thus the high point varies inversely with σ. When σ is small, the high point will be large; when σ is large, the high point will be low, as is shown in figure 11.18. This amounts to saying that σ is a measure of

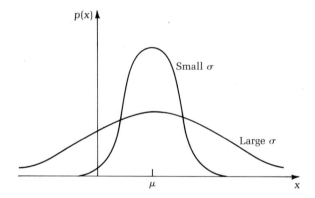

Figure 11.18

the dispersion of the distribution: the smaller is σ, the more the values cluster about the mean.

The normal distribution occurs so frequently that its areas have been tabulated. The table is given in terms of the deviations from the mean in units of σ, which is called the "standard deviation." For example, the area from $\mu + 2\sigma$ out "to infinity" is about .025, meaning that there is a low probability of exceeding this value; the area from $\mu + 3\sigma$ is about .003, and from $\mu + 4\sigma$ is less than .0001. Thus "intelligence tests" standardize the mean to 100, and σ to 15. Hence you are unusually bright if your score is 130 ($\mu + 2\sigma$), very unusually bright if it is 145, very, very unusually bright if it's 160, and so on. Similar remarks apply to the "other side," since the curve in figure 11.18 is symmetrical: 70 ($\mu - 2\sigma$) is unusually low intelligence, 55 exceptionally unusually low, and so on; but don't feel sad, because no one yet knows what intelligence tests measure. (See appendix table 7.1)

When you come to study statistics, you will make frequent use of the normal distribution, because it can be shown that the averages of random samples tend to obey the normal distribution, even when the samples are small. Thus it is known that individual incomes of citizens of the U.S. are not normally distributed, but the average incomes in a series of sample surveys will be normally distributed. In chapter 7 we showed how the normal distribution could be used to approximate the discrete binomial when np is reasonably large.

Even this brief exposure to continuous probabilities should indicate to you how the theory of discrete probabilities, based on Σ, can be extended to a theory of continuous probabilities, based on $\int$.

PROBLEMS APPENDIX 11

Chain Rule

1. If $f(y) = y^2$, and $y = x^2$, what is df/dx?

2. If $f(y) = ay + b$, and $y = cx + d$, what is df/dx?

3. If $f(x) = 2x^2 + 3x + \dfrac{1}{x}$, and $x = 3t^2 + t$, what is df/dt?

4. Suppose that sales for your company depend on consumer attitudes, which in turn depend on, among other things, the amount spent for advertising. If you could express each of these in functional form, how would you maximize sales? What rules of derivatives would you use, if any, and what would you do to determine the maximum?

5. The Dana Company has discovered empirically that its profit function can be approximated by the following: $P = 3x - 250$

$- x^2/2500$ where $P =$ profits in hundreds of dollars and $x =$ total production volume in thousands of units. The company has also discovered that its total production is related to the size of its labor force by the following equations: $x = 4y + y^2/20$, where y is the number of men employed.

a. What are the company's profits if the labor force consists of 20 men?
b. What is the rate of change of profits with respect to the number of men employed at this point? Is this rate increasing or decreasing?
c. Should more men be hired at this point?

Product and Quotient Rules

Calculate the derivative of the following functions:

1. $f(x) = x(x^2 - 1)$
2. $f(x) = (x + 1)(x - 1)$
3. $f(x) = x^3(x^2 + x)$
4. $f(x) = (2x + 3)(4x^2 - 6x + 9)$
5. $f(x) = (5x - x^2)^2(3x^2 + 2)$
6. $f(x) = x/(1 + x)$
7. $f(x) = x/(2x + 1)$
8. $f(x) = (2x^2 - x)/(4x + 1)$
9. $f(x) = (x^2 + x + 1)/(x^2 - x + 1)$
10. $f(x) = (x^2 - ax)/(x + a)$

The Partial Derivative

1. If $f(x, z) = 3x^2 + 6x + z$, what is $\delta f/\delta x$? $\delta f/\delta z$?
2. If $f(x, y) = x^4 + 4xy + y^3 + 10$, what is $\delta f/\delta x$? $\delta f/\delta y$?
3. If $f(x, y, z) = x + y + z$, what is f/x? f/y? f/z?
4. If $f(x, y, z) = 3x^2 + 6xy + (2z^2/x^3) - (x + 2)/(x - 2)$, what is $\delta f/\delta x$? $\delta f/\delta y$? $\delta f/\delta z$?

5. A department store has two departments. The earnings (gross revenues minus costs of goods sold) are given by:

$$E_1(x_1, y_1) = 4x_1 + 5y_1 + x_1y_1 - x_1^2 - y_1^2 \quad \text{for department 1}$$

and

$$E_2(x_2, y_2) = 4x_2 + 2y_2 + 2x_2y_2 - 2x_2^2 - y_2^2 - 5 \quad \text{for department 2}$$

where: E_i = earnings of department i in millions of dollars

x_i = investment in inventory by department i in millions of dollars

y_i = floor space used by department i in units of 10,000 sq. ft.

The store management wishes to determine the needs of capital and floor space to the departments in order to maximize the total earnings for the store. The total earnings are given by:

$$E(x_1, y_1, x_2, y_2) = E(x_1, y_1) + E_2(x_2, y_2)$$

so they are separable.

What are the optimal values of the four variables? What are the capital and floor space needs of the department store?

12 The Systems Approach

Throughout this text we have often mentioned the "systems approach" in a way that cast doubt on the so-called solutions to the problems. When we did so, we questioned whether the set D (decisions) really contained all the alternative decisions you could make, or whether S (states of the world) was adequately specified. We also questioned whether the value (W) of the outcomes (O) was defensible in terms of the larger system of human values.

But the "systems approach" always appeared as a question, ambiguously formulated. In chapter 2 we explained how precision always occurs as a bridge between the ambiguity of problem formulation and decision making. Now we should say some more about how this deductive process of problem formulation should be understood.

We can begin with the question that has been implicit in all our problems: What is a system? Even in chapter 1 as we examined the Route to Work problem we had to consider systemic aspects. Were you really the system? Wasn't there really a much broader perspective in which your arrival or nonarrival at work could be gauged in terms of its social worth, rather than your rather selfish expected value?

In defining a system it will be helpful to use some of the logic introduced in chapter 10. There we explained how a problem could be "decomposed" into a set of variables, and that there sometimes exists a function of these variables which can be taken as the worth of specific decisions. Thus in the very simple Super Sled problem, we assumed there were two variables, x_1 and x_2, the first representing the number of regular sleds you decide to make, and the second the number of super sleds. We assumed that the value to you of any decision you make about the size of x_1 and x_2 can be represented by a linear function, $x_1 + x_2$, which we called the "objective" function. We can now say that a "system" is a way of looking at a problem in terms of component variables, like x_1 and x_2 in the case above, which variables can be used to determine the values of alternative decisions. In real-life problems— for example, in the allocation of funds to programs in a community— there may be hundreds of variables, and the "worth" is some kind of social well-being.

You will note that we said that a "system" is a way of looking at a problem; this is important to note because later on in life you're almost bound to meet someone who will tell you that you're really running a system and that you ought to pay him for telling you how to do it. However, you should not assume that a system is "out there," but rather is itself a decision you can make or not make. A great many of our problems are not viewed as a system—for example, almost every emergency. If someone shouts, "Fire!" you'd be foolish to begin identifying alternative escape routes and trying to minimize time of flight. Instead, you go where your instinct and past experience guide you.

You should realize the power and restriction of the "systems approach." First of all, it views a problem in terms of objectives (goals, ends, purposes). But, more important, the systems approach unifies all the variety of goals into one "measure of performance." We have seen that sometimes this measure can reasonably be "expected dollars," or, as in chapter 7, expected utility, which takes into account risk aversion or risk seeking. But consider a community: Can you come up with a reasonable measure of performance of the community in which you live? Average income? Income spread? Average state of health? Educational level? Morality level? Yet community policy makers somehow do decide on the allocation of funds to various programs. At the present time, we don't understand very well how they ought to do this allocation, but if you believe in the systems approach, you believe that a measure of performance exists and you will do your best, if you are the manager or planner, to approximate the measure.

But what is the correct measure of performance? How do we decide whether a proposed measure is appropriate? There is no completely satisfactory answer to these questions, but it will help in considering them to realize that a satisfactory answer must be based on the determination of who should be served by the system. Suppose we call the people who are benefited by the system, the system "clients." The client may be a single individual, as in many of the problems of this book. Usually, however, a large group of individuals constitute the system clients, including people yet to be born, or people who have died. Thus it may seem reasonable to you to say that students — present and future—are the proper clients of the national system called the schools; or that present and future patients are the clients of the system of health services, including hospitals, clinics, doctors, and so on.

We've now come to the most crucial point about the systems approach—namely, who the clients *should* be. To illustrate this value question, suppose that in the Super Sled problem the client really should have been poor kids in your community, since you have plenty of money and don't need to make any more. See how the whole problem shifts once this value judgment is made: the measure of performance is not net dollars to you, but something like the total number of safe sleds you can make and distribute to the kids. The value of a super sled is now zero if it takes longer to make. And so on. If the proper client were poor kids, and if your problem were solved under the assumption that you were the client, then we could say that the problem was precisely "solved"—in the wrong way.

We'd like to tell you that this example is contrived, and that most of our modern systems serve the right clients, but it ain't so. Most reflective planners have come to realize that our major systems—schools, hospitals, transportation, private corporations—all serve the wrong clients. There are good political reasons why this is so, but the systems approach, which attempts to be rational, cannot accept politics alone as a justification.

But wait a bit, you'll say. How do we know who is the right or the wrong client? Isn't this an ethical judgment, and aren't all "rights" and "wrongs" relative? The answer is no, unless you want to be mentally and spiritually lazy. In the nineteenth century children worked 14 hours a day in the mines in England in order to serve the clients, who were the owners. Were the owners the only rightful clients, and was this practice right? If you say "yes," we won't penalize you. We'll just pity you, because you have no moral sense; you aren't shocked at the treatment of women and minorities; you couldn't care less how many Jews were burned in concentration camps. But if you aren't like that, and have a moral sense, then you can use it to decide who the clients ought to be. In the recent past our ancestors slaughtered the buffalo and egret almost to the extinction of the species. This was morally wrong, because we and our progeny are as much the clients of the wildlife system as they were. So are the egrets and buffalo.

Thus the appropriate clients of a system are those who have a moral right—based on justice and fairness—to be so. There is no "technique" for making the decisions about the right clients, because morality doesn't operate by techniques. But it does operate through talk; so talk it over with those whose opinions you respect, the next time you have to determine the right clients of a system.

There is a second group of people who are essential in any systems approach: the decision makers. These are the people who can make real changes by the allocation of resources, such as manpower, money, equipment, and so on. In most of this book there was a "you" who made the decisions, a single individual who controlled the resources. But in real organizations the decision maker is a complex of interacting persons, often very difficult to identify. A part of the difficulty lies in trying to determine the scope of the system. Consider a school, for example. The teacher may be the sole decision maker if we say that the decision is what happens in a classroom. But more often nowadays educational planners choose to view the whole school as a system, because what happens in one classroom may influence student and teacher performance in other classes. Of course, the choice of the size of the system does not necessarily stop at the school; perhaps it is more sensible to think of all the public schools in a region — or nationally. But why stop at schools? After all, health depends very much on education as well as recreation. So, why not say that the "system" is the complex of education, health, recreation — and a number of other things like income, pollution, population, and so on? In recent years, there have even been attempts to model the whole world for centuries ahead.

As the scope of the system becomes larger, the nature and composition of the decision makers becomes more and more complicated and difficult to identify. If the choice is to view the nation as a system, for example, then almost every adult is in the act of deciding. It also becomes very much more difficult to specify what decisions are possible — that is, to define the set D.

However the choice of a system is made, there will always be relevant aspects of a problem which are not controlled by the decision makers but which do influence the outcomes and hence the measure of performance: the weather, other nations' policies, politics, and so on. These aspects belong in the *environment* of the system. Thus we can begin to visualize the decision makers' task: it is to use the available *resources* in the right way, so that the resources plus the environment produce a measure of performance that is as high as one can expect. In the case of linear programming (LP) in chapter 10, the resources were the variables x_1, x_2, etc., and the environment was described by the constraint equations. It is worth noting that in LP and related systems approaches, everything has a price. Thus if there is a moral constraint (for example, not to cheat the customers) and it can be written into a constraint equation, then (using the dual) we can calculate the price of remaining moral. Even lives have a price in this kind of systems approach. But there are other systems approaches in which not everything can be priced — for example, systems where moral laws play a dominant role.

Before leaving decision makers, we should emphasize once more that very important aspect — information. For example, if you decide to take a two-week vacation from your business, what does it cost you? You might be tempted just to add the travel, hotels, meals, etc. But this "information" would be very weak. What the question asks, from the systems point of view, is the most you could have earned if you had not taken a vacation (assuming that your measure of performance is earnings). We call the "cost" of the vacation an *opportunity* cost. You should realize that the information about opportunity costs is not gained by simply going out and observing. For example, you wouldn't necessarily be able to estimate the vacation cost by observing how much you earn in two weeks when you're on the job, because you may be earning far less than you can earn. In effect, information for decision making is not descriptive or predictive information, but rather is based on a judgment about the value of alternative courses of action. Information for decision making is value loaded, not value free. If you ever undertake to adopt a systems approach to your favorite system, expect your neck to become very sore, because you'll be constantly sticking it out. In making your opportunity cost estimates, you'll find you have to talk with a lot of people, use your best judgment, imagination, intuition, and then guess.

This remark brings us to the third of the cast of characters of the systems approach. Besides the clients and decision makers, there is the group of persons who invent a systems approach. For lack of a better name, suppose we call them planners. One of the necessary but most difficult aspects of the systems approach is self-understanding—that is, understanding what you are like as a planner. It would be very nice just to say that you are "objective," apart from it all, observing without bias, without value involvement. But from what we have just said, you can see how ridiculous any such claim would be.

You can never escape from your own intellectual and feeling background. Eventually you come to see the world in one particular way, and this way of seeing it tells you what "reality" really is. The German philosophers called such a way of seeing the world a Weltanschauung. You will have arrived at the systems approach once you realize your own Weltanschauung and how it differs from others. The economists like linear programming, preference orderings, expected values, because in this way they see the world of decision making as made up of prices. But engineers may see society as a machine and thus see that the "real" problem is to get the parts running together smoothly. Another of a different persuasion says "No, it's not a machine, it's a brain, so let's see how a brain 'really' works and apply this knowledge to re-designing society." "No," says the biologist, "society is a biological organism, so we need a general systems theory to tell us how it really works." "Wait a minute," says another, "the important thing is getting changes to occur in society; otherwise, all the theory is a waste of time.

Hence social psychology is the secret of the systems approach." "True," chirps his neighbor, "but the secret is 'organizational development' (OD) which emphasizes leadership and responsibility." The anthropologist is amused at all this, because he sees that all of this quarreling is a result of modern-day cultural forces, especially those of a technological society. The radical really knows the answer: every academic is working for the establishment. And the religious person finds the secret in each individual's relationship to the Divine, the Whole, the Complete—God. The philosopher is even more amused; each of them is captured by his own Weltanschauung, as is the philosopher himself, of course.

Thus, you, as a student, are bound to be confused as you read in the systems approach. You can probably make your life easier if you don't seek one answer, but use your readings to suit your own style. These readings may include the past, because as we said in chapter 1 the systems approach is at least as old as the *I Ching*. Also, you should keep in mind that the systems approach is only one approach to societal problems and progress. Politics, for example, and art are other possibilities.

But what should you read? A few ancient writings like Plato's *Republic*, the *I Ching*, and Aristotle's *Ethics* may be appropriate. More modern writings by Spinoza, Kant, Marx, Bentham, and J. S. Mill, all describe systems approaches.

Some relevant recent works are C. W. Churchman's *The Systems Approach* (New York, Delacorte, 1969); S. Beer's *Decisions and Control* (New York, Wiley, 1966); and R. L. Ackoff's *Redesigning the Future* (New York, Wiley, 1974).

Above all, you should take the systems approach seriously (albeit, with a modicum of humor) because it may well be the only way in which humanity can save itself from destruction. Very possibly it is the only way we can reassemble the pieces of our fragmented world: the only way we can create coherence out of chaos.

Short Answers to Odd-Numbered Problems

Problems 1.1

1. Quantitative methods enter into the decision by consideration of tuition charges, number of students in classes, level of difficulty, region, etc.
3. One way: fill the 5-quart can and use it to fill the 4-quart, leaving 1 quart in the 5. Dump the 4-quart, and put the 1 quart into it. Fill the 5 and dump as much as possible into the 4; i.e., dump 3 quarts into the 4. What remains in the 5 is 2 quarts.
5. The net increase is $240, which is probably peanuts for a $30,000 a year family.
7. **a.** flexible and very imprecise **c.** inflexible and fairly precise **e.** somewhat flexible and precise **g.** flexible and rather imprecise

Problems 1.3

1. All cats eventually die.
3. Nothing can be deduced from these assumptions, although the FBI may keep storing such "facts" in its files.
5. Improbable events are probable. But you should sense that the meaning of "probable" and "improbable" has shifted in the second assumption.

Problems 1.4

1.

	State of the World	
Decision	Job for less than a year	Job for the whole year
Job 1	6000	10,000
Job 2	5000	8000

3. D is the total purchases you make at a given time (in dollars). S is the balance at any time (one number). O is "underdrawn" or "overdrawn." W is zero or the penalty for overdrawing the account.

5. Outcome table:

Decision	State of the World	
	s_1 = no bonus in job A	s_2 = bonus in job A
d_1 = accept A	$15,000 poor region	$17,000 poor region
d_2 = accept B	$14,000	$14,000

Payoff table:

Decision	State of the World	
	s_1 = no bonus in job A	s_2 = bonus in job A
d_1 = accept A	w_1 = $15,000, worth of poor region	w_2 = $17,000, worth of poor region
d_2 = accept B	w_3 = $14,000, worth of good region	w_4 = $14,000, worth of good region

Problems 1.5

1. Categorical, descriptive (Possibly, there is the implied prescription: "Abolish all governments.")
3. Categorical, descriptive – but note that the statement strongly implies a prescription: "There shouldn't be too many cooks."
5. Categorical, prescriptive
7. The first part is categorical prescriptive; the second is categorical descriptive.

Problems 1.6

1. To "make the most", you'd accept the order.

Problems 1.7

1. $2.00
3. $3.50
5. Expected income from job 1 = $7600; expected income from job 2 = $8200; so, choose job 2, assuming you must choose one of the jobs, and you should "make the most."
7. Go to court.
9. Expected value of the bet is −$5; so don't bet.

Problems 1.8

1. a. when someone shouts "Fire!"   **c.** when someone swerves toward you on the road

Problems 2.2.1

1. 2 is the successor of 1; all positive whole numbers can now be defined.

Problems 2.2.2

1. For example, that a degree from the school qualifies you for a job; that you find good friends and teachers, that it's the cheapest way to get an education.
3. Assumptions about fads, changing styles, permanent styles, competitor's marketing strategies, etc.

Problems 2.2.3

1. Fallacious. Such communication is estimated to be very costly. To justify the "therefore" we'd have to assume that the funds don't have a better use.
3. This works.
5. No go

Problems 2.3

1. Because of the "double entry" convention of accounting. The axiom is "true" because it is useful. It is a pragmatic truth.
3. The reason could be regarded as conventional, but is more likely pragmatic because the legislative sessions begin in January, and this allows time for hearings and other inquiries.
5. There is no convincing argument we know of why the cause has to precede the event in time.

Problems Appendix 2.1

1. a. $U = \{a,d,s\}$ **c.** $\{a,d\}, \{a, s\}, \{d, s\}, \{a\}, \{d\}, \{s\}, \{\phi\}$

3. a. $0 = \{(s_1, s_2, s_3), (s_1, s_2, u_3), (s_1, u_2, s_3), (s_1, u_2, u_3), (u_1, s_2, s_3), (u_1, u_2, s_3), (u_1, s_2, u_3), (u_1, u_2, u_3)\}$ **c.** d_1 is more expensive than d_2 because of a possible shortage of raw material and the return expenditure

5. a. $0 = 0,1,2,\ldots\ldots,15$ **c.** E consists of the following. N of customers contacted on the first day: 0 0 2 1 1 0; second day 0 2 0 1 0 1; third day 2 0 0 0 1 1.   **e.** first day: 0 0 2; second day: 0 2 0; third day: 2 0 0   **g.** Impossible: $E \cap F = \phi$

7. The set D of decisions consists of: $d_1 =$ drive your car and park in the city lot; $d_2 =$ drive your car and park in the 2-hour zone; $d_3 =$ take a cab. (See top of the following page for set S.)
Payoff table:

Decision	State of the World		
	s_1	s_2	s_3
d_1	$5.00	$5.60	$6.20
d_2	$1.50	$1.50	$6.50
d_3	$17.00	$17.00	$17.00

The set S of states of the world consists of: s_1 = performance starts on time; s_2 = performance is 1/2 hour late; s_3 = performance starts 1 hour late.

9. a. d_1 = grow wheat in Santa Cruz; d_2 = raise chickens in Santa Cruz; d_3 = grow wheat in Monterey; d_4 = raise chickens in Monterey; d_5 = do not farm

c.

Decision	State of the World		
	s_1 = poor weather	s_2 = average	s_3 = excellent
d_1	.3 × 10,000 − 9000 = −$6000	.5 × 18,000 − 9000 = $0	.2 × 25,000 − 9000 = −$4000
d_2	18,000 − 7000 = $11,000	18,000 − 7000 = $11,000	18,000 − 7000 = $11,000
d_3	.3 × 6000 − 8500 = −$6700	.5 × 15,000 − 8500 = −$1000	.2 × 35,000 − 8500 = −$1500
d_4	18,000 − 7000 = $11,000	18,000 − 7000 = $11,000	18,000 − 7000 = $11,000
d_5	not known	not known	not known

Problems 3.2

1. Some examples of criteria for ordering Presidents: was stronger in defending the country from its enemies; was more egalitarian; was more responsive to public needs; was more honest.

3. In the history of philosophy, assumption (b) has been most frequently attacked, by the argument that existence is not a (positive) property. But (a) has also been attacked by the argument that the "definition is either hopelessly vague or self-contradictory.

Problems 3.3

1. $f(3) = 23$; $f(18) = 98$
3. $f(4) = 46$; $f(0) = 2$; $f(-2) = 4$
5. $f(4,3) = 53$; $f(0,1) = 21$; $f(0,0) = 15$
7. $h(3) = 2$; $h(0) = -7$; $h(-4) = 37$
9. $f(3) = \dfrac{7}{45}$; $f(-6) = \dfrac{17}{57}$; $f(4) = \dfrac{1}{6}$
11. **a.** $x = \dfrac{9}{4}$ **c.** $x = 5\dfrac{1}{2}$ **e.** $\therefore x = -1$ **g.** $\therefore x = 2$ or $x = -2$
13. Not necessarily, because x can also take on certain fractional values
15. **a.** $x^2(1 + x)$ **c.** $\dfrac{1}{x}$

Problems 3.6

1. **a.** The measure avoids completely the quality (value) of the education for the student.   **c.** discussion question

3. probably not
5. *aspirin*: time for relief of pain and (sometimes) purity   *laundry soap*: whiteness; brightness   *toothpaste*: minus number of cavities and (sometimes) whiteness

Problems 3.7

1. Dept. A, 3 million; Dept. B, 2 million; the sixth million can be allocated to any of the three departments.
3. Four conveyors from supplier 3; one conveyor from supplier 1; one conveyor from supplier 2
5. The additional labor should be assigned as follows: one each to departments 1, 3, and 4, and two to department 2.

Problems 4.2

1. **a.** $= 36$ **c.** $= 246$
3. **a.** $= 6$ **c.** $= 30$
5. **a.** 89   **c.** 41

Problems 4.3

1. **a.** 36,450   **c.** 115,600
3. $a_5 = a_0 = 5d$; $d = -800$; depreciation is \$800 a year.
5. **a.** You will need 4000 beds 10 years from now.   **c.** That the rate of growth will remain constant over the next 10 years

Problems 4.4

1. **a.** a geometric series; $a_0 = 1$ and $q = 2$ **c.** a geometric series; $a_0 = 4$ and $q = 1.5$
3. plan I
5. \$2,377,592.20

Problems 4.5

1. **a.** 8150   **c.** 12,480
3. 17,035
5. **a.** 13,740   **c.** 13,351
7. **a.** 313,147

Problems 4.6

1. **a.** 115,000   **c.** 958,000
3. The solution depends on the discount rate used.
5. $$a_0 = \frac{a_i - d\left(\dfrac{q^i - 1}{q - 1}\right)}{q^i}$$

Problems 5.1

1. By looking at past weather situations and examining under what conditions they occurred

3. Yes, in (1) we deal with a sample of past data to estimate, whereas in (2) we have complete information.

5. For the three customers waiting there are a total of 3! = 6 different sequences in which they can be serviced. Draw one at random.

Problems 5.2

1. a. Two atomic events: heads and tails. **c.** (i) $\frac{3}{4}$; (iii) $\frac{3}{4}$; (v) $\frac{1}{4}$

3. ∴ $E(w_1) = \frac{1}{8}$; $E(w_2) = \frac{3}{4}$; $E(w_3) = -\frac{3}{8}$; $E(w_4) = 0$. Since $E(w_2)$ is the highest, you should make the bet; i.e., at least 2 heads.

5. Play in the 3-die game, since the expected gain is higher.

Problems 5.3

1. No, because it may not be possible to get all the data needed or to know what factors in the past to look for.

3. (a–d) The events are equiprobable and independent.

Problems 5.4.1

1. $\frac{1}{36}$

3. $\frac{1}{225}$

5. a. 17,576,000 different plates **c.** 2,159,206,300 plates

7. $\frac{1}{1,679,616}$

9. a. Three outcomes are favorable to your enrichment. **c.** Total expected payoff = 1.10.

Problems 5.4.2

1. 3,628,800 different ways

3. 20

5. 120 different orders; the probability of each order is $\frac{1}{120}$.

7. .0965

9. 271,667

Problems 5.4.3

1. The number of possible distinct 3-card hands is 22,100, and the probability of each hand is $\frac{1}{22,100}$.

3. $\frac{1}{2,598,960}$

5. The daily expected profits would decrease by $5.

7. It should take $\frac{1}{2}$ the time to make the million or about 100 days.

Problems 5.4.4

1. .308
3. No

Problems 6.1

1. a.

x	$P(X = x)$
0	1/16
1	4/16
2	6/16
3	4/16
4	1/16

c.

0	1/2
1	1/2

Problems 6.1.1

1. No
3. Examples are: no. of dots in toss of one die $(P = 1/6)$; no. of heads in flip of one coin $(P = 1/2)$; a number on a roulette wheel which has 36 slots $(P = 1/36)$.

Problems 6.1.2

1. $P(X = 0) = 1/2$ (for heads); $P(X = 1) = 1/2$ (for tails)

3. a. $X = \begin{cases} 1 \text{ if defective} & P(X = 1) = 1/100 \\ 0 \text{ if not defective} & P(X = 0) = 99/100 \end{cases}$

c. $X = \begin{cases} 1 \text{ if the day is rainy} & P(X = 1) = .3 \\ 0 \text{ otherwise} & P(X = 0) = .7 \end{cases}$

Problems 6.1.3

1. $n = 3$ and $p = .5$
3. $P(X \geq 3)$ when $p = .05$ is .0116; when $p = .20$ is .3222
5. The probability of such a feat is approximately .0005.
7. The probability of getting one or more defective fuses is .096.
9. X is the number of seeds that will germinate.
$$P(X \geq 180) = \sum_{X=180}^{200} \binom{200}{X} (.95)^X (.05)^{200-X} = .99$$

Problems 6.1.4

1. $P(X_1 = 1, X_2 = 2, X_3 = 5, X_4 = 2) = \dfrac{10!}{1!2!5!2!} (.4)^1 (.3)^2 (.2)^5 (.1)^2 \approx .099$

3. $P(X_1 = 0, X_2 = 4, X_3 = 46) = \dfrac{50!}{0!4!46!} (.02)^0 (.06)^4 (.92)^{46} \approx .064$

5. $P(X_1 = 4, X_2 = 6, X_3 = 90) = \dfrac{100!}{4!6!90!}(.01)^4(.05)^6(.94)^{90} \approx .002$

Problems 6.2

1. a. .50   **c.** The difference of .1 represents the probability that $C = 5$.   **e.** .76
g. .16   **i.** .23
3. X = no. of heads $P(X \le x)$ $P(1 \le X \le) = 15/16$

0	1/16
1	5/16
2	11/16
3	15/16
4	16/16 = 1

5. .001
7. The tank should be built so that it can hold at least 4000 gallons.

Problems 7.1

1. 5.62
3. Your standard price recommendation should be .80.
5. Your friend should not have expected more favorable results.
7. Be indifferent between buying fire insurance only and buying no insurance.

Problems 7.2

The questions in this section are designed to introduce the student to the concepts of risk and utility, which are discussed later in the book. Thus, they should be viewed as starting points for discussion.

Problems 7.3

1.

maximum value of X	minimum value of X	range
a. 18	3	15
c. 7	0	7
e. 12	0	12

3. $\dfrac{15}{16}$

Problems 7.4

1. $E|x\text{-mean}| = 2.6000$; $E|x\text{-median}|$: 2.60
3. .5
5. The expected deviations from the standard is .55; the expected absolute deviation is .575.

Problems 7.5

1. The variance is .437500; the standard deviation is .66144.

3. The variance is 1.25.

5. I might, since the variance of X is less than the variance of Y. It would depend to what extent I was a "risk averter."

7. Your solution would be the same as 6.

Problems 7.7

1.

no. of σ from mean	Chebyshev's inequality	normal distribution
1	1.00	.3174
2	.25	.0456
3	.111	.0026
4	.0625	.0000

3. The 5 cases would represent $\left(\dfrac{5-\frac{2}{3}}{316}\right) = .01$ standard deviations which has a high probability of occurring. Thus, you would not alert anybody. It would be wrong to use the normal in this case because np is very small.

5. a. Since $np = 5$ is small, tell him to use the Poisson distribution.
   c. $P(X \le 12) = .0054$

Problems 7.8

1. a. $E(Y) = 19.5$ c. $E(Y) = 22.5$

3.

(3) = (2) + (10) cost of repair with fixed costs	10	13	16	19	22	25	28	31	34	37	40
(4) probability table	.5987	.3151	.0746	.0105	.0010	.0001	.00	.00	.00	.00	.00

5. 5.35

7. 2.5

Problems 7.9

1. The expected value is 5% and the variance would be zero since a savings account is a "sure" investment.

3. Probably not, because all factors of the economy interact.

5. The investments below the frontier are 3, 4, 5, 9, 12.

7. Compare return/risk tradeoff.

Problems 7.10

1. This would be done by constructing a "risk lovers" type of utility curve, which would indicate preference for risky or expected dollars over sure dollars.

3. You might not.

5. discussion question

Problems 8.2

1. .74

3. You might define the expected value of complete information as follows. The value

$$\sum_i W(d_i^*|s_i)P(s_i) - \sum_i W(d^*)P(s_i)$$

where d_i^* represents the best decision if s_i occurs and d^* represents the d_j that maximizes the following:

$$\sum_i W(d_j|s_i)P(s_i)$$

5. The expected value with the device would be 54, which is less than 68 by more than 10 (the cost of the device). So buy the device.

7. The most E. John could charge would be $80,000.

Problems 8.3

1. a. .27   **c.** $\dfrac{4}{11}$

3. a. It doesn't pay to bet because you would expect to lose $3\dfrac{1}{8}$ dollars.

5. a. .2   **c.** .1   **e.** .85

7. a. .075

Problems 8.4

1. Accept the bet.

3. Investigate to determine the cause of the deviation.

5. 46.15%

7. 3.14

9. discussion question

Problems 8.5

1. a. $\dfrac{3}{4}$ **c.** $\dfrac{5}{8}$ **e.** $\dfrac{3}{8}$

3. a. $P(x=10) = .151$; $P(x=11) = .240$; $P(x=12) = .228$; $P(x=13) = .239$; $P(x=14) = .142$ **c.** .137   **e.** The probability is 0 since x is never negative.

5. a.

X	0	1	2	3	4	5	6	7	8	9	10
given misty	$\dfrac{13}{51}$	$\dfrac{4}{51}$	$\dfrac{2}{51}$	$\dfrac{1}{51}$	$\dfrac{7}{51}$	$\dfrac{2}{51}$	$\dfrac{3}{51}$	$\dfrac{5}{51}$	$\dfrac{5}{51}$	$\dfrac{3}{51}$	$\dfrac{6}{51}$

c. $P(\text{rain}|x=4) = \dfrac{6}{13}$; $P(\text{mist}|x=4) = \dfrac{7}{13}$; $P(\text{clear}|x=4) = 0$.

7.

sales	0	1	2	3	4	5	6
probability	$\dfrac{12}{183}$	$\dfrac{27}{183}$	$\dfrac{41}{183}$	$\dfrac{34}{183}$	$\dfrac{28}{183}$	$\dfrac{24}{183}$	$\dfrac{17}{183}$

9. a. Your revised probabilities would be: unemployment, 13.6%; partial unemployment, 45.5%; full employment, 40.9%.

11. a clear day, 3.40; a misty day, 4.49; not raining, 7.89

Problems 8.6

1. relevant
3. relevant

Problems 8.7

1. The expected value of the survey is 126,062, which is $(125,062 - 110,500) = 15,562$ higher than the payoff without the survey. Since the survey only cost \$5000, you should commission it.
3. The expected value with the survey would be 33,180. Since $33,180 > 10,000$ (the expected value without the survey) by more than 4000, you would conduct the survey.
5,7. discussion questions

Problems 9

1. a. $x = \dfrac{13}{32}$ **c.** $x = 22$ **e.** $x = \dfrac{30}{19}$; $y = \dfrac{13}{9}$
3. Break-even quantity is 500 units; produce 1000 units to make \$50 daily profit.
5. Ship 30,000 barrels to California and 20,000 barrels to Seattle.
7. a. The number of adults attending the evening show is 280 and the number of children is 46.   **c.** You would know one of them has made a mistake because working out the calculation would result in a solution having $\dfrac{2}{3}$ and $\dfrac{1}{3}$ of a person in it, which is impossible.
9. The specifications asked for are not possible to fulfill.
11. a. There is no unique solution.   **c.** $x_1 = x_2 = x_3 = 1$
13. \$215,800
15. discussion question
17,19 Solutions for these questions will vary.

Problems 10.2

1. a. $x_1 = 3$; $x_2 = 2^*$ (*optimal solution)
3. a. They should sell 2.5 packages of Herzlia and 10 packages of Oded; profit will be 6,500.

Problems 10.3

1. It is the highest price you would pay for one more unit of packing facilities.

3. The shadow prices are $\dfrac{5}{14}$ and $1\dfrac{1}{14}$.

5.

primal corner solutions	primal objective function
$x_1 = \dfrac{15}{7}$ $x_2 = \dfrac{8}{7}^*$	$42\dfrac{6}{7}^*$

dual corner solutions	dual objective function
$y_1 = \dfrac{15}{7}$ $y_2 = \dfrac{12}{7}$	$42\dfrac{6}{7}^*$

7. a. Let the right side of the constraint equations in the dual be the coefficient of the x's in the objective function. The coefficients of y_1 and y_2 in the dual objective function now become the right-hand side of the constraint equation; and the coefficients in the new constraint equation 1 and the coefficients of y_2 become the coefficient in the new constraint equation 2. Thus, we have the original primal. **c.** Follow the above process.

Problems 10.4

1. The problem can be formulated as: minimize $.9x_{11} + x_{12} + 1.3x_{13} + x_{21} + 1.4x_{22} + x_{23} + x_{31} + .8x_{32} + .8x_{33}$

3. Let x_{ij} represent an assignment of section i to classroom j. If it is assigned, $x_{ij} = 1$. Otherwise, it is 0.
Let a_{ij} represent the "cost" of assigning section i to class j. For those assignments that are ruled out, let a_{ij} be a very large number. If the assignment is feasible, $a_{ij} = 1$. The problem then becomes to minimize

$$\sum_{\text{all } i} \sum_{\text{all } j} a_{ij} x_{ij}$$

subject to

$$\sum_{i=1}^{28} x_{ij} = 1 \text{ for all } j \ (j = 1, 2, \ldots\ldots28)$$

and

$$\sum_{j=1}^{28} x_{ij} = 1 \text{ for all } i \ (i = 1, 2, \ldots\ldots28); \ x_{ij} = 1 \text{ or } x_{ij} = 0 \text{ for all } i, j$$

5. discussion problem

Problems 11.1

1,3. discussion questions
5. $5

Problems 11.2

1. a. $3x^2$ **c.** $e^x + a$ **e.** 0 **g.** $-\dfrac{a}{x^2} + \dfrac{6}{x^4}$ **i.** $\dfrac{2ax + b}{5}$ **j.** $\dfrac{-6}{x^3}$

3. 200; the increase therefore is 200 dollars.

5. MR is 0 at all qualtities.

Problems 11.3

1. a. $f'(x) = 3; f''(x) = 0$ **c.** $f'(x) = 2x - 2$ **e.** $f'(x) = \dfrac{-a}{x^2} - \dfrac{3a}{x^4}; f''(x) = \dfrac{a}{x^3} + \dfrac{12a}{x^5}$

3. $-dp/dv = 96 - 48v$; the maximum profit is at a volume of 2000 units.

5. He should keep the cattle for $66\frac{2}{3}$ days before selling them. If it costs .09 per day per pound to feed the cattle, then it doesn't even pay to buy the cattle, as your costs increase faster than your revenue.

7. The order size should be 300 units

Problems 11.4

1. a. $2x + K$ **c.** $ax + K$ **e.** $K = -\dfrac{5}{x} + K$ **g.** $\dfrac{2x^n}{3n} + K$ **i.** $2x^2 + \dfrac{1}{2x} + K$

3. a. 922,733,955.41

   c. 8,236,165

5. Accept the order, since profit will be 2500.

Problems Appendix 11

Chain Rule

1. $4x^3$

3. $\left[4(3t^2 + t) + 3 - \dfrac{1}{(3t^2 + t)^2}\right](6t + 1)$

5. a. 46   **c.** Yes

Product and Quotient Rule

1. $3x^2 - 1$

3. $5x^4 + 4x^3$

5. $(5x - x^2)^2 (6x) + (3x^2 + 2) [2(5x - x^2) (5 - 2x)]$

7. $\dfrac{1}{(2x + 1)^2}$

9. $\dfrac{-2(x + 1)}{(x^2 - x + 1)^2}$

The Partial Derivative

1. $\dfrac{df(x,z)}{dx} = 6x + 6$

3. $\dfrac{df(x,y,z)}{dx} = 1$

5. Department 1 requires $4\frac{1}{3}$ million dollars of inventory and 86,667 sq. ft. Department 2 requires 3 million dollars in inventory and 40,000 sq. ft.

Glossary of Important Symbols

(Page number indicates where symbol is first introduced, defined, or explained.)

MIS (management information system) 10

D (set of decisions) 11

d (member of D) 11

O (set of outcomes) 12

o (member of O) 13

S (set of states of the world) 11

s (member of S) 12

W (set of payoffs) 13

w (member of W) 14

! (factorial) 18

$\subset$ (containment in set) 44

$=$ (two sets have the same membership) 45

U (universal set) 45

ϕ (empty or null set) 45

$\sim$ (complement of a set) 46

$\cap$ (intersection of two sets) 46

$\cup$ (union of two sets) 48

$-$ (difference between two sets) 50

XBy (better than) 64

XWy (worse than) 64

XIy (indifference) 64

X_{max} (best) 65

f(x) (function of one variable) 68

f(x,y, . . .) function of several variables 69

π (ratio of circumference to diameter) 91

e (base of natural logs) 91

x_i, x_{i+1} (sequence of values) 94

$\sum\limits_{i=1}^{n} a_i$ (summation) 94

$\sum\limits_{i=1}^{n} i(i+1)$ (summation of products) 95

d (difference in arithmetic series) 98

q (ratio in geometric series) 103

r (interest rate) 107

$(1 + r)^n$ (n-year interest) 107

P or PV (present value) 109

P_r^k (permutations) 146

C_r^k (combinations) 150

$P(X = X_i)$ (probability) 163

$X \sim B(n,p)$ (binomial distribution) 169

c.d.f. (cumulative probability distribution) 179

σ_x^2 or Var [X] (variance of X) 201

Note: Common arithmetical symbols, such as $+, -, \times, \div, <, >$, are not given.

σ_x (standard deviation)   203

$E[U(X)]$ (expected utility)   228

$P(A|K)$ (conditional probability)   252

LP   (linear programming)   341

Δt (increment of time)   368

$\dfrac{dft}{dt}$ (derivative)   369

$\dfrac{d^2t}{dt^2}$ (second derivative)   382

$\int f(t)dt$ (integral)   389

$P(t)$ (cumulative continuous function)   406

$p(t)$ (continuous probability density)   407

μ (mean of continuous p(t)   408

Index to Problems

Index

Sponsoring Editor:	**Paul Kelly**
Project Editor:	**Sara Boyd**
Designer:	**Rick Chafian**
Illustrator:	**Judith McCarty**

Thinking for Decisions was set in Melior body
and display type by Applied Typographic
Systems, Mountain View, California. The book
was printed and bound by Kingsport Press,
Kingsport, Tennessee.